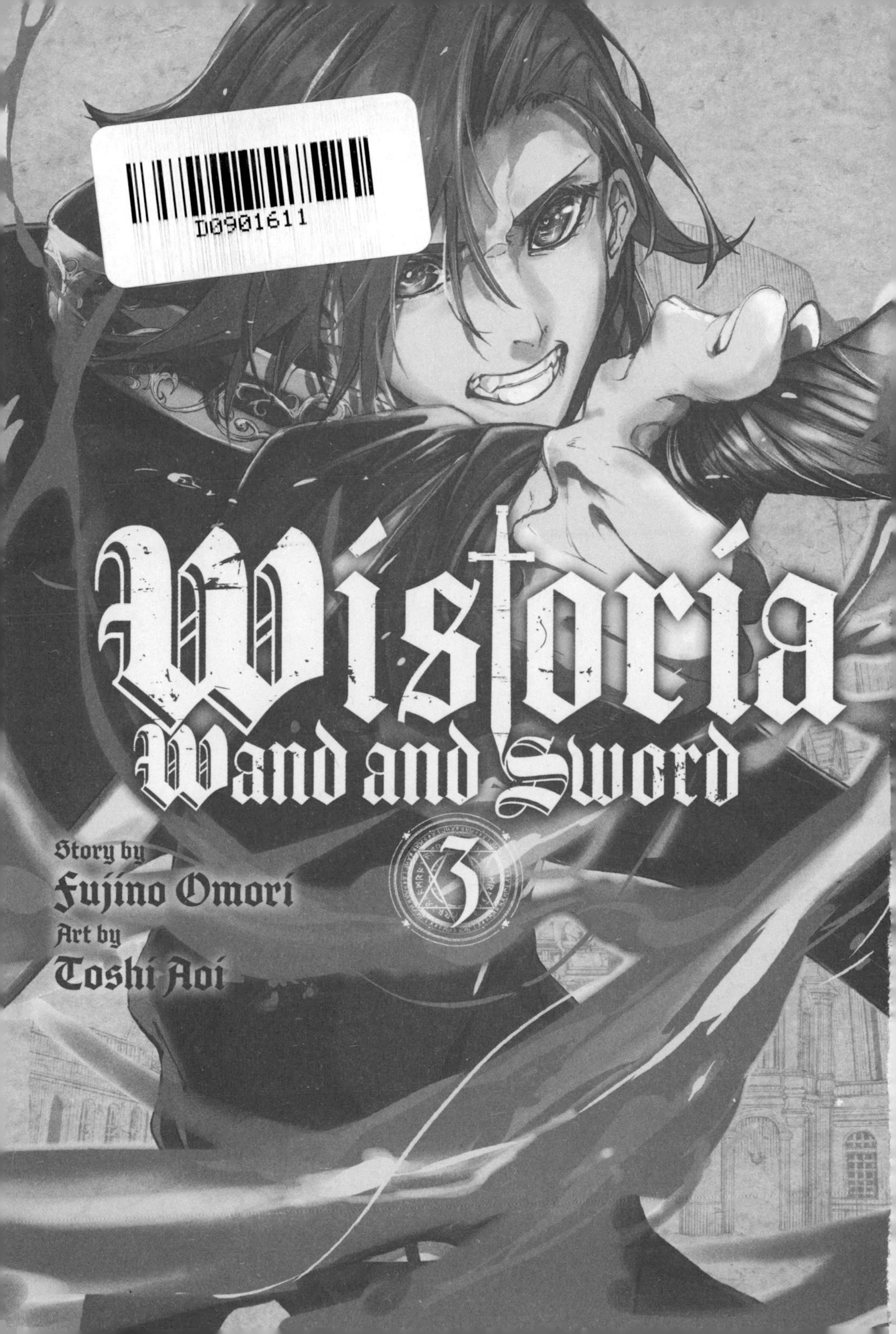
Wistoria
Wand and Sword
3
Story by
Fujino Omori
Art by
Toshi Aoi

Fujino Omori Toshi Aoi

Wistoria
Wand and Sword
3

contents

Chapter 9: El Glace Frosse 003

Chapter 10: Festival Finale 051

Chapter 11: Shall We Date? 099

Chapter 12: Dungeon Dive! 141

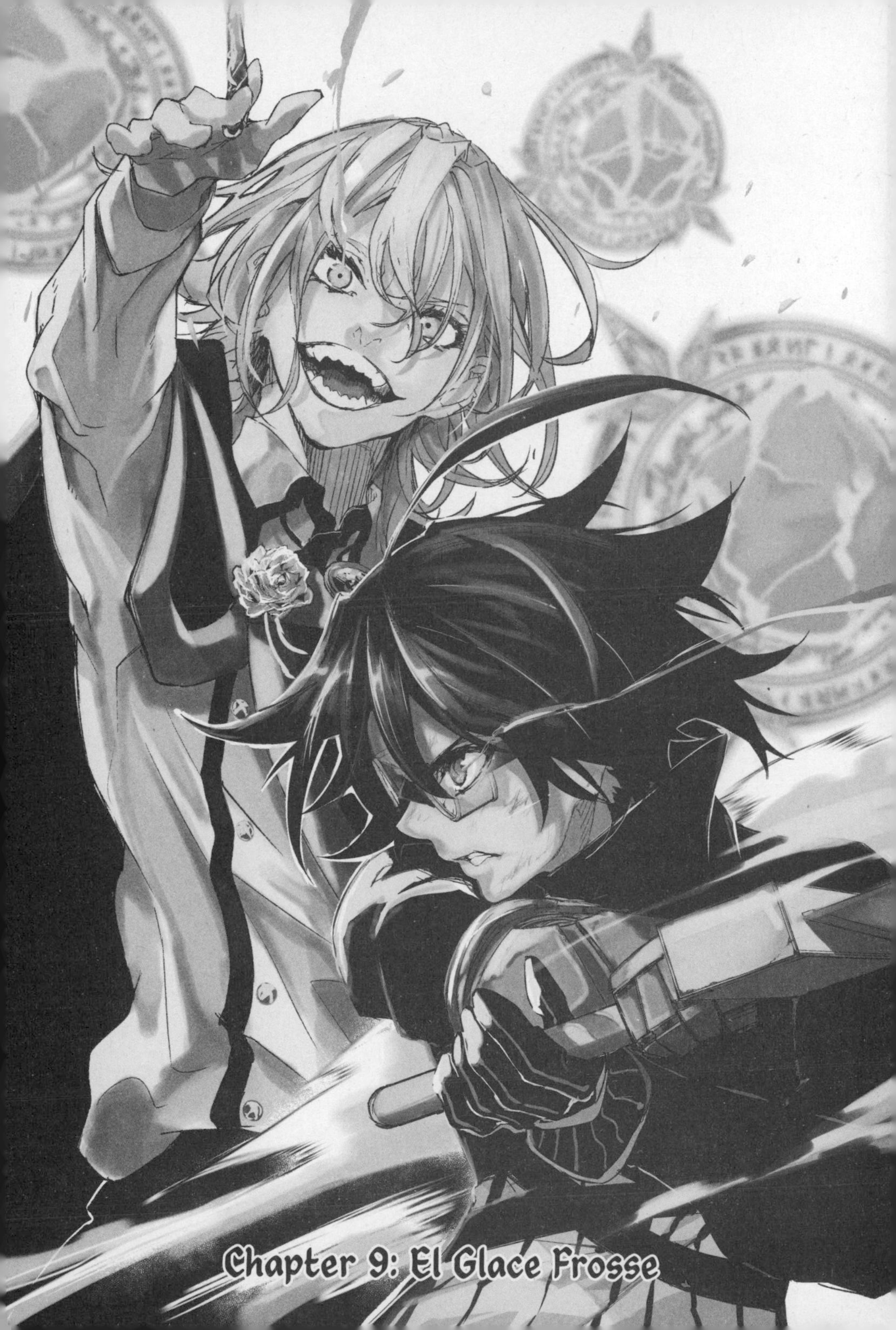
Chapter 9: El Glace Frosse

Wistoria
Wand and Sword

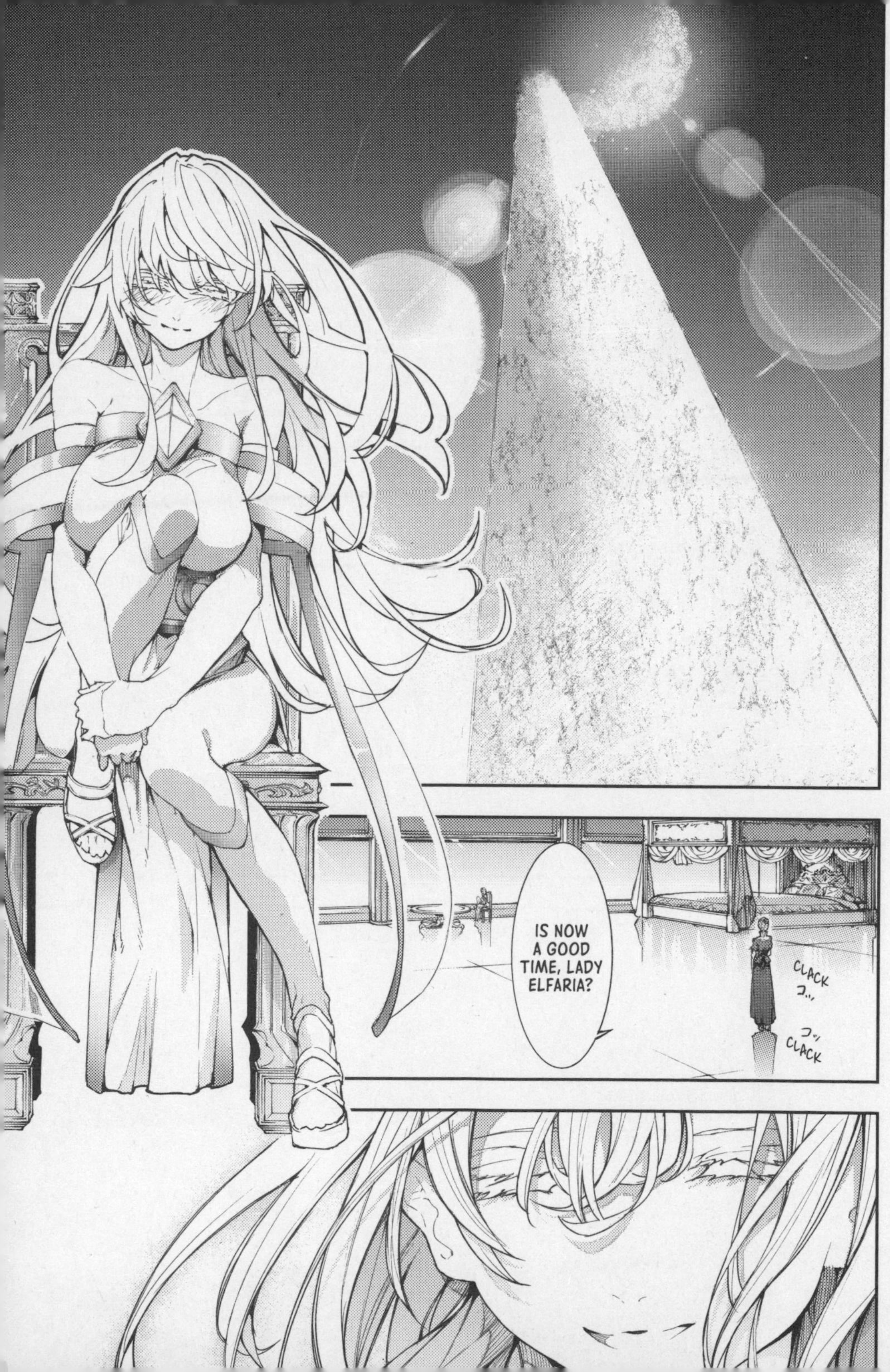
IS NOW A GOOD TIME, LADY ELFARIA?
CLACK
コッ
コッ
CLACK

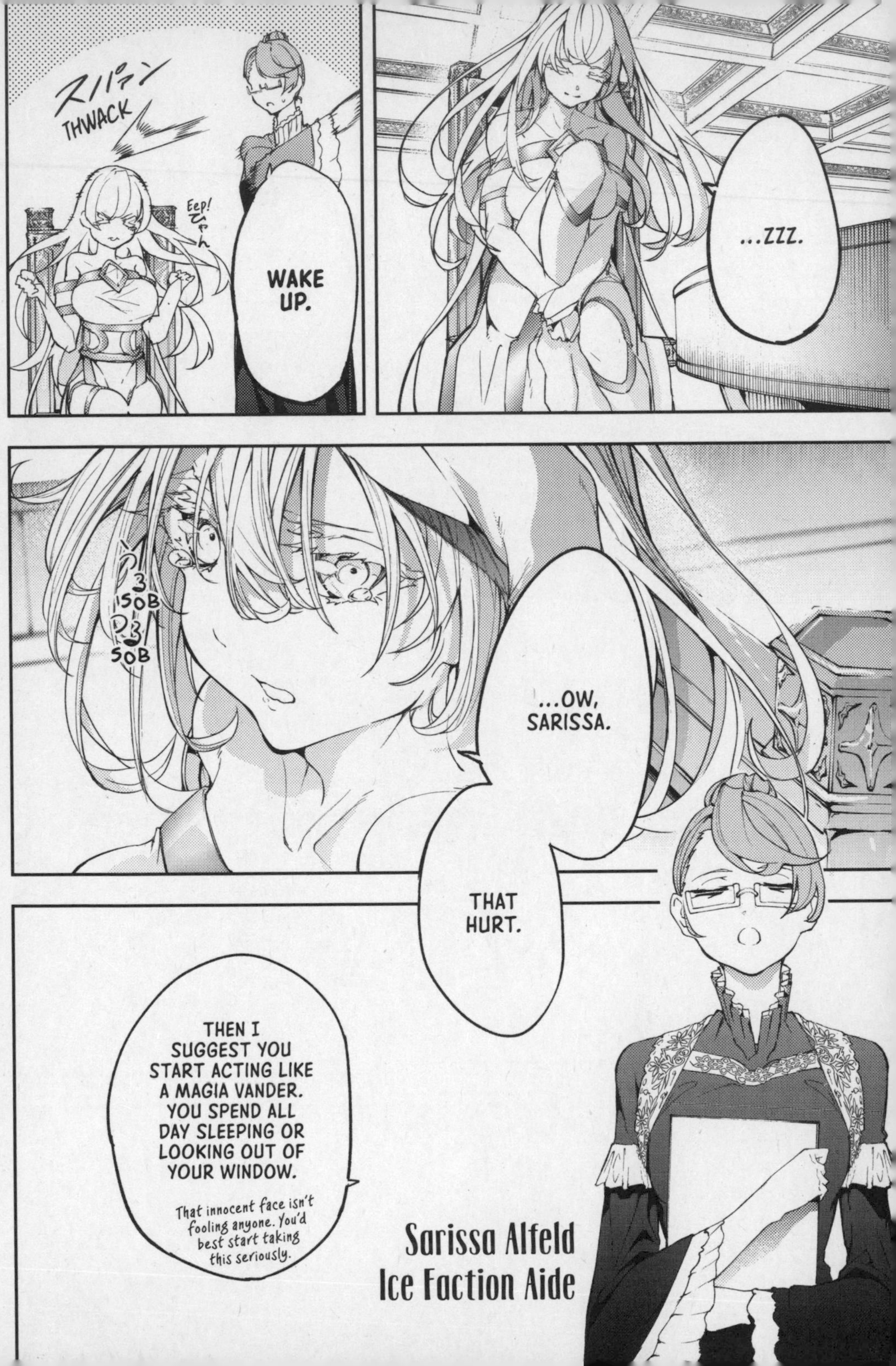
...ZZZ.
スパァン
THWACK
Eep!
びゃん
WAKE UP.
ぐすっ
SOB
ぐすっ
SOB
...OW, SARISSA.
THAT HURT.
THEN I SUGGEST YOU START ACTING LIKE A MAGIA VANDER. YOU SPEND ALL DAY SLEEPING OR LOOKING OUT OF YOUR WINDOW.
That innocent face isn't fooling anyone. You'd best start taking this seriously.
Sarissa Alfeld
Ice Faction Aide

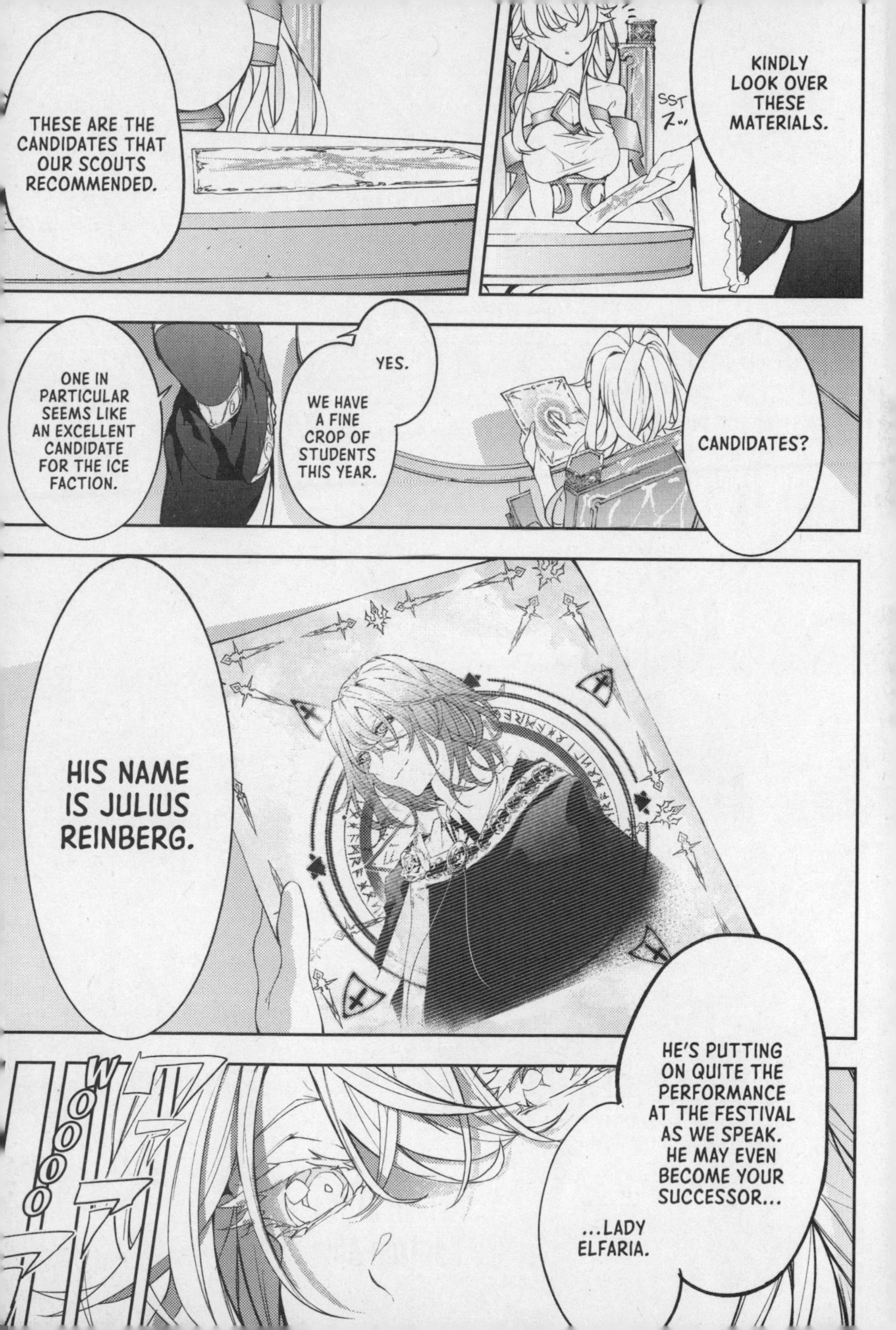
KINDLY LOOK OVER THESE MATERIALS.
SST
THESE ARE THE CANDIDATES THAT OUR SCOUTS RECOMMENDED.
CANDIDATES?
YES.
WE HAVE A FINE CROP OF STUDENTS THIS YEAR.
ONE IN PARTICULAR SEEMS LIKE AN EXCELLENT CANDIDATE FOR THE ICE FACTION.
HIS NAME IS JULIUS REINBERG.
HE'S PUTTING ON QUITE THE PERFORMANCE AT THE FESTIVAL AS WE SPEAK. HE MAY EVEN BECOME YOUR SUCCESSOR...
...LADY ELFARIA.
WOOOOO

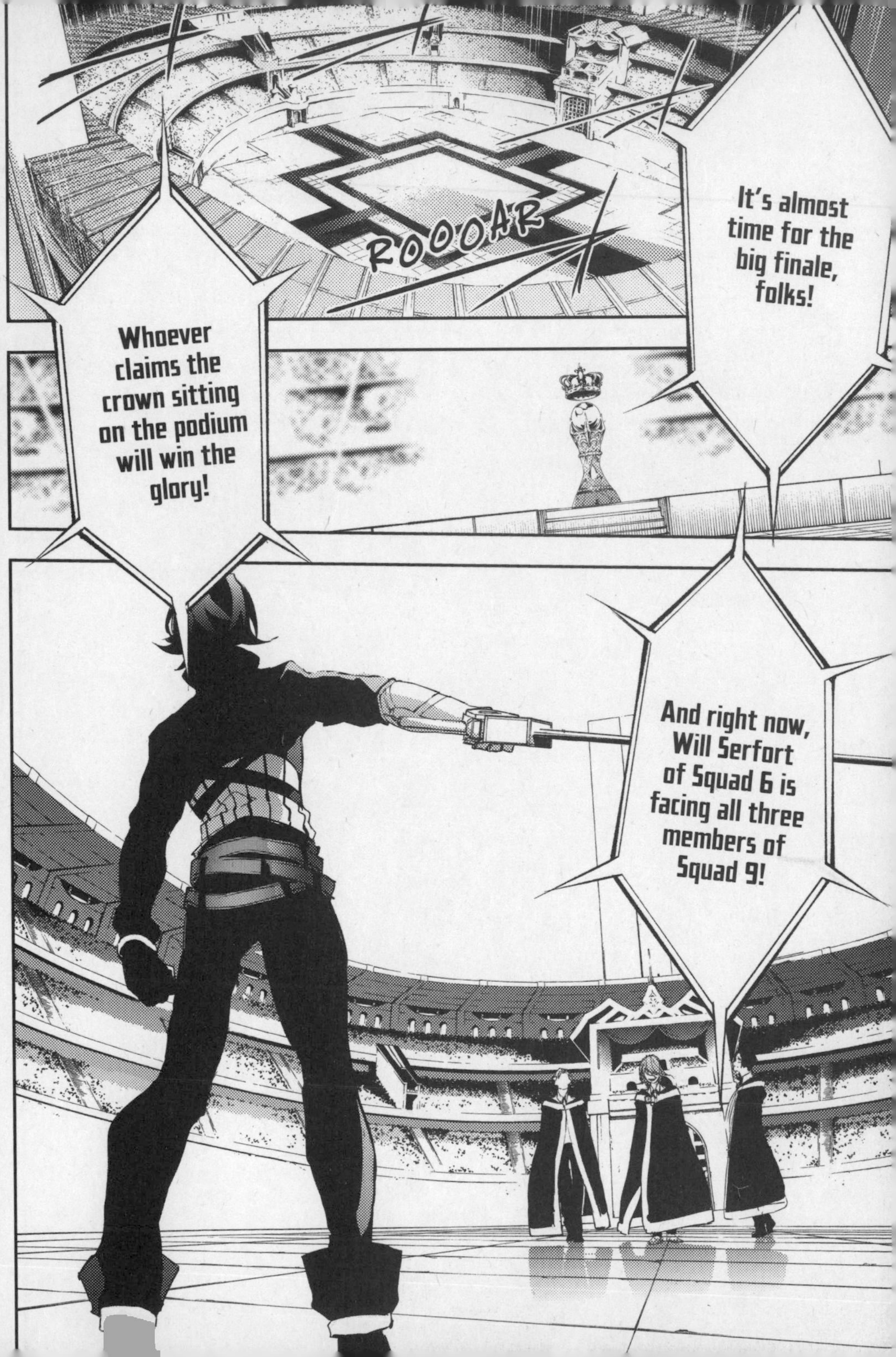
It's almost time for the big finale, folks!
ROOOAR
Whoever claims the crown sitting on the podium will win the glory!
And right now, Will Serfort of Squad 6 is facing all three members of Squad 9!

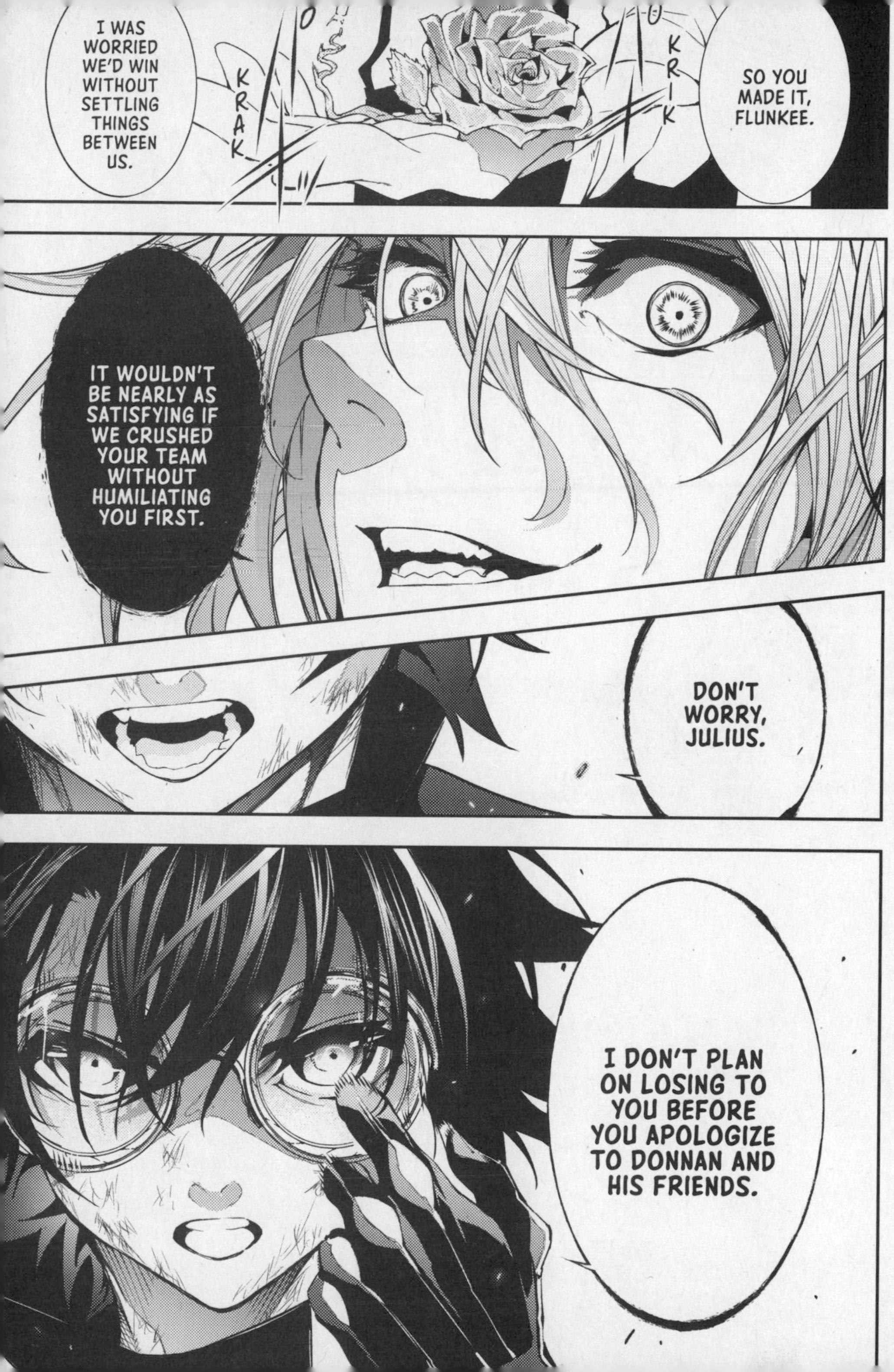
SO YOU MADE IT, FLUNKEE.
KRIK
KRAK
I WAS WORRIED WE'D WIN WITHOUT SETTLING THINGS BETWEEN US.
IT WOULDN'T BE NEARLY AS SATISFYING IF WE CRUSHED YOUR TEAM WITHOUT HUMILIATING YOU FIRST.
DON'T WORRY, JULIUS.
I DON'T PLAN ON LOSING TO YOU BEFORE YOU APOLOGIZE TO DONNAN AND HIS FRIENDS.

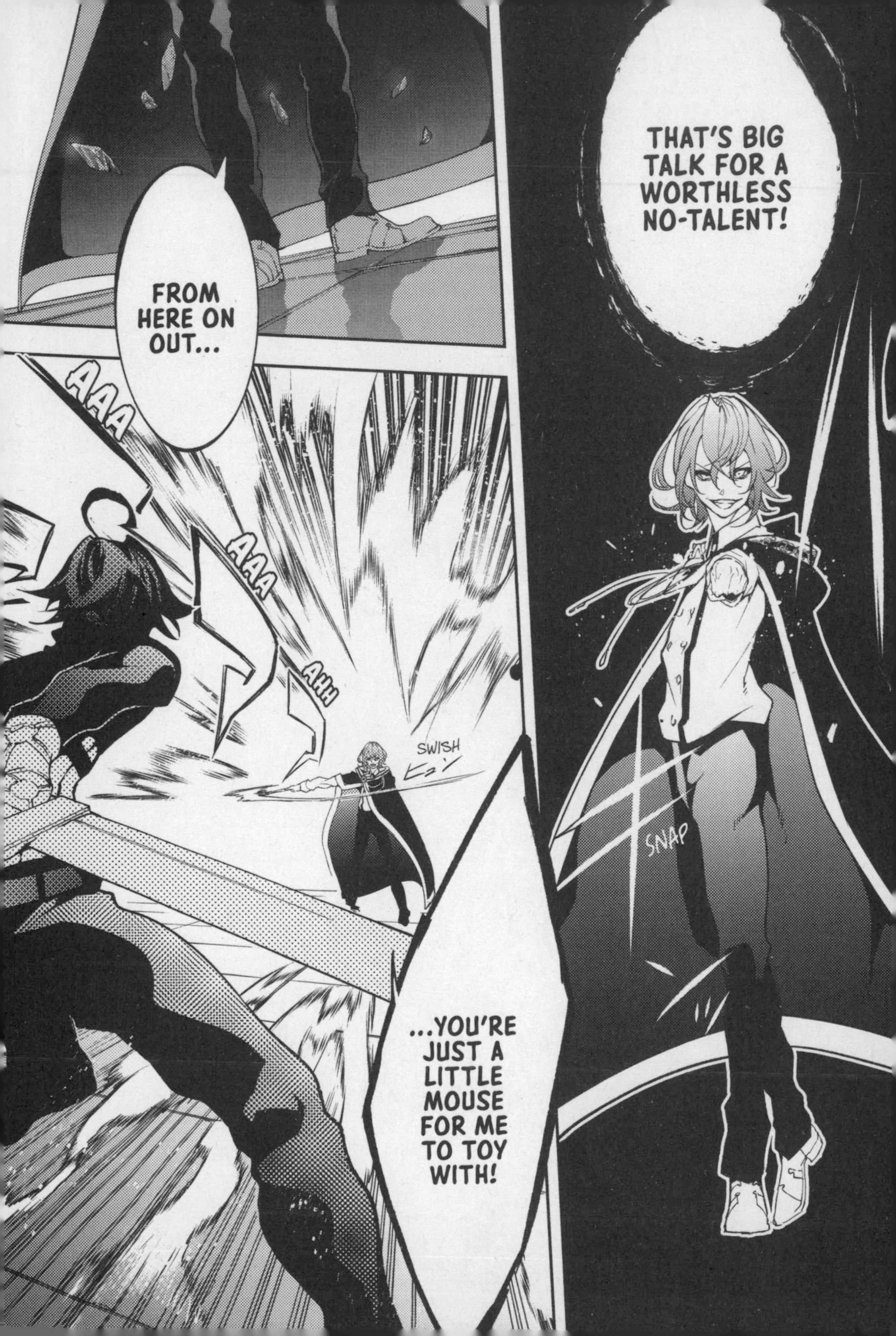
THAT'S BIG TALK FOR A WORTHLESS NO-TALENT!
SNAP
FROM HERE ON OUT...
AAA
AAA
AHH
SWISH
...YOU'RE JUST A LITTLE MOUSE FOR ME TO TOY WITH!

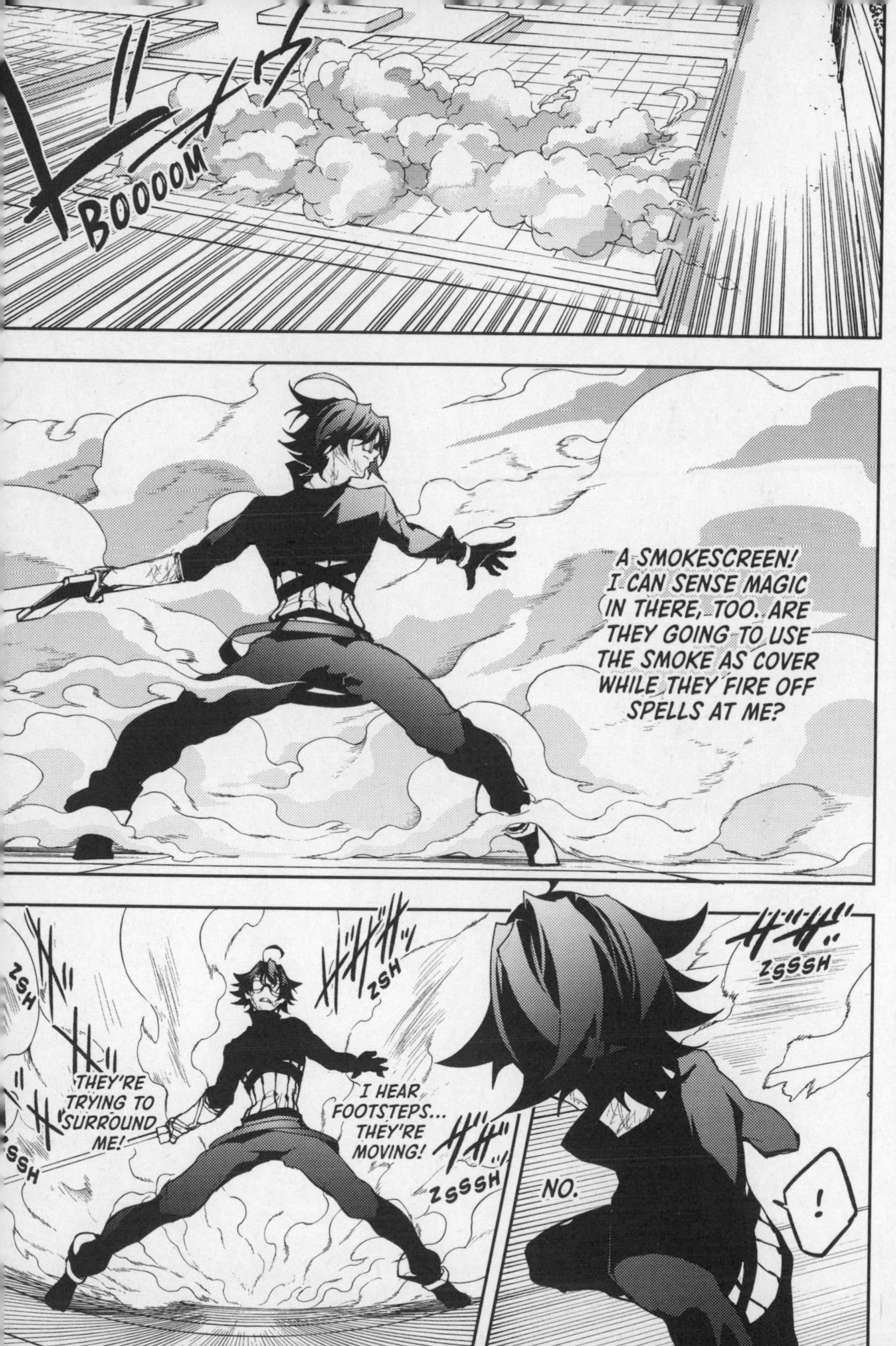
BOOOOM
A SMOKESCREEN! I CAN SENSE MAGIC IN THERE, TOO. ARE THEY GOING TO USE THE SMOKE AS COVER WHILE THEY FIRE OFF SPELLS AT ME?
ZSSSH
NO.
!
ZSH
I HEAR FOOTSTEPS... THEY'RE MOVING!
ZSSSH
ZSH
THEY'RE TRYING TO SURROUND ME!
SSH

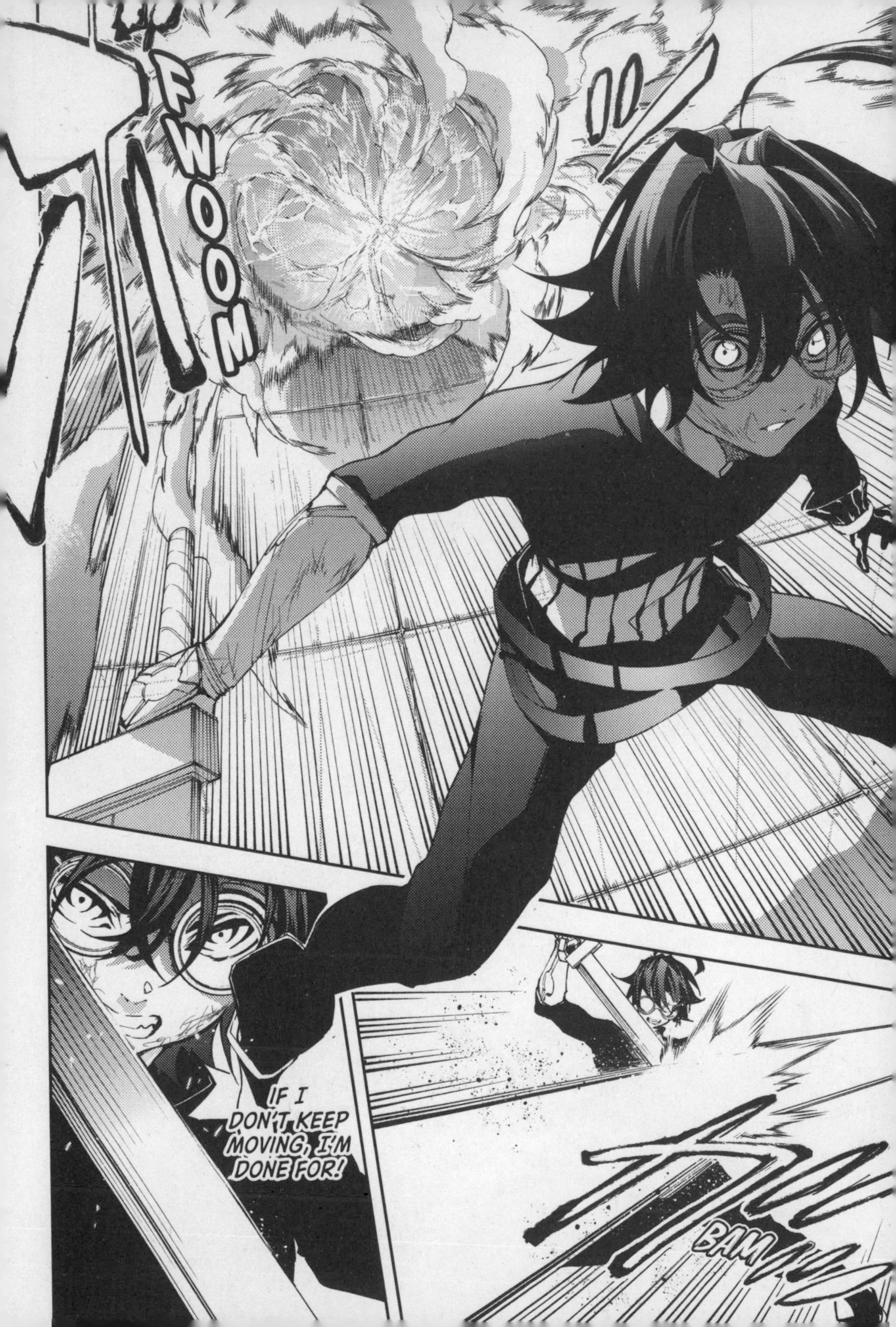
FWOOM
BAM
IF I DON'T KEEP MOVING, I'M DONE FOR!

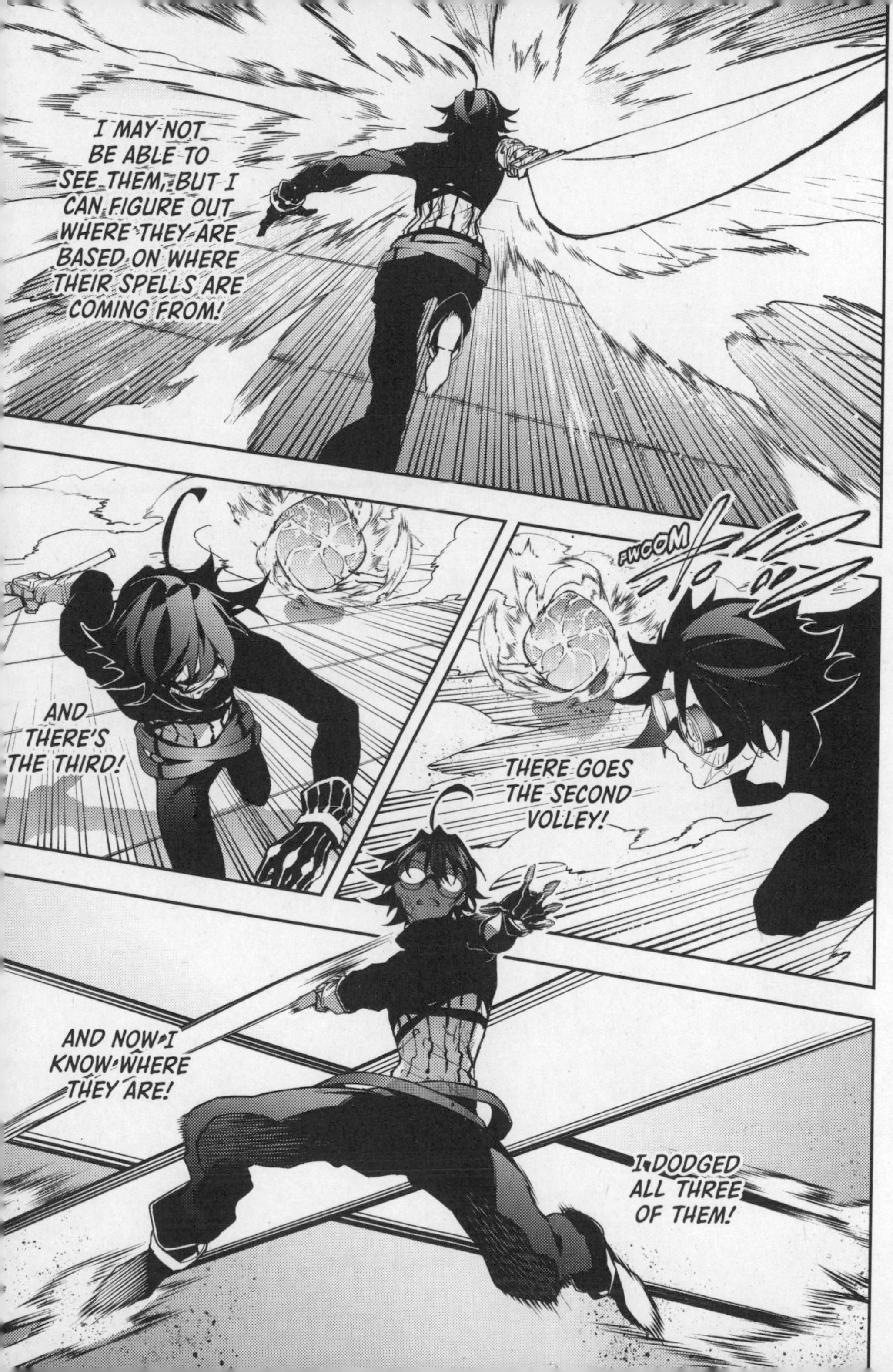
I MAY NOT BE ABLE TO SEE THEM, BUT I CAN FIGURE OUT WHERE THEY ARE BASED ON WHERE THEIR SPELLS ARE COMING FROM!
FWOOM
THERE GOES THE SECOND VOLLEY!
AND THERE'S THE THIRD!
I DODGED ALL THREE OF THEM!
AND NOW I KNOW WHERE THEY ARE!

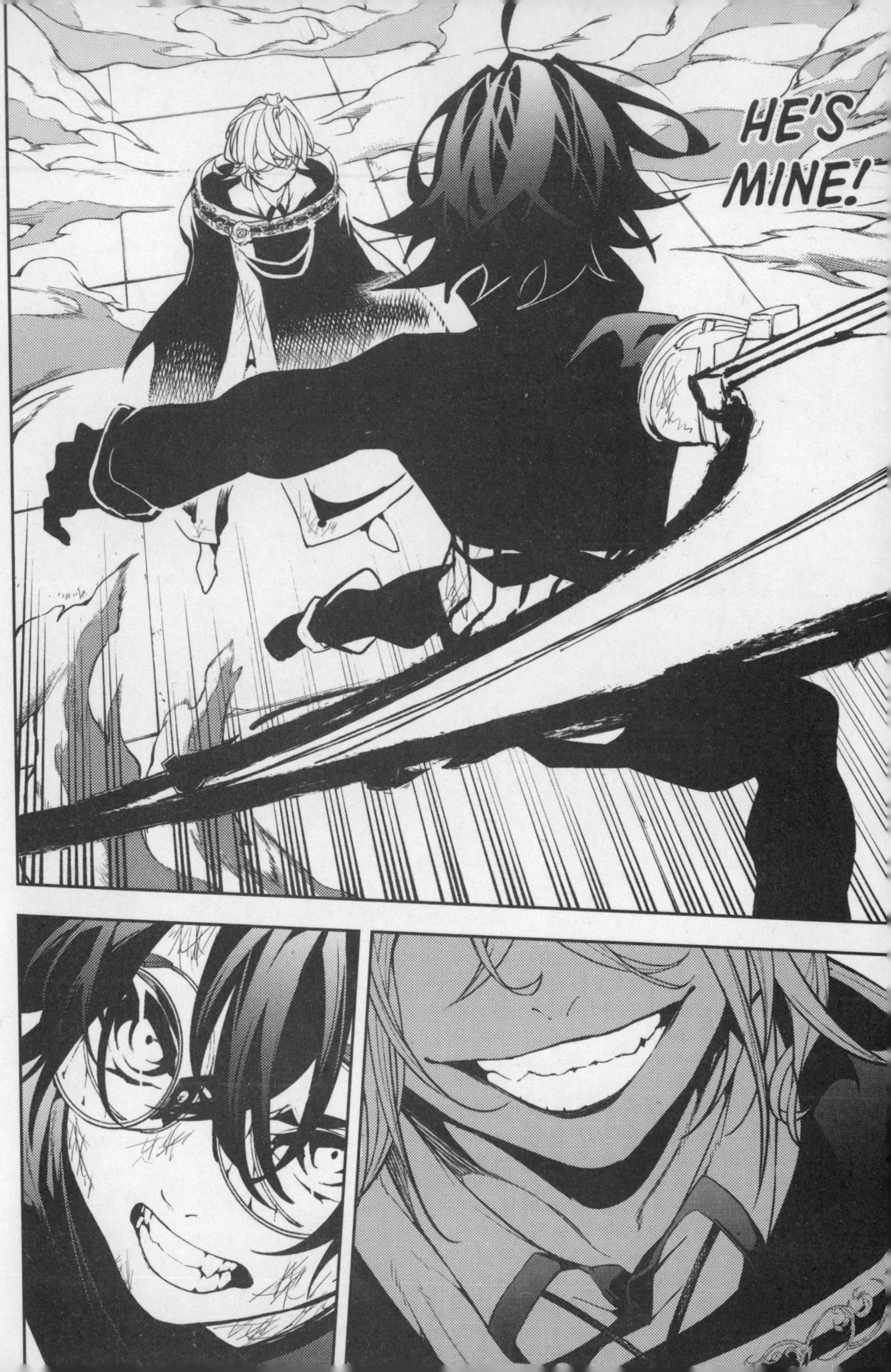
HE'S MINE!

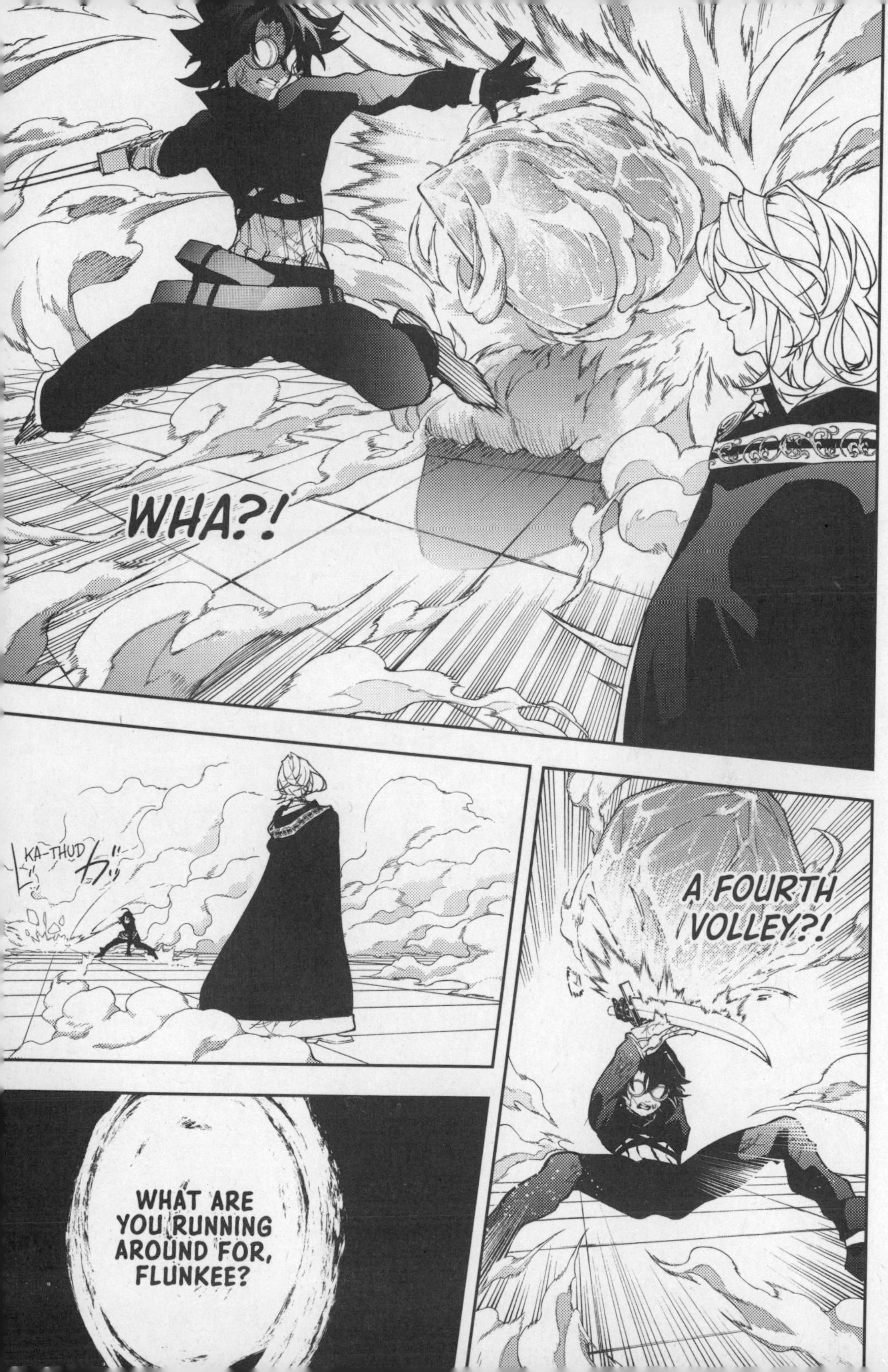
WHA?!
A FOURTH VOLLEY?!
KA-THUD
WHAT ARE YOU RUNNING AROUND FOR, FLUNKEE?

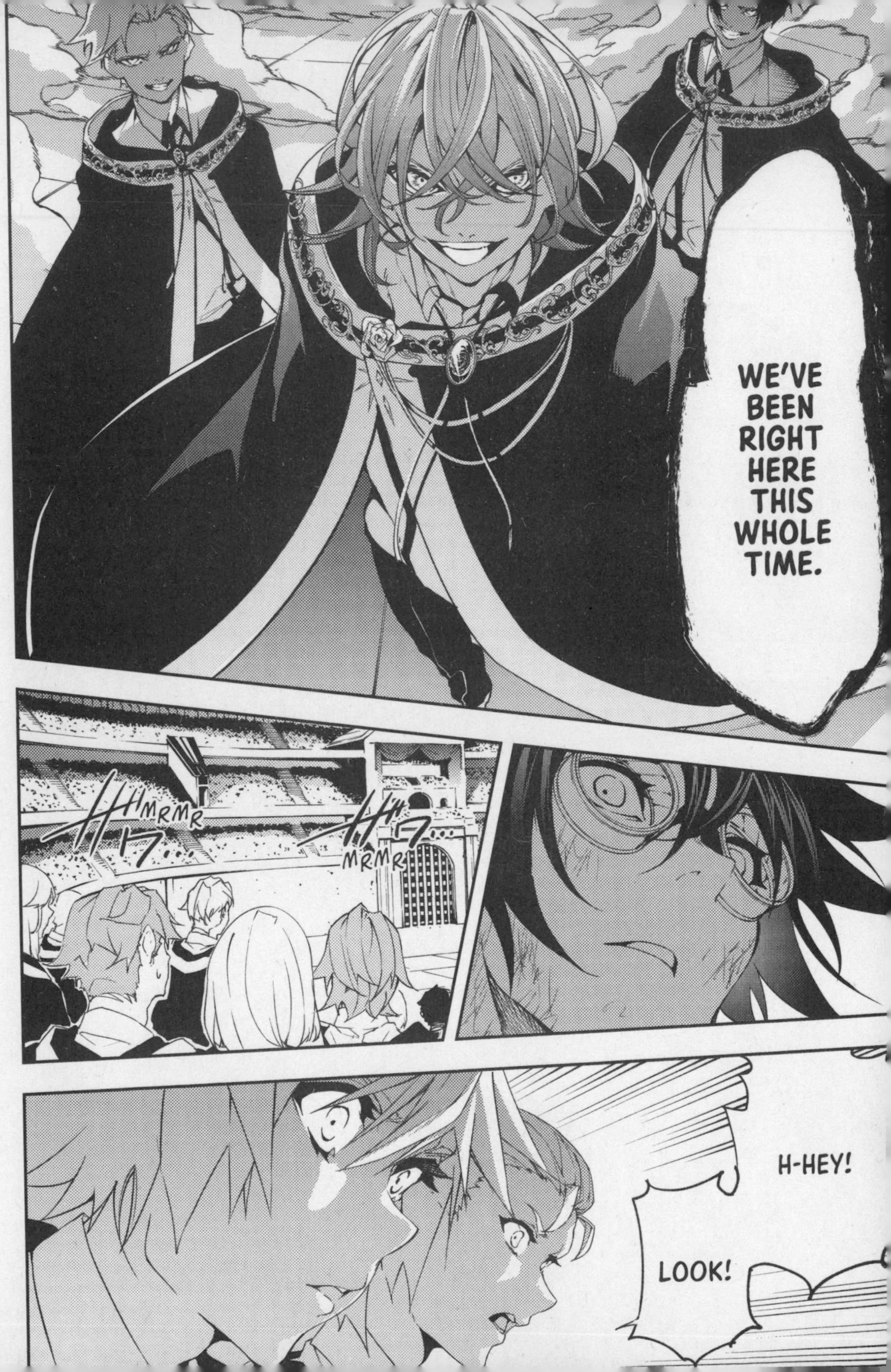
WE'VE BEEN RIGHT HERE THIS WHOLE TIME.
HMRMR
MRMR
H-HEY!
LOOK!

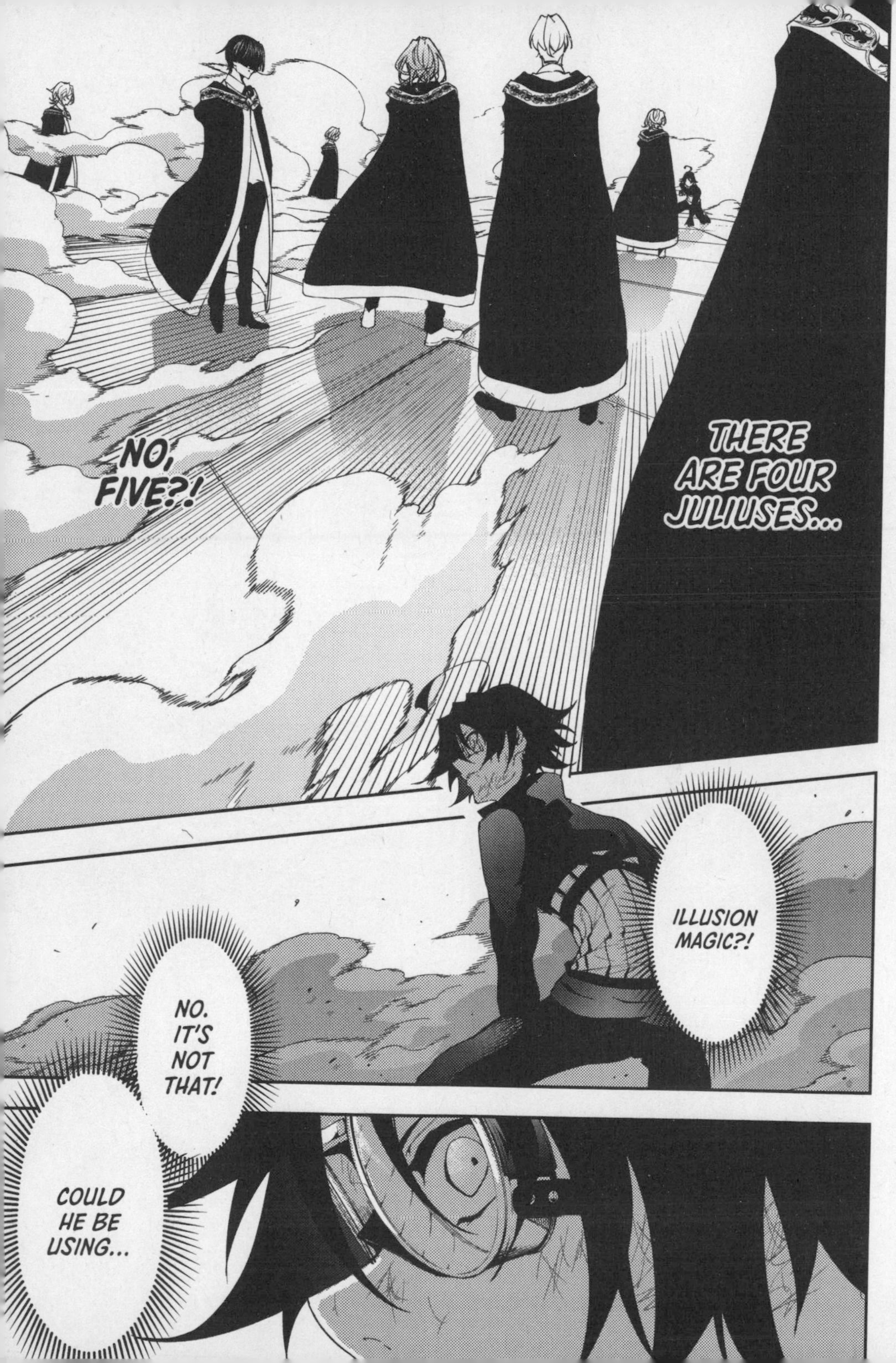
THERE ARE FOUR JULIUSES...
NO, FIVE?!
ILLUSION MAGIC?!
NO. IT'S NOT THAT!
COULD HE BE USING...

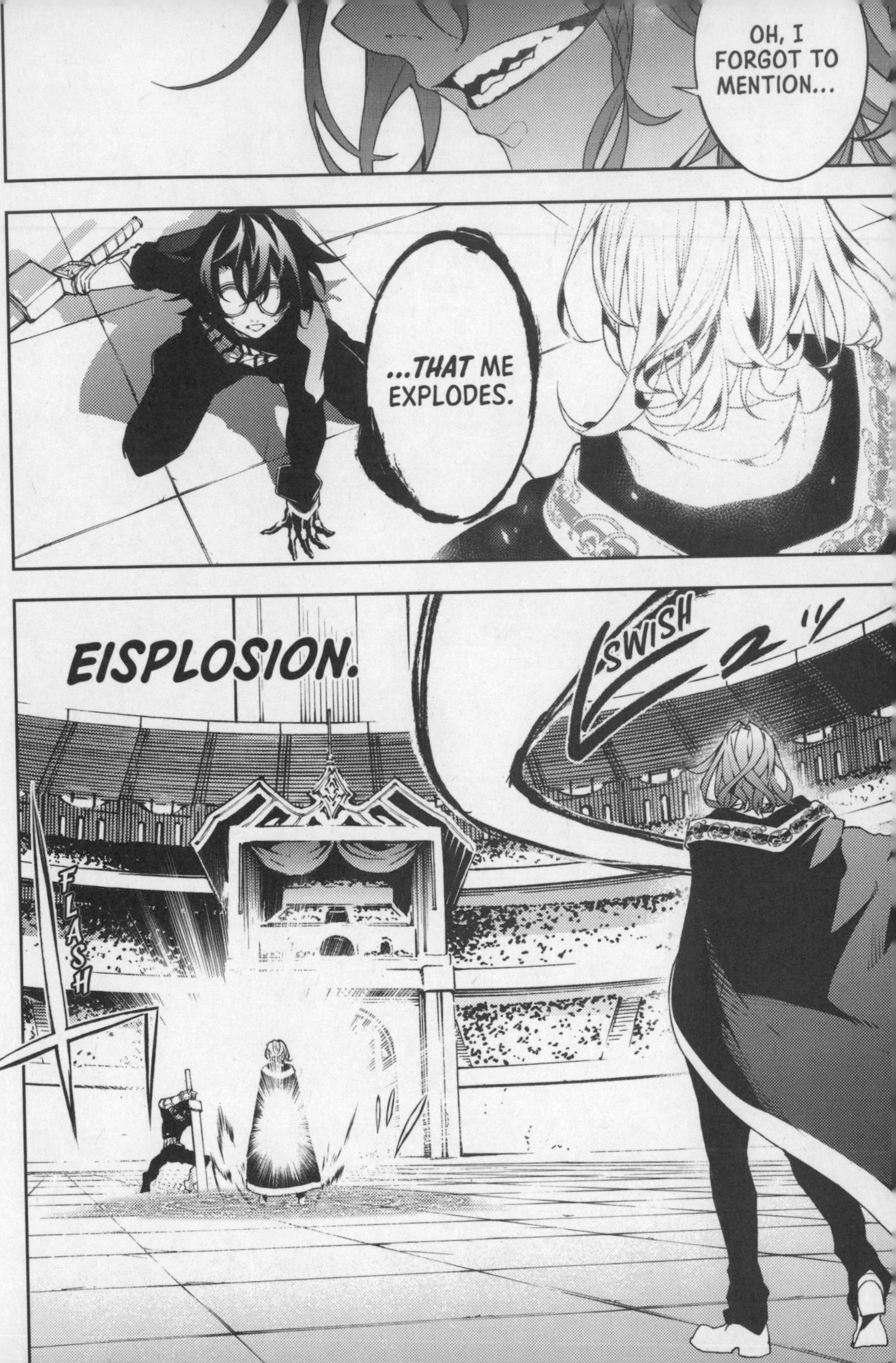
OH, I FORGOT TO MENTION...
...THAT ME EXPLODES.
SWISH
EISPLOSION.
FLASH

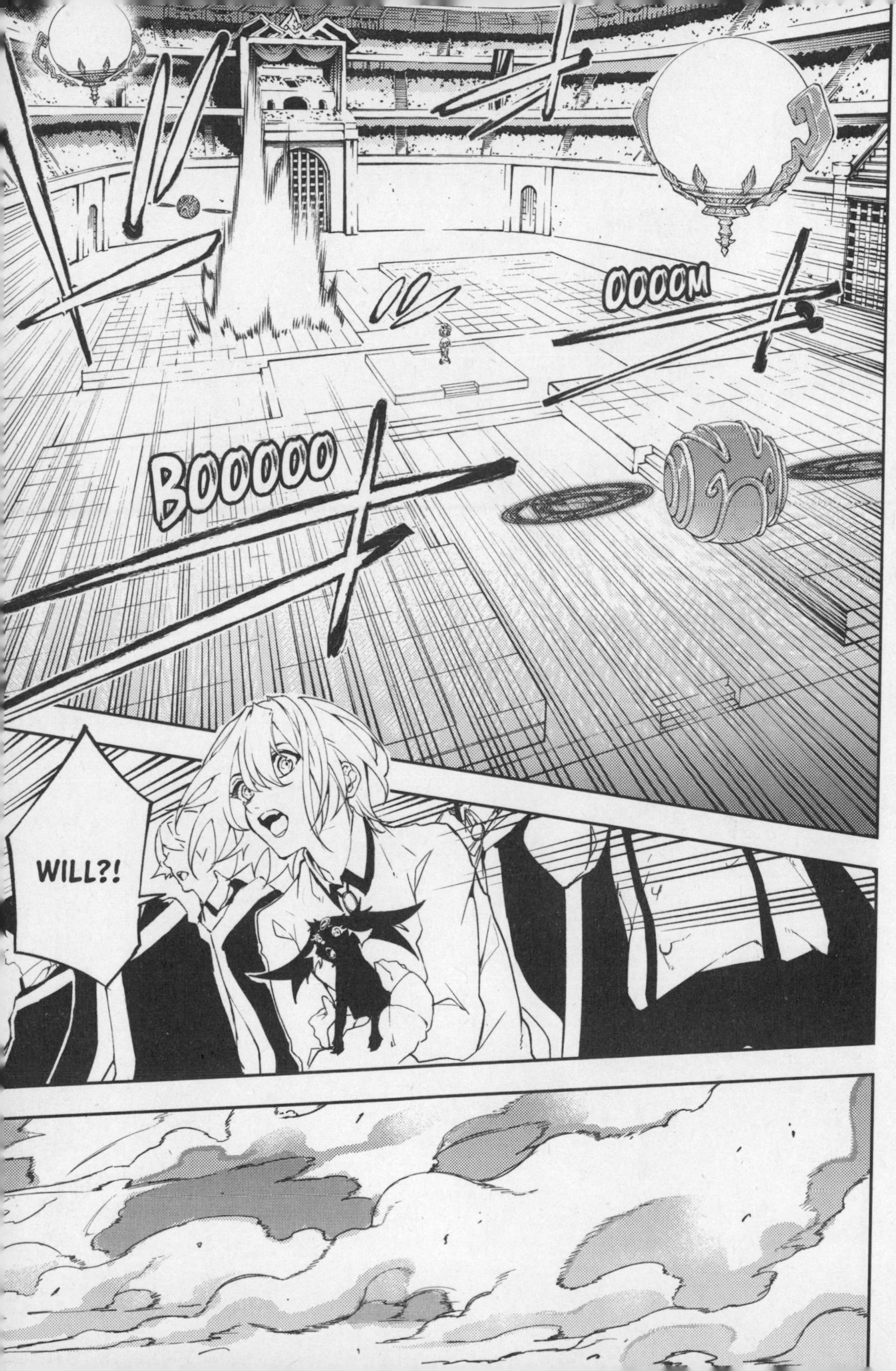
BOOOOO
OOOOM
WILL?!

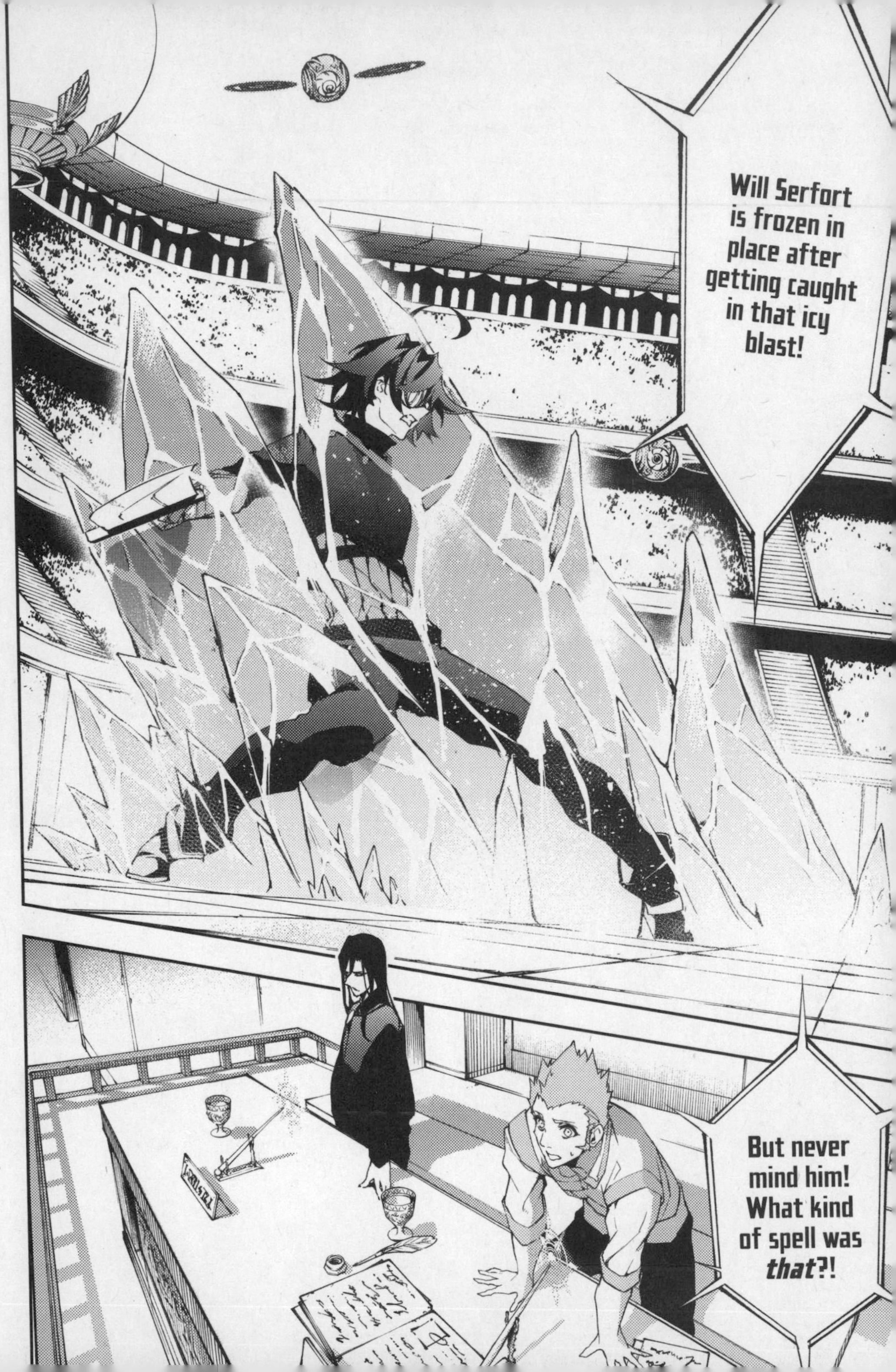
Will Serfort is frozen in place after getting caught in that icy blast!
But never mind him! What kind of spell was *that*?!

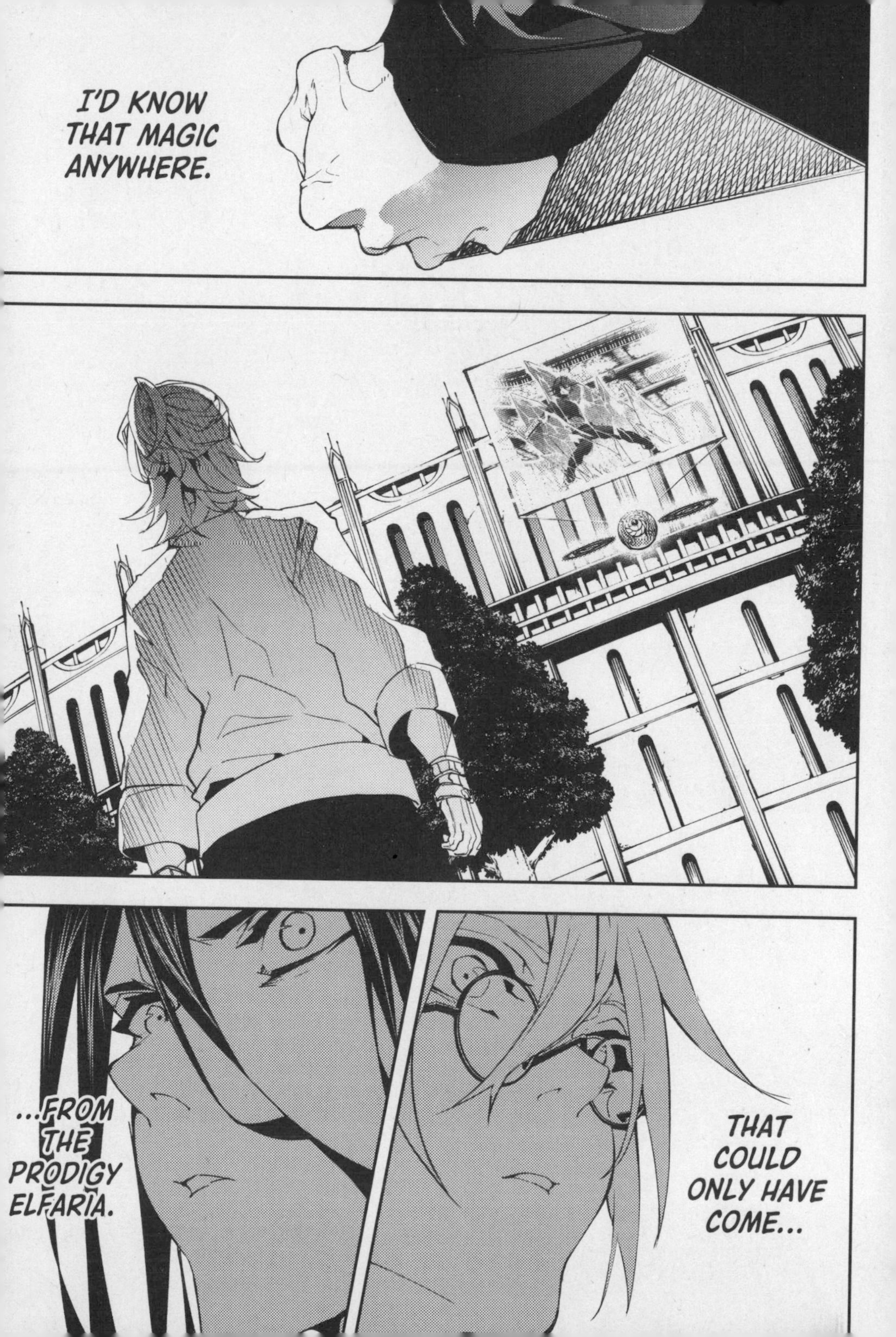
I'D KNOW THAT MAGIC ANYWHERE.
THAT COULD ONLY HAVE COME...
...FROM THE PRODIGY ELFARIA.

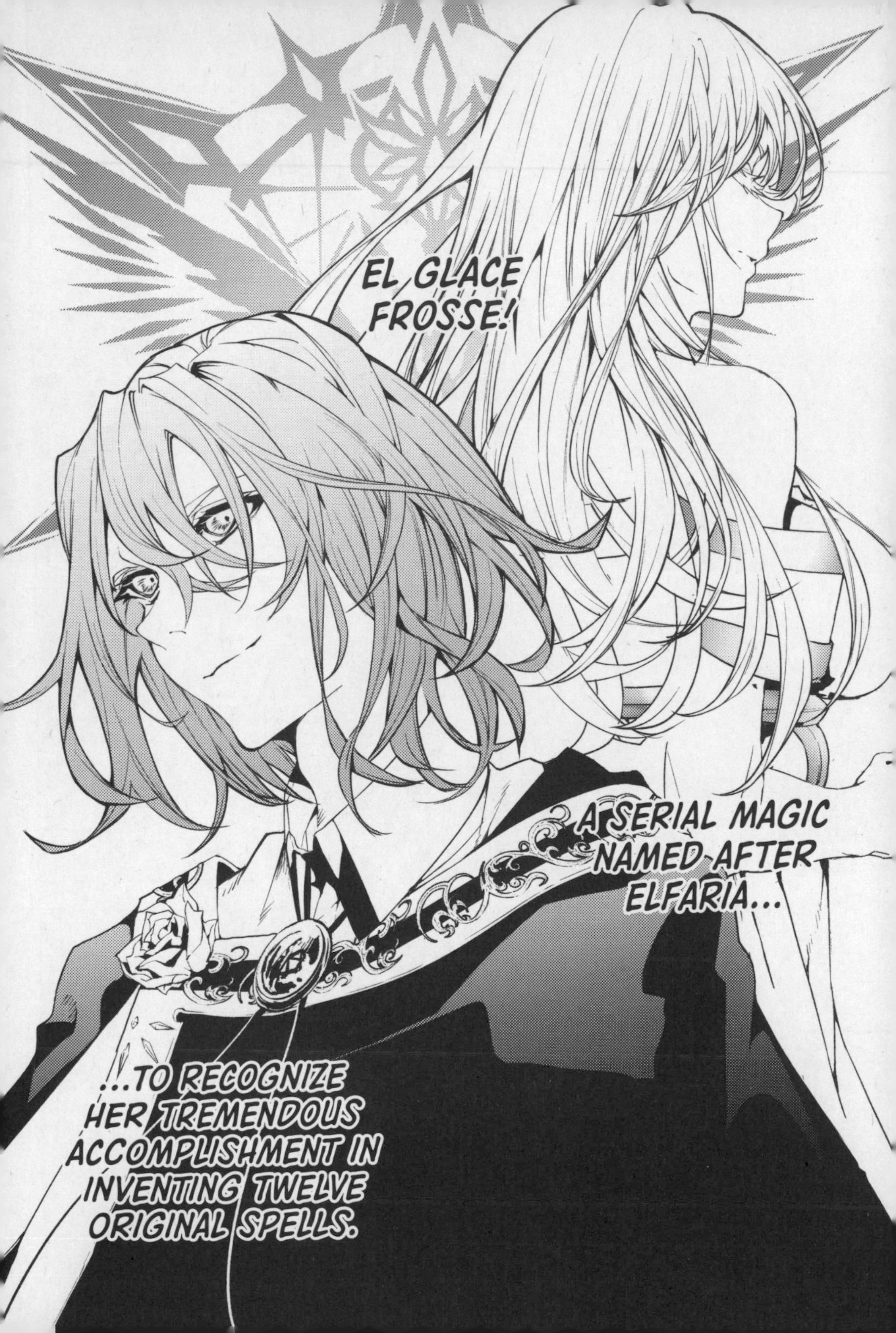
EL GLACE FROSSE!
A SERIAL MAGIC NAMED AFTER ELFARIA...
...TO RECOGNIZE HER TREMENDOUS ACCOMPLISHMENT IN INVENTING TWELVE ORIGINAL SPELLS.

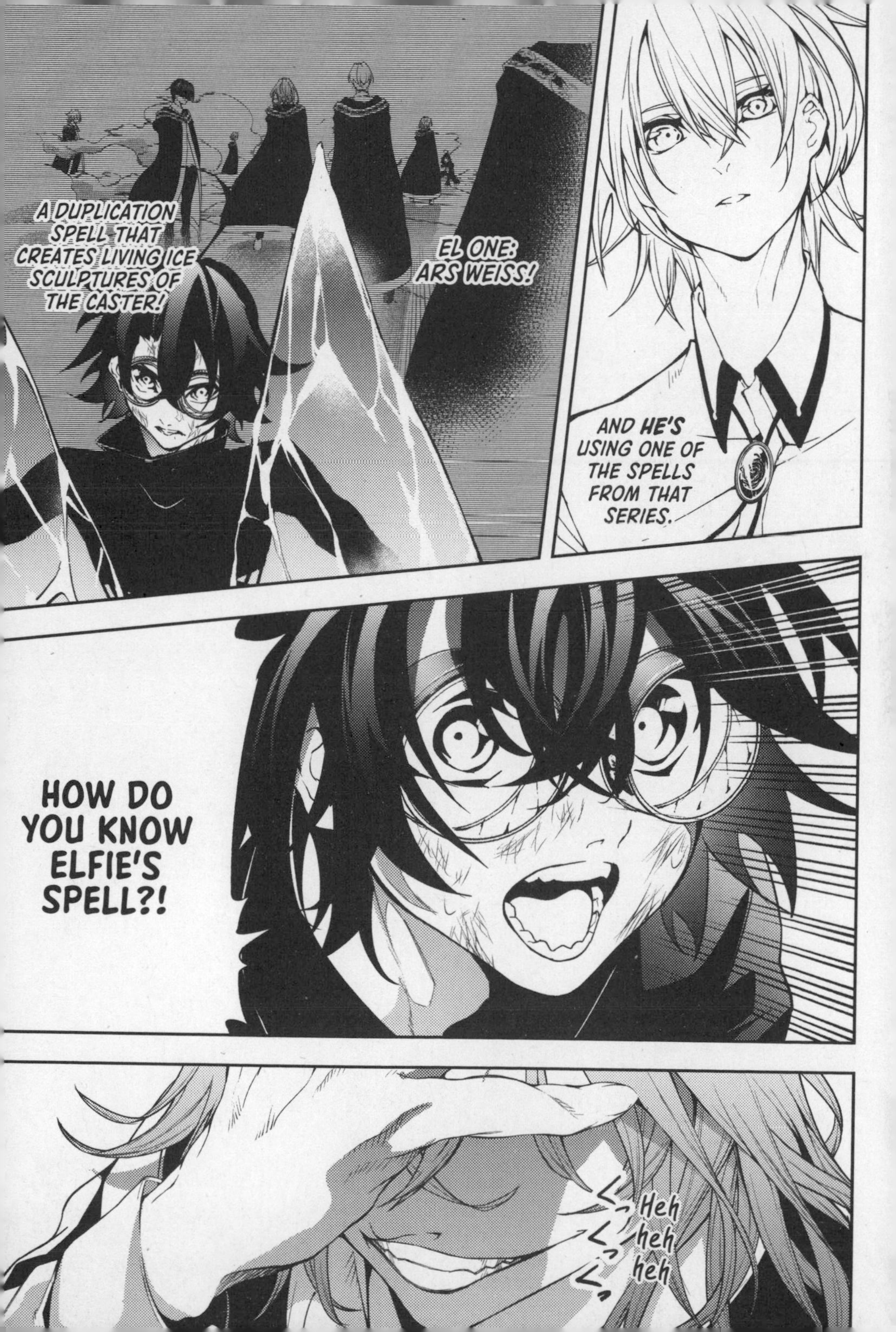
AND HE'S USING ONE OF THE SPELLS FROM THAT SERIES.
EL ONE: ARS WEISS!
A DUPLICATION SPELL THAT CREATES LIVING ICE SCULPTURES OF THE CASTER!
HOW DO YOU KNOW ELFIE'S SPELL?!
Heh heh heh

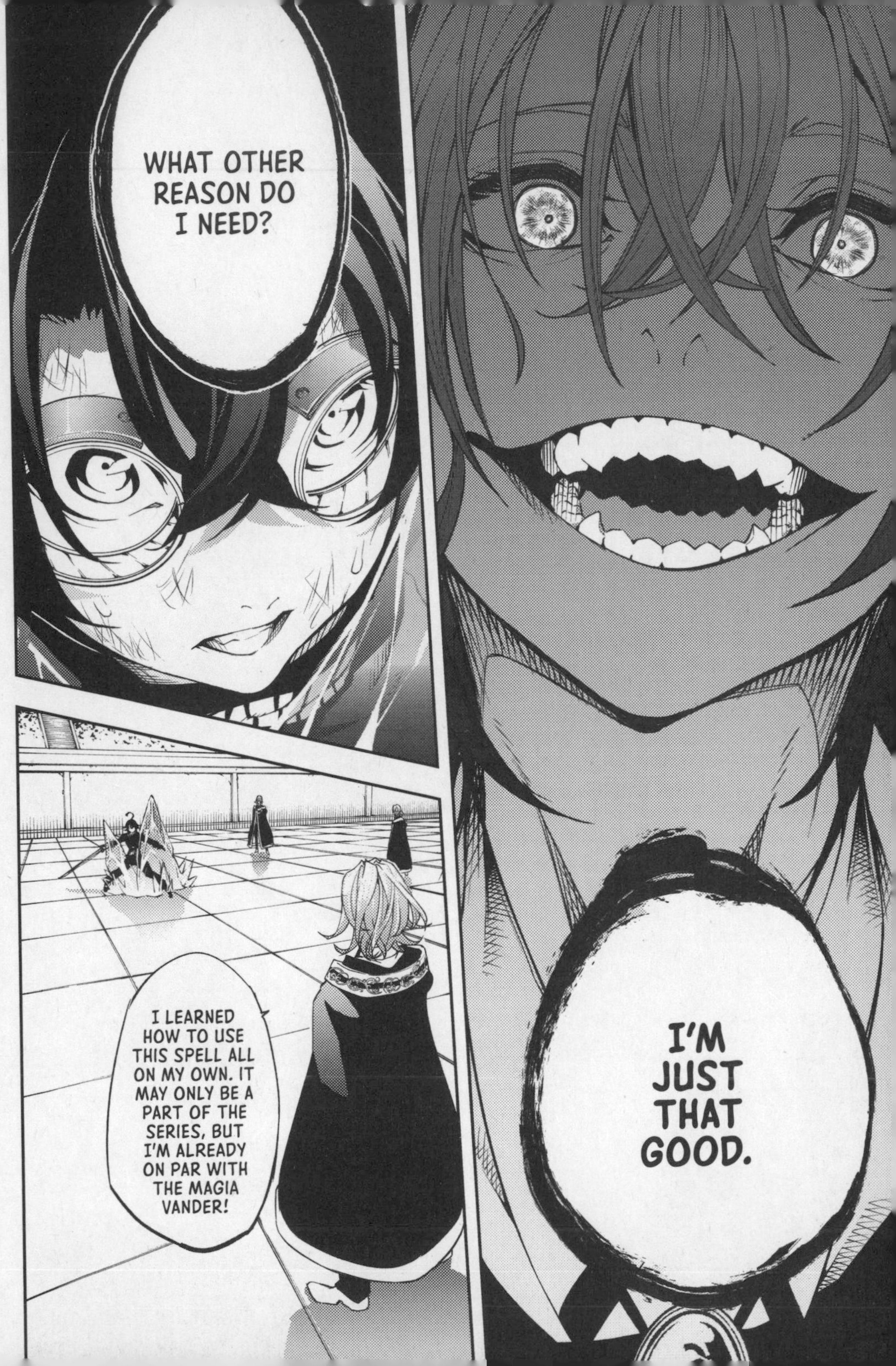
I'M JUST THAT GOOD.
WHAT OTHER REASON DO I NEED?
I LEARNED HOW TO USE THIS SPELL ALL ON MY OWN. IT MAY ONLY BE A PART OF THE SERIES, BUT I'M ALREADY ON PAR WITH THE MAGIA VANDER!

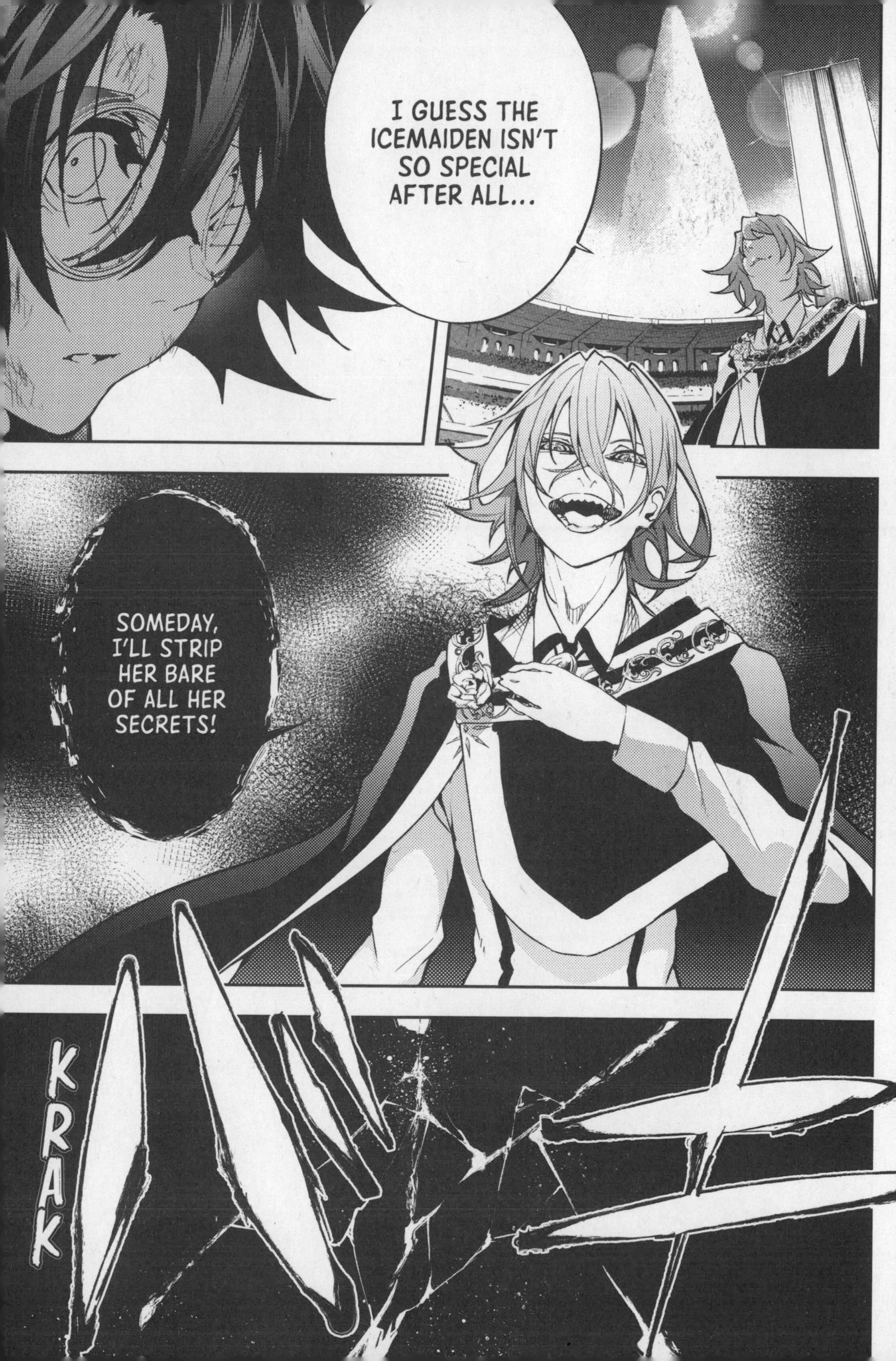
I GUESS THE ICEMAIDEN ISN'T SO SPECIAL AFTER ALL...
SOMEDAY, I'LL STRIP HER BARE OF ALL HER SECRETS!
KRAK

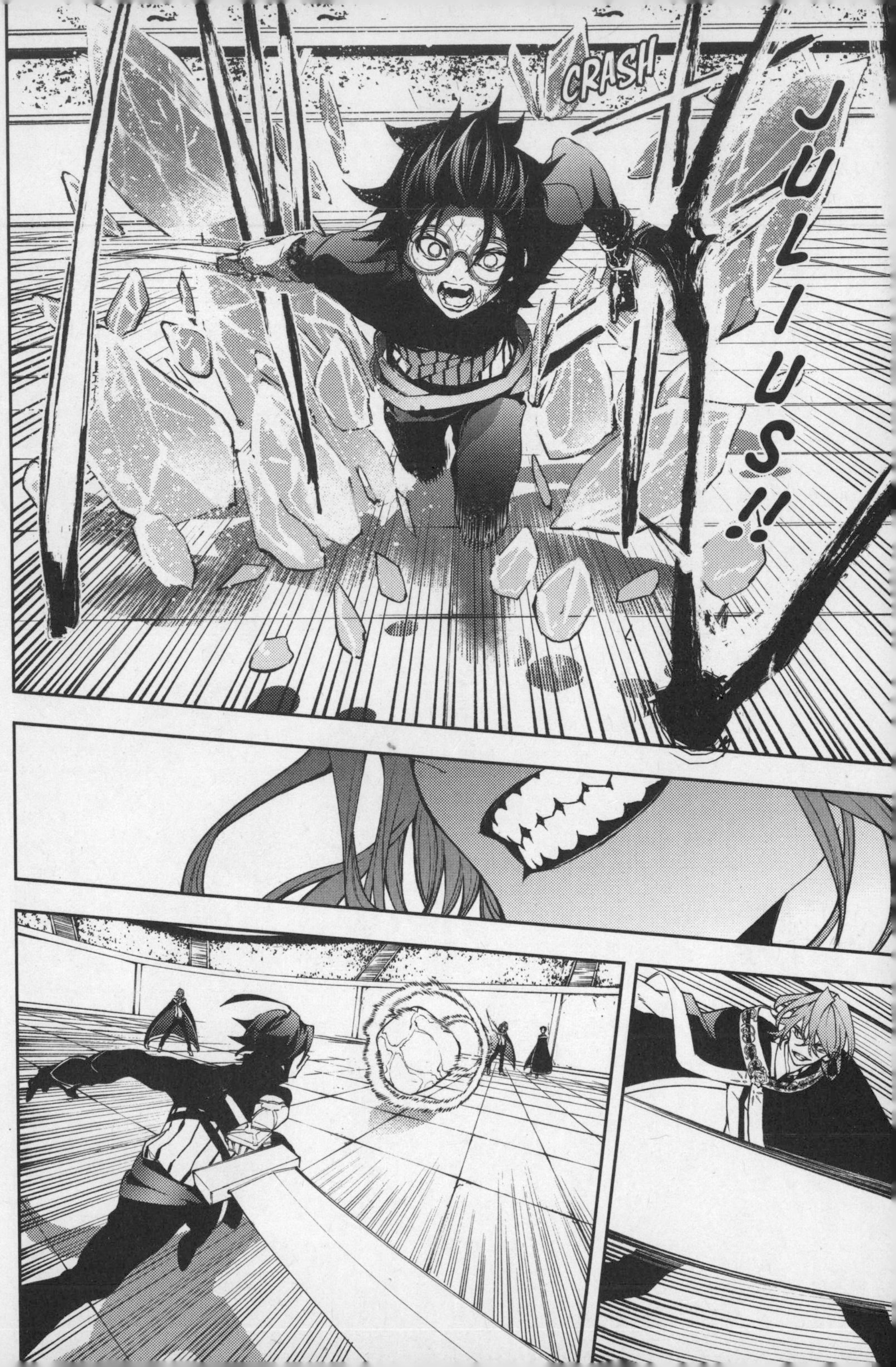
CRASH
JULI-I-US!!

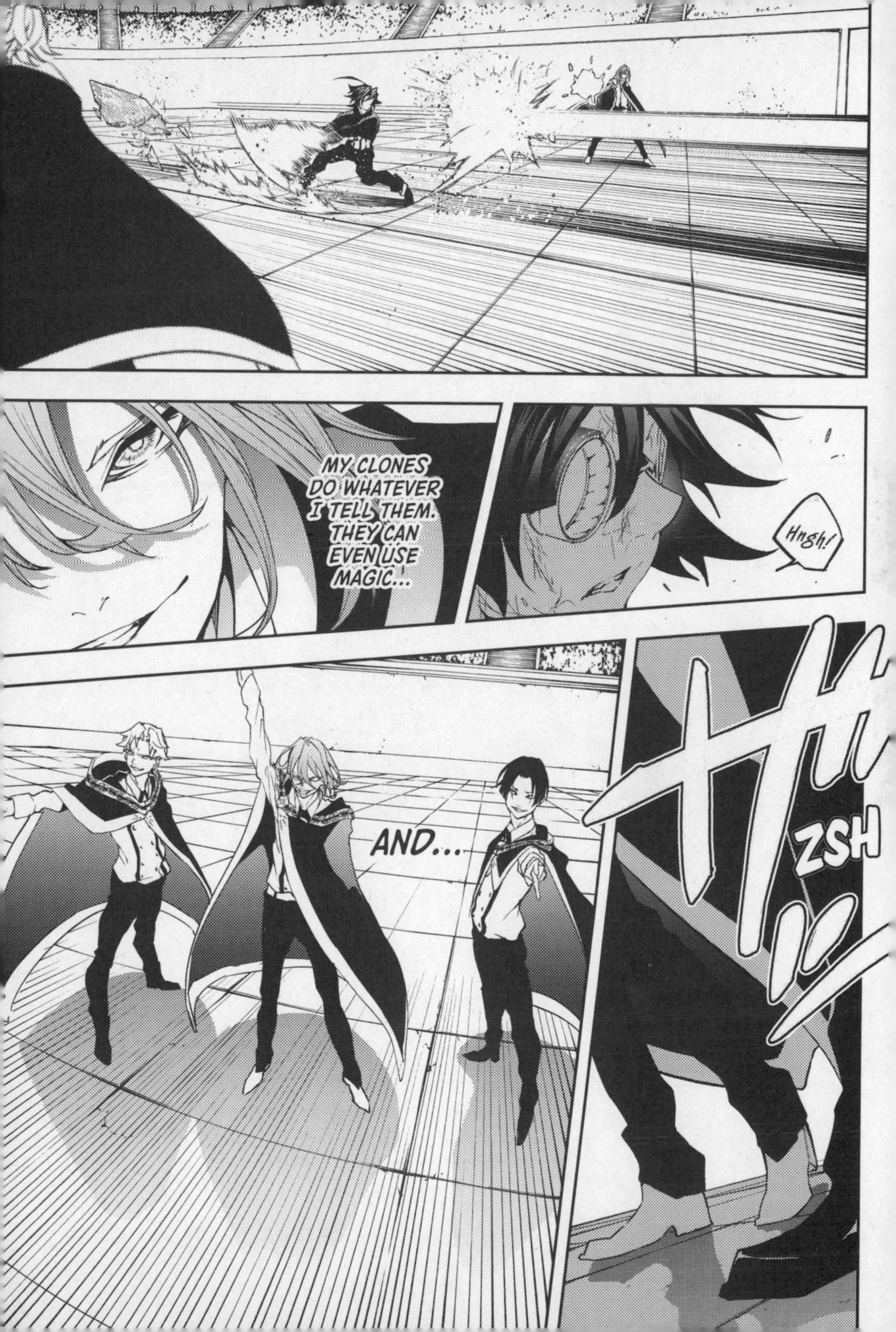
Hngh!
MY CLONES DO WHATEVER I TELL THEM. THEY CAN EVEN USE MAGIC...
ZSH
AND...

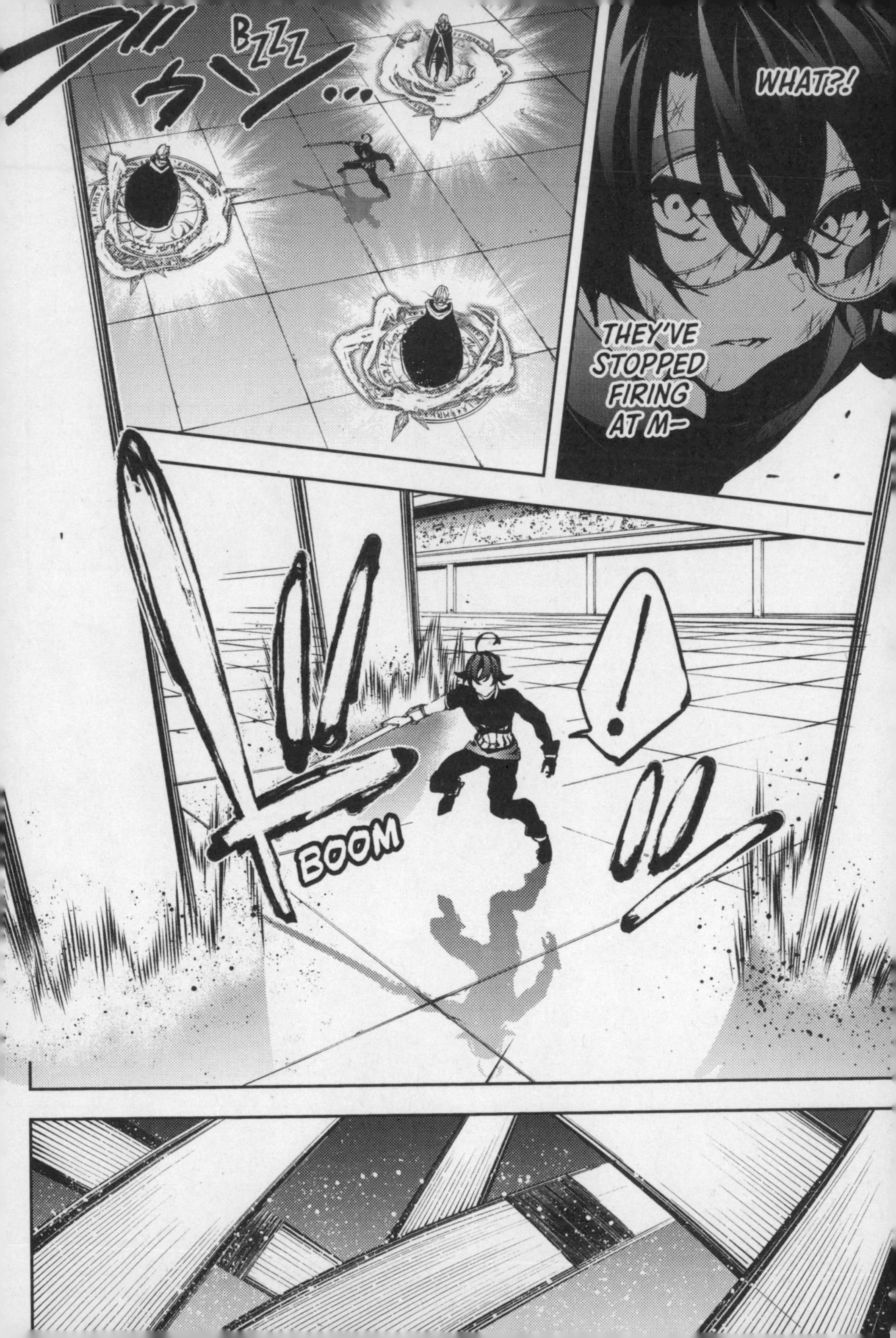
WHAT?!
THEY'VE STOPPED FIRING AT M—
BZZZ...
BOOM

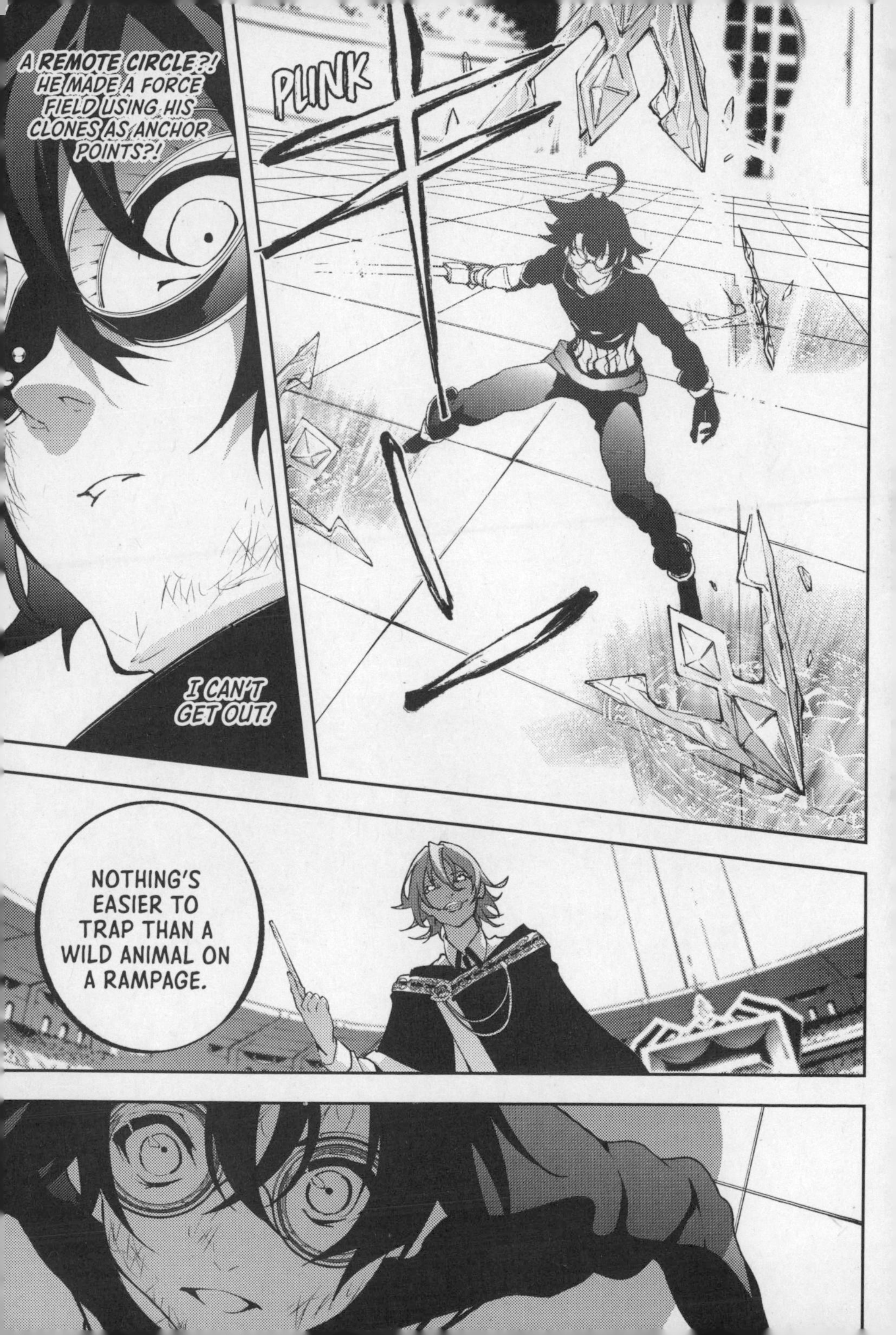
PLINK
A REMOTE CIRCLE?! HE MADE A FORCE FIELD USING HIS CLONES AS ANCHOR POINTS?!
I CAN'T GET OUT!
NOTHING'S EASIER TO TRAP THAN A WILD ANIMAL ON A RAMPAGE.

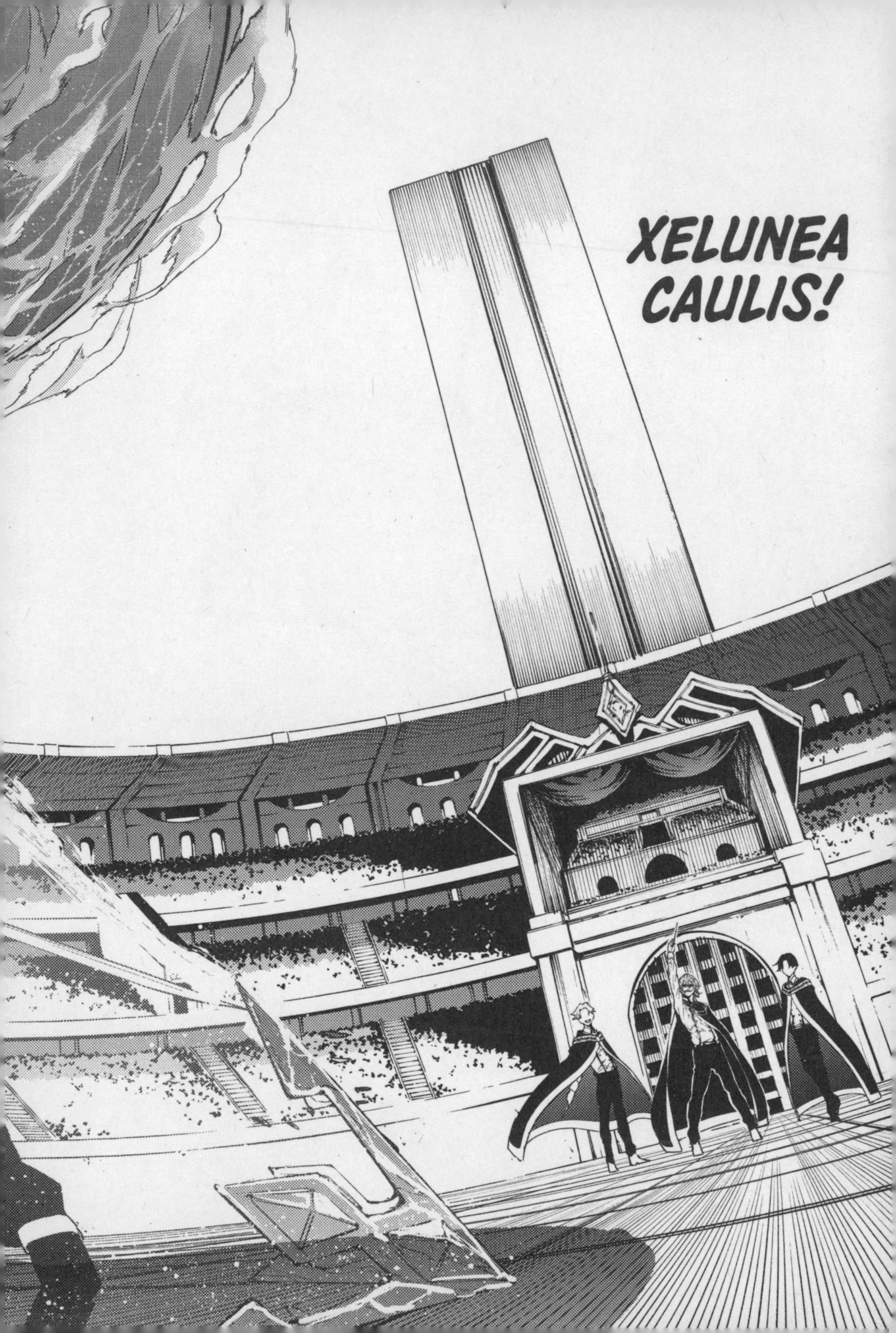
XELUNEA CAULIS!

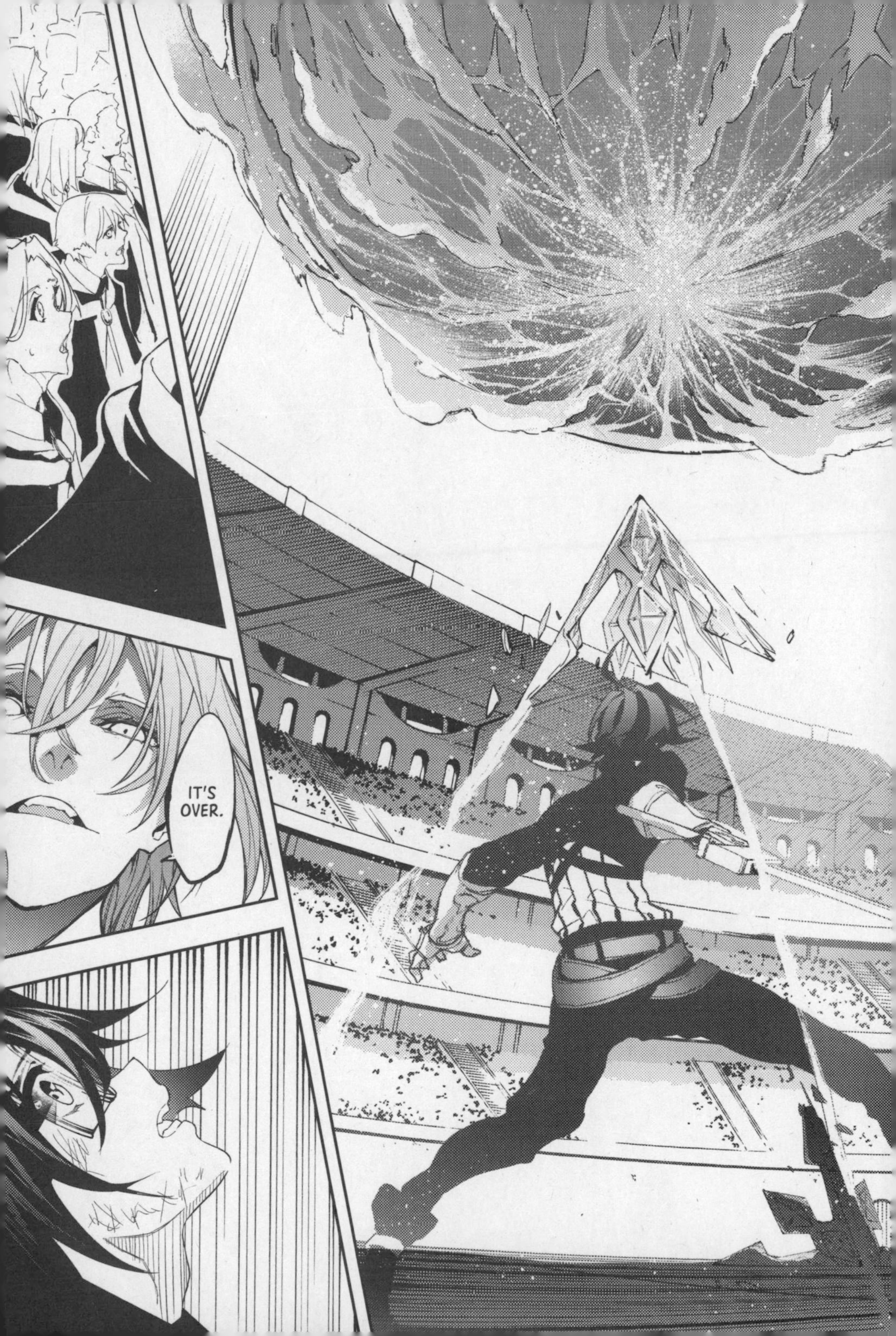
IT'S OVER.

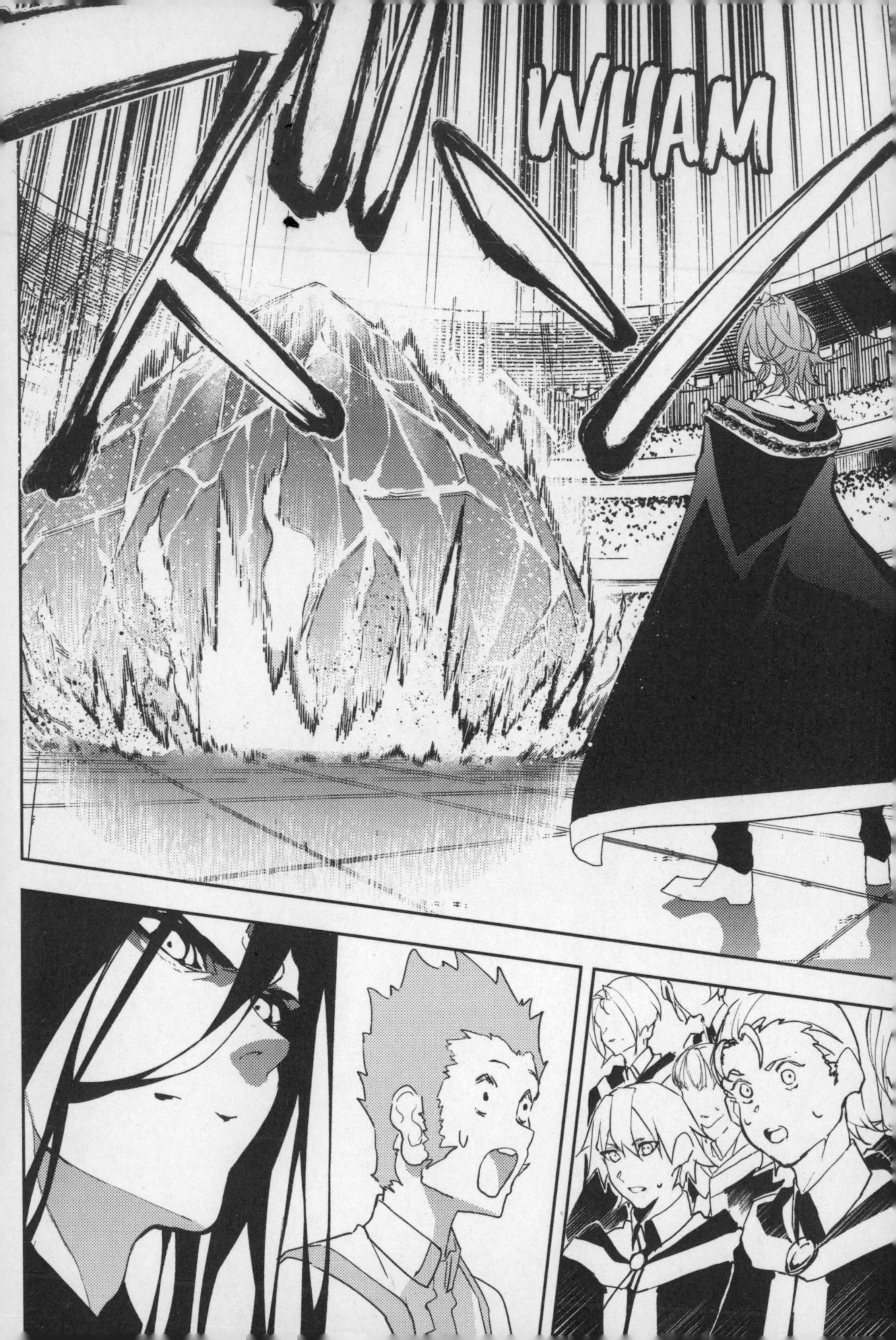
WHAM

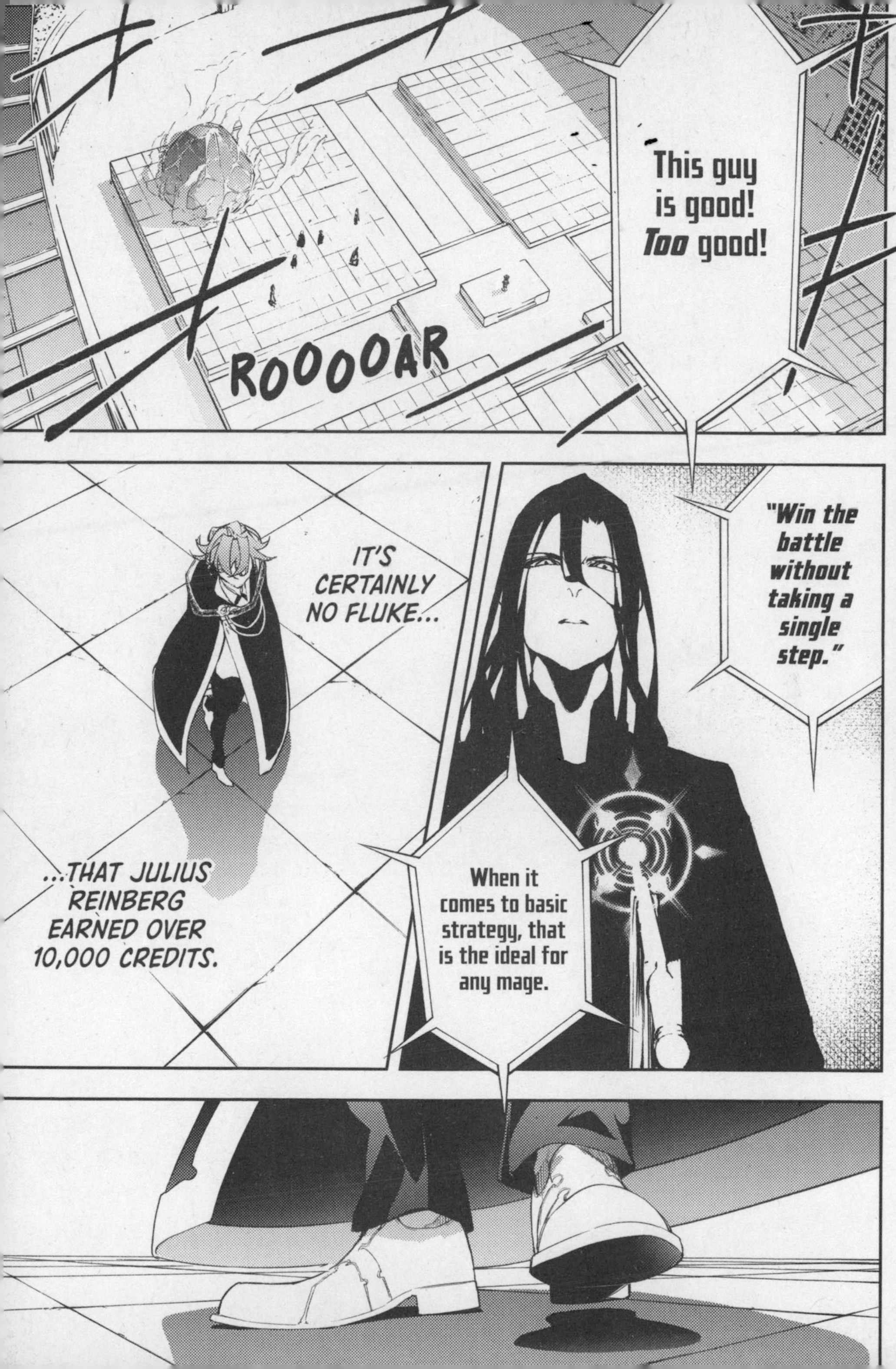
This guy is good! *Too* good!
ROOOOAR
"Win the battle without taking a single step."
When it comes to basic strategy, that is the ideal for any mage.
IT'S CERTAINLY NO FLUKE...
...THAT JULIUS REINBERG EARNED OVER 10,000 CREDITS.

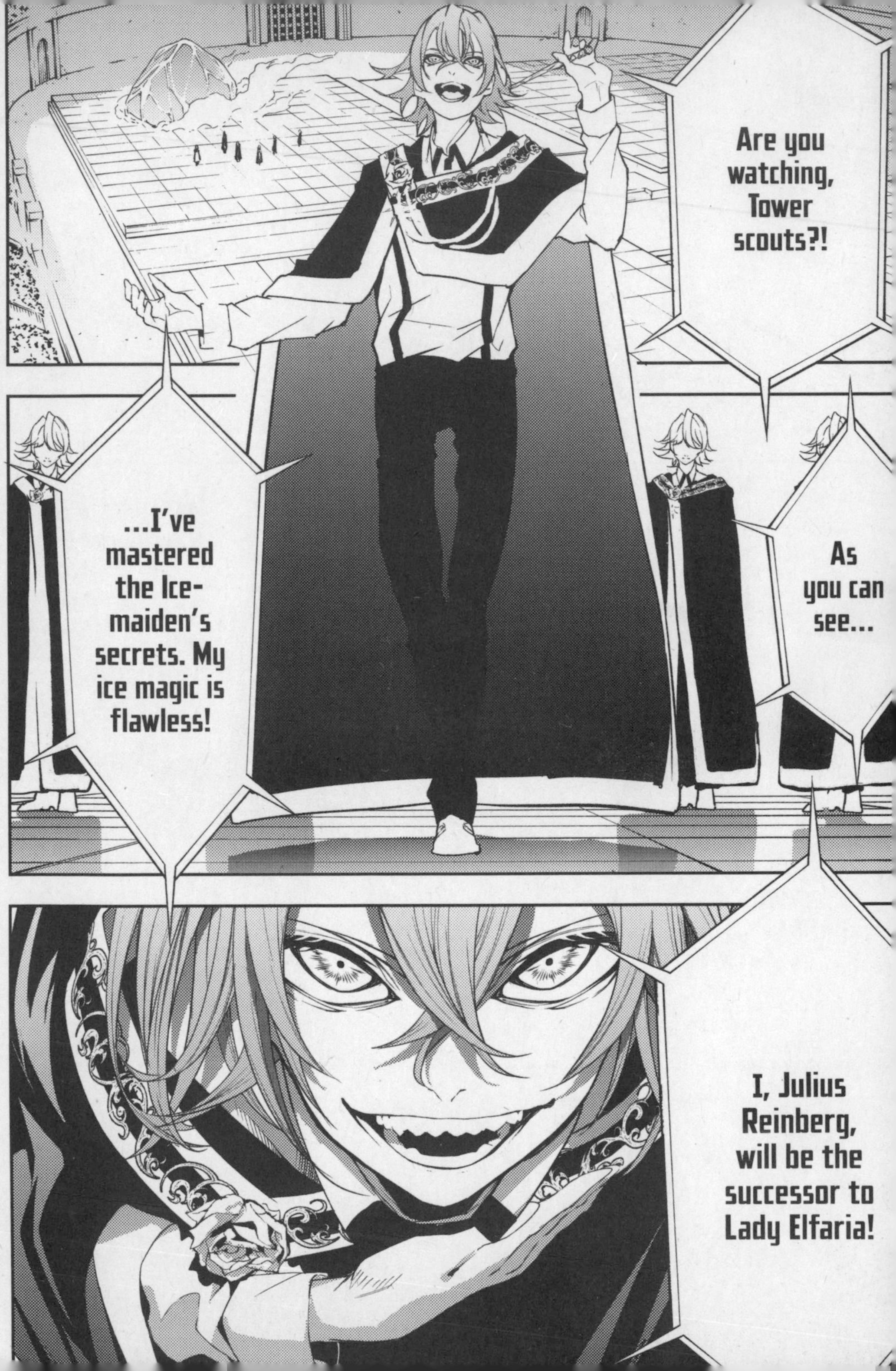
Are you watching, Tower scouts?!
As you can see...
...I've mastered the Ice-maiden's secrets. My ice magic is flawless!
I, Julius Reinberg, will be the successor to Lady Elfaria!

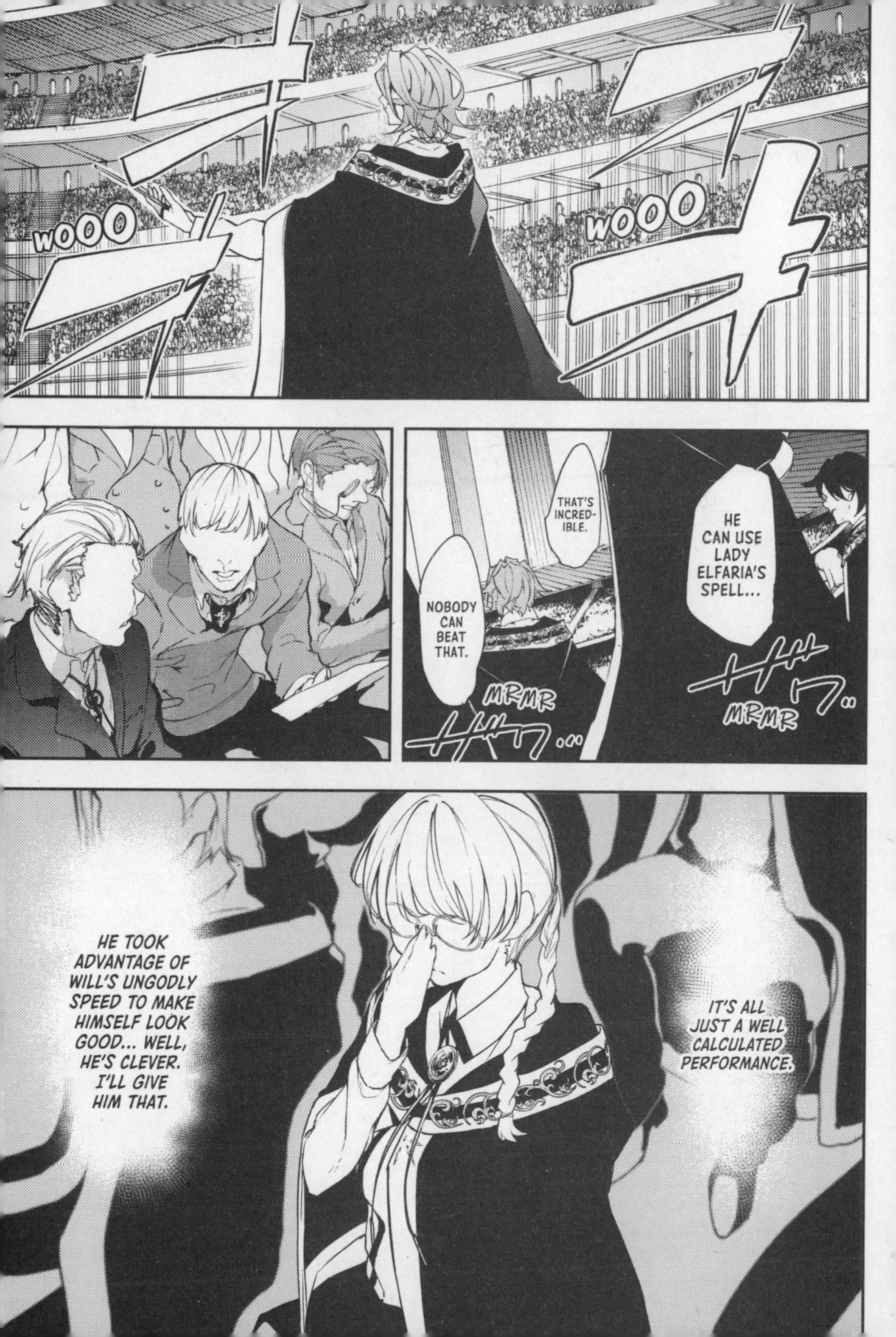
WOOO
WOOO
HE CAN USE LADY ELFARIA'S SPELL...
MRMR
THAT'S INCREDIBLE.
NOBODY CAN BEAT THAT.
MRMR
HE TOOK ADVANTAGE OF WILL'S UNGODLY SPEED TO MAKE HIMSELF LOOK GOOD... WELL, HE'S CLEVER. I'LL GIVE HIM THAT.
IT'S ALL JUST A WELL CALCULATED PERFORMANCE.

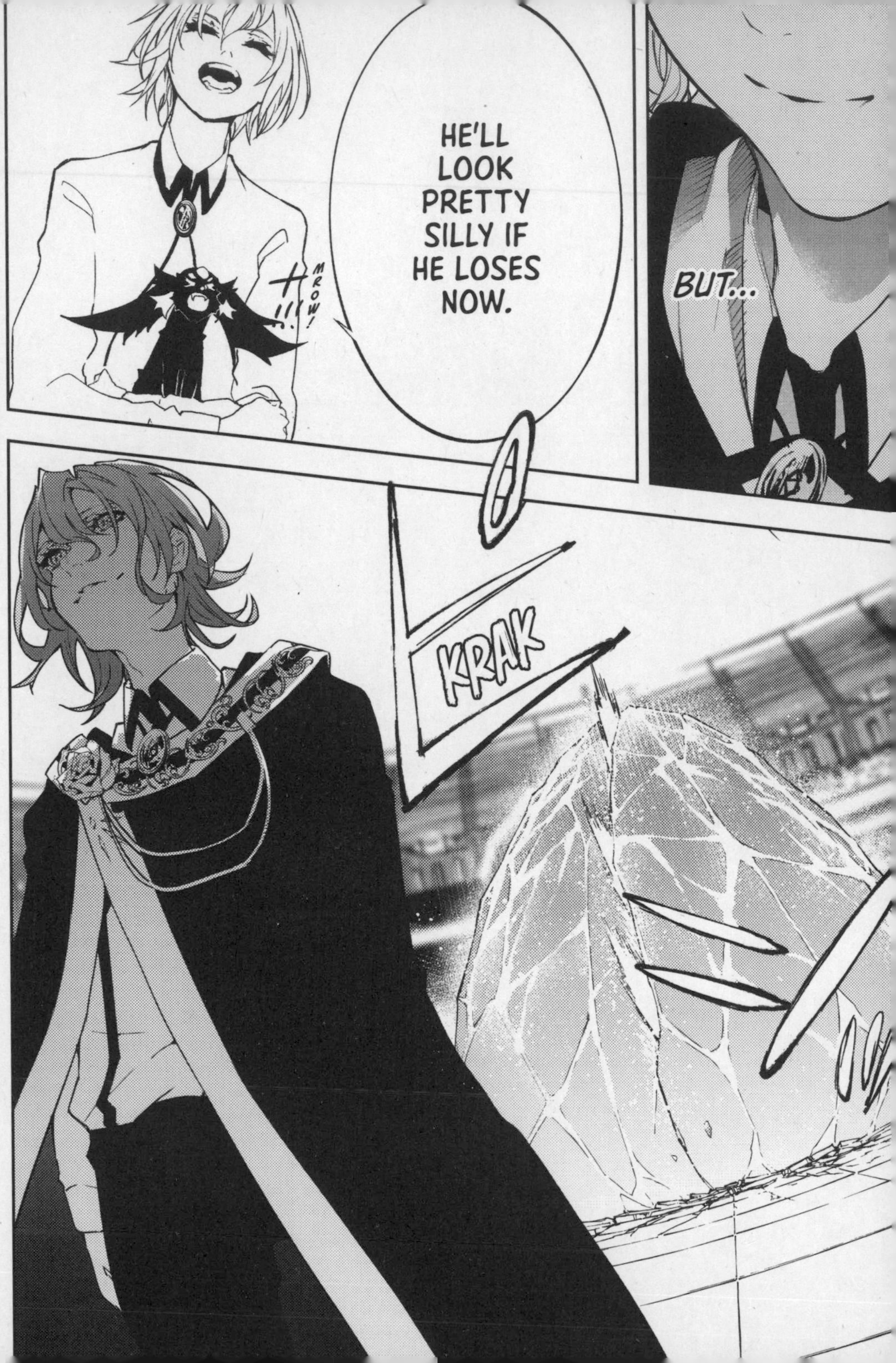
BUT...
HE'LL LOOK PRETTY SILLY IF HE LOSES NOW.
MROW!!!
KRAK

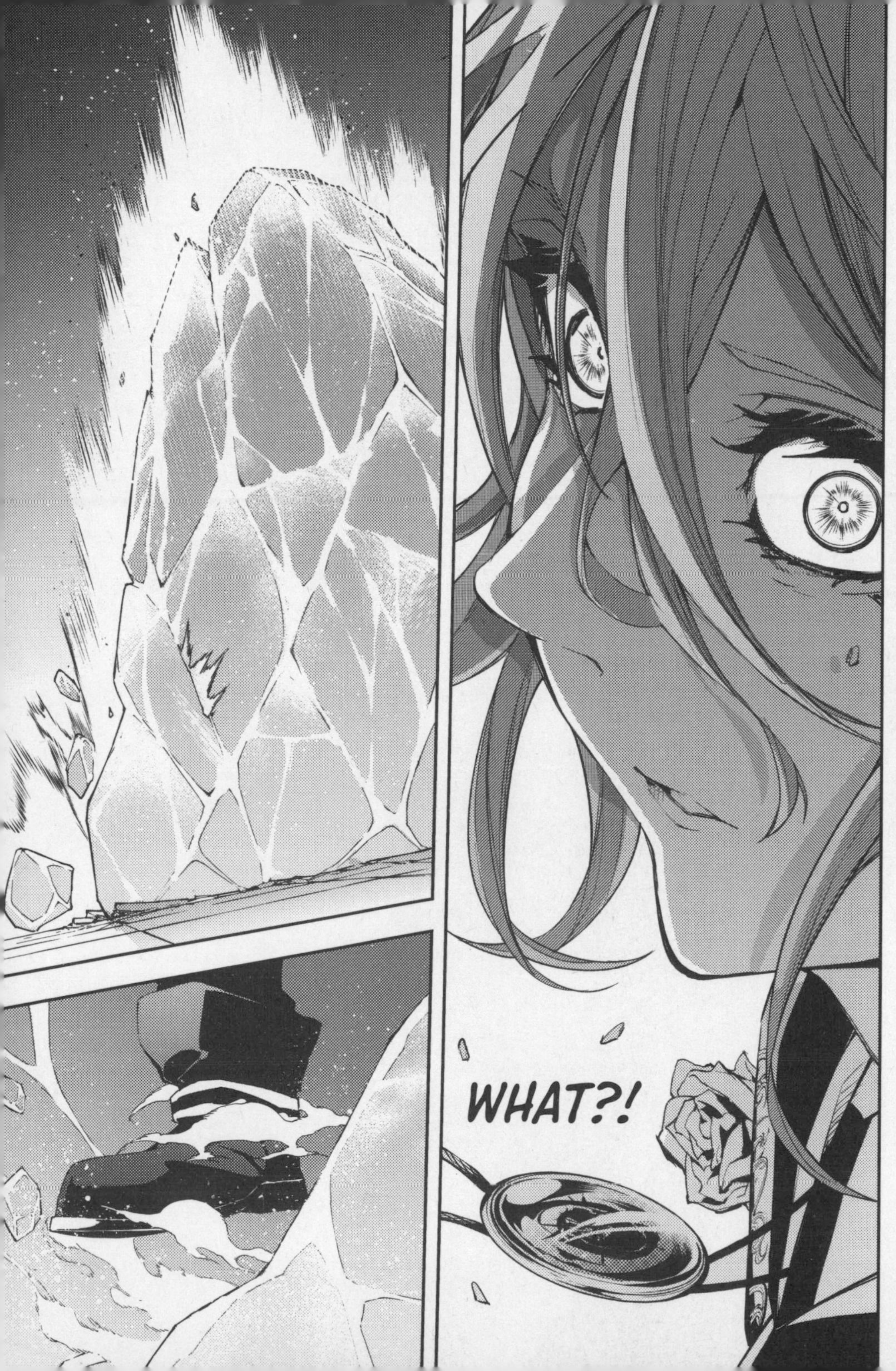
WHAT?!

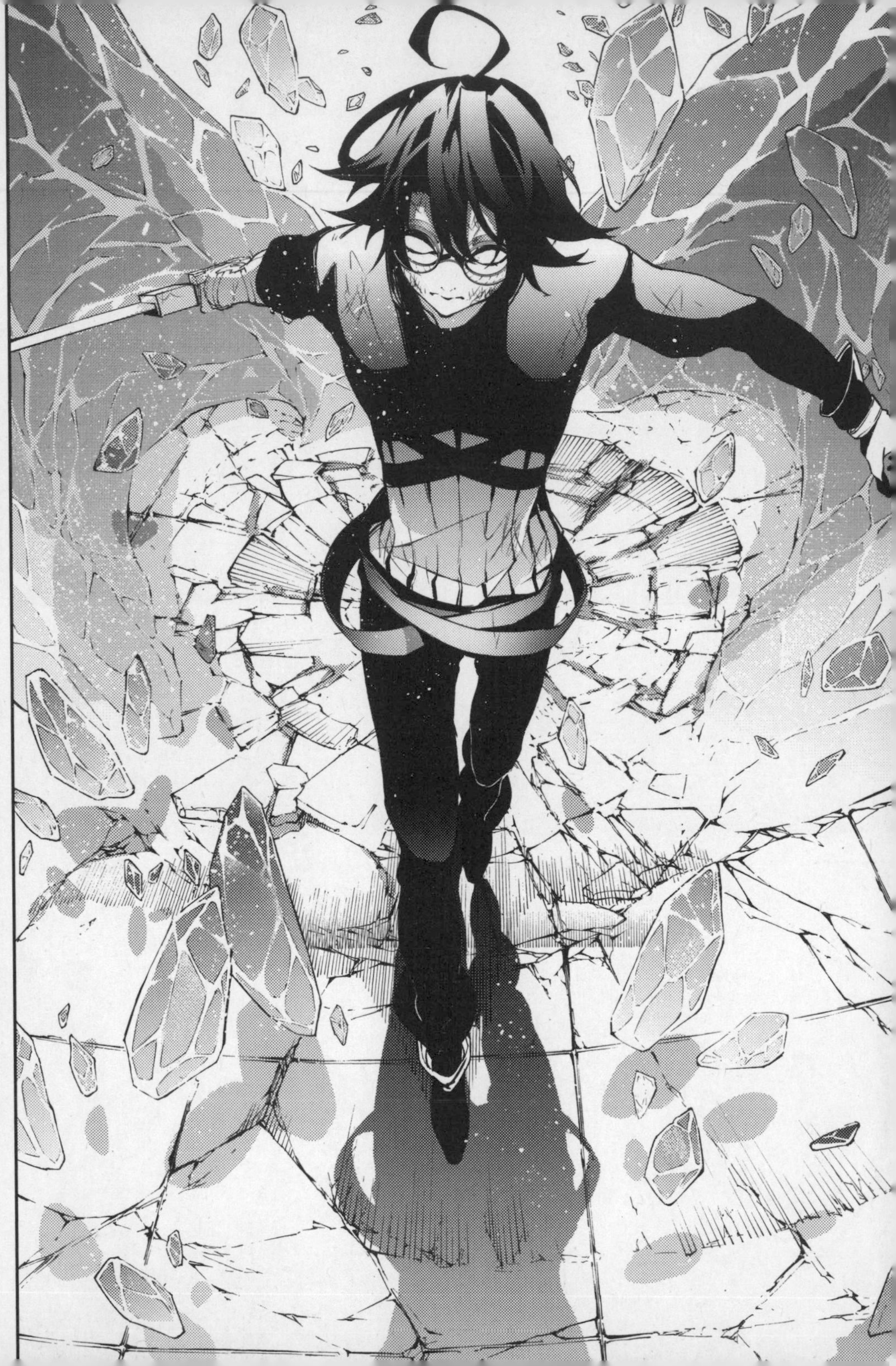

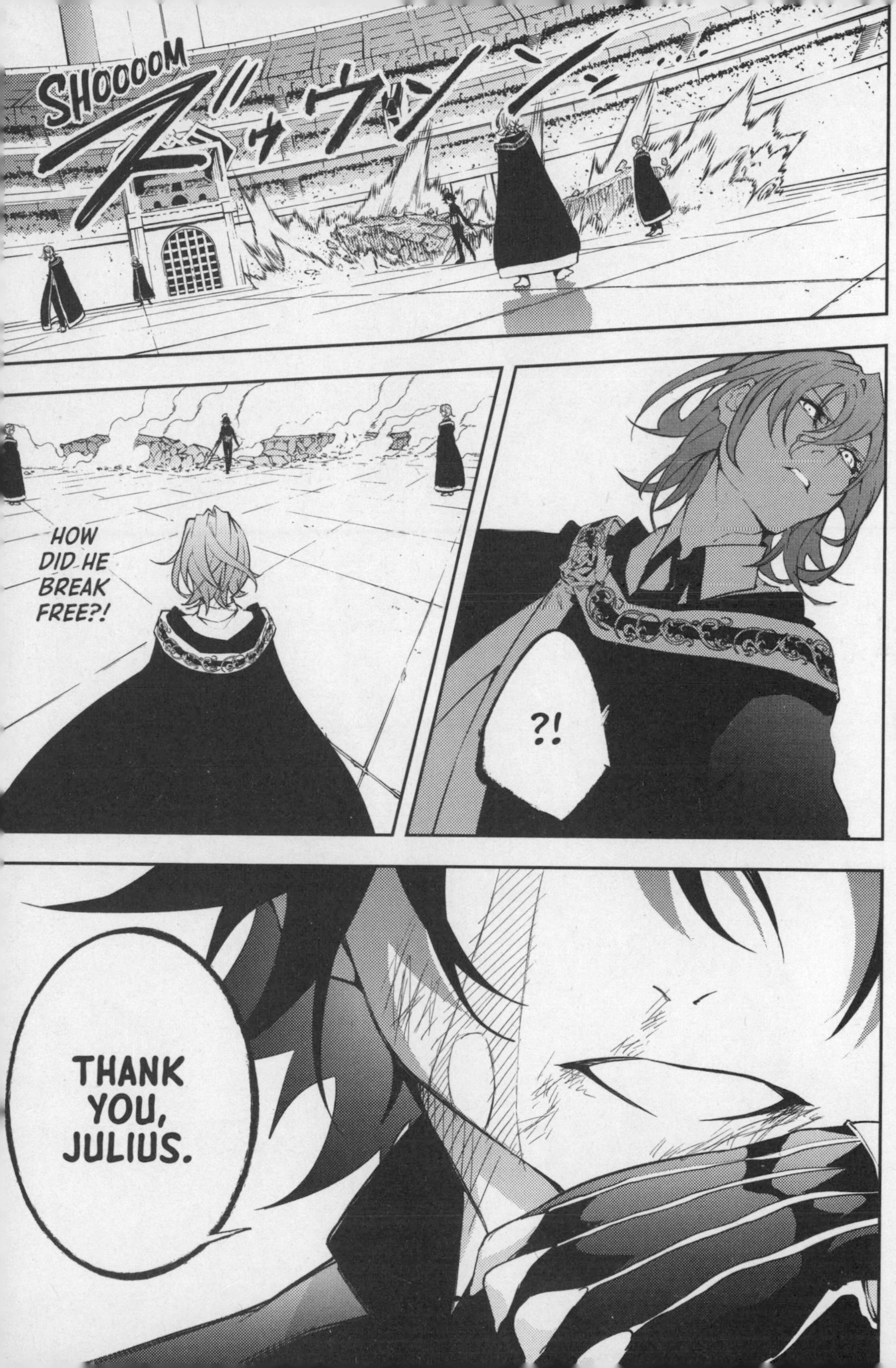
SHOOOOM
?!
HOW DID HE BREAK FREE?!
THANK YOU, JULIUS.

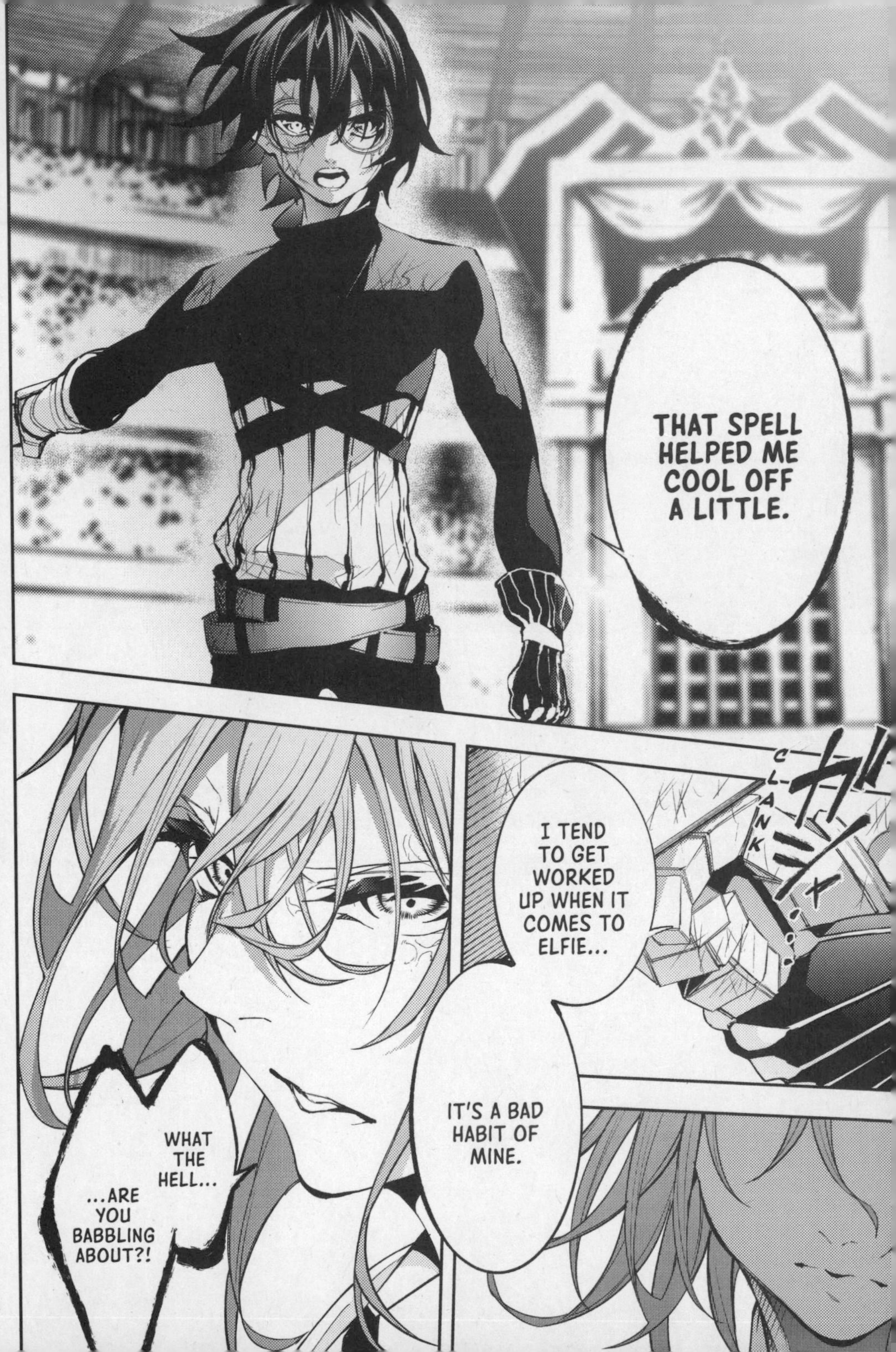
THAT SPELL HELPED ME COOL OFF A LITTLE.
CLANK
I TEND TO GET WORKED UP WHEN IT COMES TO ELFIE...
IT'S A BAD HABIT OF MINE.
WHAT THE HELL...
...ARE YOU BABBLING ABOUT?!

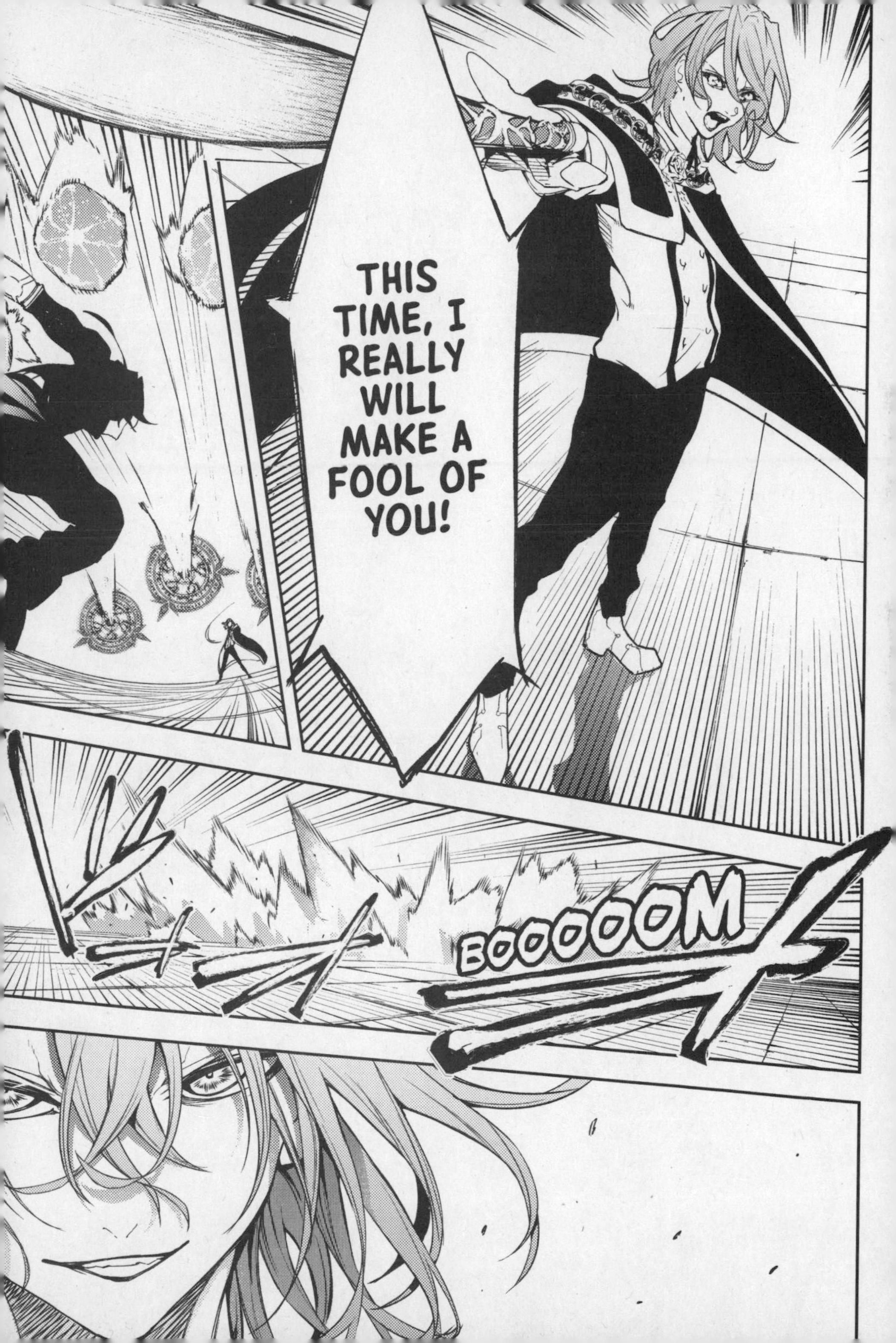
THIS TIME, I REALLY WILL MAKE A FOOL OF YOU!
BOOOOOOM

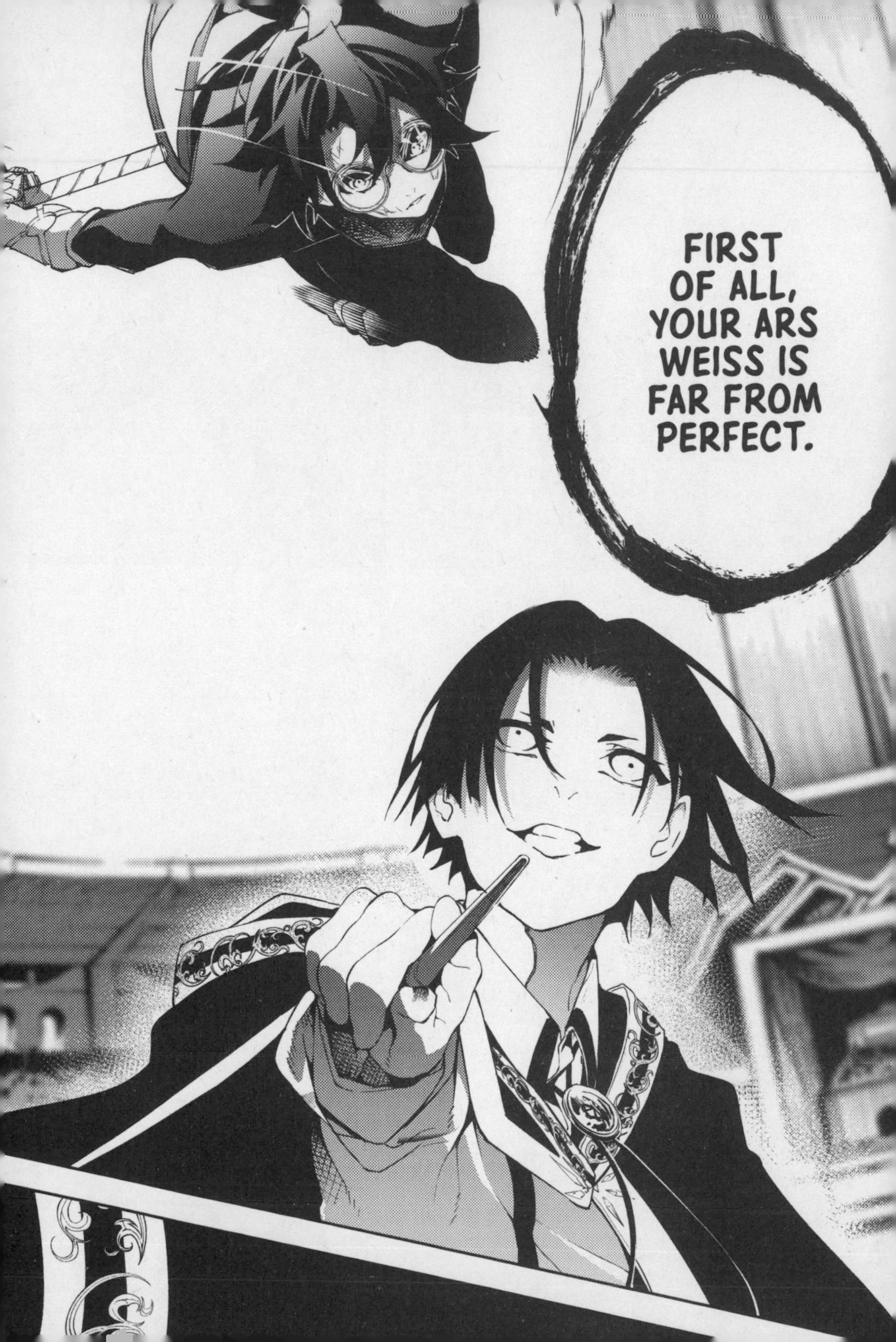
FIRST OF ALL, YOUR ARS WEISS IS FAR FROM PERFECT.

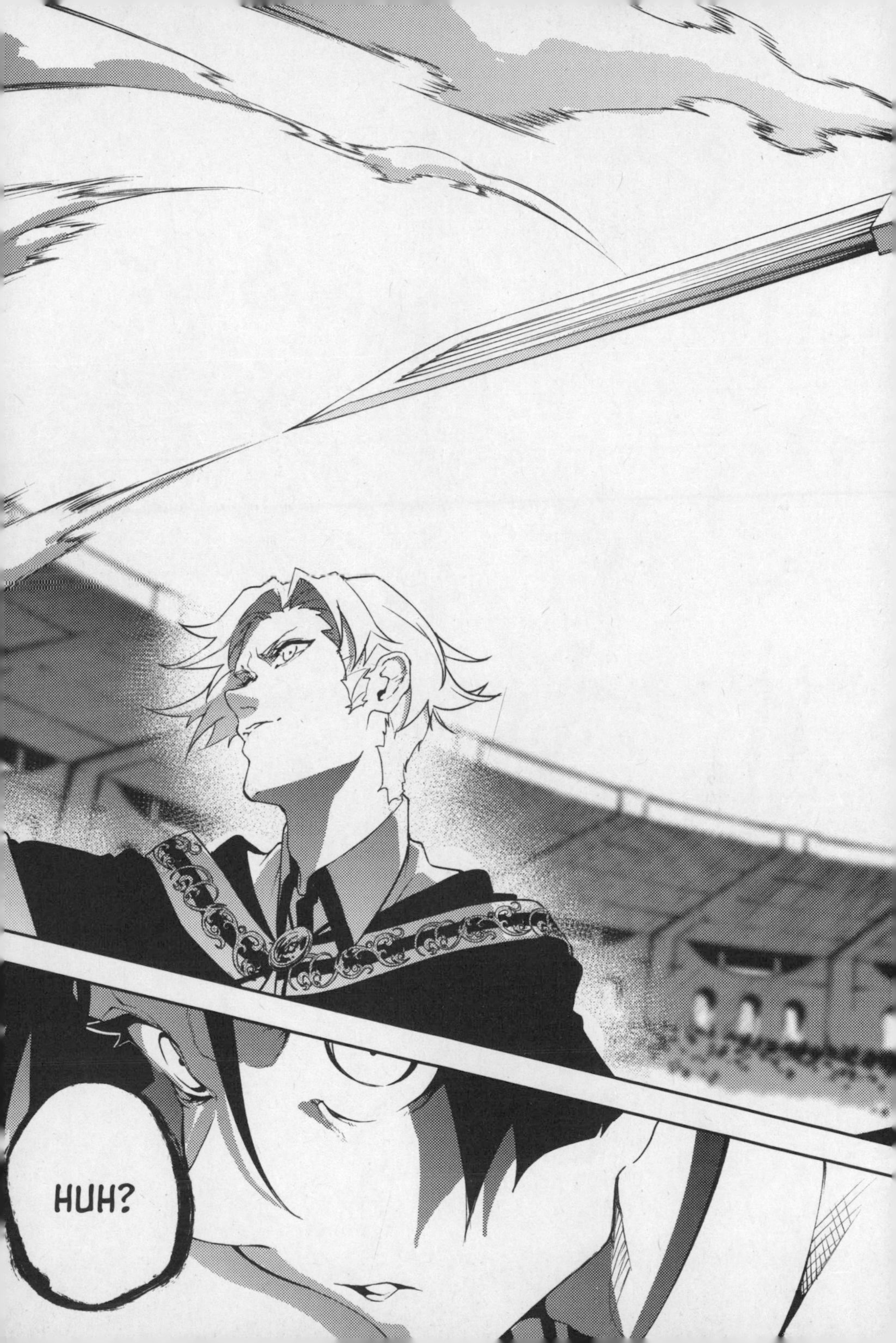
HUH?

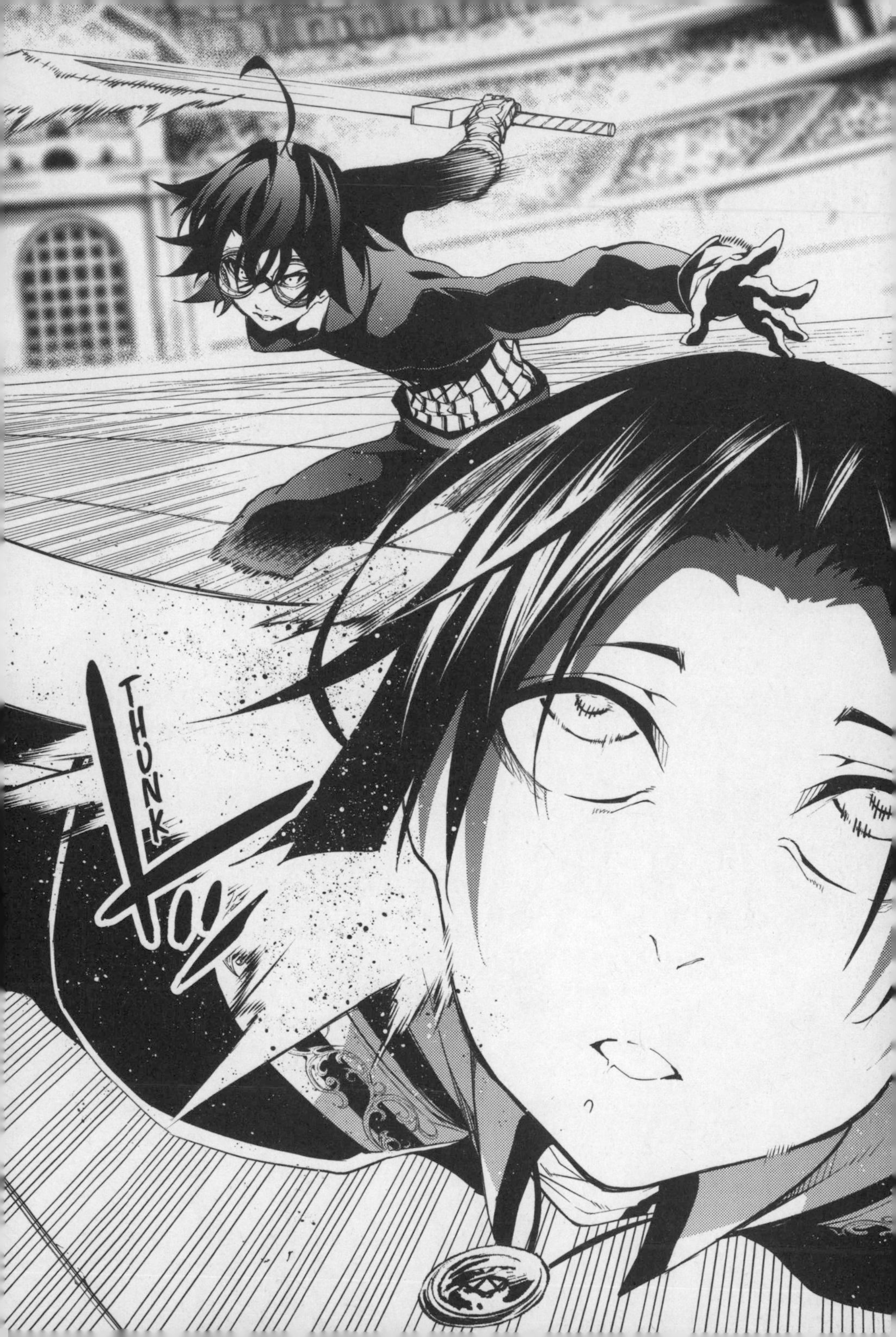
THUNK

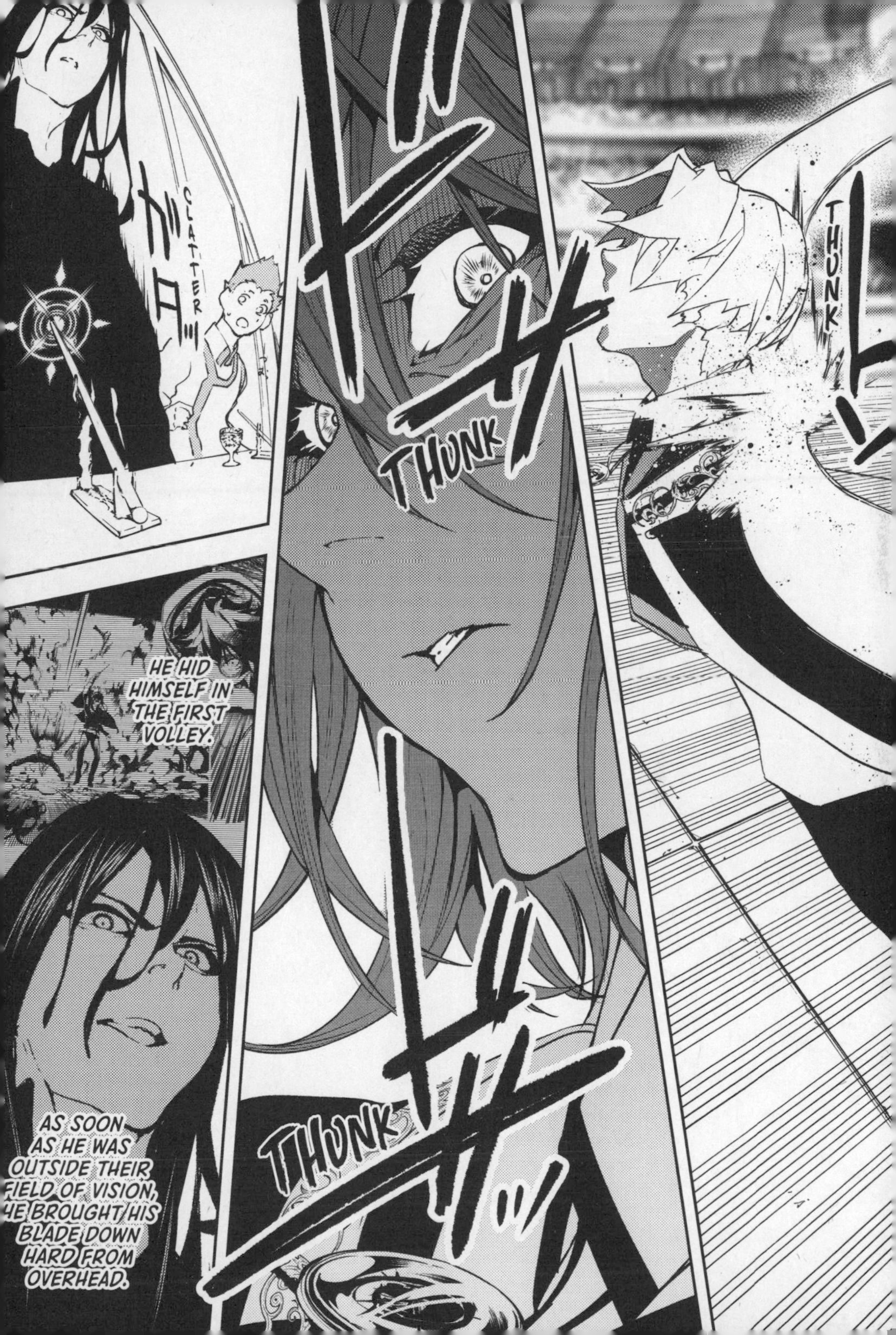
THUNK
THUNK
THUNK
CLATTER
HE HID HIMSELF IN THE FIRST VOLLEY.
AS SOON AS HE WAS OUTSIDE THEIR FIELD OF VISION, HE BROUGHT HIS BLADE DOWN HARD FROM OVERHEAD.

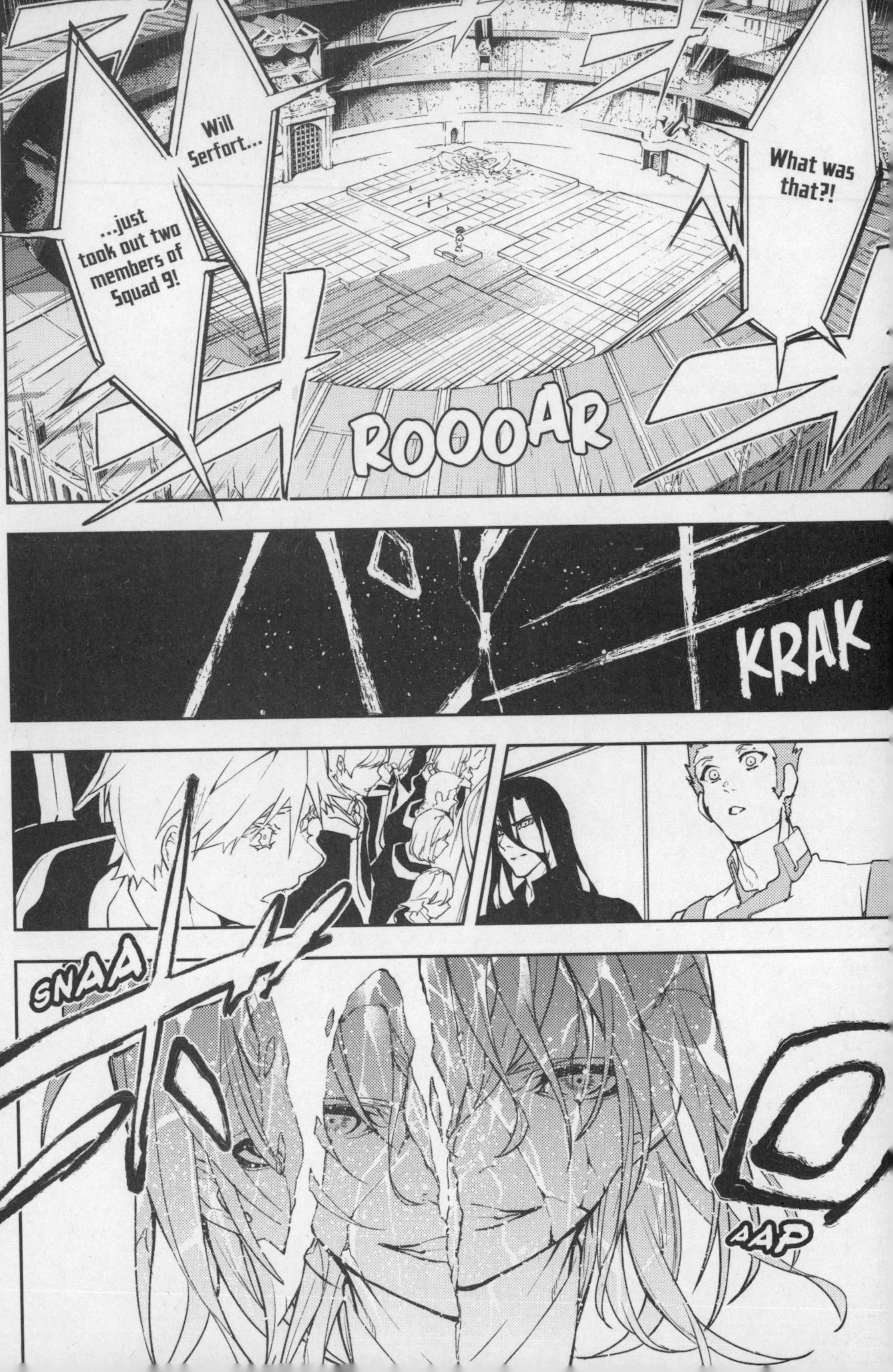
What was that?!
Will Serfort...
...just took out two members of Squad 9!
ROOOAR
KRAK
SNAA
AAP

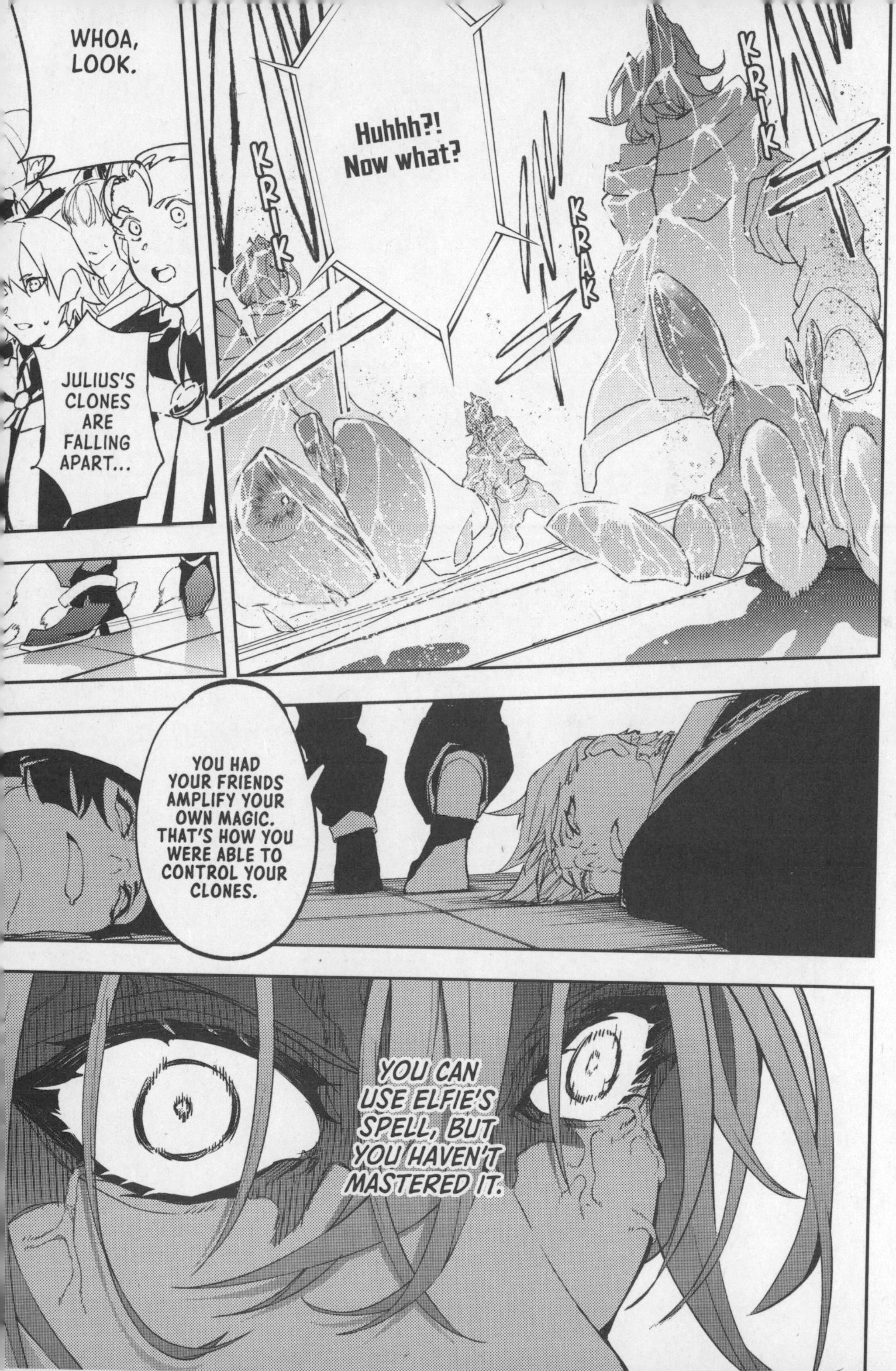
KRIK
KRAK
Huhhh?! Now what?
KRIK
WHOA, LOOK.
JULIUS'S CLONES ARE FALLING APART...
YOU HAD YOUR FRIENDS AMPLIFY YOUR OWN MAGIC. THAT'S HOW YOU WERE ABLE TO CONTROL YOUR CLONES.
YOU CAN USE ELFIE'S SPELL, BUT YOU HAVEN'T MASTERED IT.

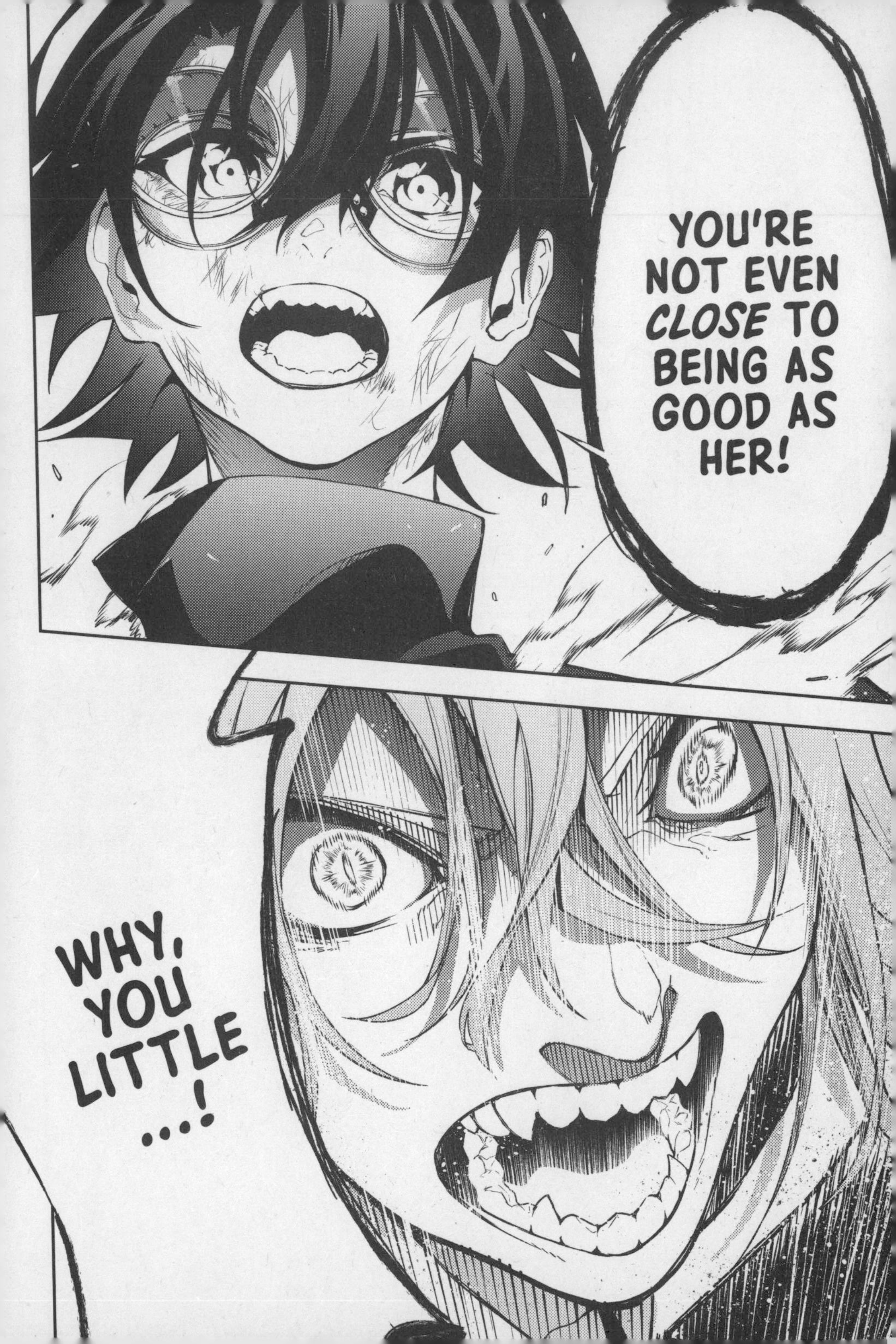
YOU'RE NOT EVEN CLOSE TO BEING AS GOOD AS HER!
WHY, YOU LITTLE ...!

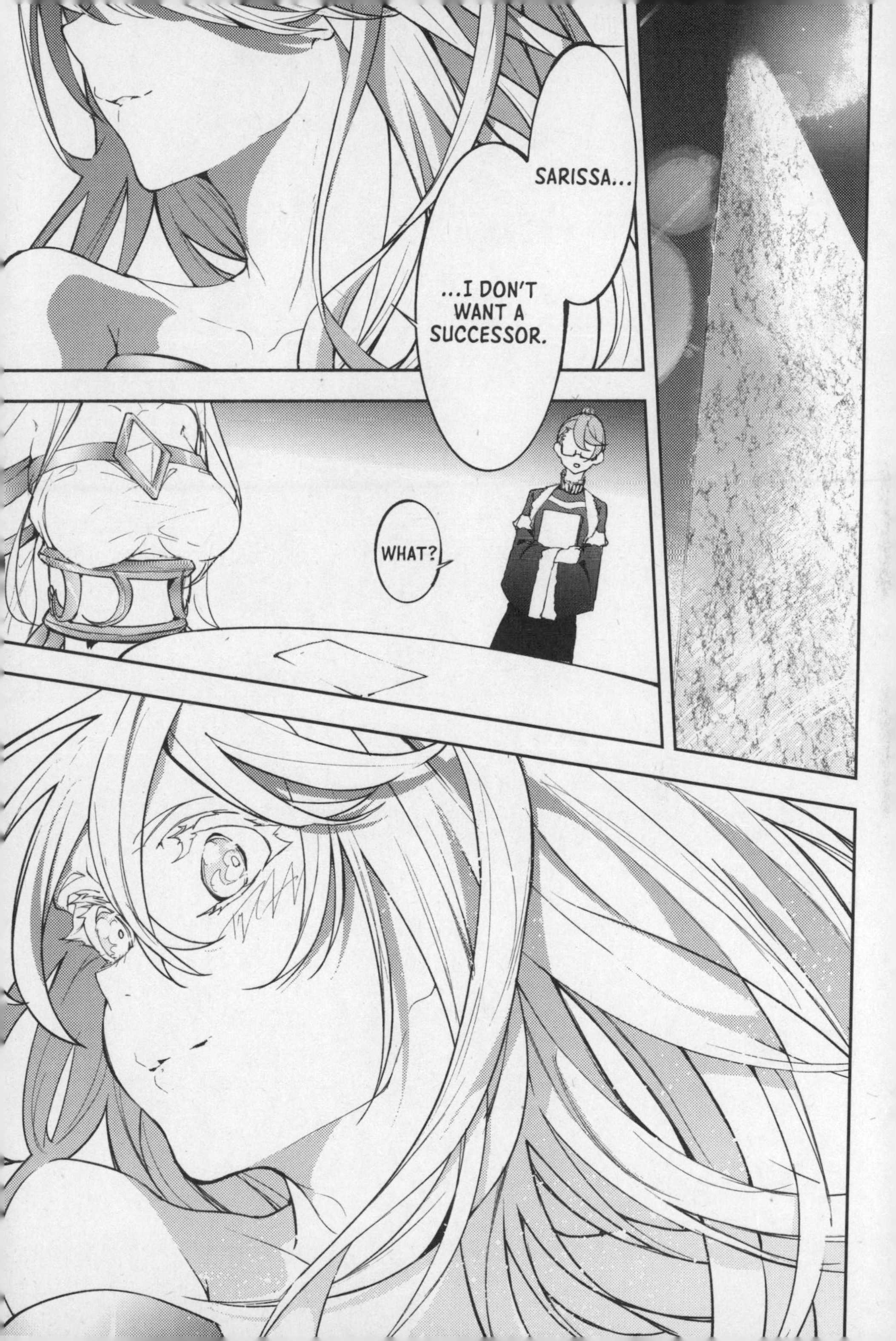
SARISSA...
...I DON'T WANT A SUCCESSOR.
WHAT?

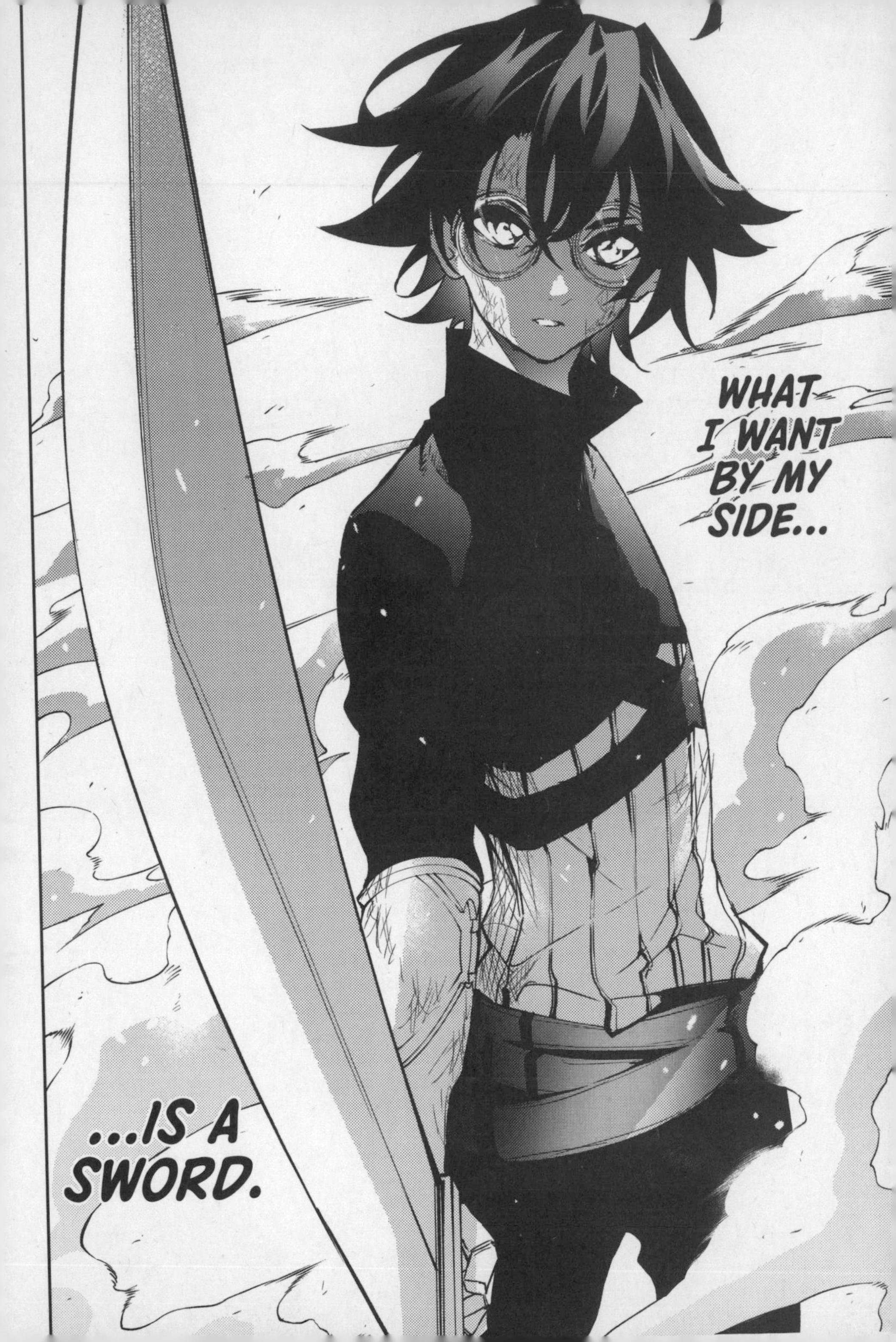
WHAT I WANT BY MY SIDE...
...IS A SWORD.

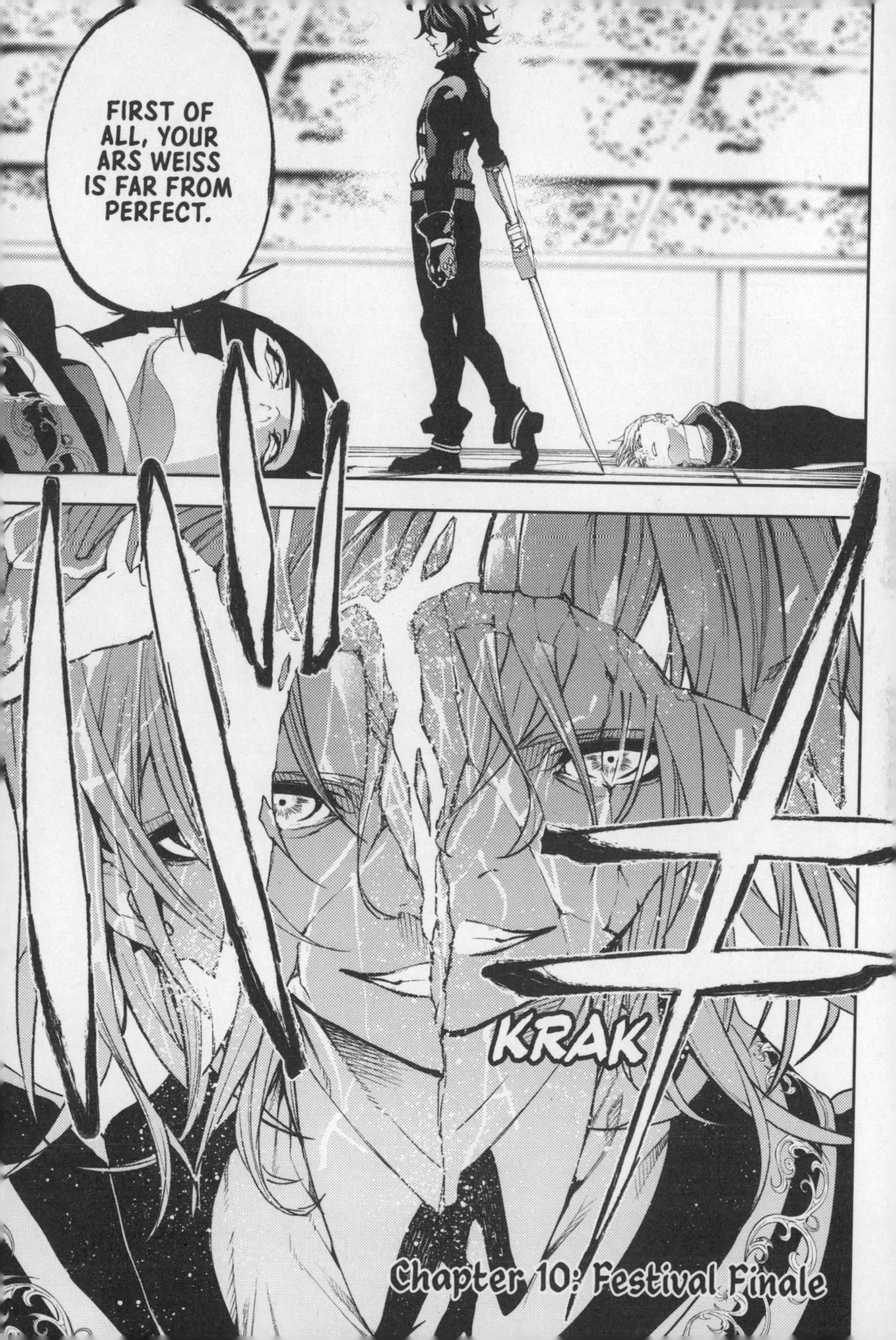
FIRST OF ALL, YOUR ARS WEISS IS FAR FROM PERFECT.
KRAK
Chapter 10: Festival Finale

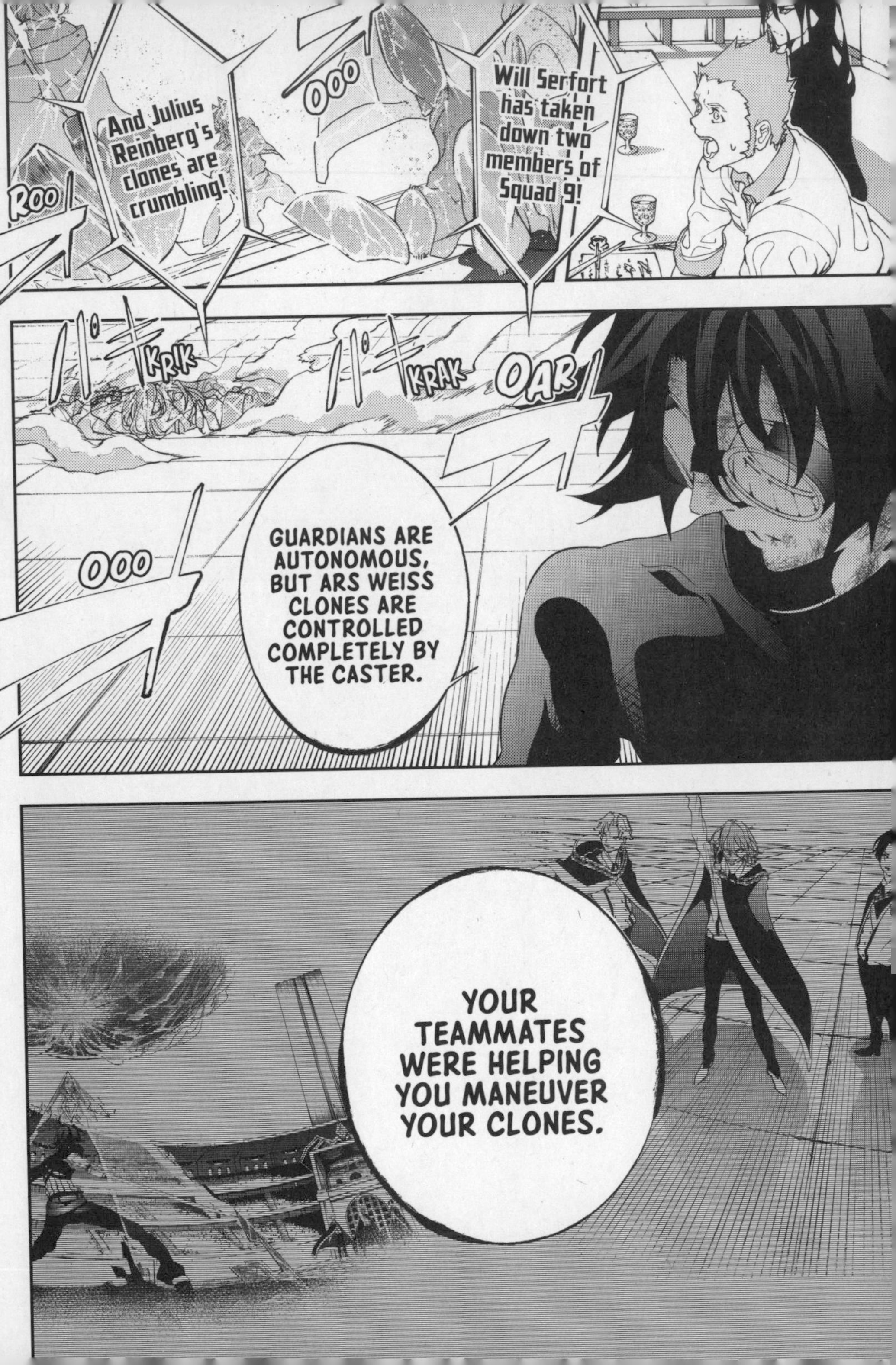
Will Serfort has taken down two members of Squad 9!
OOO
And Julius Reinberg's clones are crumbling!
ROO
OAR
KRAK
KRIK
GUARDIANS ARE AUTONOMOUS, BUT ARS WEISS CLONES ARE CONTROLLED COMPLETELY BY THE CASTER.
OOO
YOUR TEAMMATES WERE HELPING YOU MANEUVER YOUR CLONES.

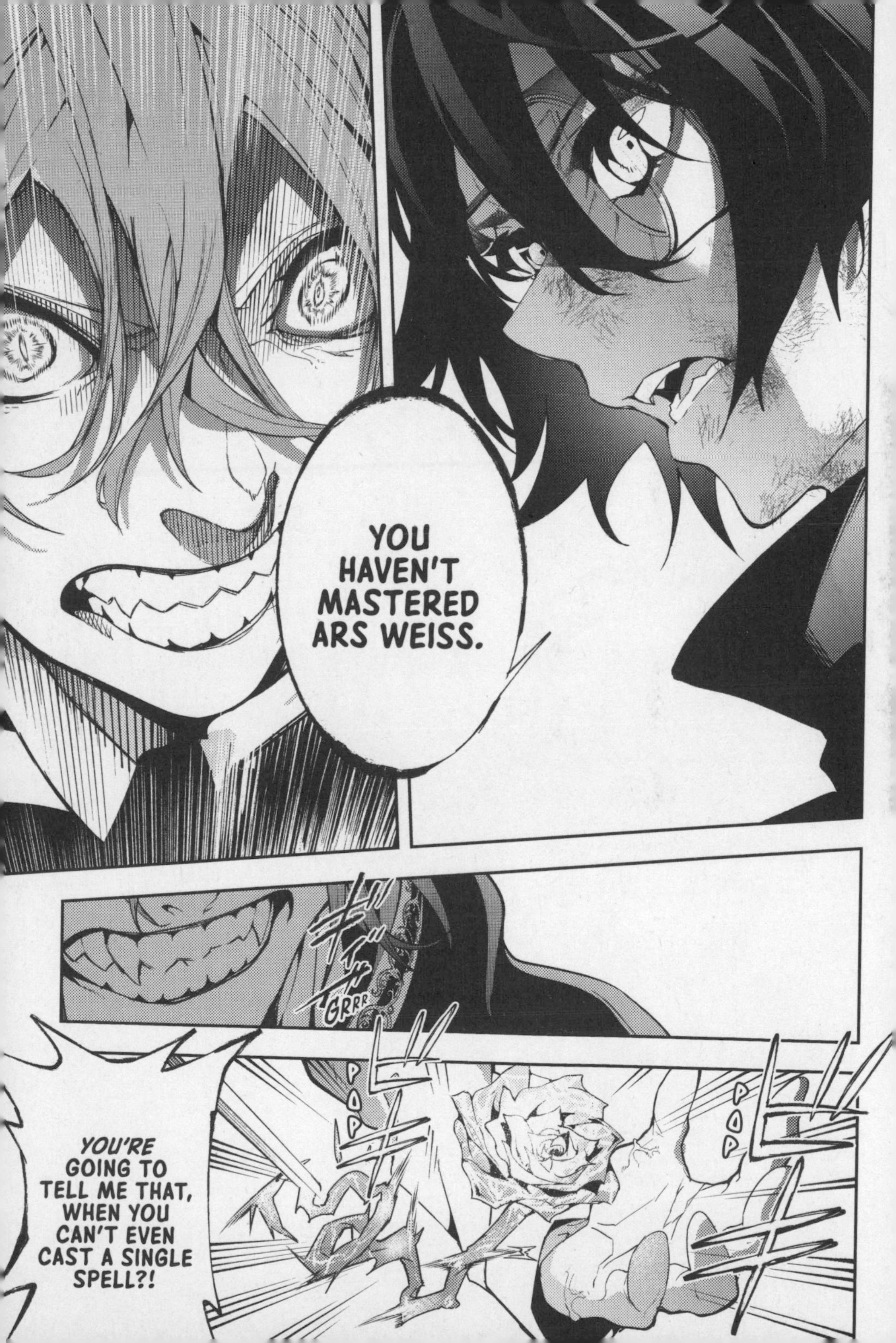
YOU HAVEN'T MASTERED ARS WEISS.
GRRR
POP
POP
YOU'RE GOING TO TELL ME THAT, WHEN YOU CAN'T EVEN CAST A SINGLE SPELL?!

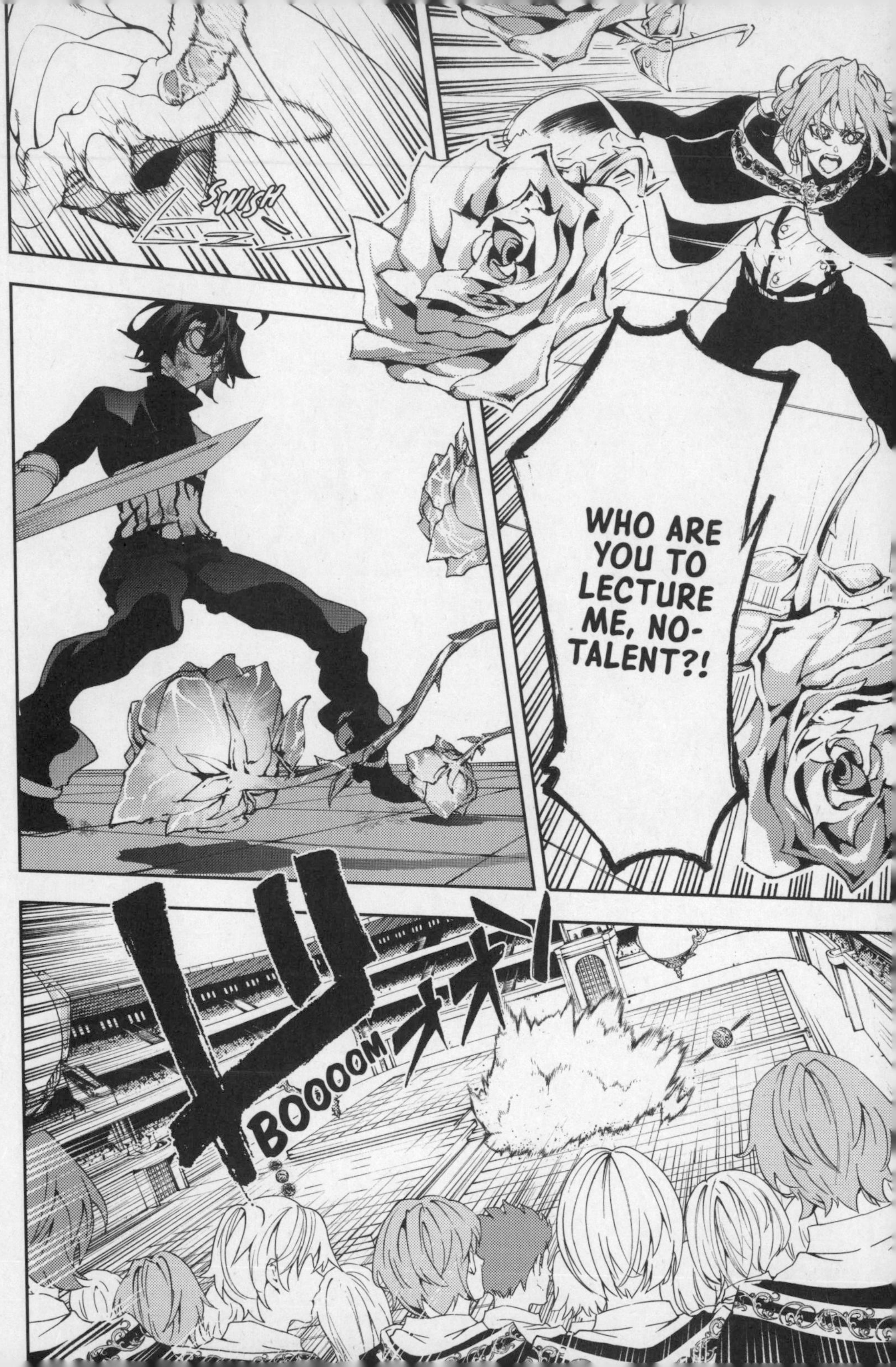
SWISH
WHO ARE YOU TO LECTURE ME, NO-TALENT?!
ドッ
BOOOOM
ォォ

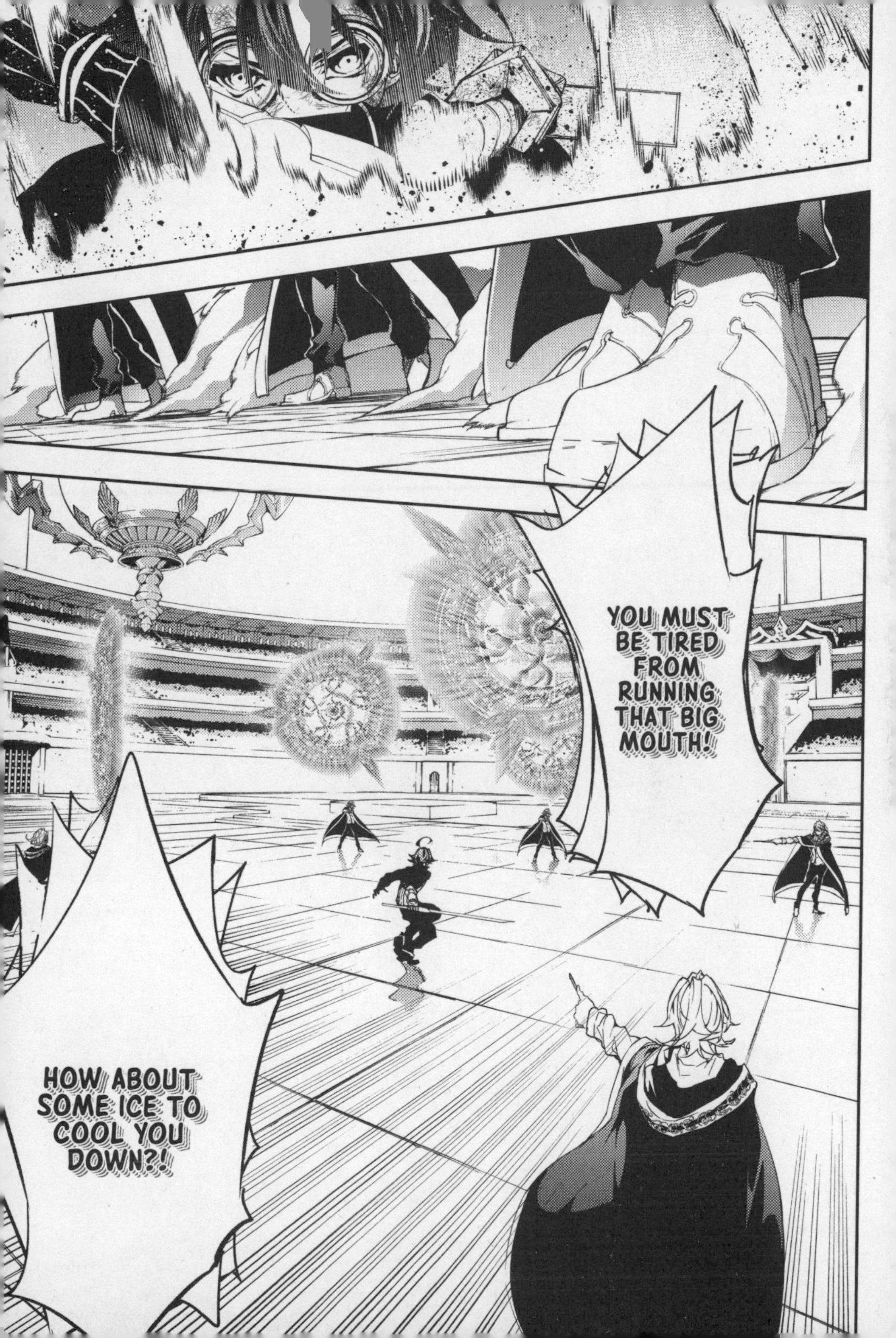
YOU MUST BE TIRED FROM RUNNING THAT BIG MOUTH!
HOW ABOUT SOME ICE TO COOL YOU DOWN?!

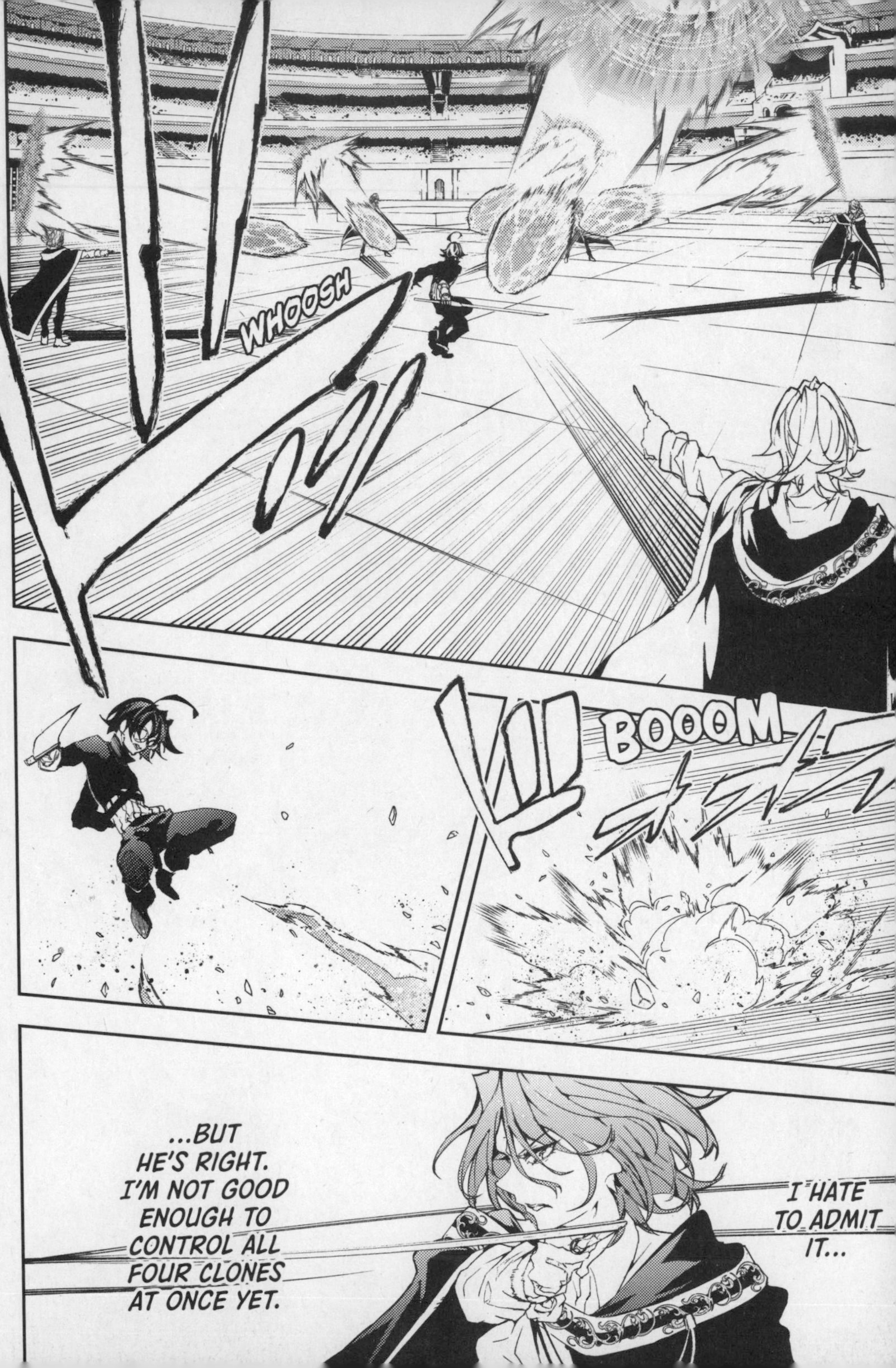
WHOOSH
BOOOM
I HATE TO ADMIT IT...
...BUT HE'S RIGHT. I'M NOT GOOD ENOUGH TO CONTROL ALL FOUR CLONES AT ONCE YET.

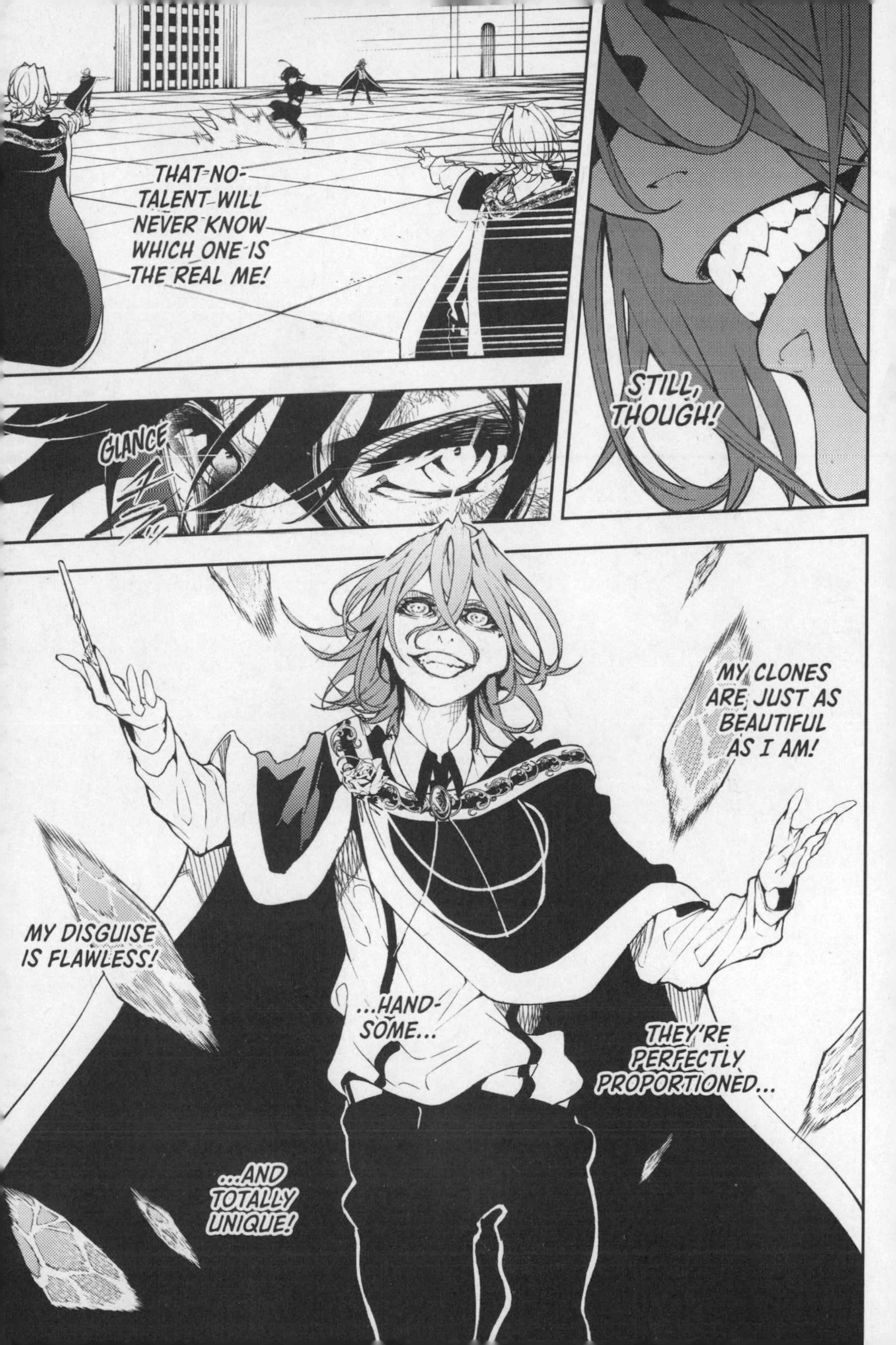
STILL, THOUGH!
THAT-NO-TALENT-WILL NEVER-KNOW WHICH-ONE-IS THE-REAL ME!
GLANCE
MY CLONES ARE JUST AS BEAUTIFUL AS I AM!
MY DISGUISE IS FLAWLESS!
...HAND-SOME...
THEY'RE PERFECTLY PROPORTIONED...
...AND TOTALLY UNIQUE!

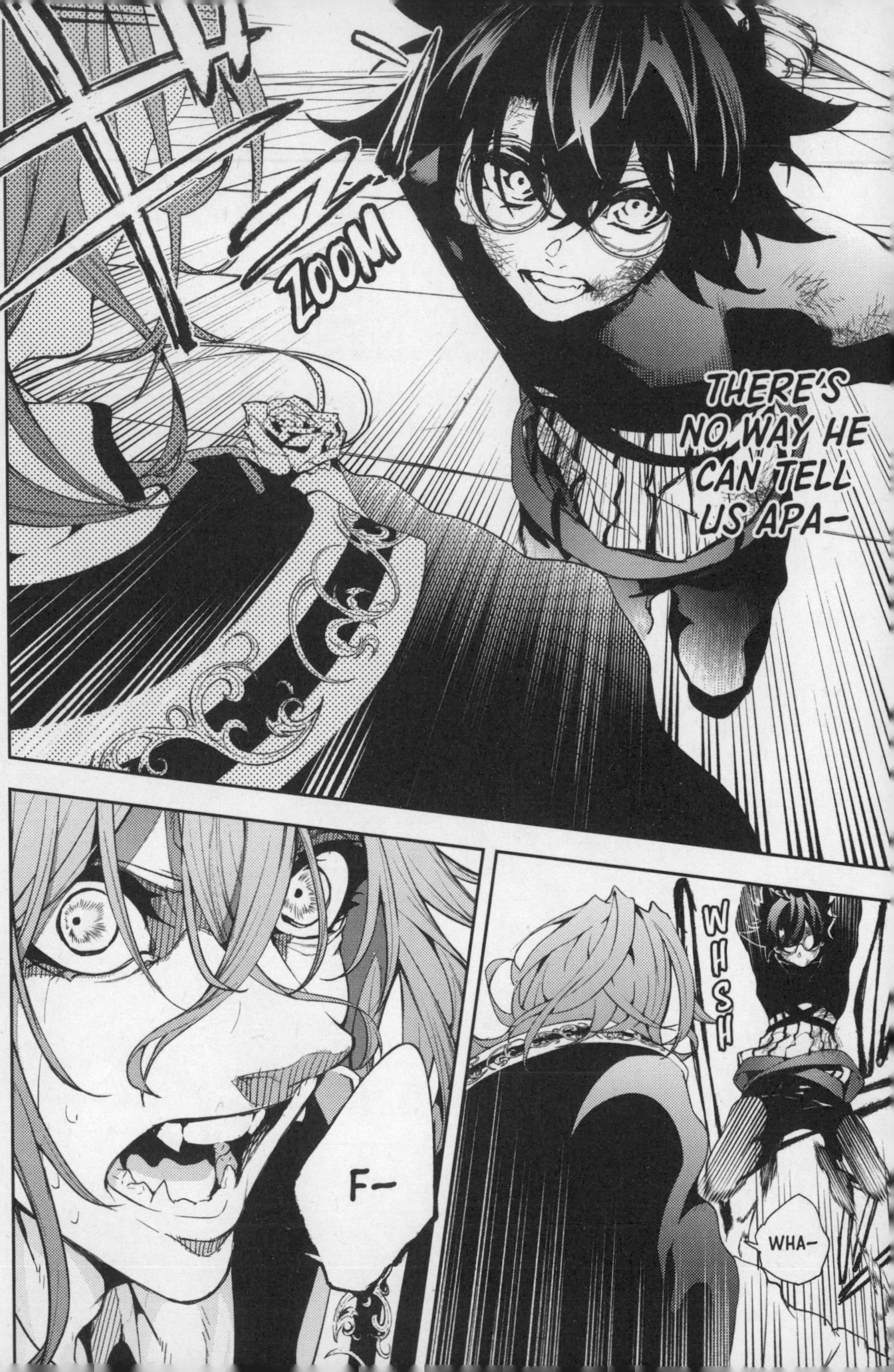
ZOOM
THERE'S NO WAY HE CAN TELL US APA—
WHSH
WHA—
F—

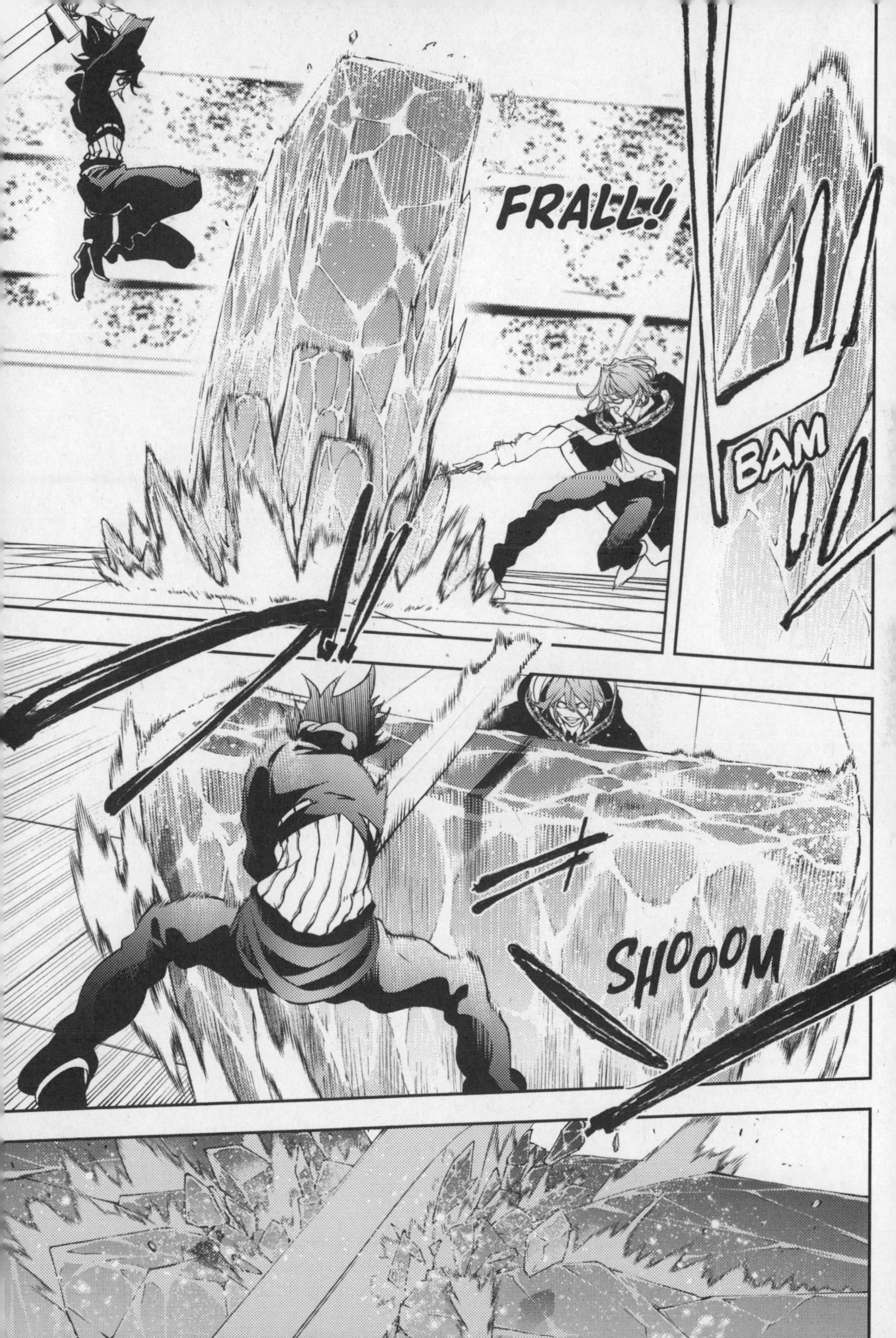
BAM
FRALL!!
SHOOOM

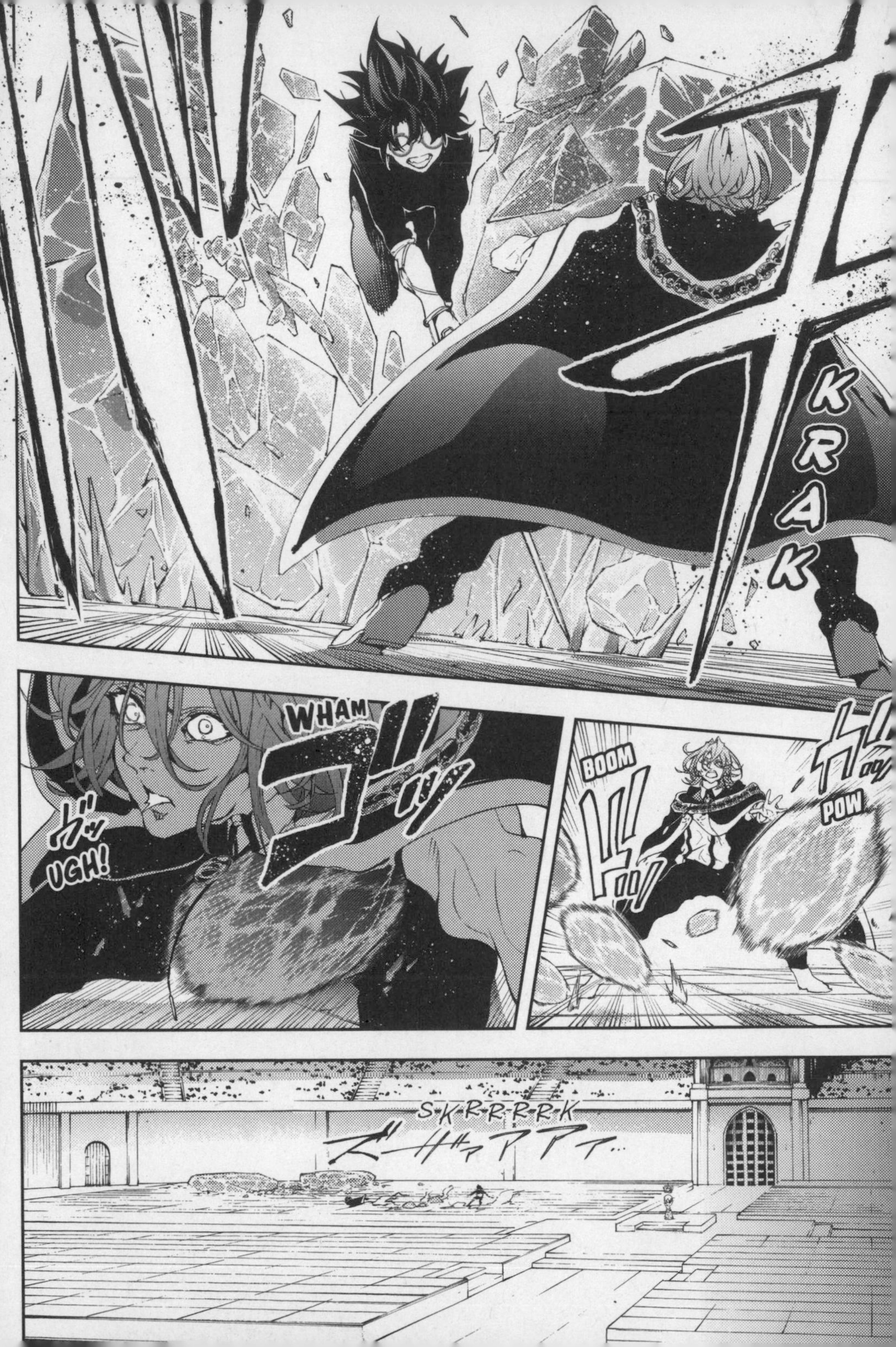
KRAK
BOOM
POW
WHAM
UGH!
S-K-R-R-R-R-K

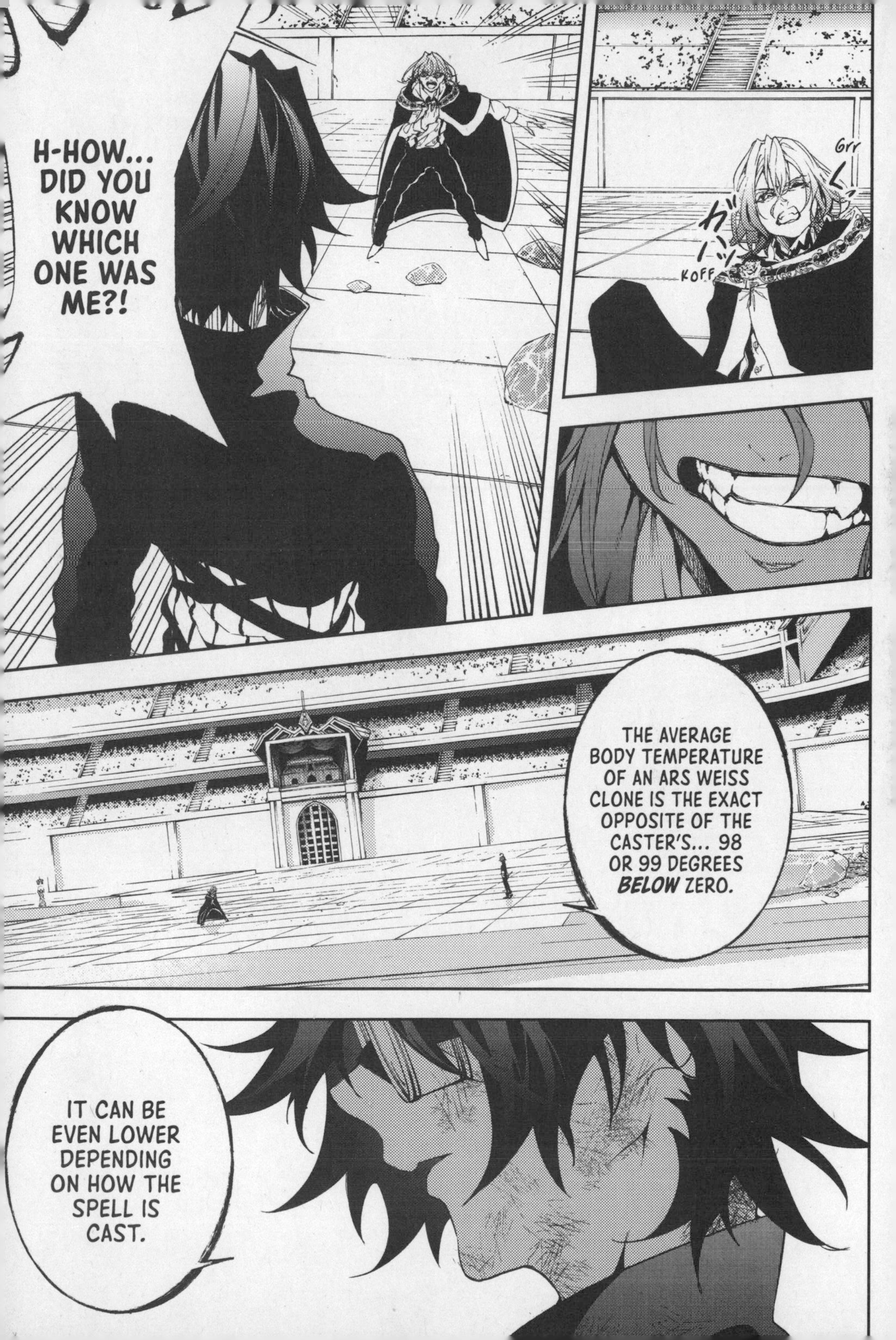
Grr
KOFF
H-HOW... DID YOU KNOW WHICH ONE WAS ME?!
THE AVERAGE BODY TEMPERATURE OF AN ARS WEISS CLONE IS THE EXACT OPPOSITE OF THE CASTER'S... 98 OR 99 DEGREES BELOW ZERO.
IT CAN BE EVEN LOWER DEPENDING ON HOW THE SPELL IS CAST.

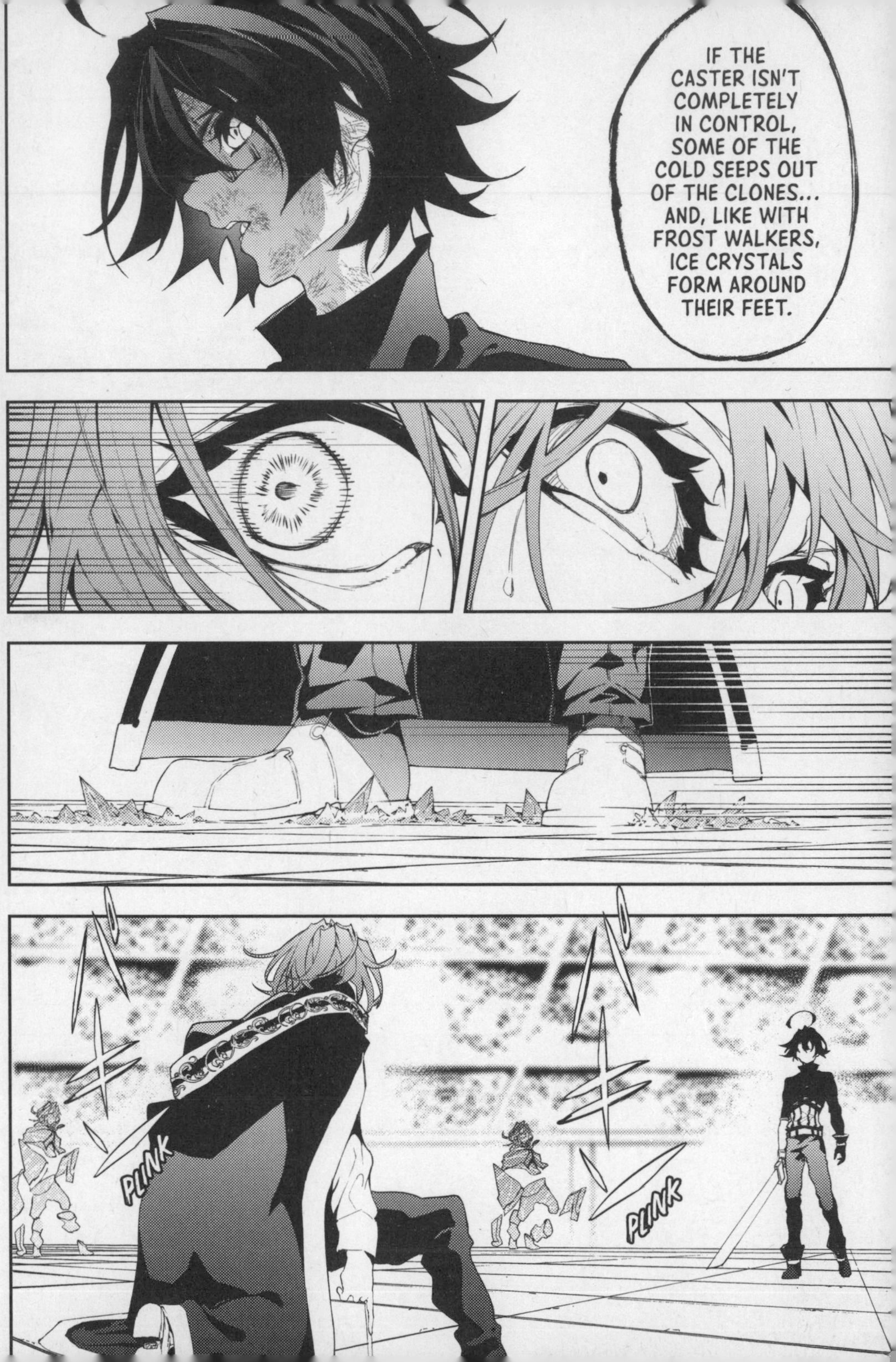
IF THE CASTER ISN'T COMPLETELY IN CONTROL, SOME OF THE COLD SEEPS OUT OF THE CLONES... AND, LIKE WITH FROST WALKERS, ICE CRYSTALS FORM AROUND THEIR FEET.
PLINK
PLINK

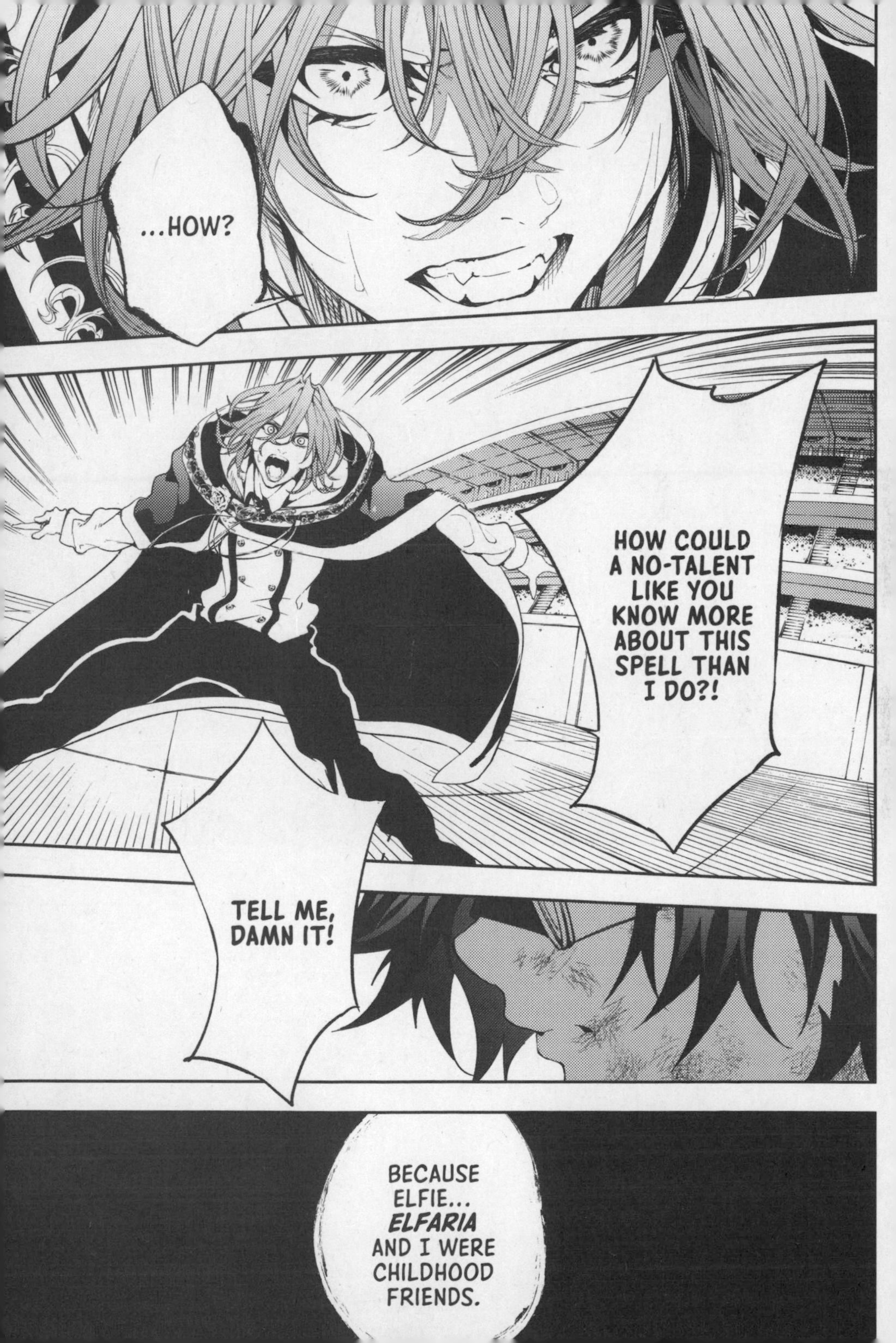
...HOW?
HOW COULD A NO-TALENT LIKE YOU KNOW MORE ABOUT THIS SPELL THAN I DO?!
TELL ME, DAMN IT!
BECAUSE ELFIE... *ELFARIA* AND I WERE CHILDHOOD FRIENDS.

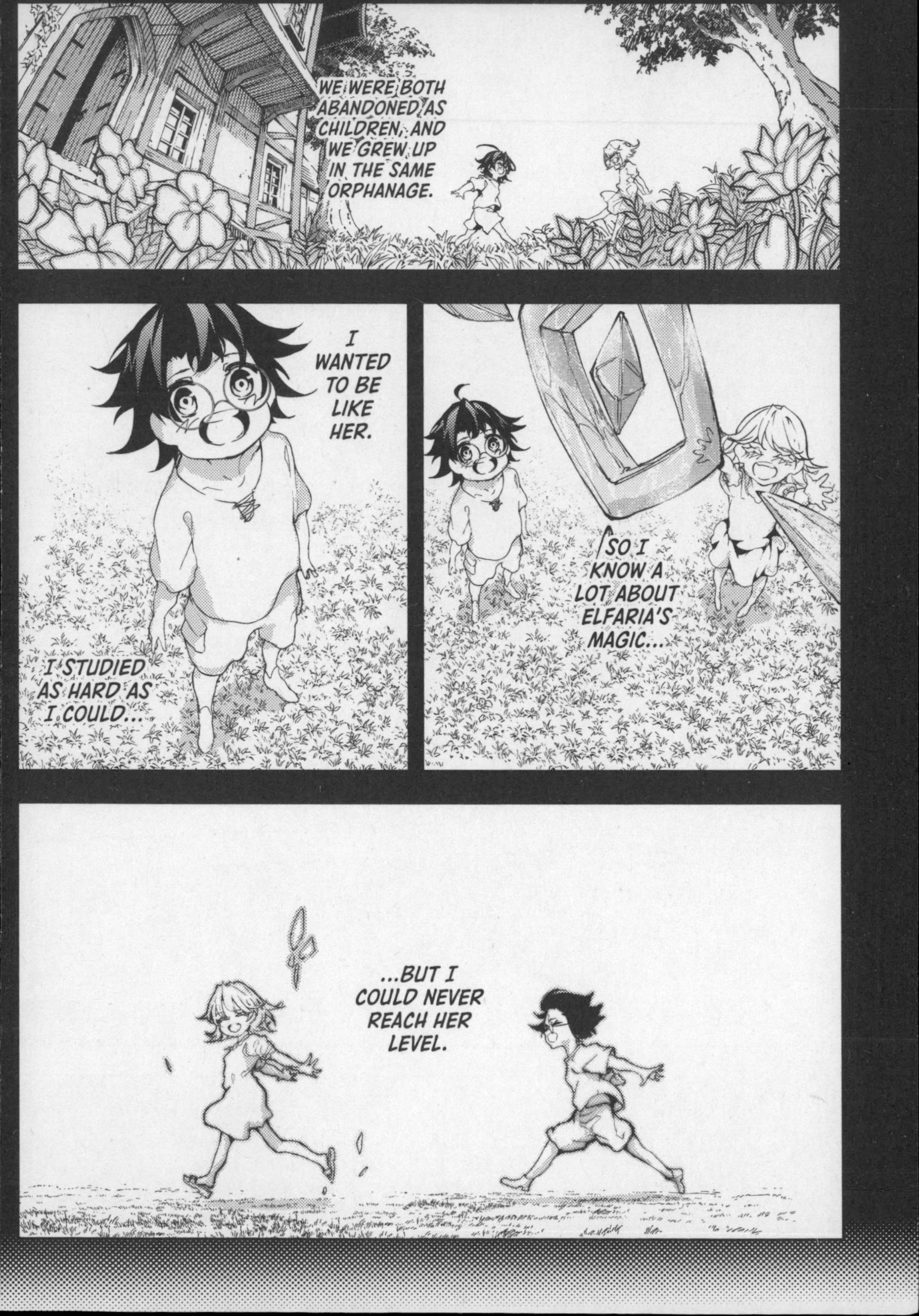
WE WERE BOTH ABANDONED AS CHILDREN, AND WE GREW UP IN THE SAME ORPHANAGE.
SO I KNOW A LOT ABOUT ELFARIA'S MAGIC...
I WANTED TO BE LIKE HER.
I STUDIED AS HARD AS I COULD...
...BUT I COULD NEVER REACH HER LEVEL.

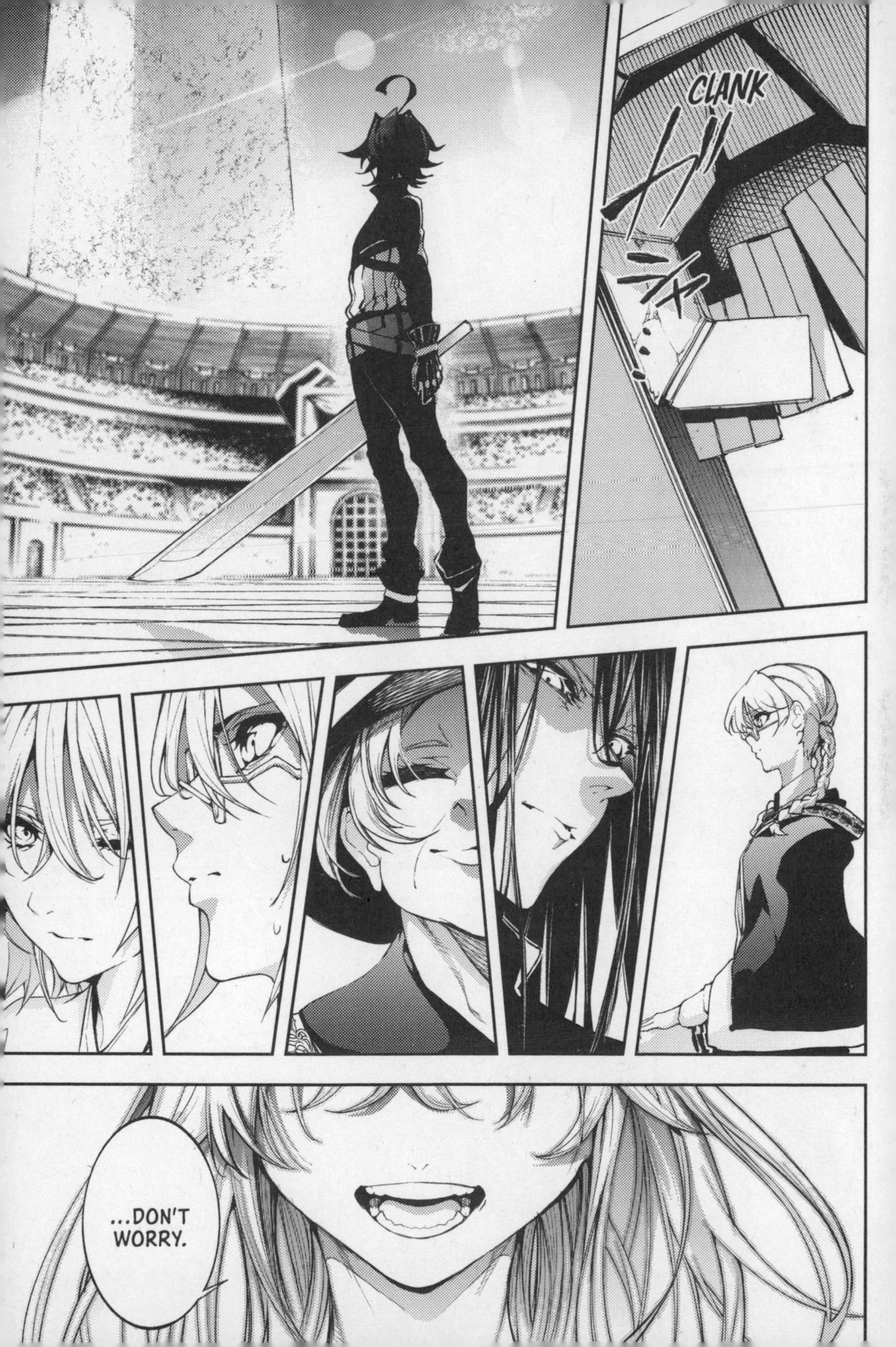
CLANK
...DON'T WORRY.

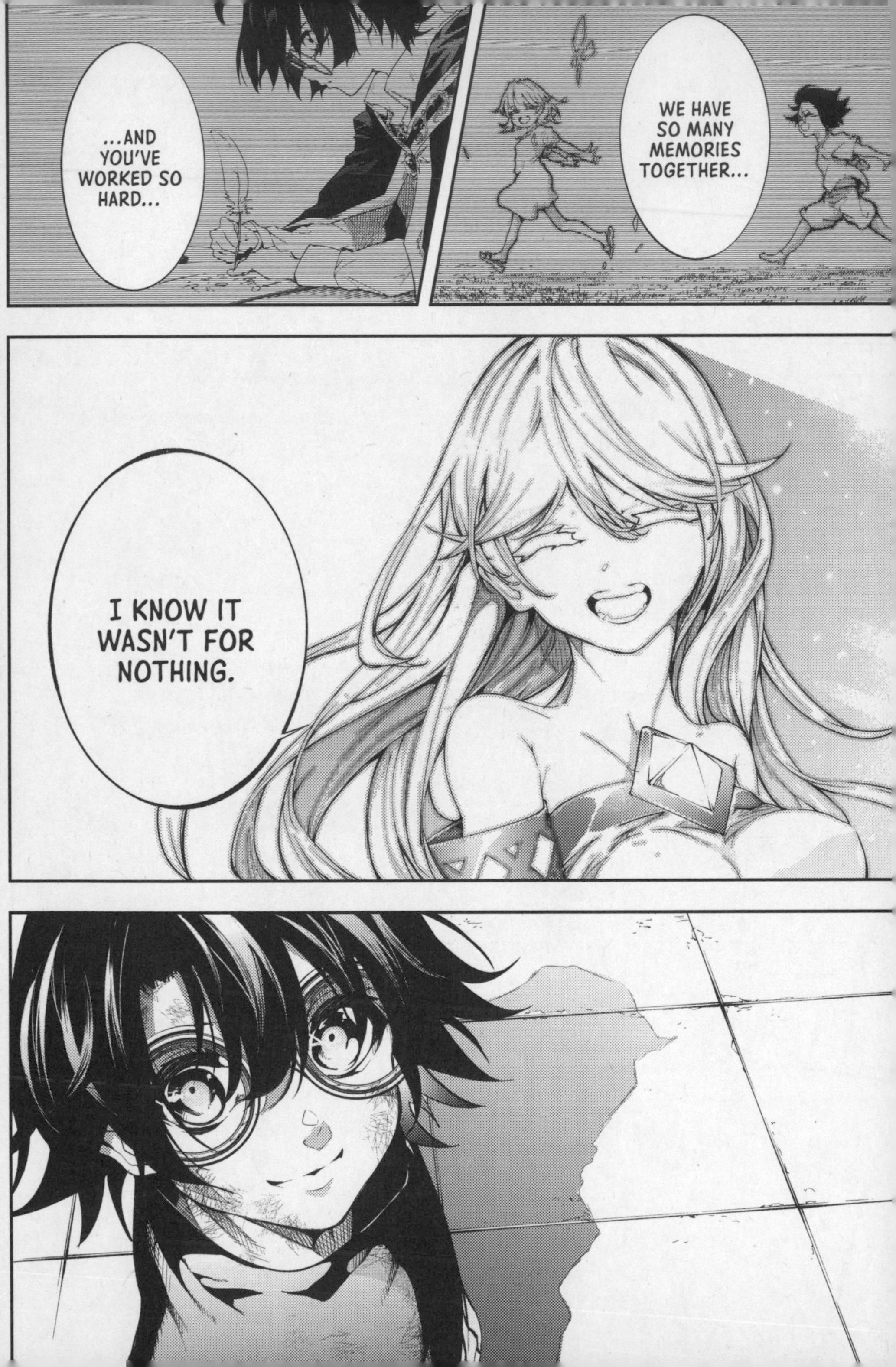
WE HAVE SO MANY MEMORIES TOGETHER...
...AND YOU'VE WORKED SO HARD...
I KNOW IT WASN'T FOR NOTHING.

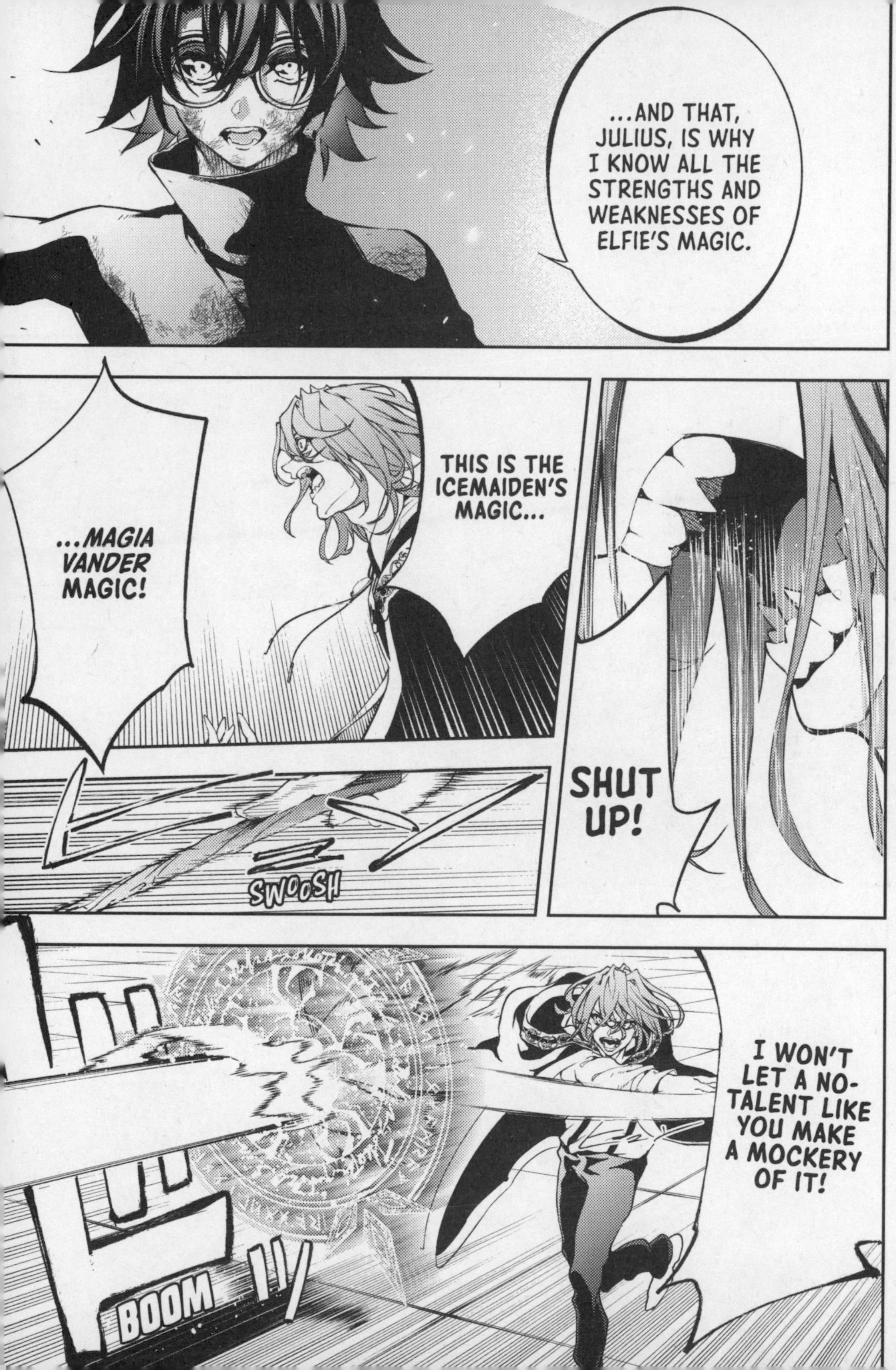
...AND THAT, JULIUS, IS WHY I KNOW ALL THE STRENGTHS AND WEAKNESSES OF ELFIE'S MAGIC.
SHUT UP!
THIS IS THE ICEMAIDEN'S MAGIC...
...MAGIA VANDER MAGIC!
SWOOSH
I WON'T LET A NO-TALENT LIKE YOU MAKE A MOCKERY OF IT!
BOOM

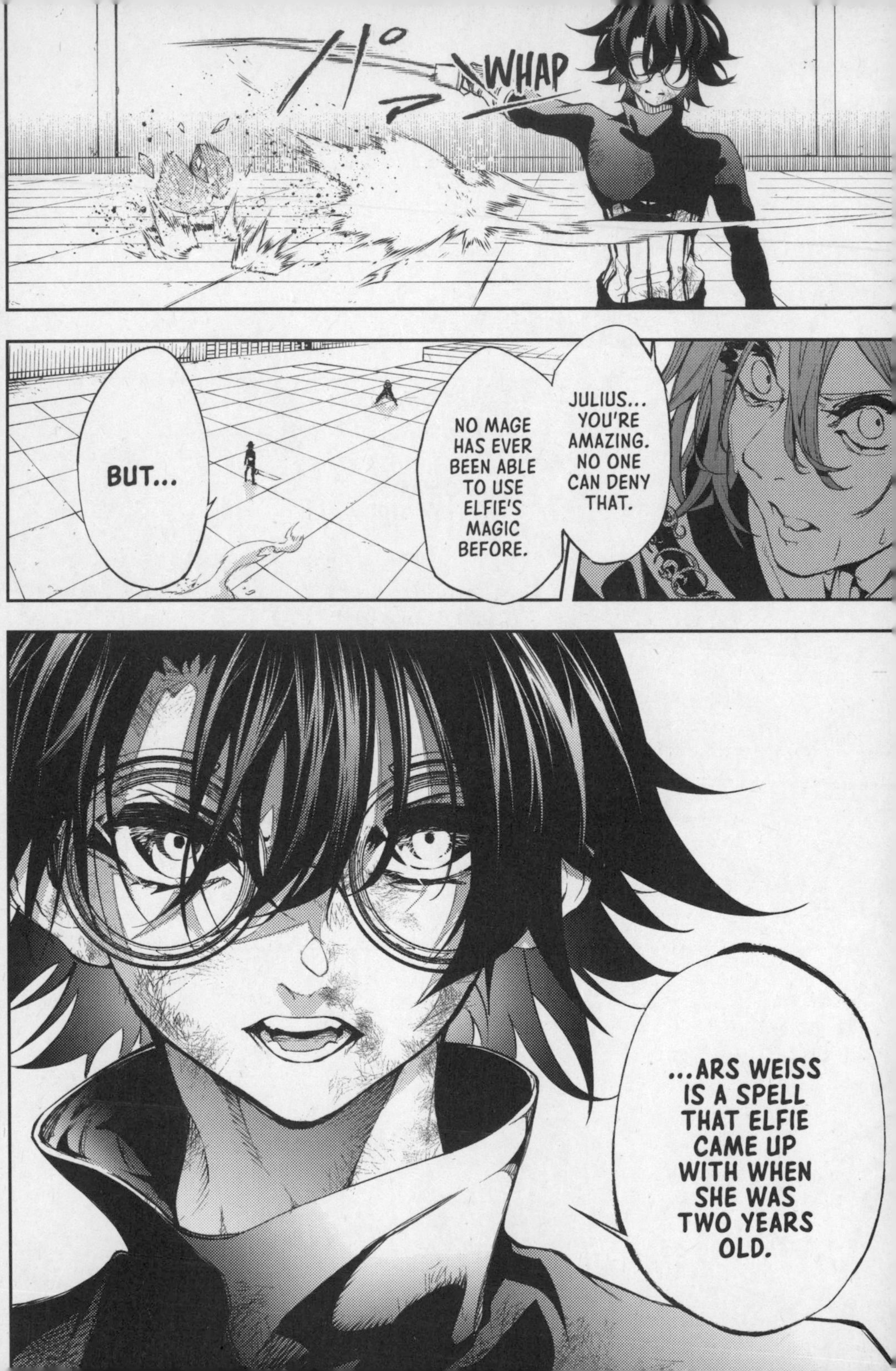
WHAP
JULIUS... YOU'RE AMAZING. NO ONE CAN DENY THAT.
NO MAGE HAS EVER BEEN ABLE TO USE ELFIE'S MAGIC BEFORE.
BUT...
...ARS WEISS IS A SPELL THAT ELFIE CAME UP WITH WHEN SHE WAS TWO YEARS OLD.

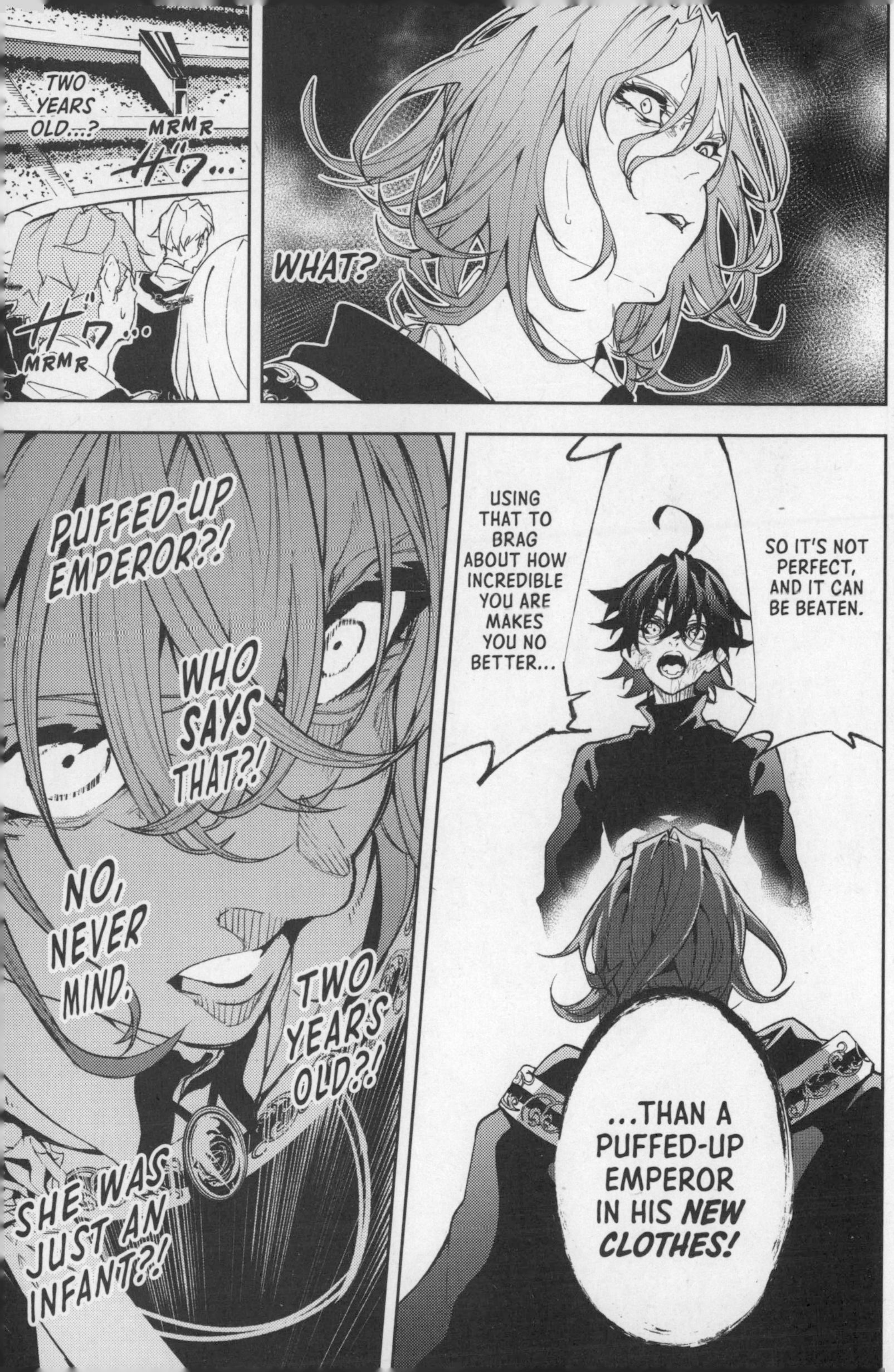
WHAT?
TWO YEARS OLD...?
MRMR
ザワ...
ザワ...
MRMR
SO IT'S NOT PERFECT, AND IT CAN BE BEATEN.
USING THAT TO BRAG ABOUT HOW INCREDIBLE YOU ARE MAKES YOU NO BETTER...
...THAN A PUFFED-UP EMPEROR IN HIS *NEW CLOTHES!*
PUFFED-UP EMPEROR?!
WHO SAYS THAT?!
NO, NEVER MIND.
TWO YEARS OLD?!
SHE WAS JUST AN INFANT?!

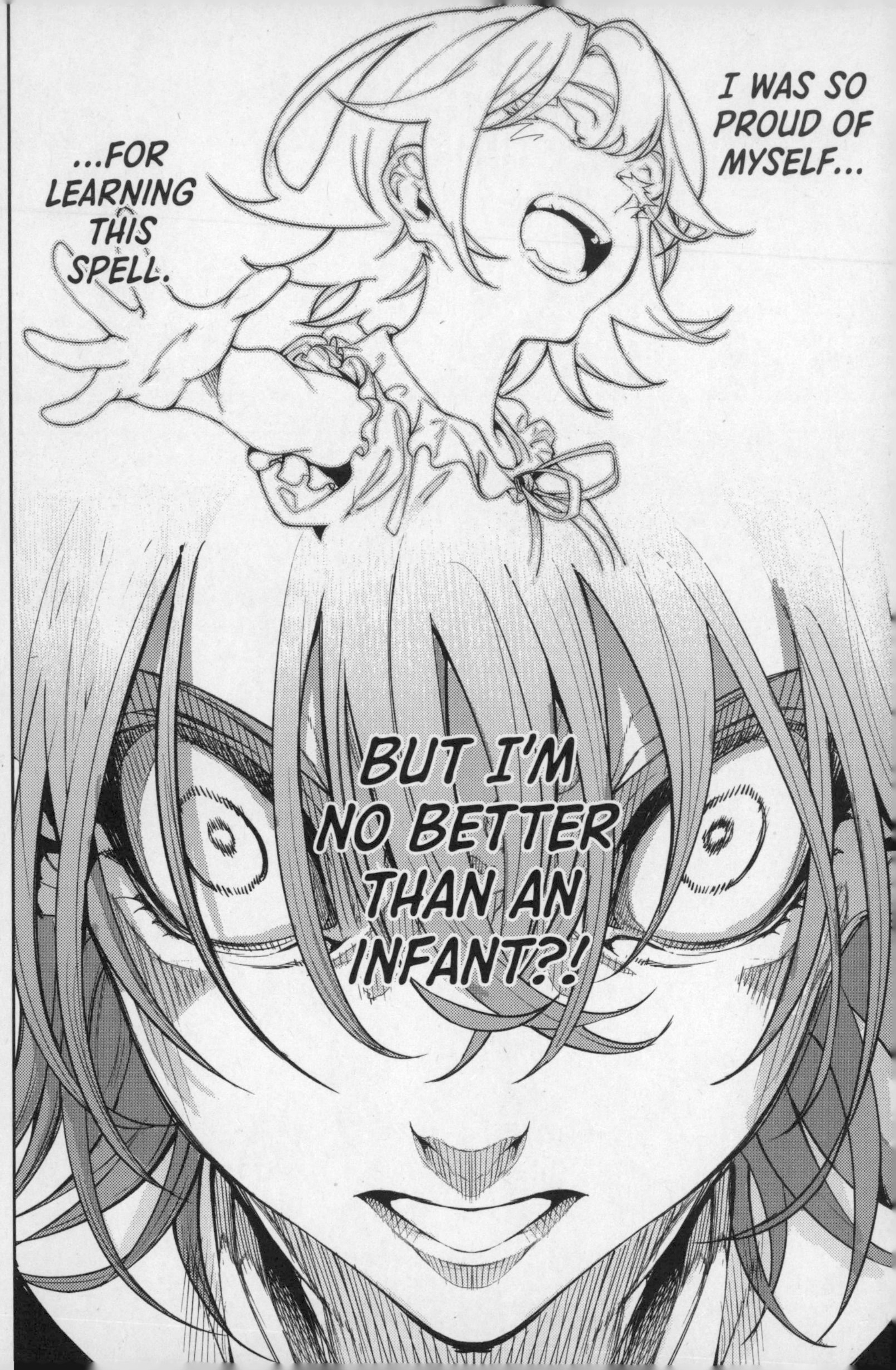
I WAS SO PROUD OF MYSELF...
...FOR LEARNING THIS SPELL.
BUT I'M NO BETTER THAN AN INFANT?!

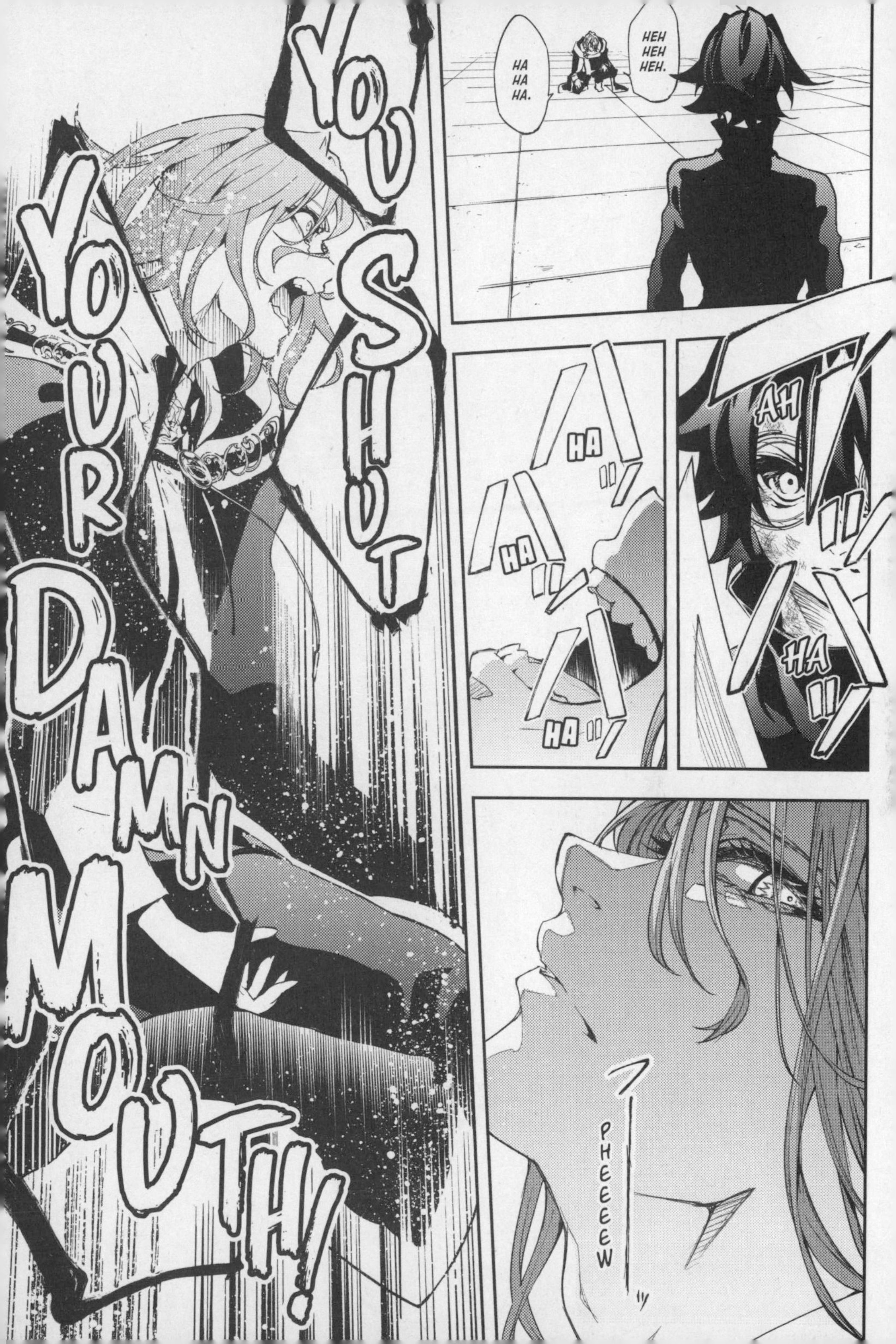
HEH HEH HEH.
HA HA HA.
AH!
HA!!
HA!!
HA!!
HA!!
PHEEEEW
YOU SHUT
YOUR DAMN MOUTH!

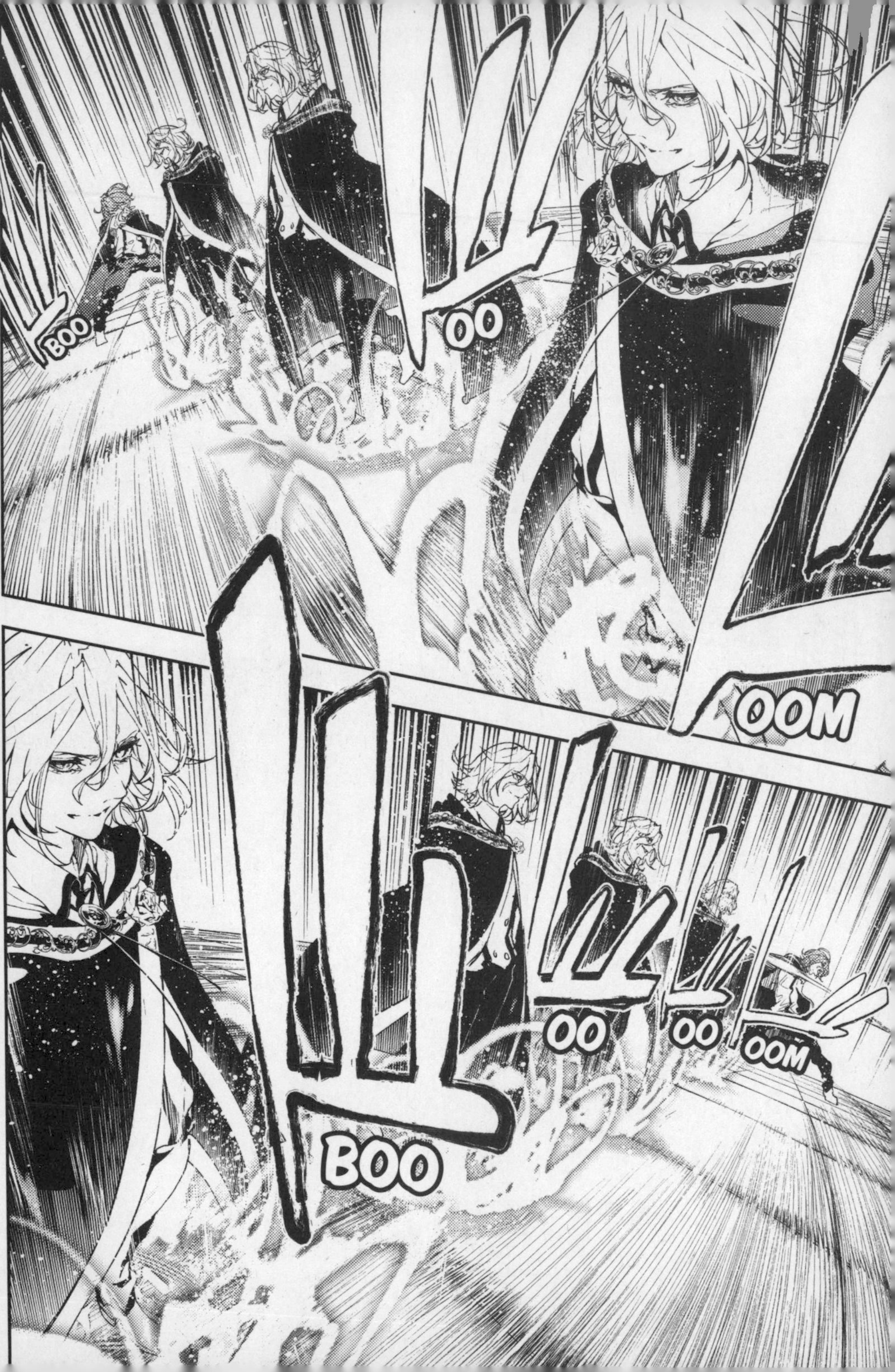
BOO
OO
OOM
BOO
OO
OO
OOM

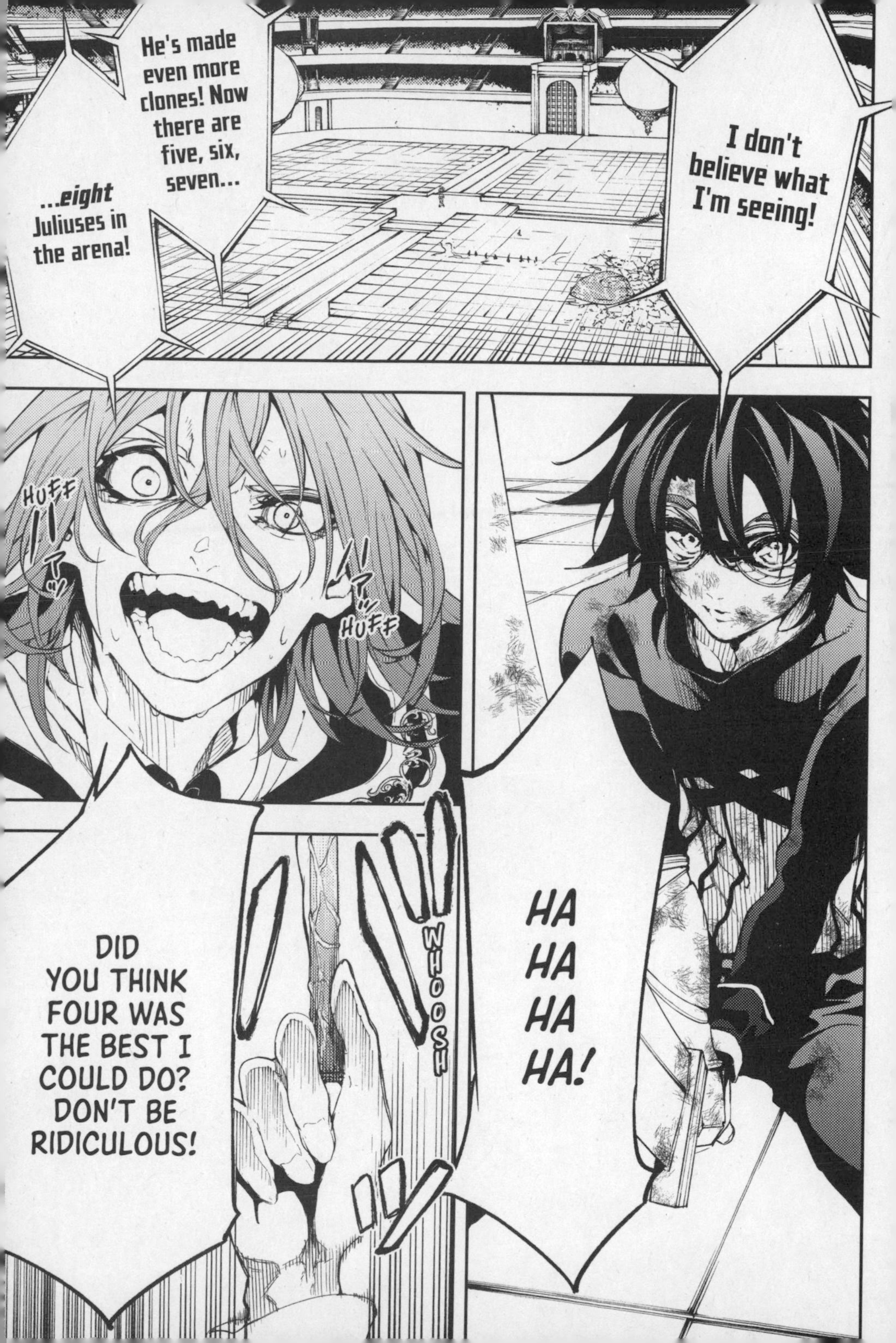
I don't believe what I'm seeing!
He's made even more clones! Now there are five, six, seven...
...eight Juliuses in the arena!
HA HA HA HA!
HUFF
HUFF
WHOOOSH
DID YOU THINK FOUR WAS THE BEST I COULD DO? DON'T BE RIDICULOUS!

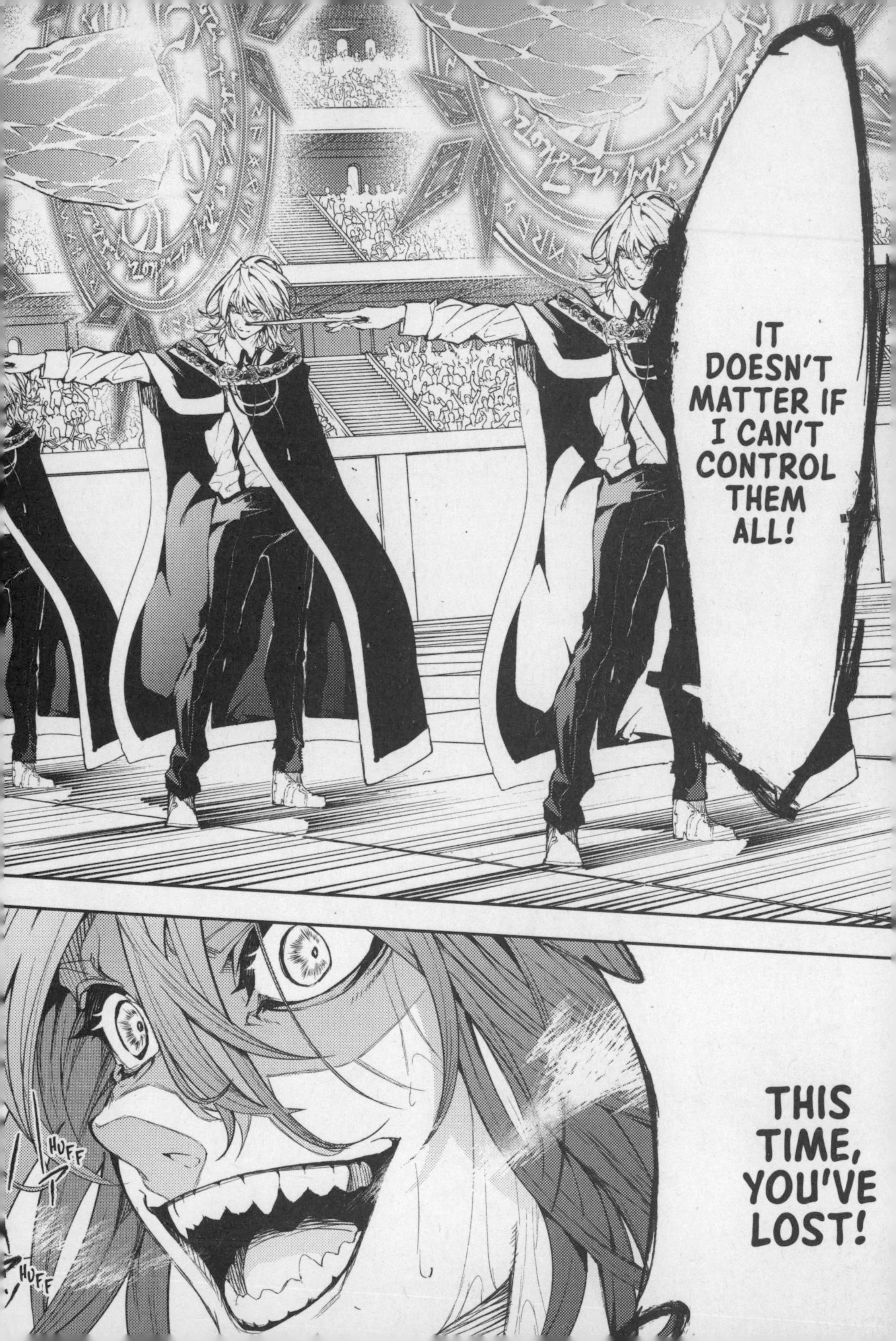
IT DOESN'T MATTER IF I CAN'T CONTROL THEM ALL!
THIS TIME, YOU'VE LOST!
HUFF
HUFF

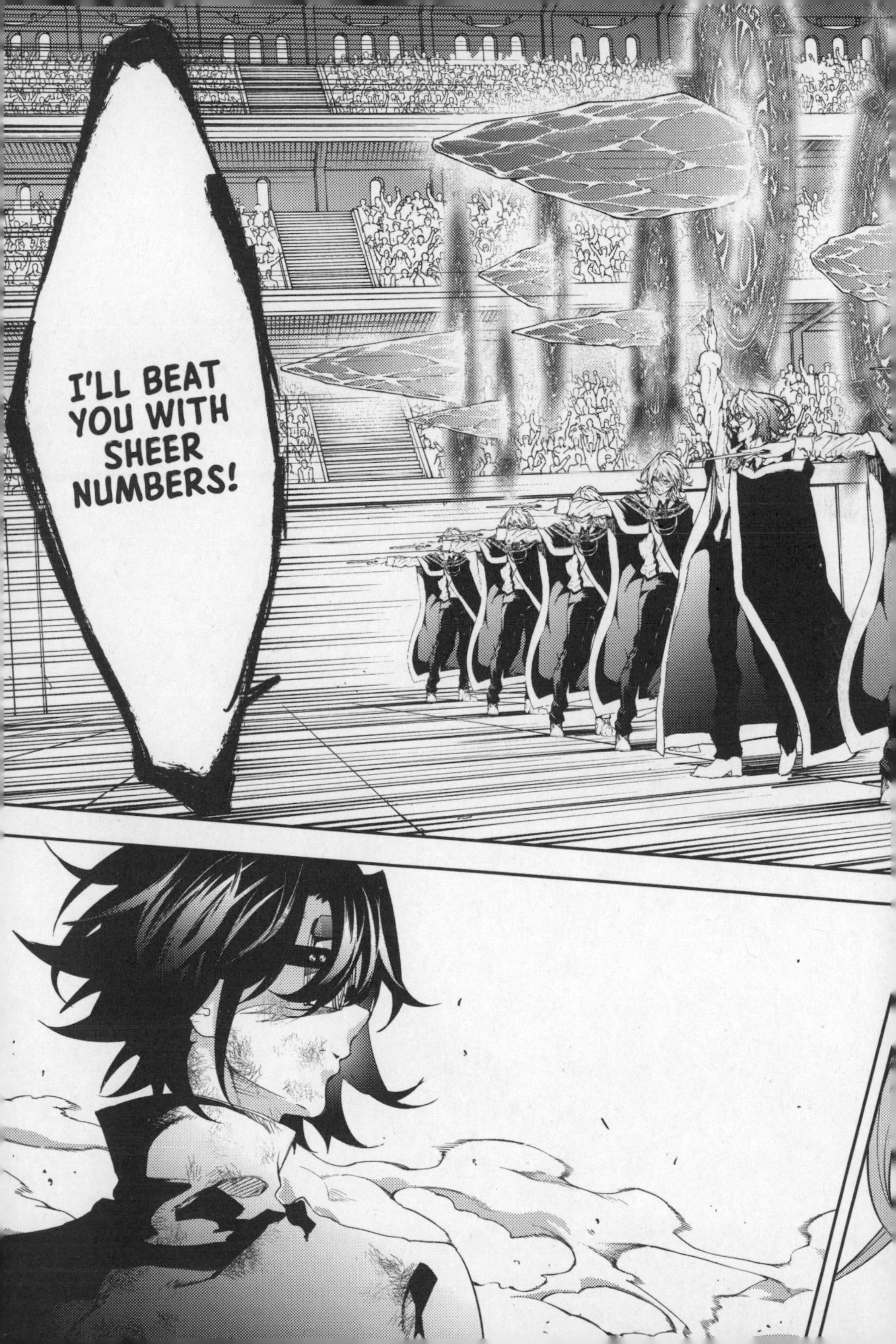
I'LL BEAT YOU WITH SHEER NUMBERS!

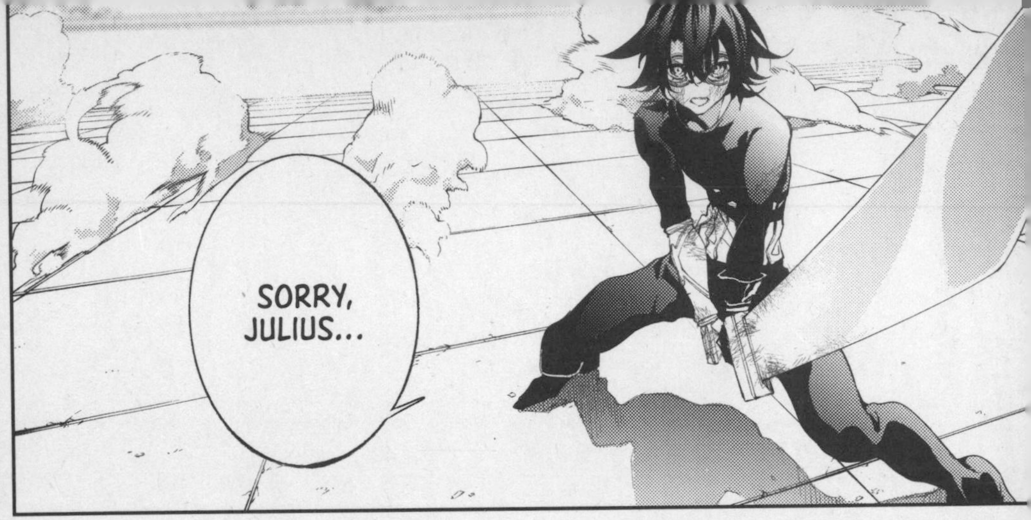
SORRY, JULIUS...

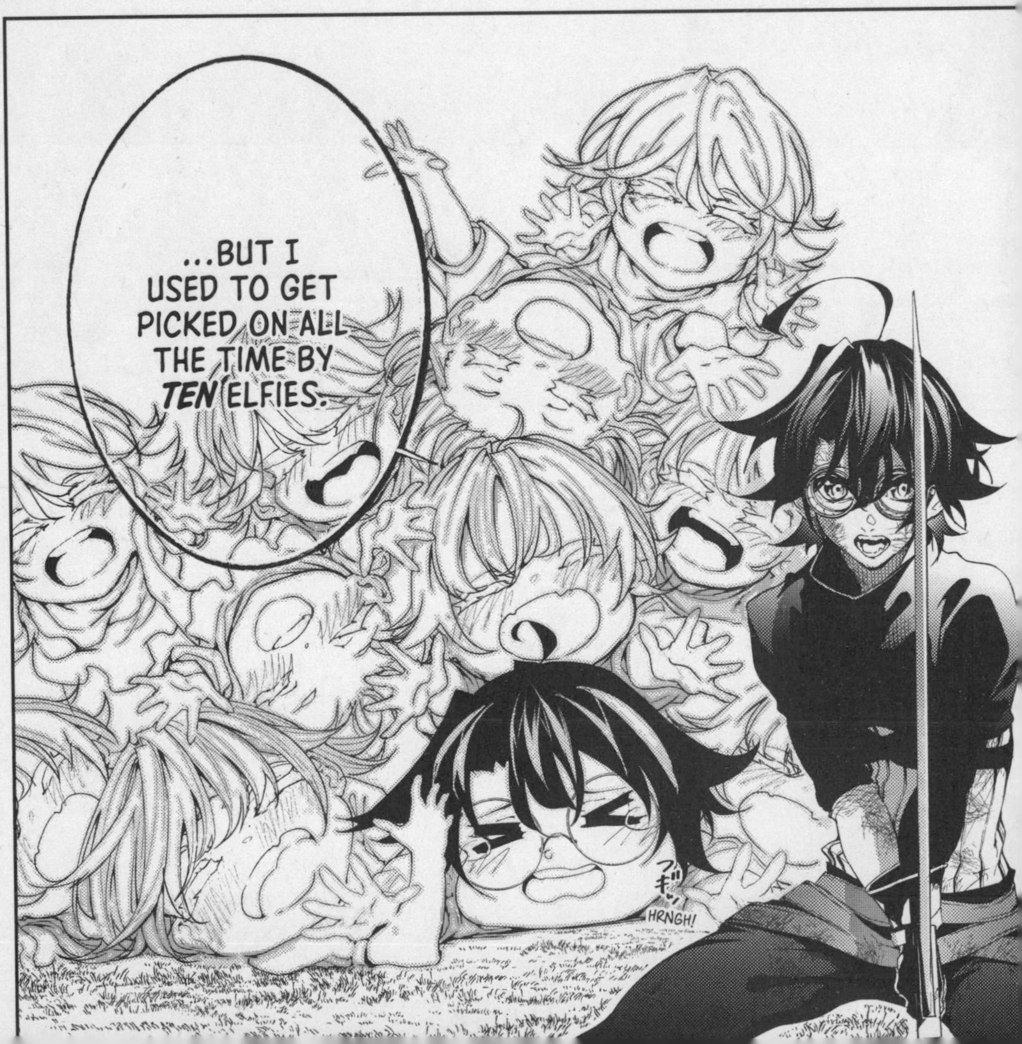
...BUT I USED TO GET PICKED ON ALL THE TIME BY *TEN* ELFIES.
HRNGH!

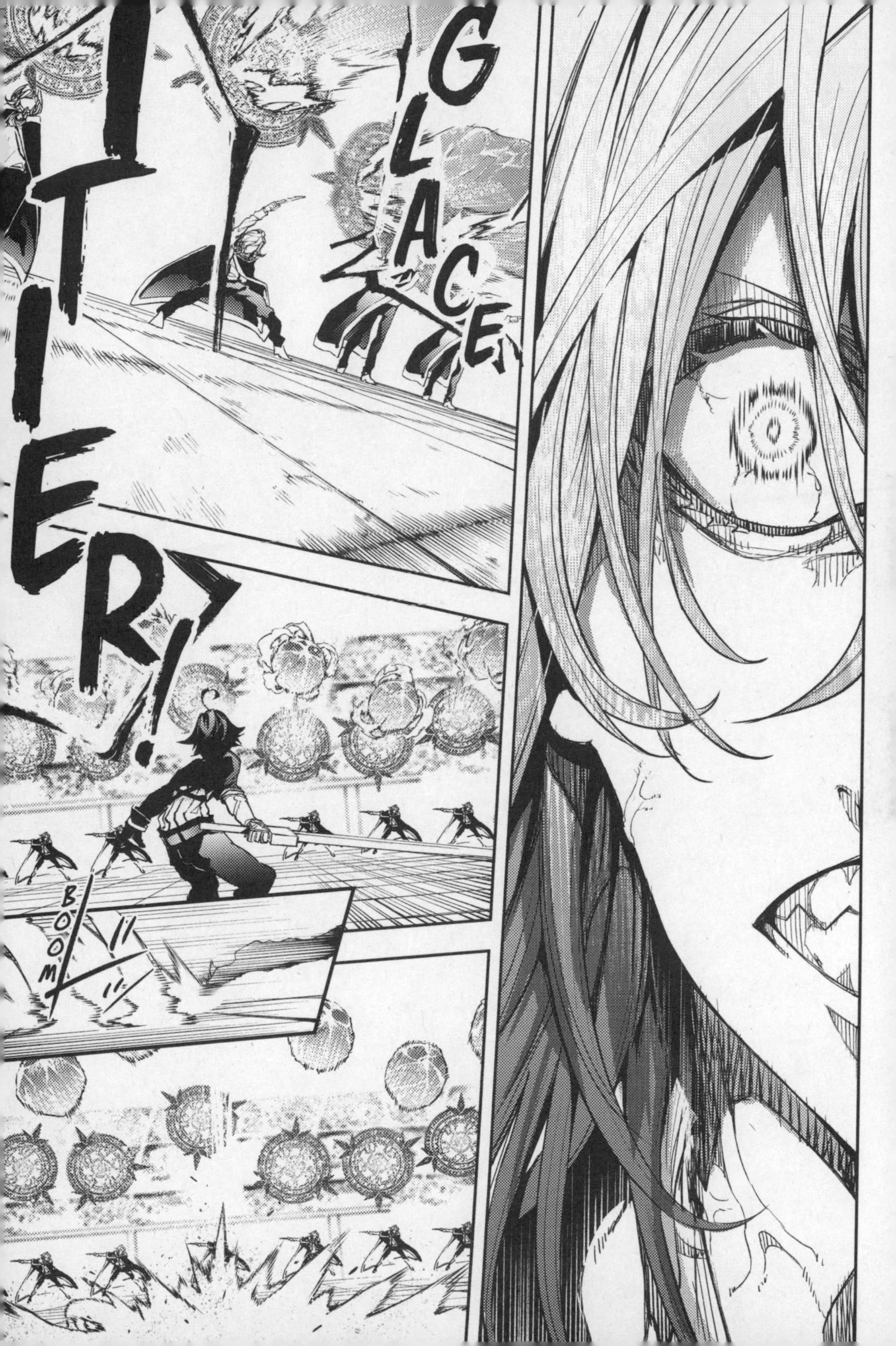
GLACE
ITIER!
BOOM

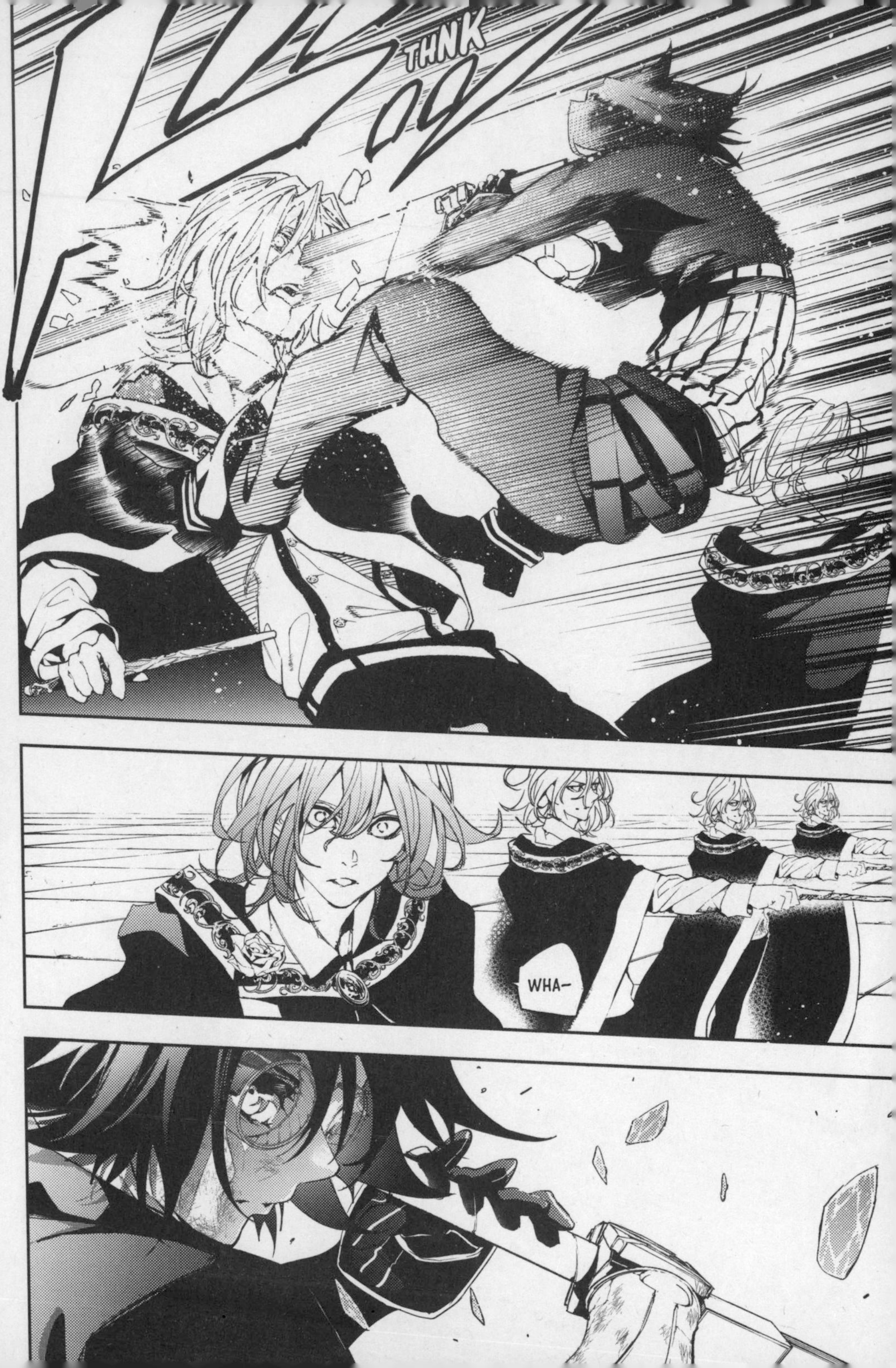
THNK
WHA-

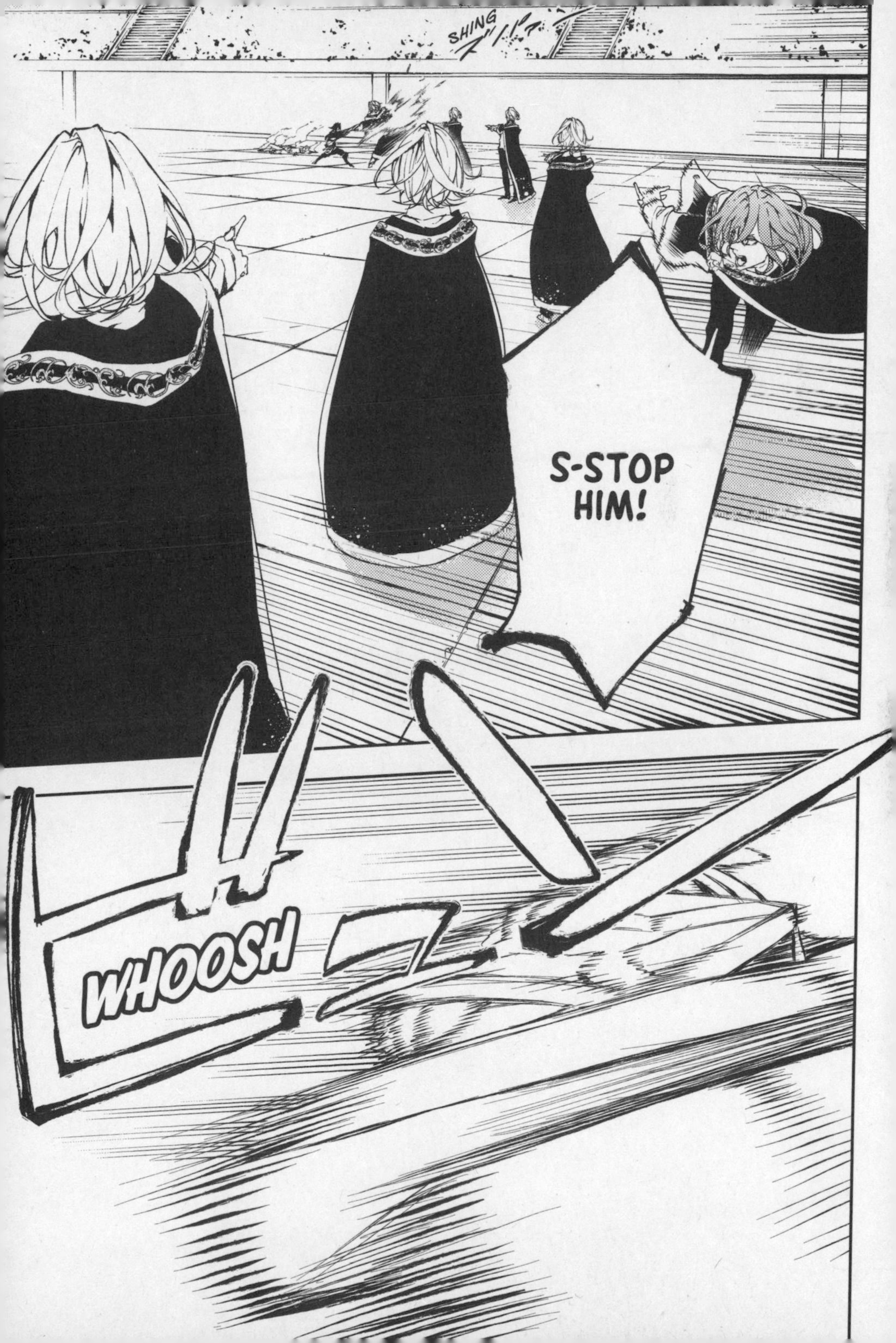
SHING
S-STOP HIM!
WHOOSH

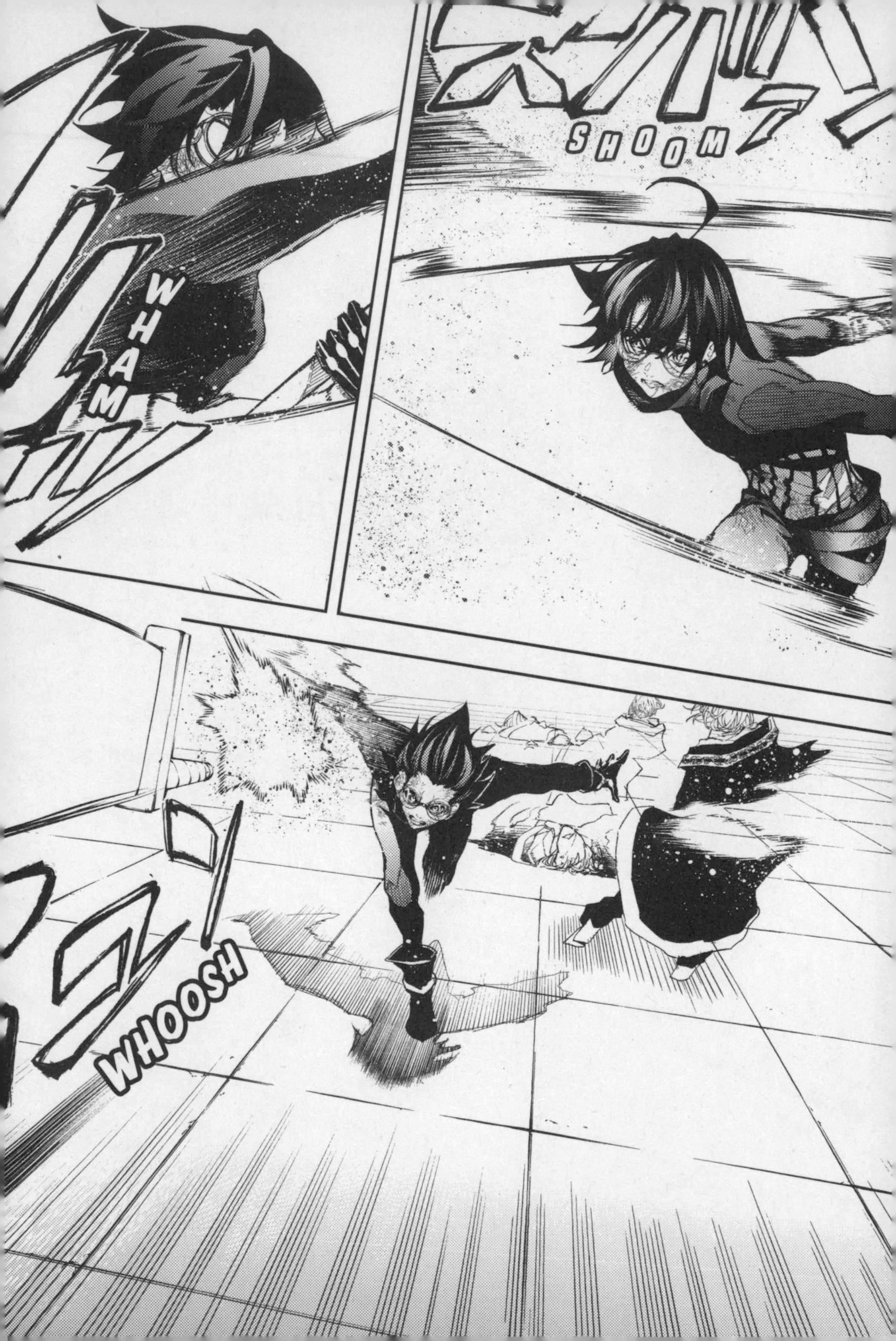
SHOOM
WHAM
WHOOSH

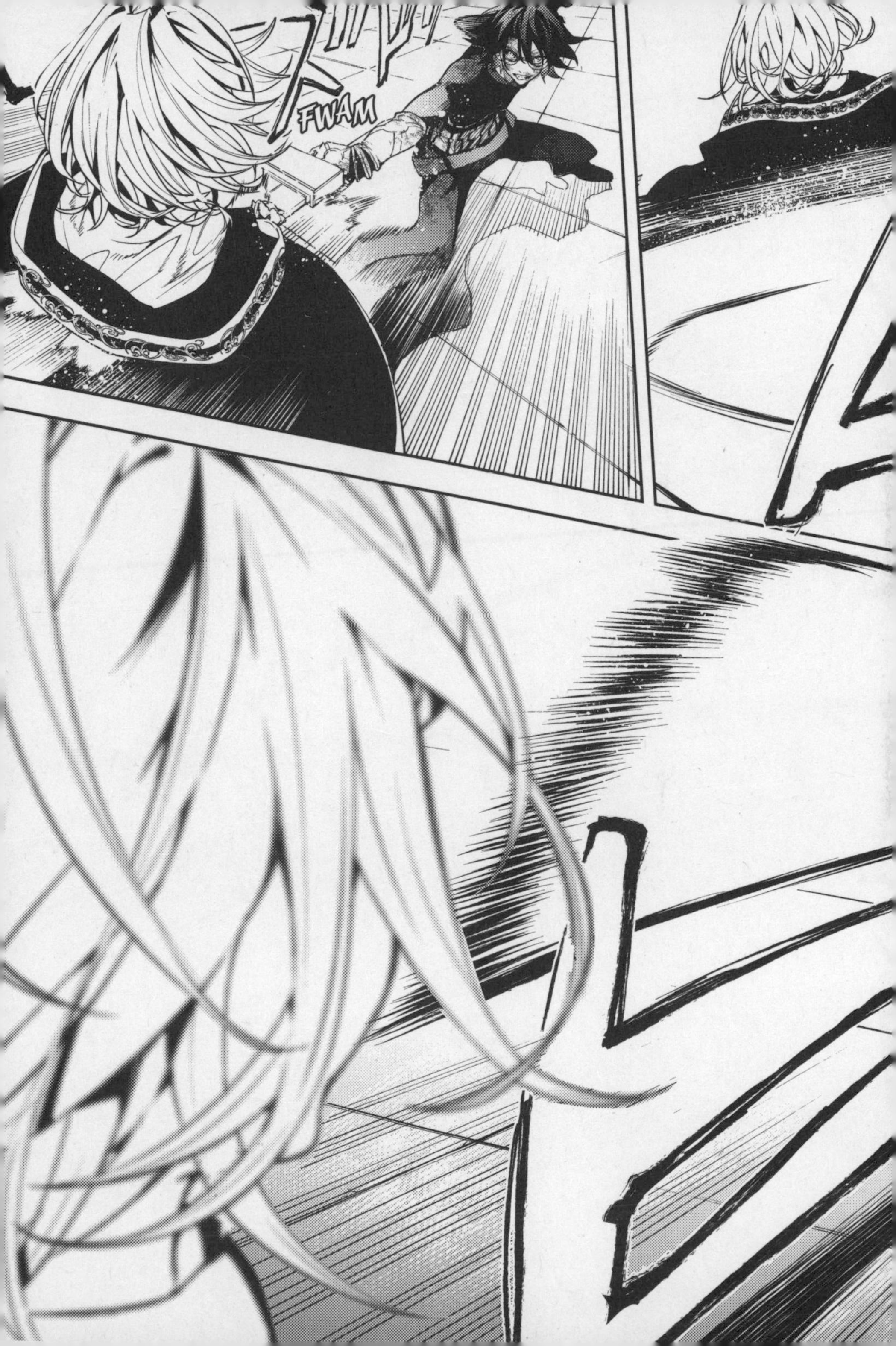
FWAM

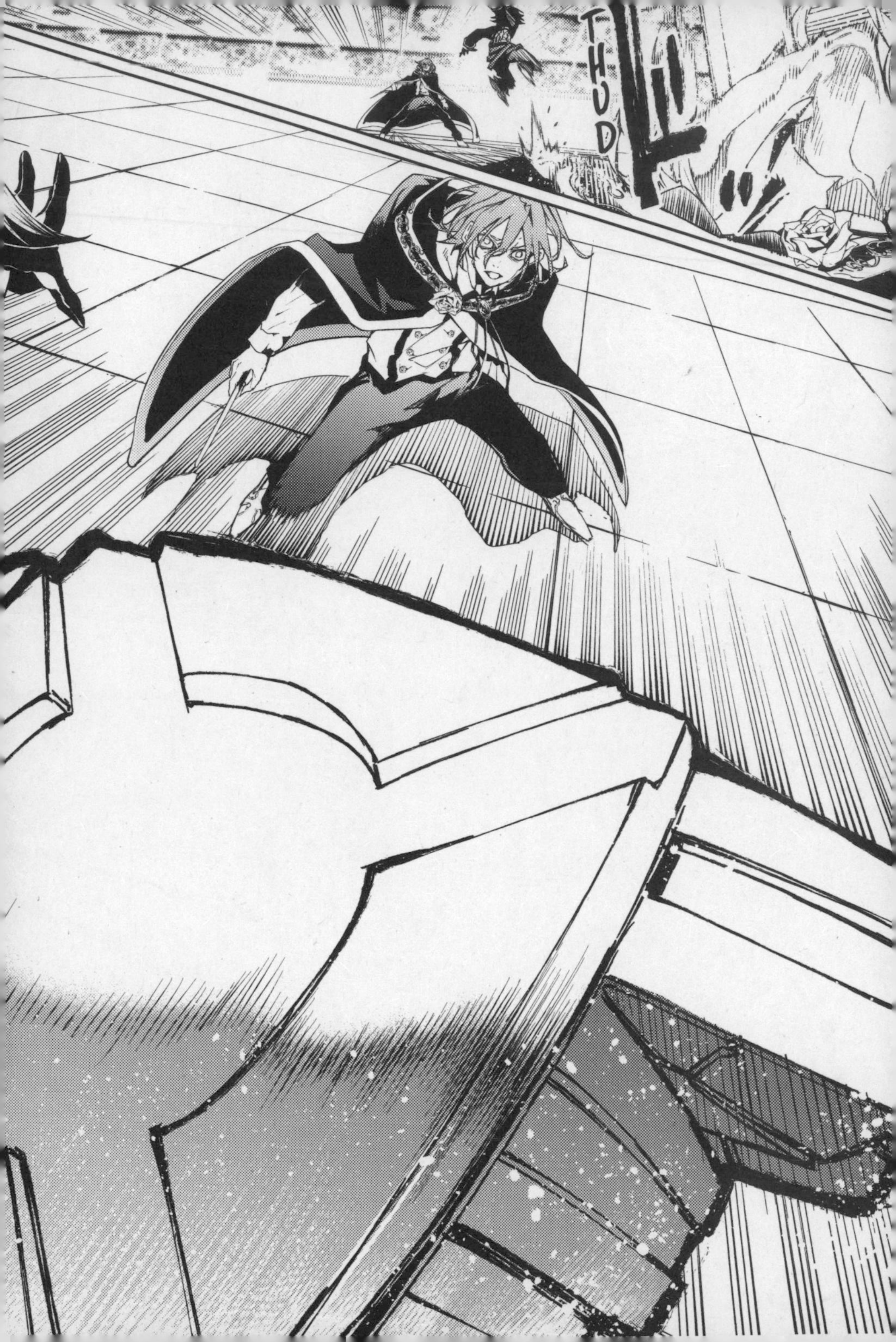
THUD

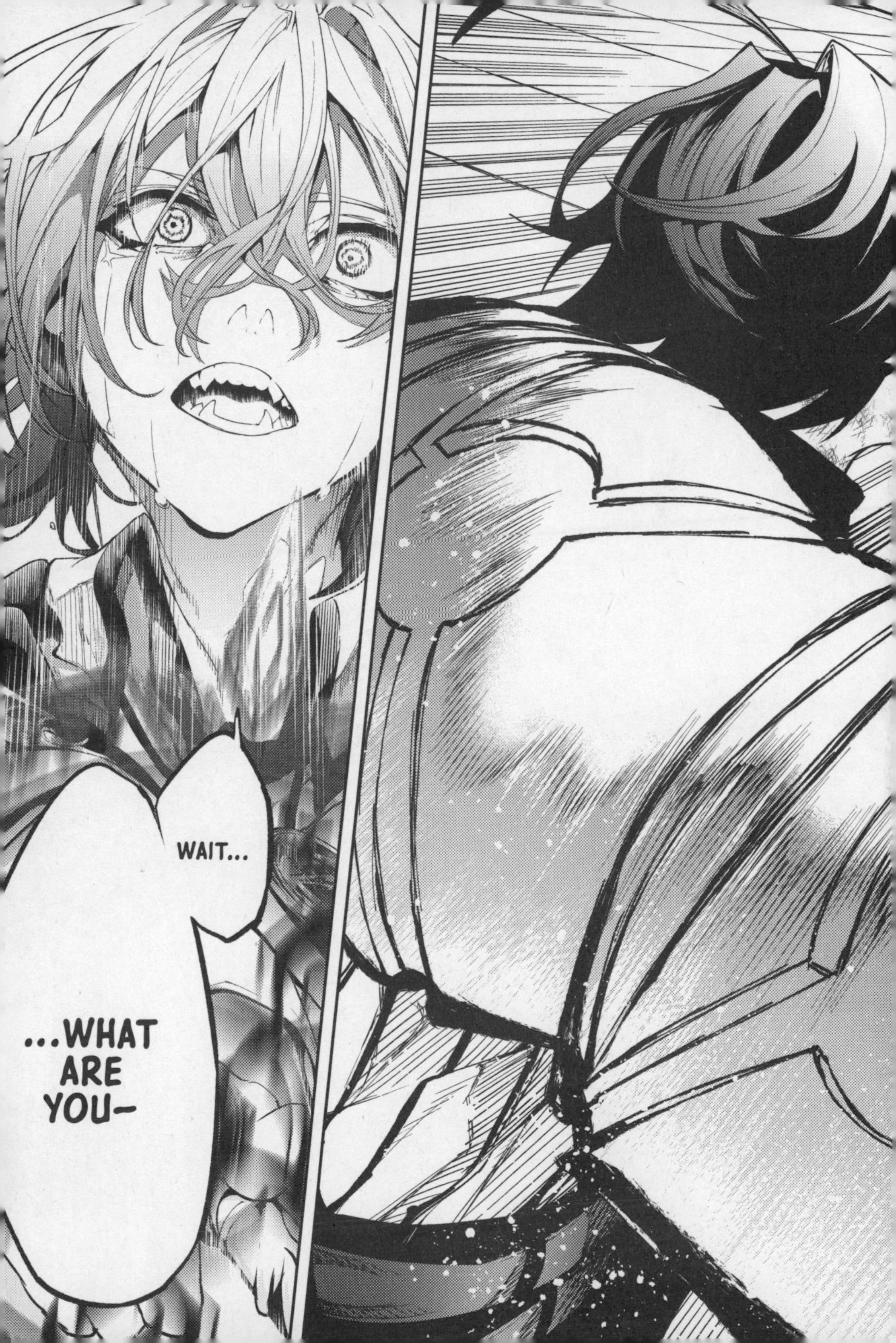
WAIT...
...WHAT ARE YOU-

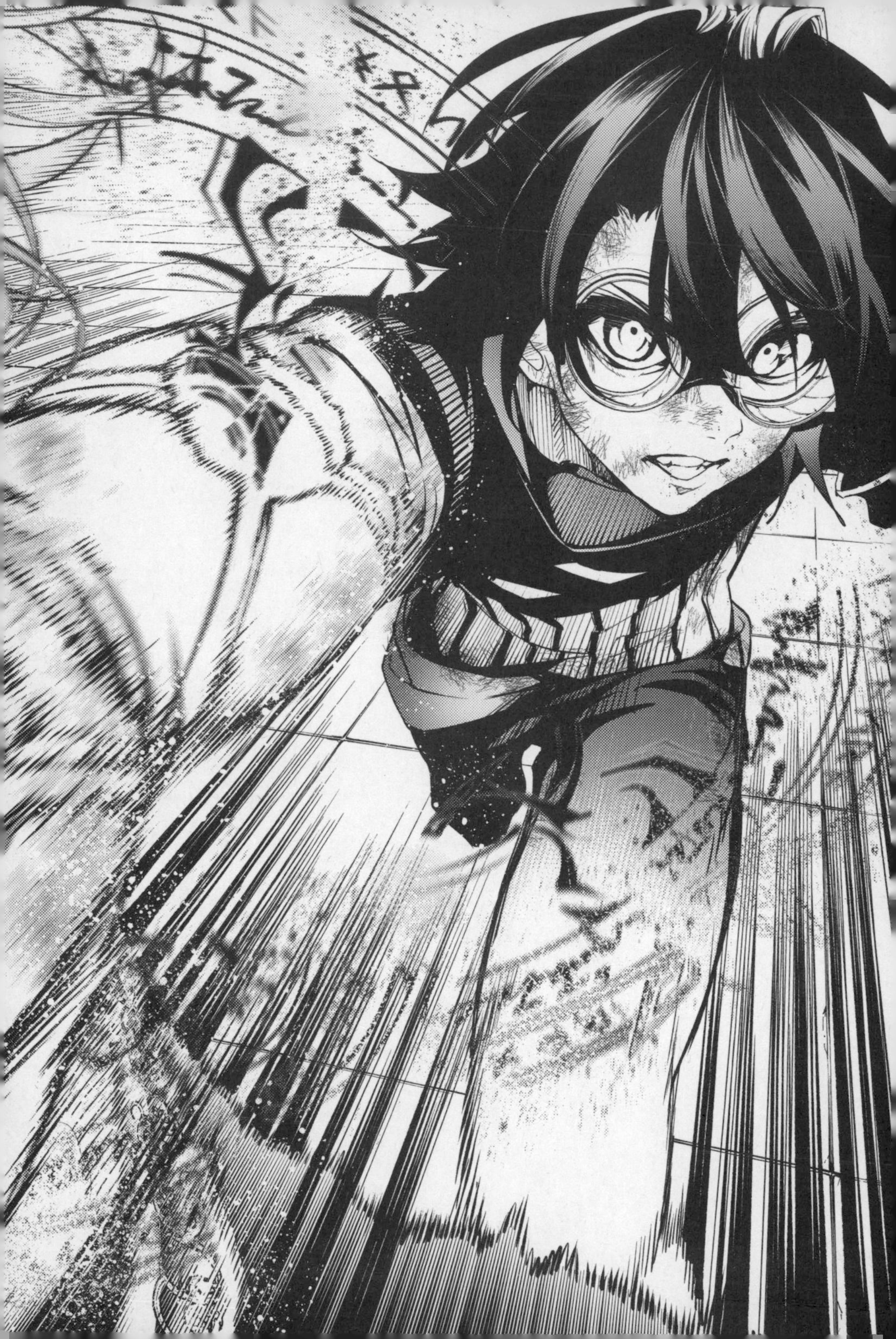

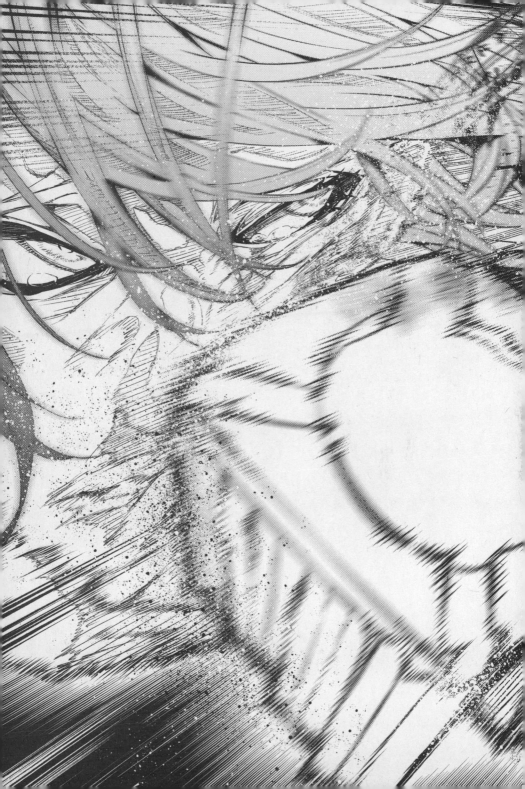

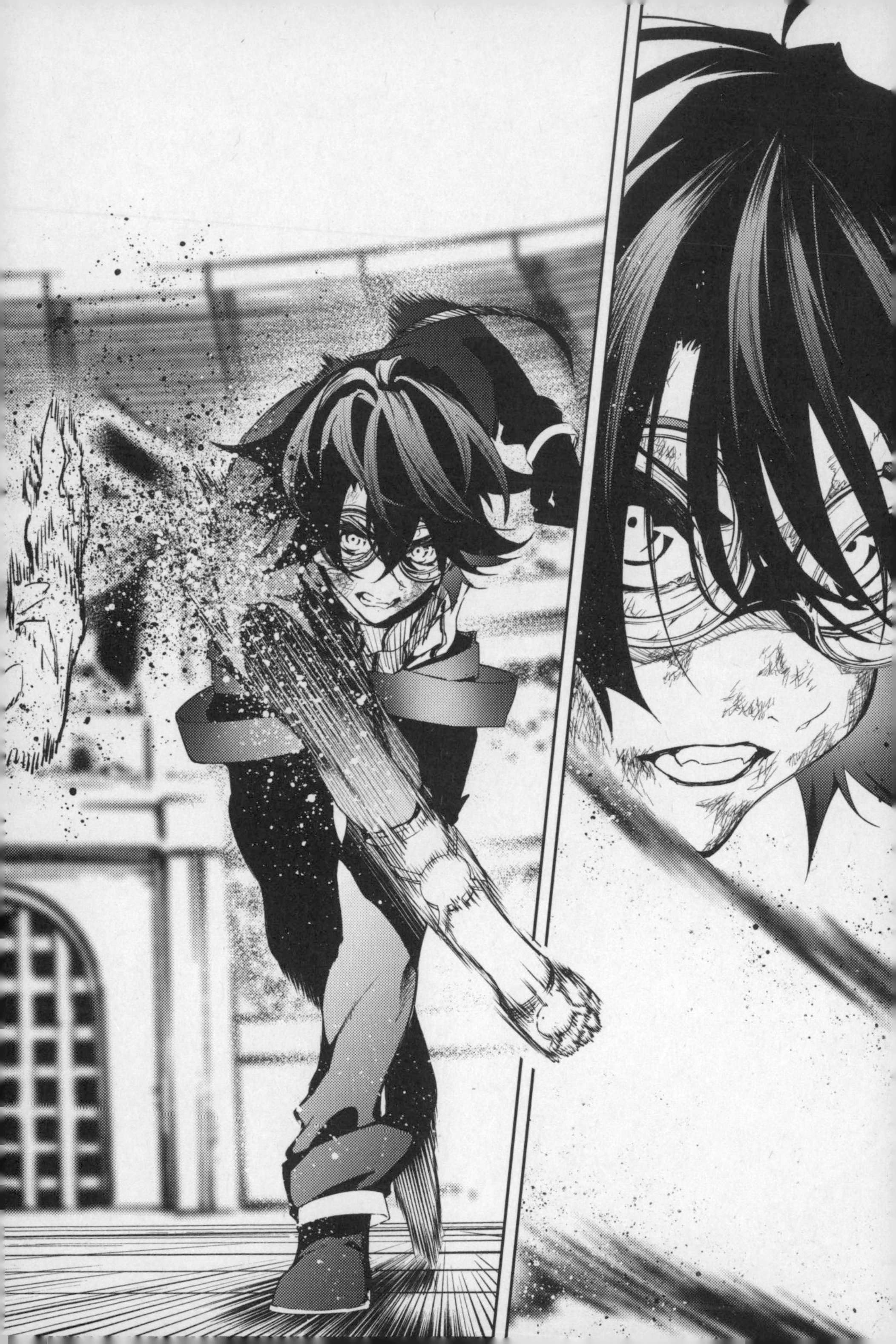

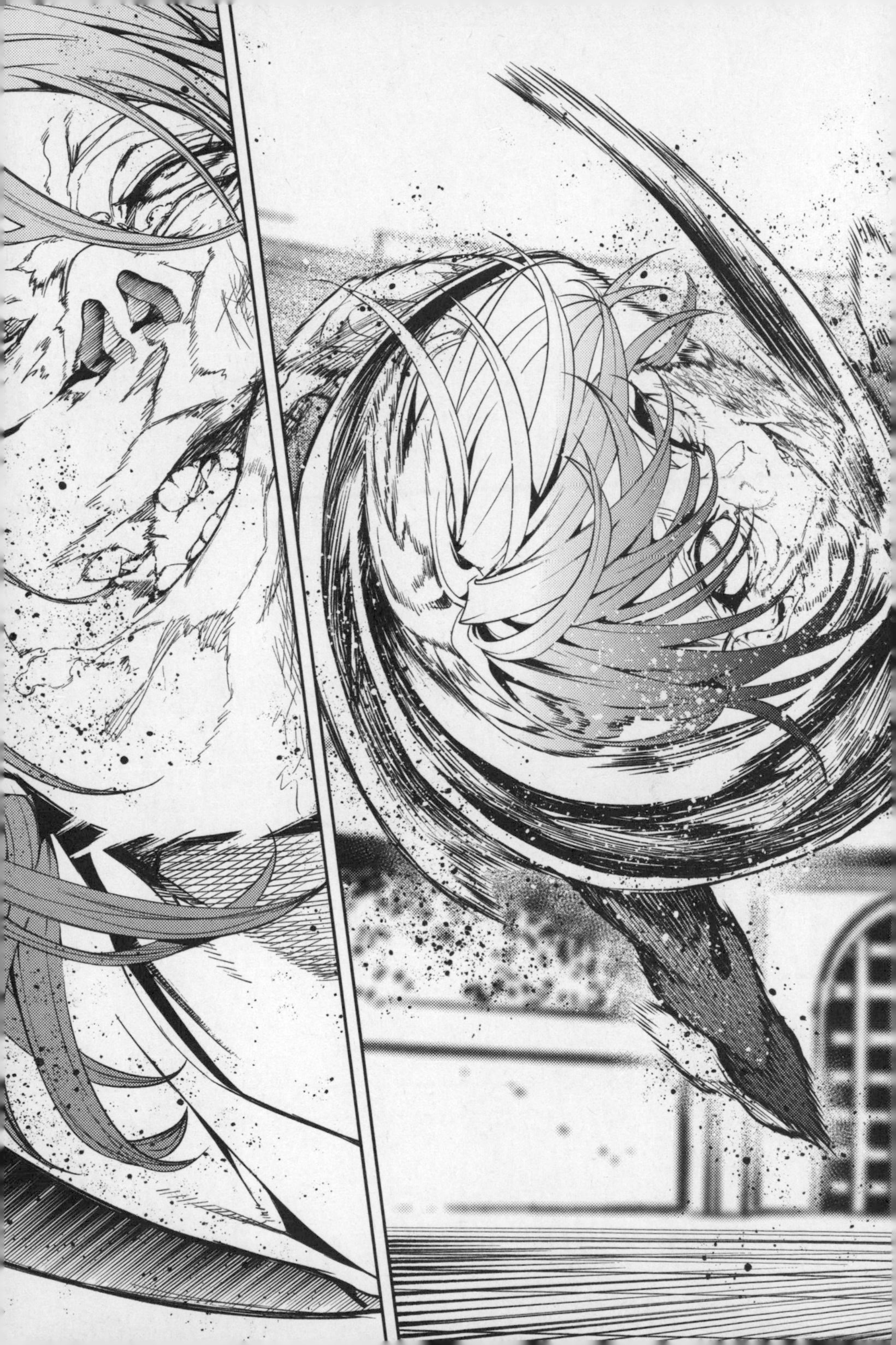

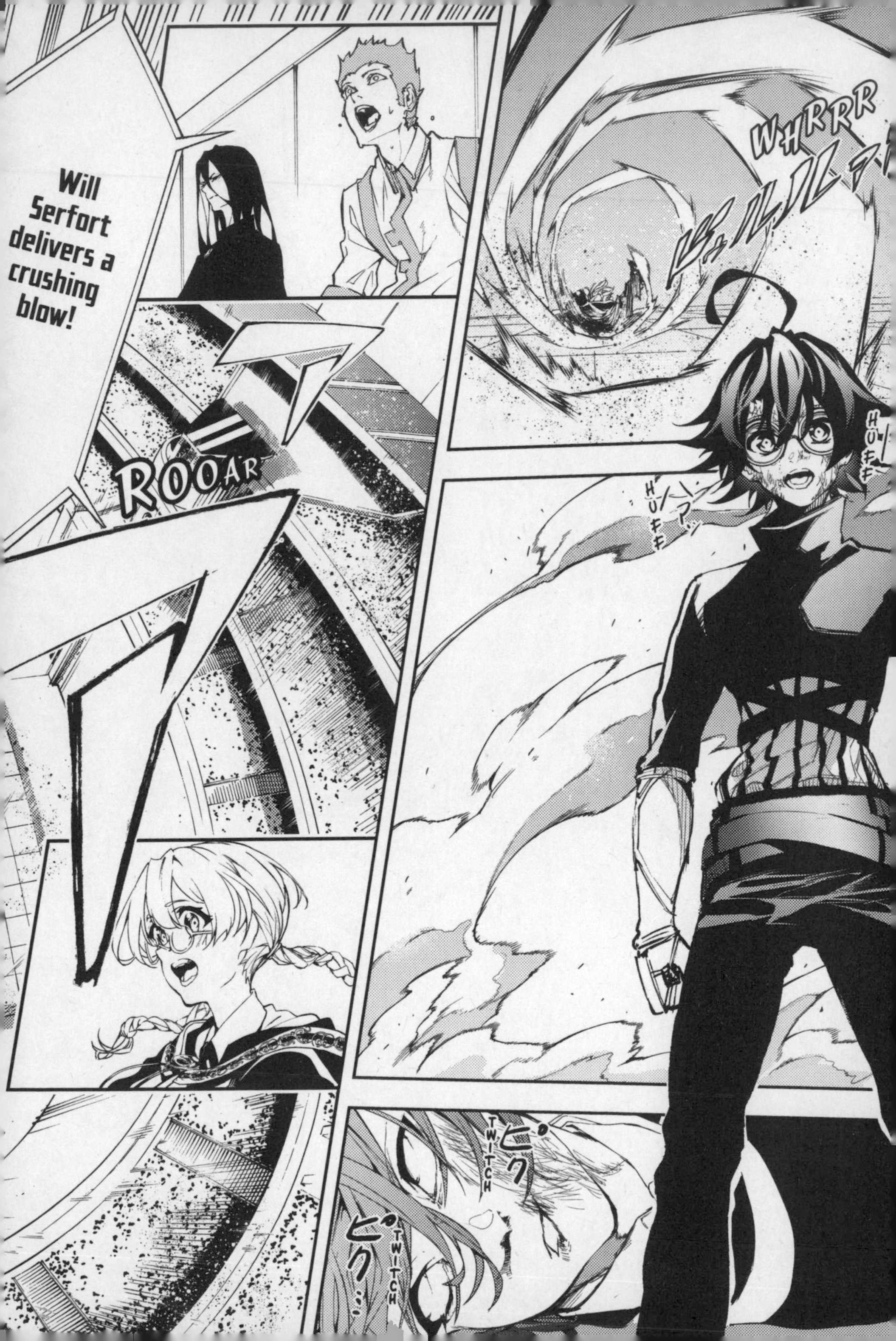
WHRRR
HUFF
HUFF
ピク
TWITCH
ピク
TWITCH
ROOAR
Will Serfort delivers a crushing blow!

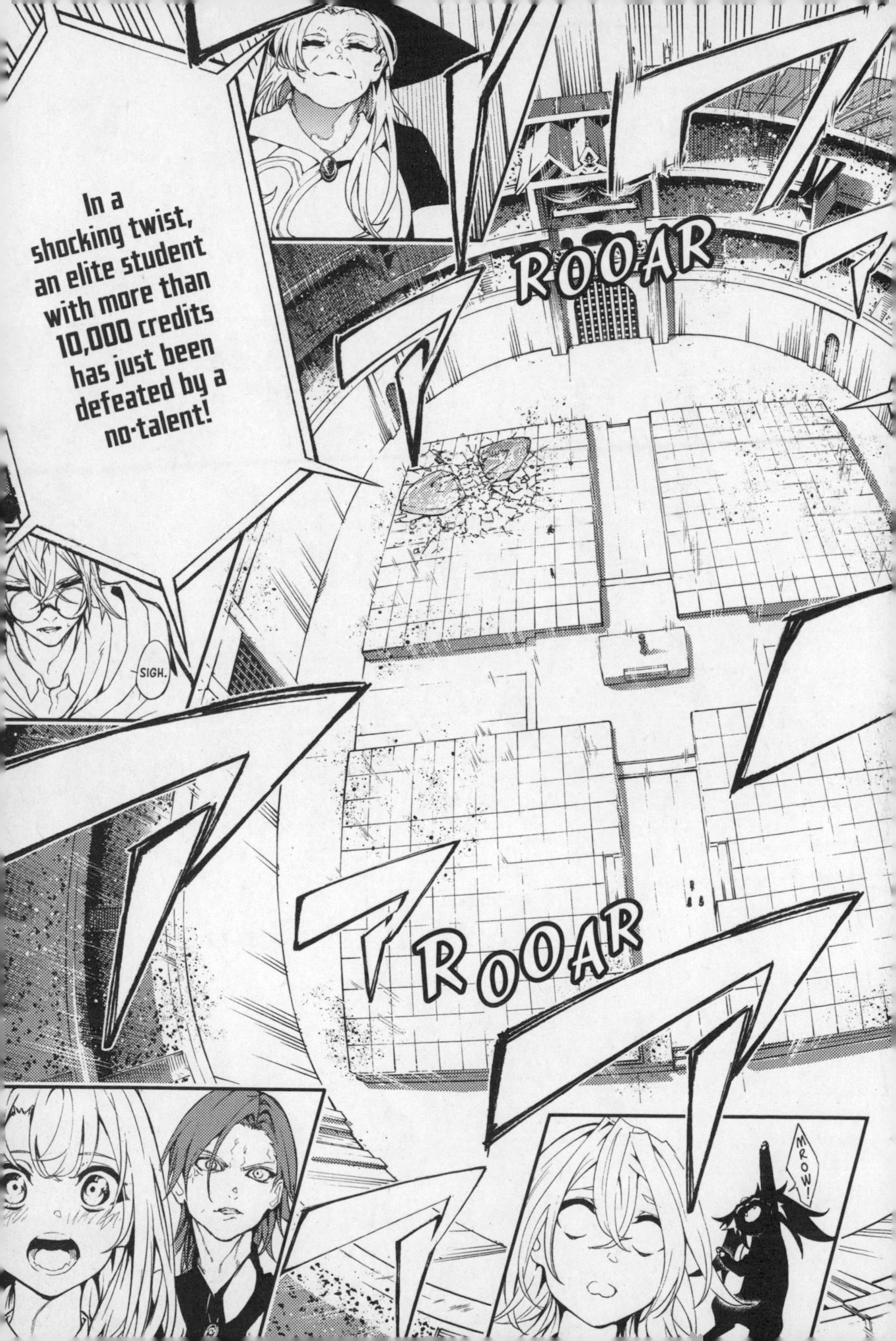
ROOAR
In a shocking twist, an elite student with more than 10,000 credits has just been defeated by a no-talent!
SIGH.
ROOAR
MROW!

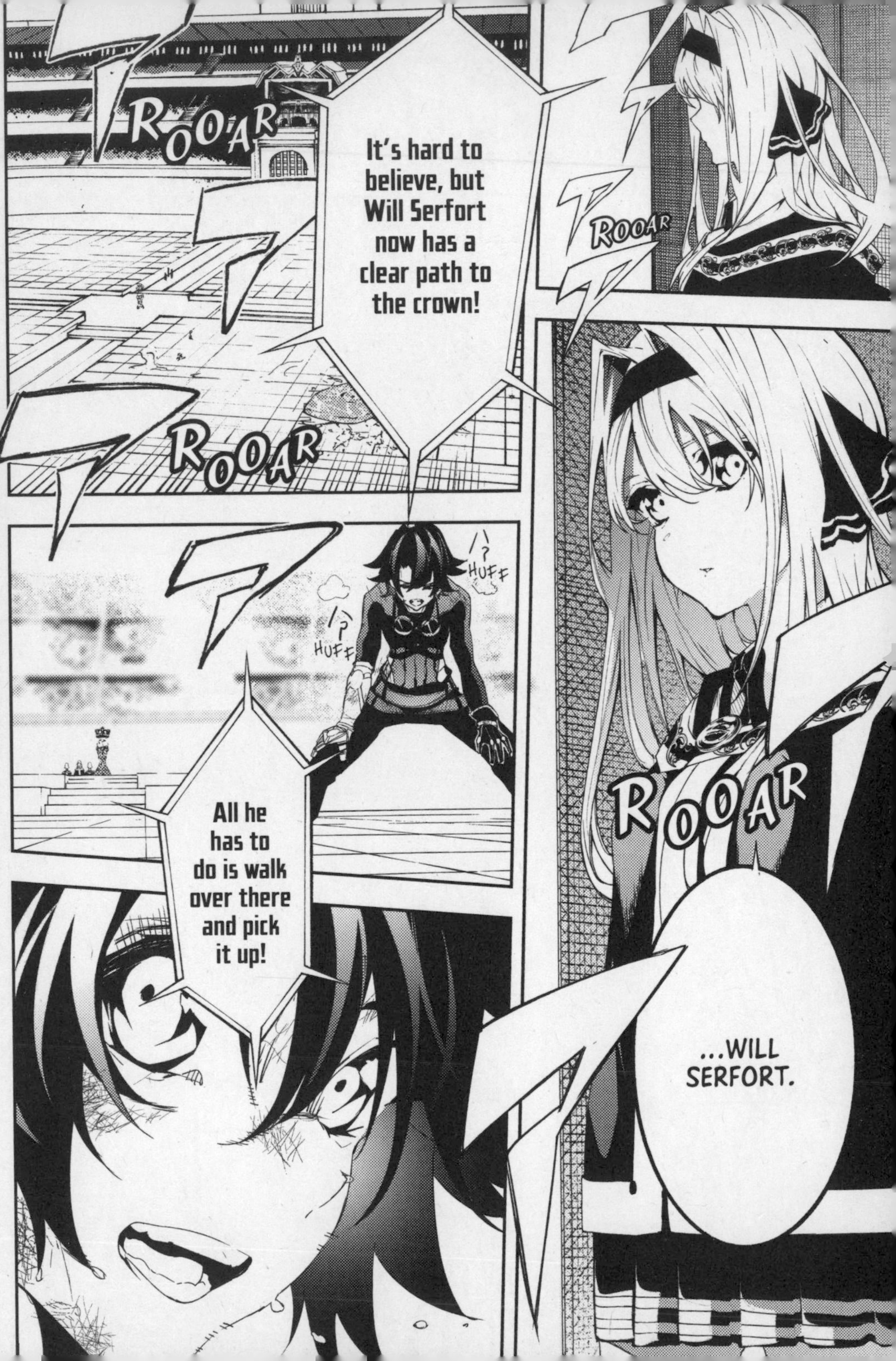
ROOAR
ROOAR
It's hard to believe, but Will Serfort now has a clear path to the crown!
ROOAR
ROOAR
...WILL SERFORT.
HUFF
HUFF
All he has to do is walk over there and pick it up!

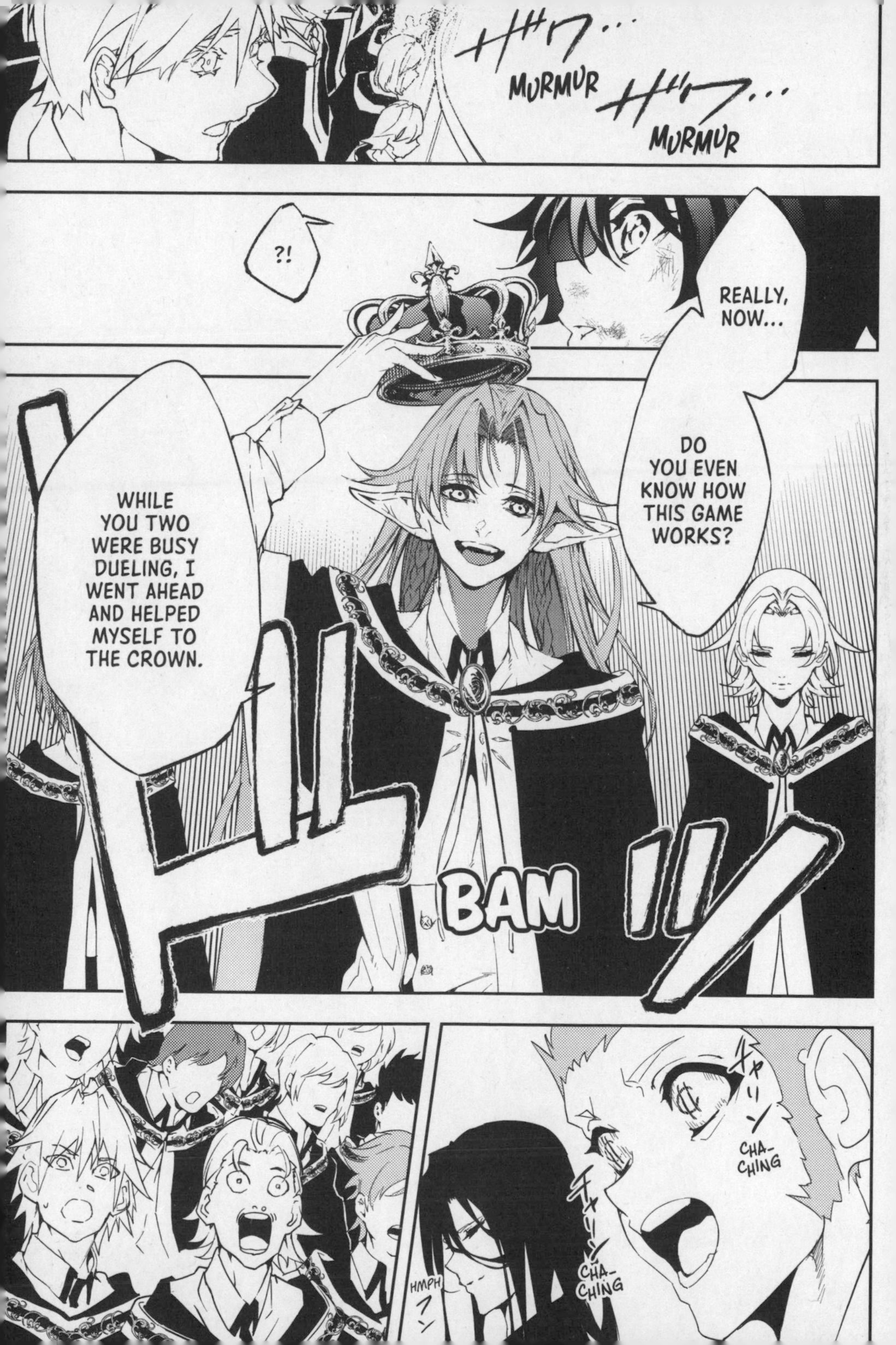
ザワ…
MURMUR
ザワ…
MURMUR
REALLY, NOW... DO YOU EVEN KNOW HOW THIS GAME WORKS?
?!
WHILE YOU TWO WERE BUSY DUELING, I WENT AHEAD AND HELPED MYSELF TO THE CROWN.
BAM
CHA-CHING
CHA-CHING
HMPH

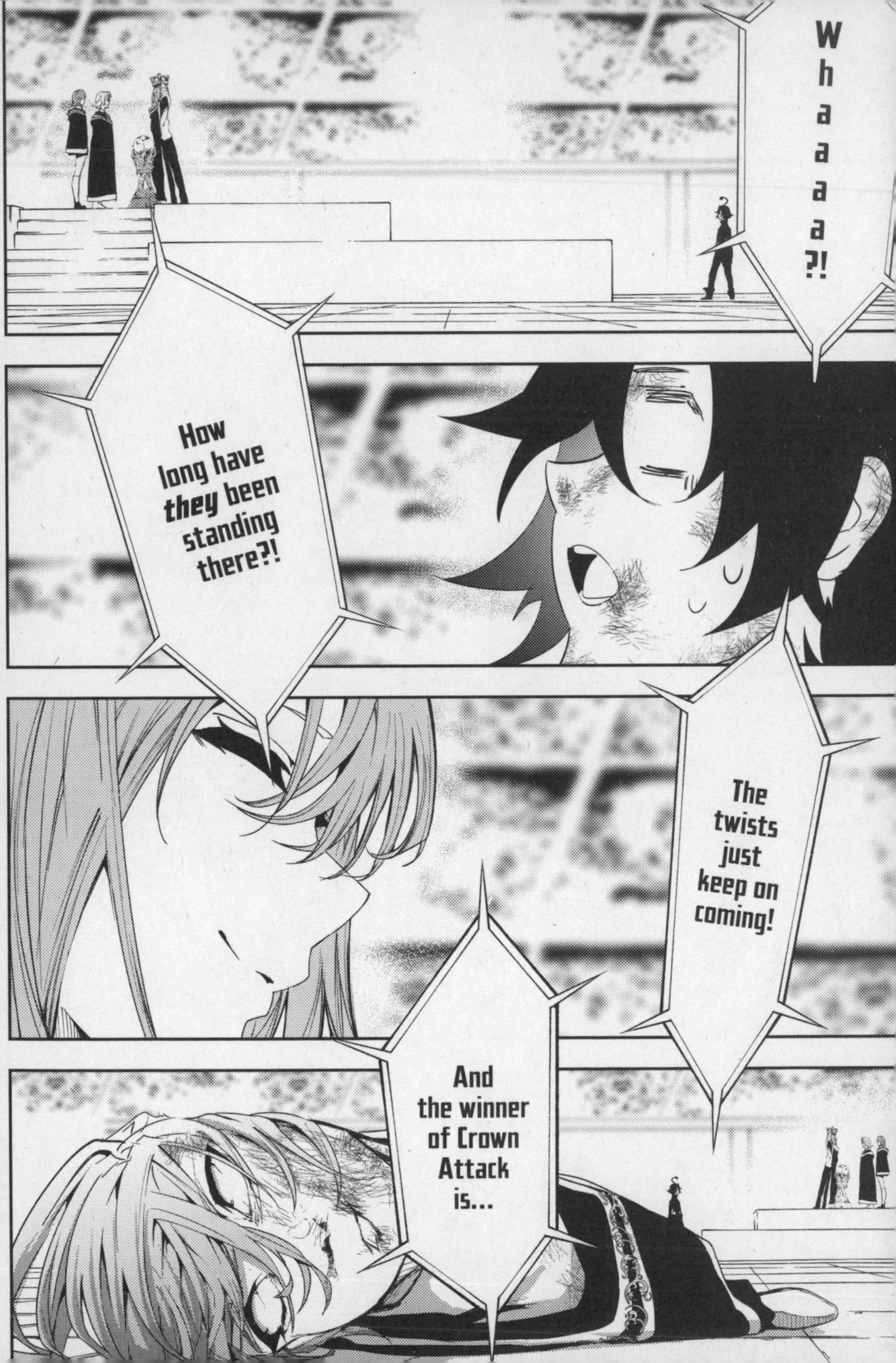
Whaaaaa?!
How long have *they* been standing there?!
The twists just keep on coming!
And the winner of Crown Attack is...

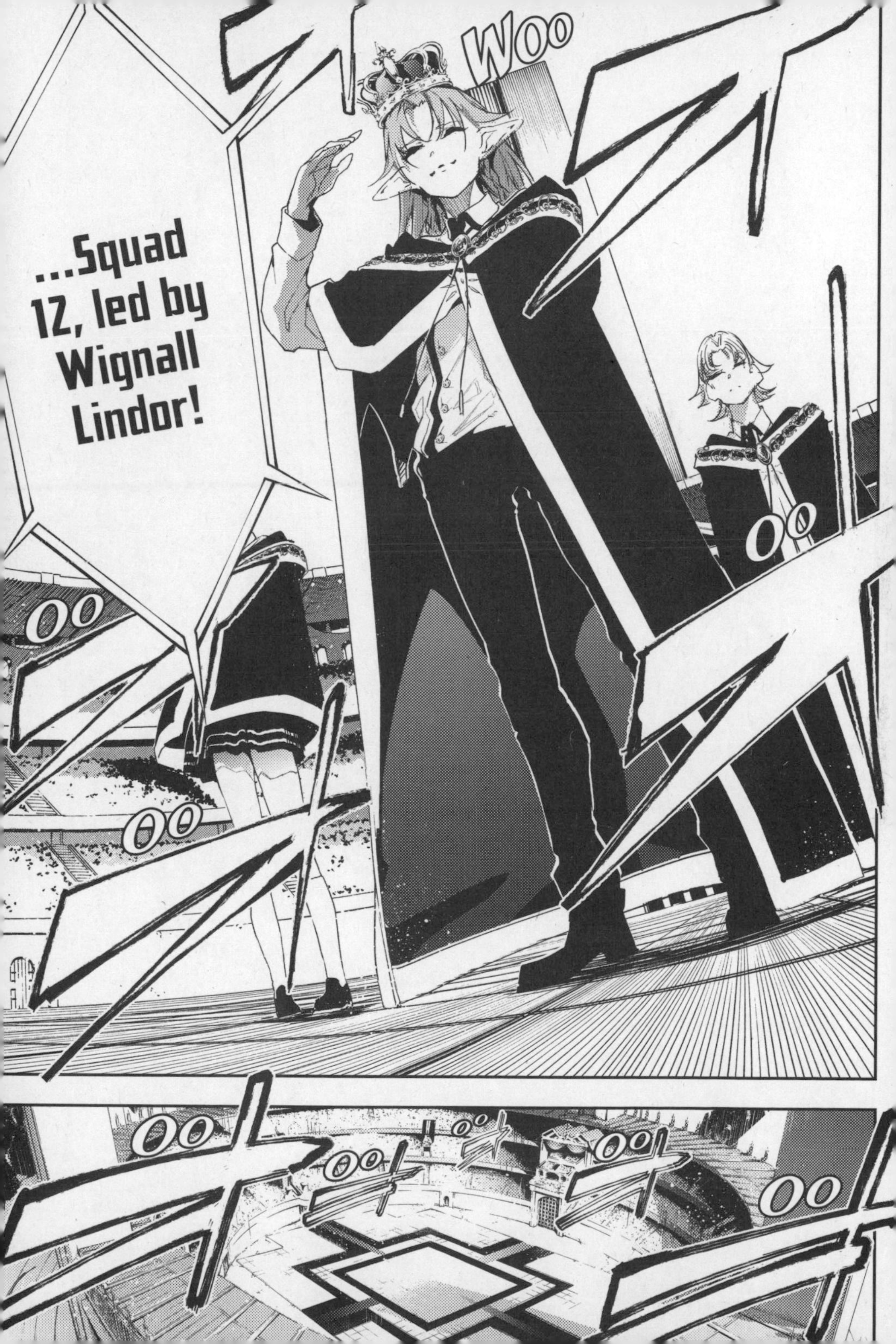
WOO
OO
...Squad 12, led by Wignall Lindor!
OO
OO
OO
OO
OO
OO
OO

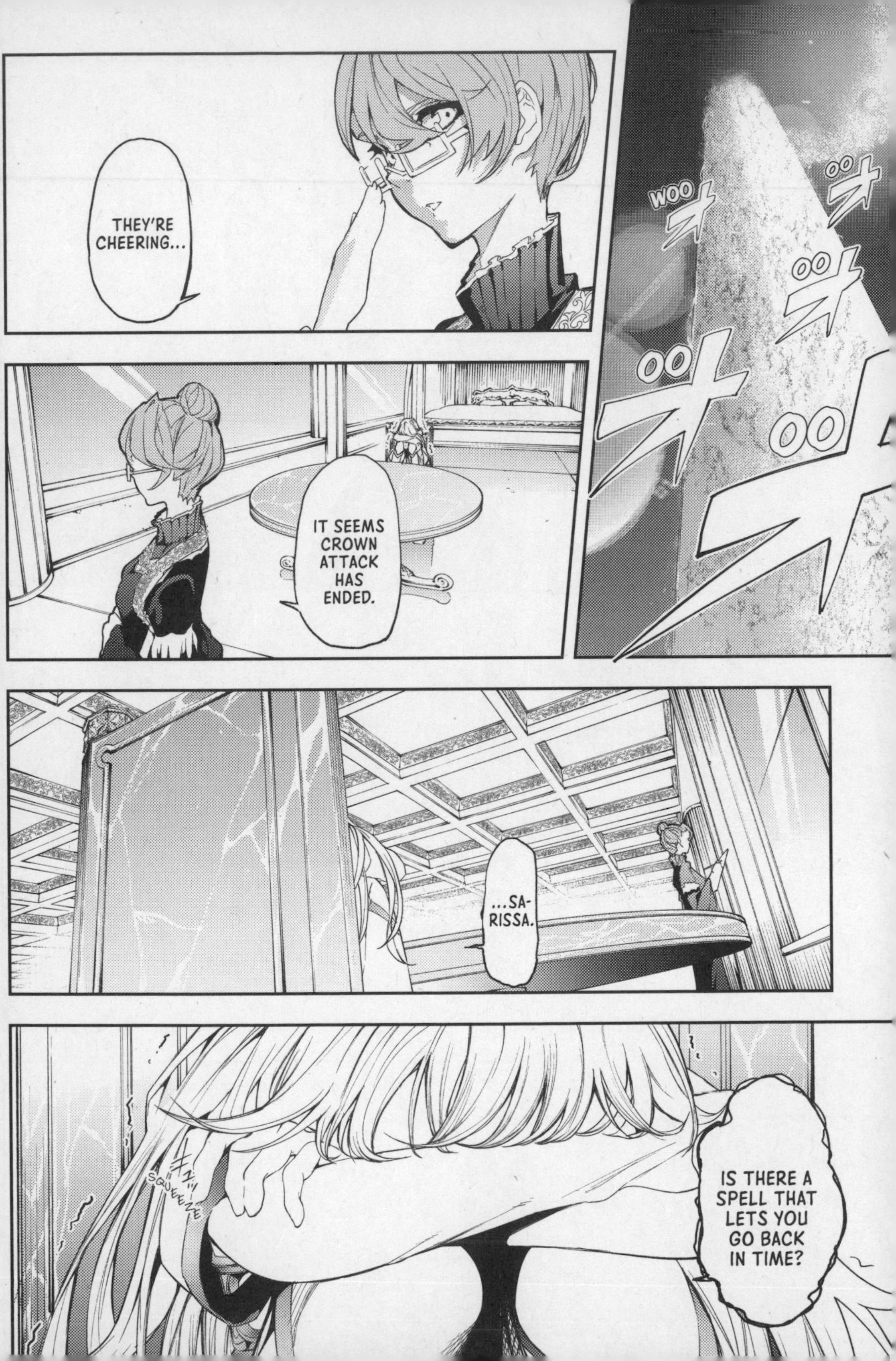
WOO
OO
OO
OO
OO
THEY'RE CHEERING...
IT SEEMS CROWN ATTACK HAS ENDED.
...SA-RISSA.
IS THERE A SPELL THAT LETS YOU GO BACK IN TIME?
SQUEEZE

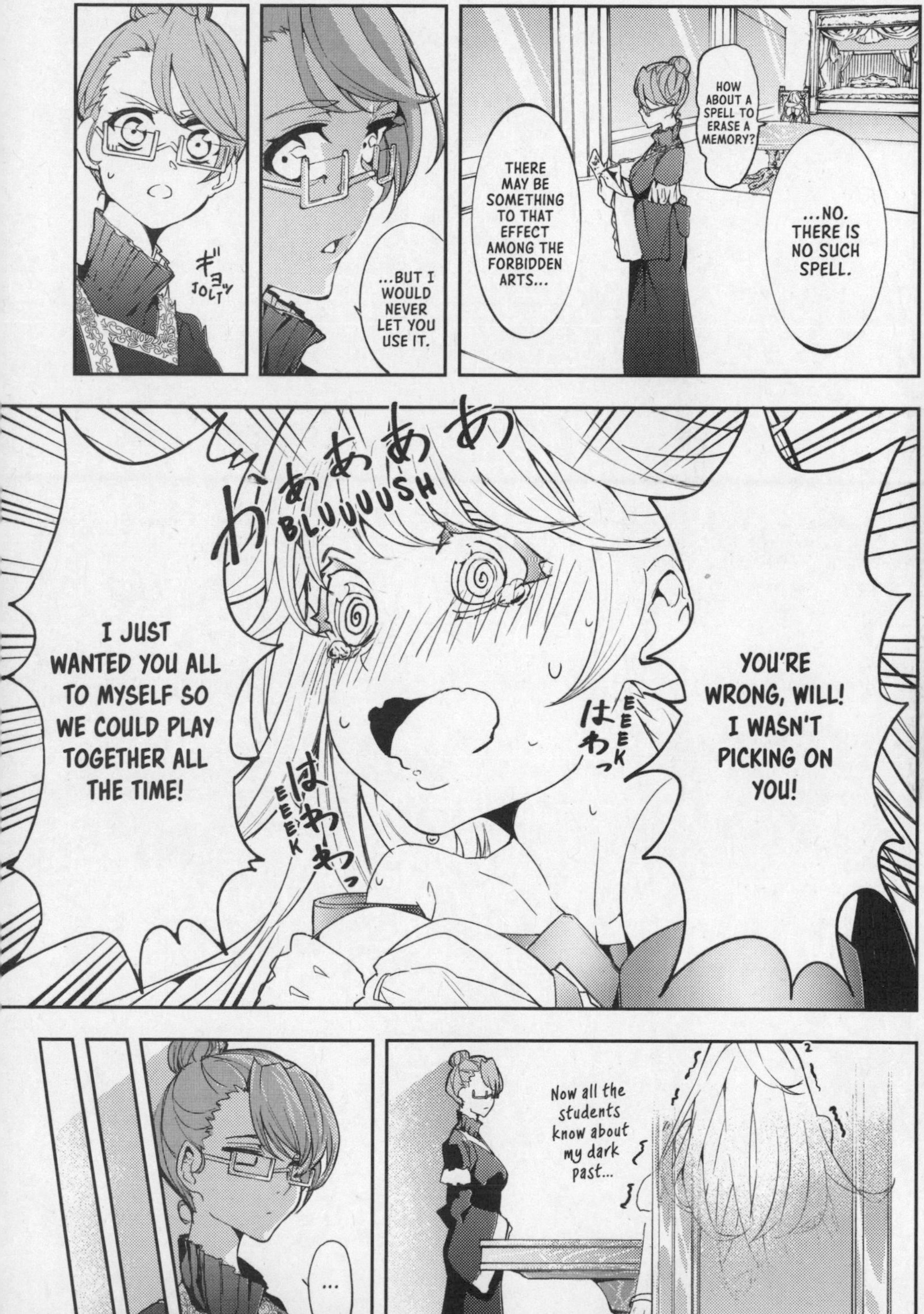

HOW ABOUT A SPELL TO ERASE A MEMORY?
...NO. THERE IS NO SUCH SPELL.
THERE MAY BE SOMETHING TO THAT EFFECT AMONG THE FORBIDDEN ARTS...
...BUT I WOULD NEVER LET YOU USE IT.
ギョッ
JOLT
わああああ
BLUUUUSH
YOU'RE WRONG, WILL! I WASN'T PICKING ON YOU!
はわっ
EEEK
はわわっ
EEEK
I JUST WANTED YOU ALL TO MYSELF SO WE COULD PLAY TOGETHER ALL THE TIME!
Now all the students know about my dark past...
...

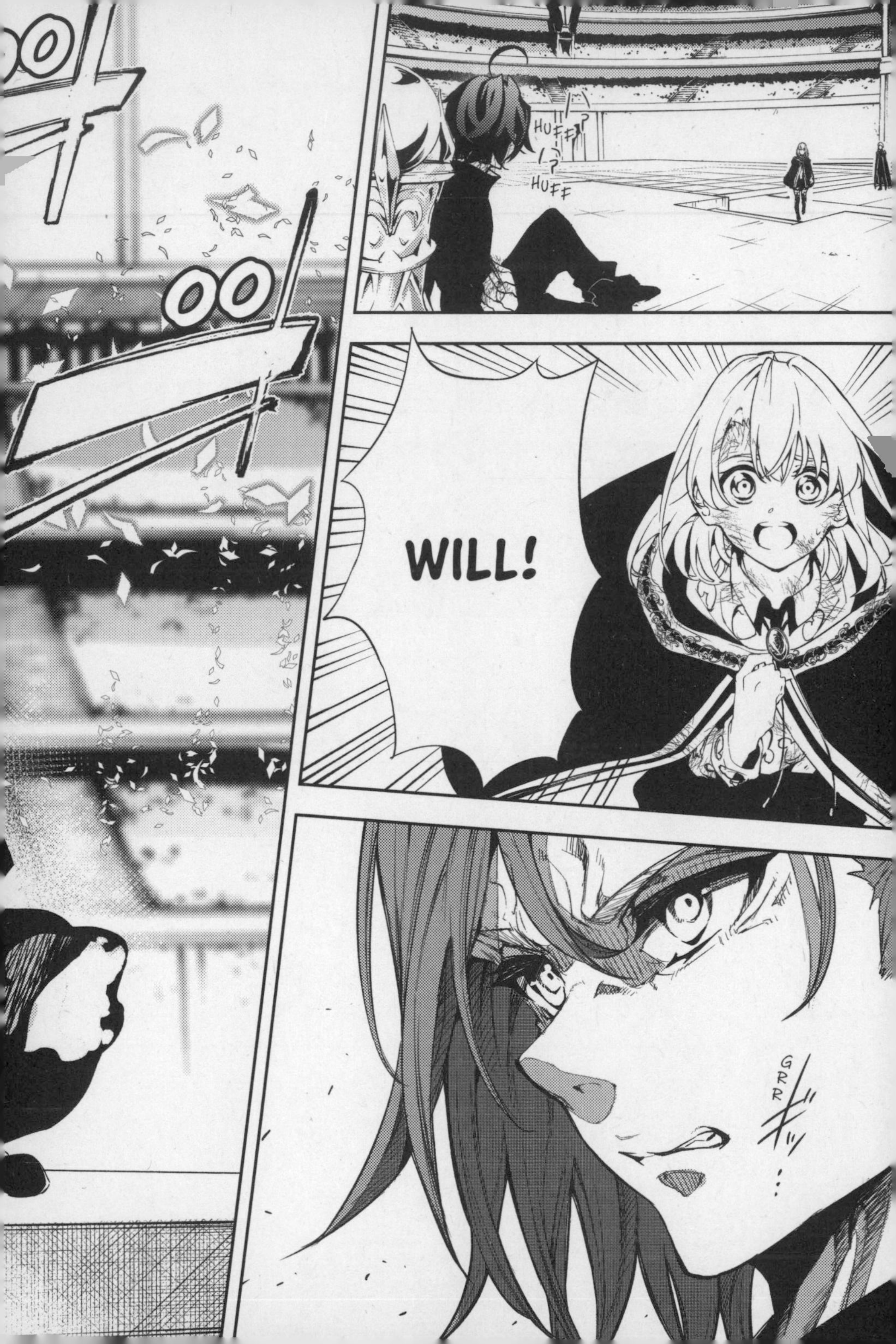
HUFF
HUFF
WILL!
GRR

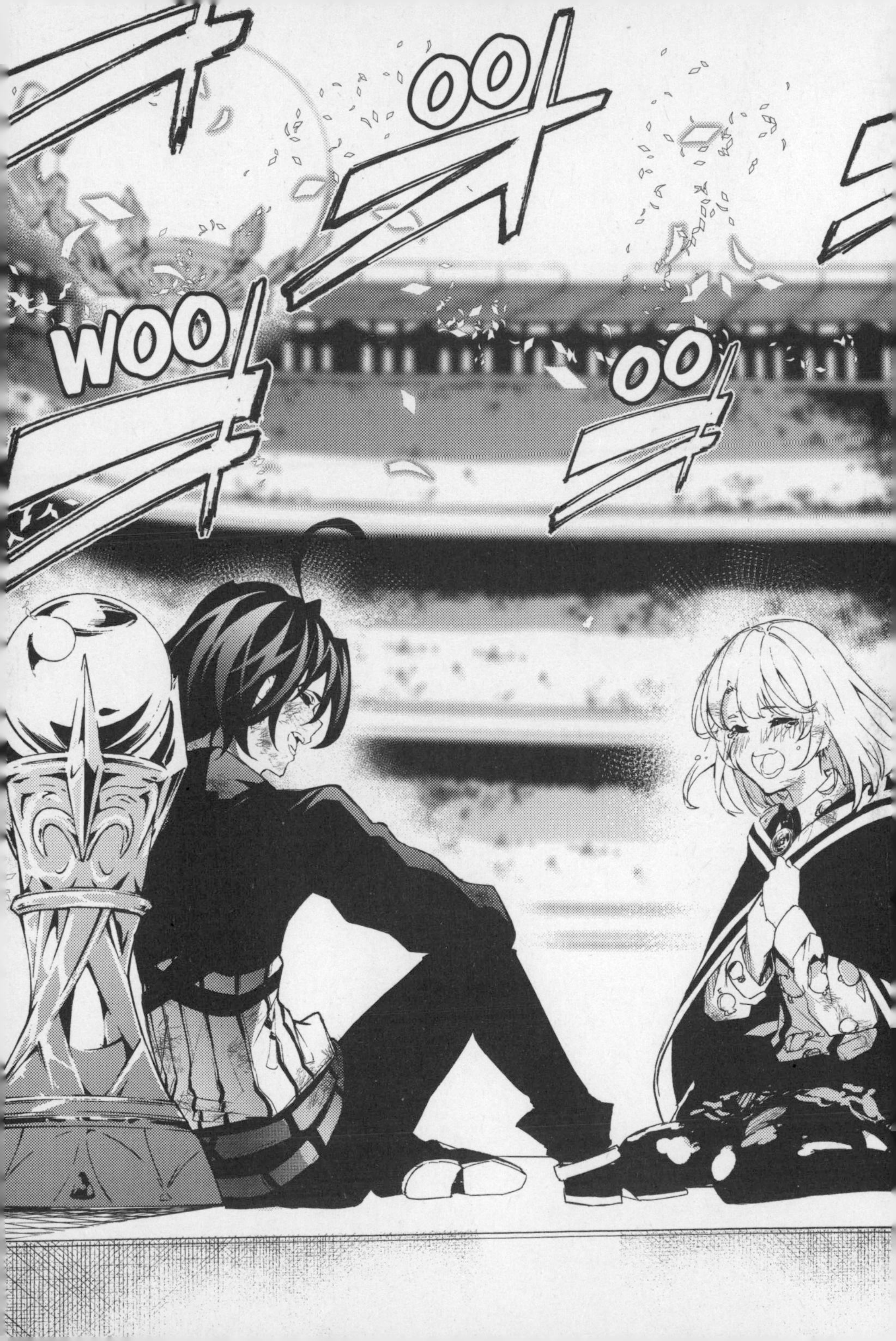
OO
OO
WOO

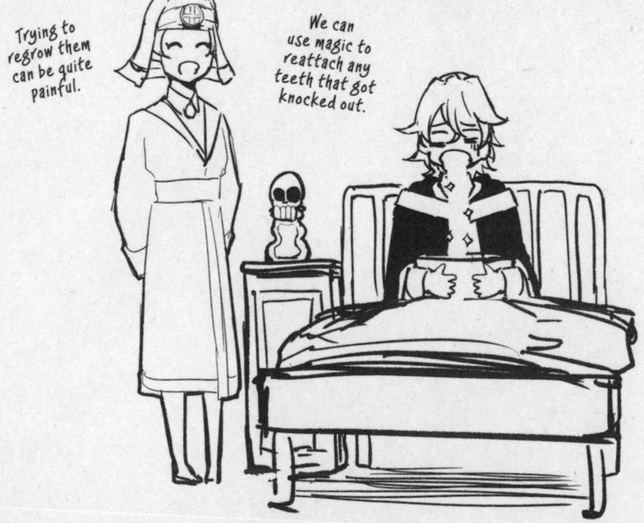
We can use magic to reattach any teeth that got knocked out.
Trying to regrow them can be quite painful.

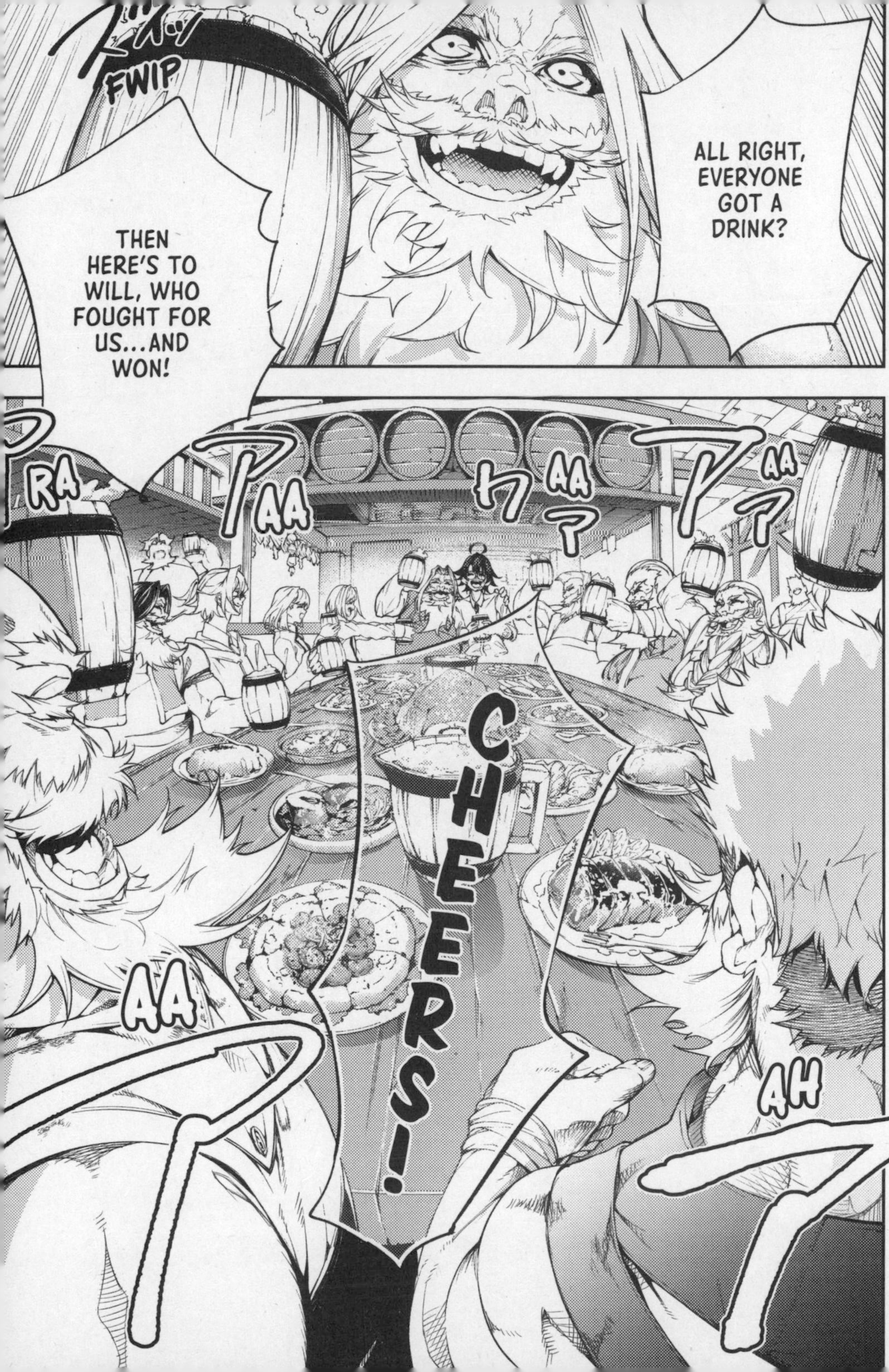

ALL RIGHT, EVERYONE GOT A DRINK?
FWIP
THEN HERE'S TO WILL, WHO FOUGHT FOR US...AND WON!
AA
AA
AA
RA
CHEERS!
AH
AA

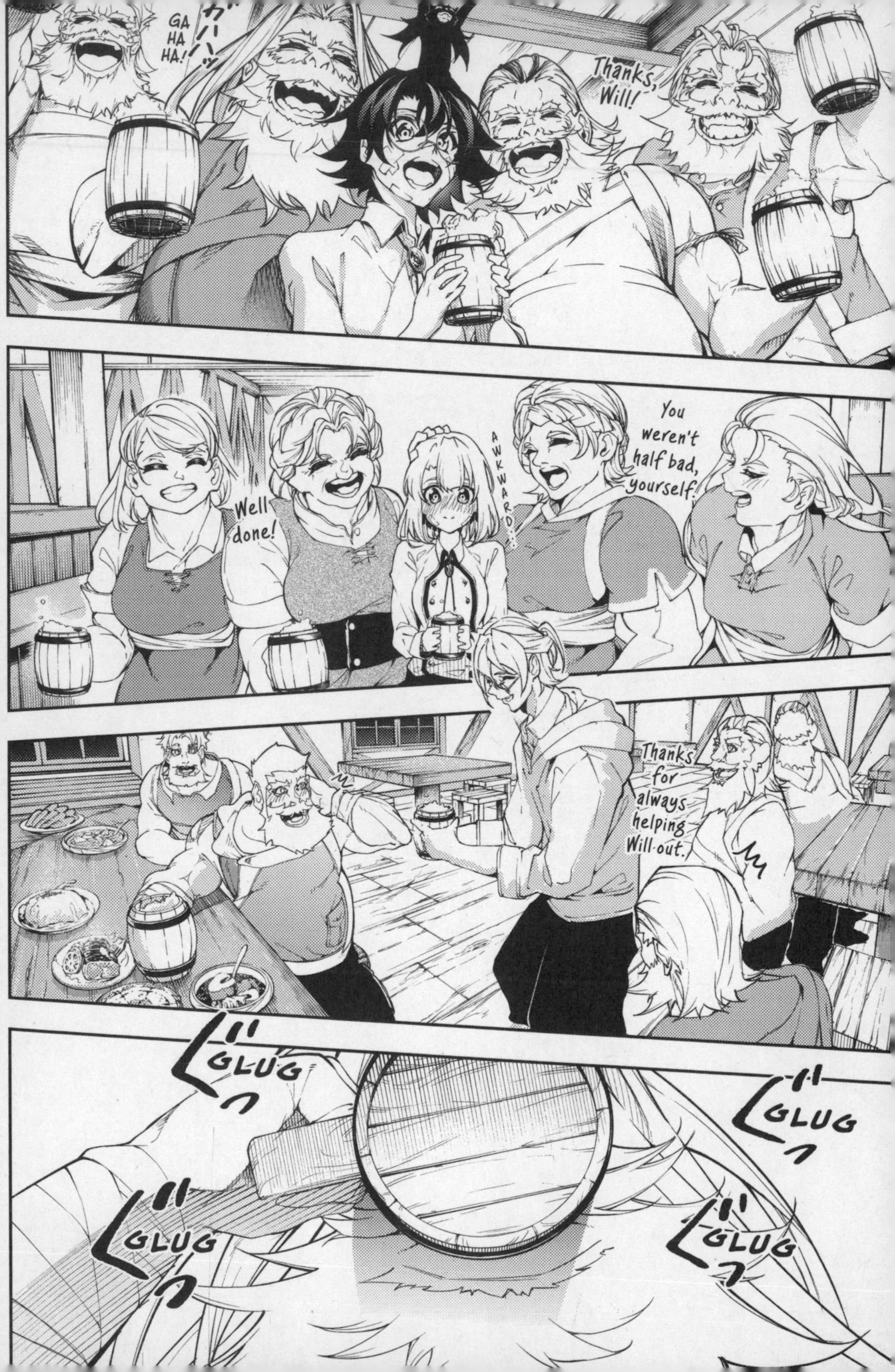
Thanks, Will!
ガハハッ
GA HA HA!
You weren't half bad, yourself.
AWKWARD...
Well done!
Thanks for always helping Will out.
GLUG
GLUG
GLUG
GLUG

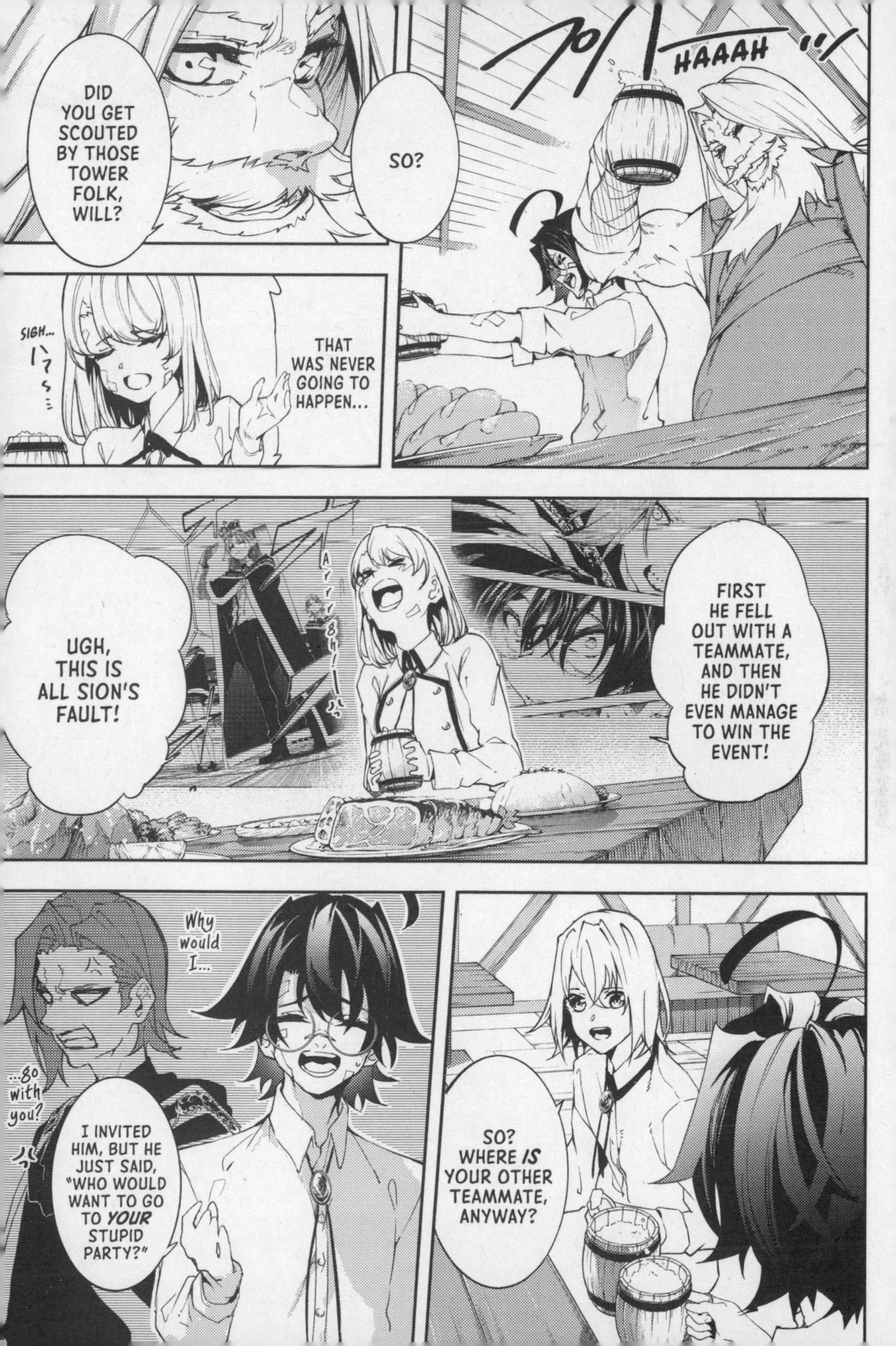
HAAAH
SO?
DID YOU GET SCOUTED BY THOSE TOWER FOLK, WILL?
THAT WAS NEVER GOING TO HAPPEN...
SIGH...
FIRST HE FELL OUT WITH A TEAMMATE, AND THEN HE DIDN'T EVEN MANAGE TO WIN THE EVENT!
Arrrgh!
UGH, THIS IS ALL SION'S FAULT!
SO? WHERE *IS* YOUR OTHER TEAMMATE, ANYWAY?
Why would I...
I INVITED HIM, BUT HE JUST SAID, "WHO WOULD WANT TO GO TO *YOUR* STUPID PARTY?"
...go with you?

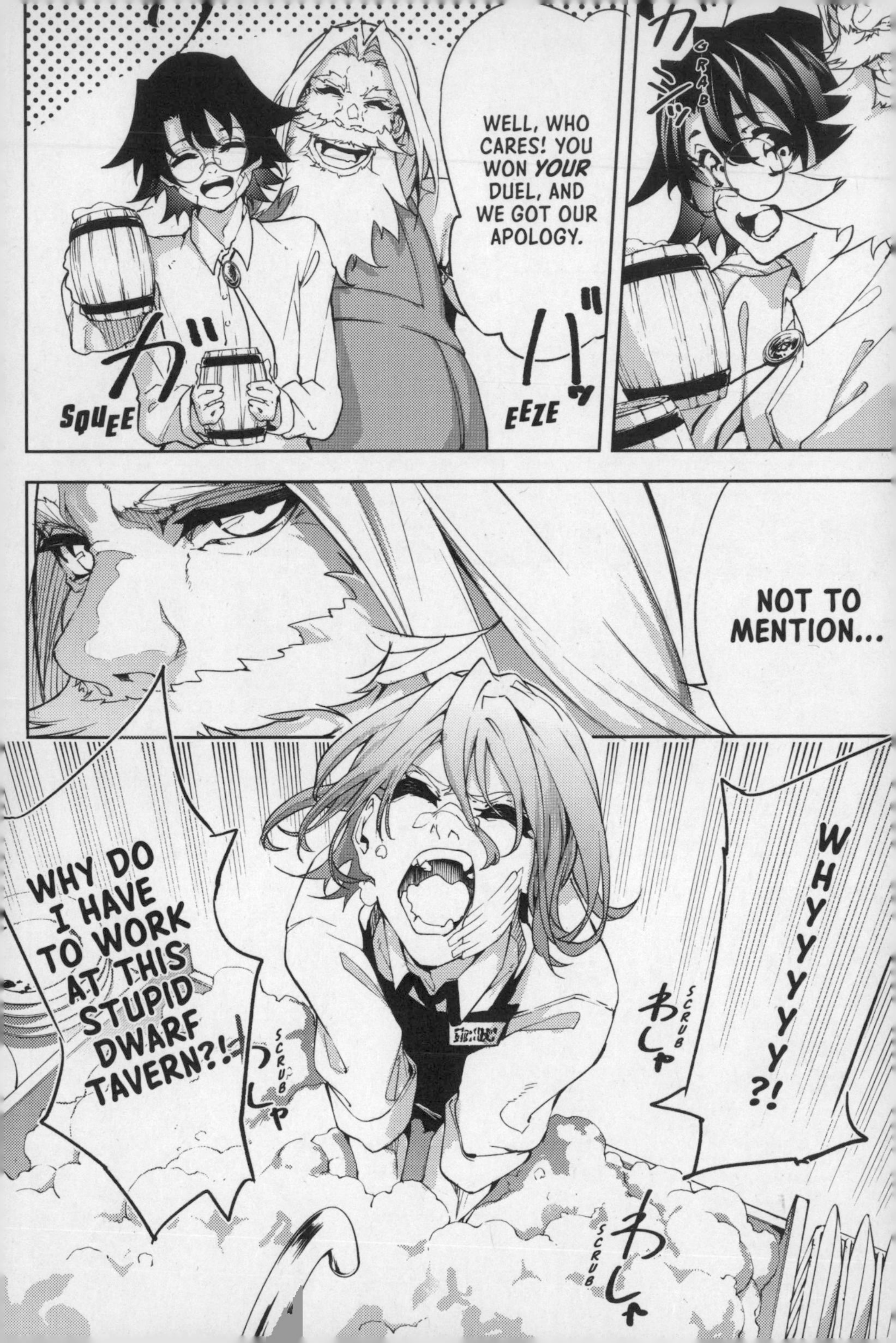
GRAB
WELL, WHO CARES! YOU WON *YOUR* DUEL, AND WE GOT OUR APOLOGY.
SQUEEZE
NOT TO MENTION...
WHYYYYYYY?!
SCRUB
SCRUB
WHY DO I HAVE TO WORK AT THIS STUPID DWARF TAVERN?!
SCRUB

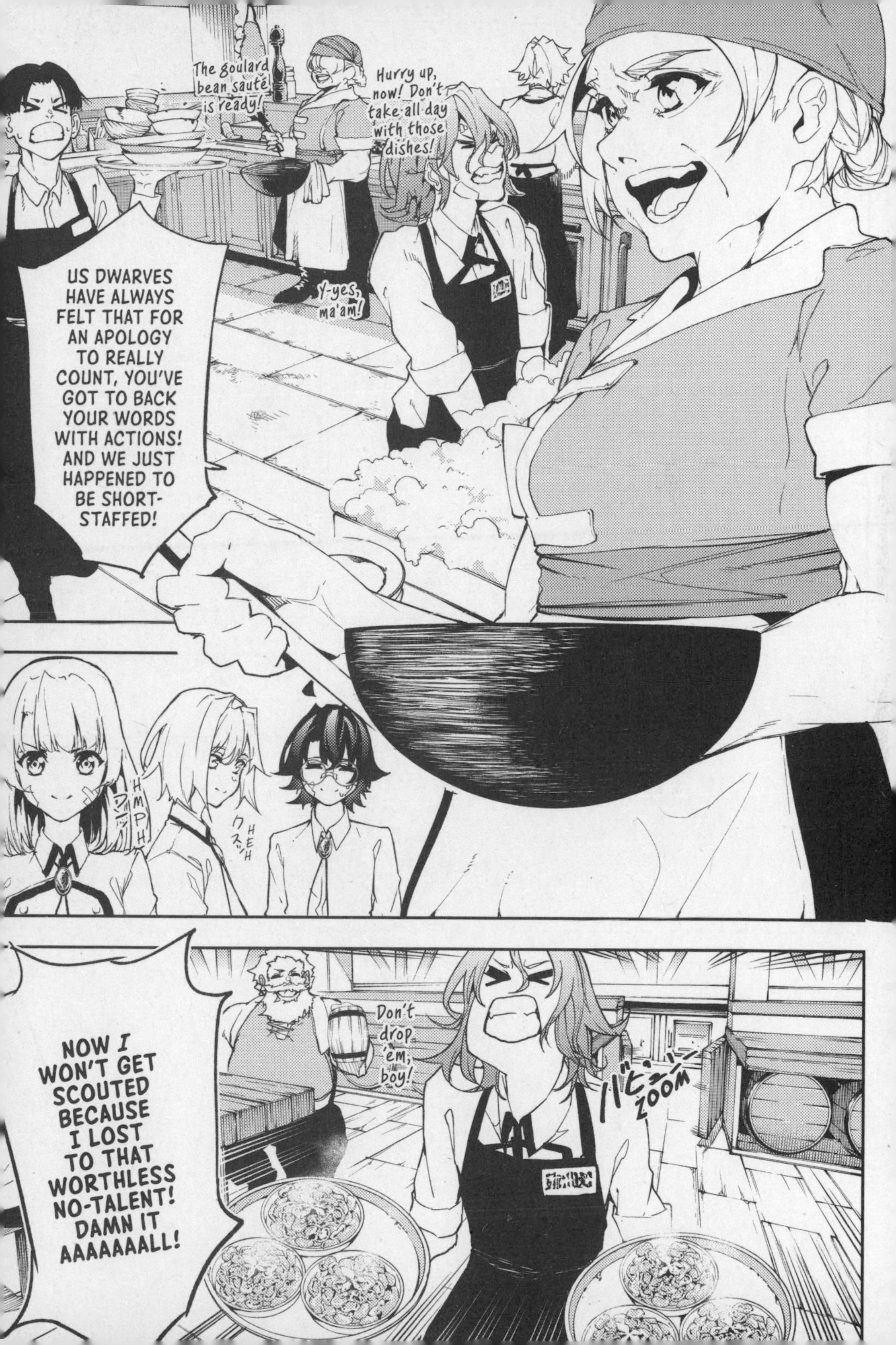
Hurry up, now! Don't take all day with those dishes!
The goulard bean sauté is ready!
Y-yes, ma'am!
US DWARVES HAVE ALWAYS FELT THAT FOR AN APOLOGY TO REALLY COUNT, YOU'VE GOT TO BACK YOUR WORDS WITH ACTIONS! AND WE JUST HAPPENED TO BE SHORT-STAFFED!
HEH
HMPH
ZOOM
Don't drop 'em, boy!
NOW I WON'T GET SCOUTED BECAUSE I LOST TO THAT WORTHLESS NO-TALENT! DAMN IT AAAAAAALL!

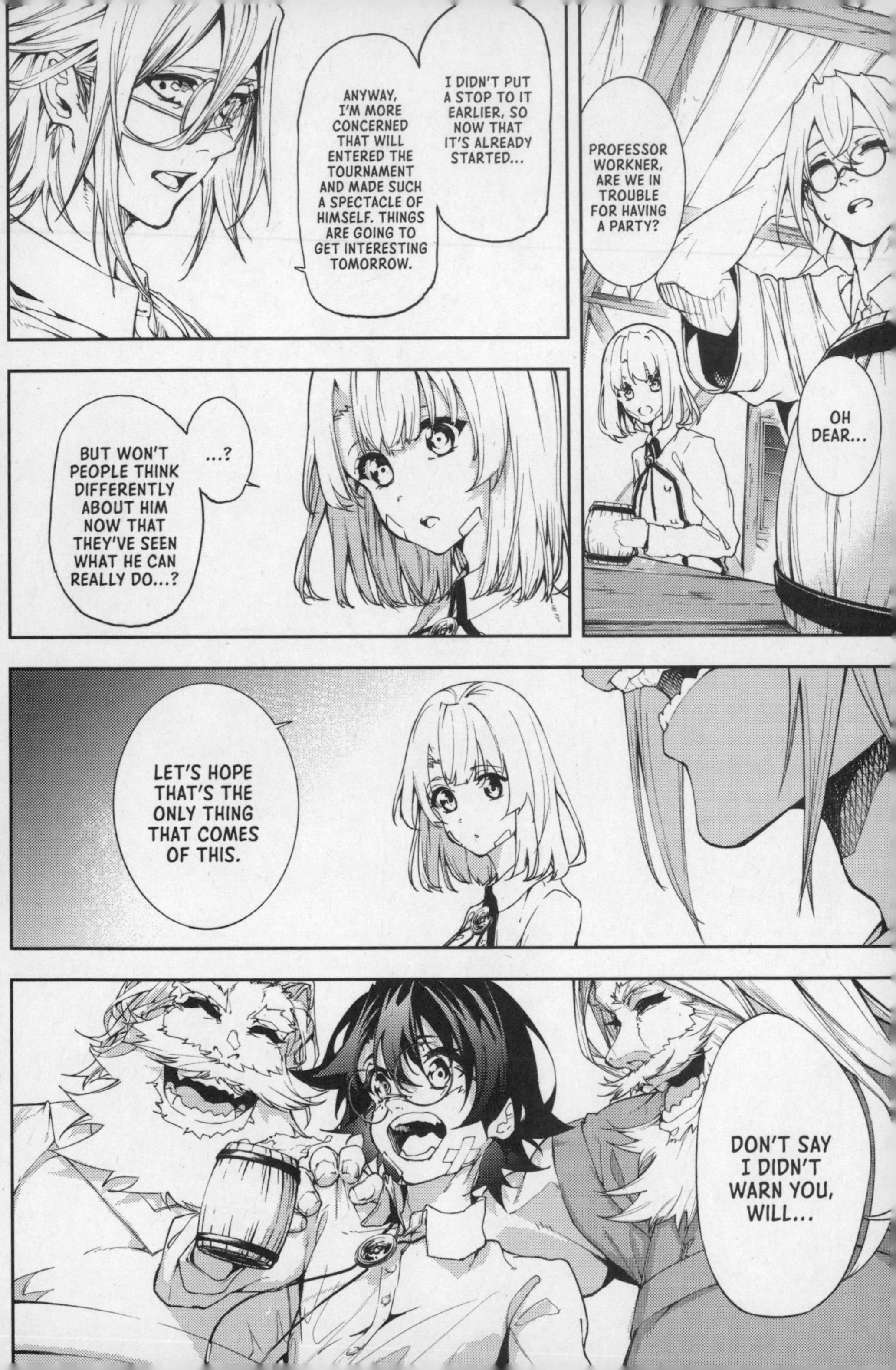
PROFESSOR WORKNER, ARE WE IN TROUBLE FOR HAVING A PARTY?
OH DEAR...
I DIDN'T PUT A STOP TO IT EARLIER, SO NOW THAT IT'S ALREADY STARTED...
ANYWAY, I'M MORE CONCERNED THAT WILL ENTERED THE TOURNAMENT AND MADE SUCH A SPECTACLE OF HIMSELF. THINGS ARE GOING TO GET INTERESTING TOMORROW.
...?
BUT WON'T PEOPLE THINK DIFFERENTLY ABOUT HIM NOW THAT THEY'VE SEEN WHAT HE CAN REALLY DO...?
LET'S HOPE THAT'S THE ONLY THING THAT COMES OF THIS.
DON'T SAY I DIDN'T WARN YOU, WILL...

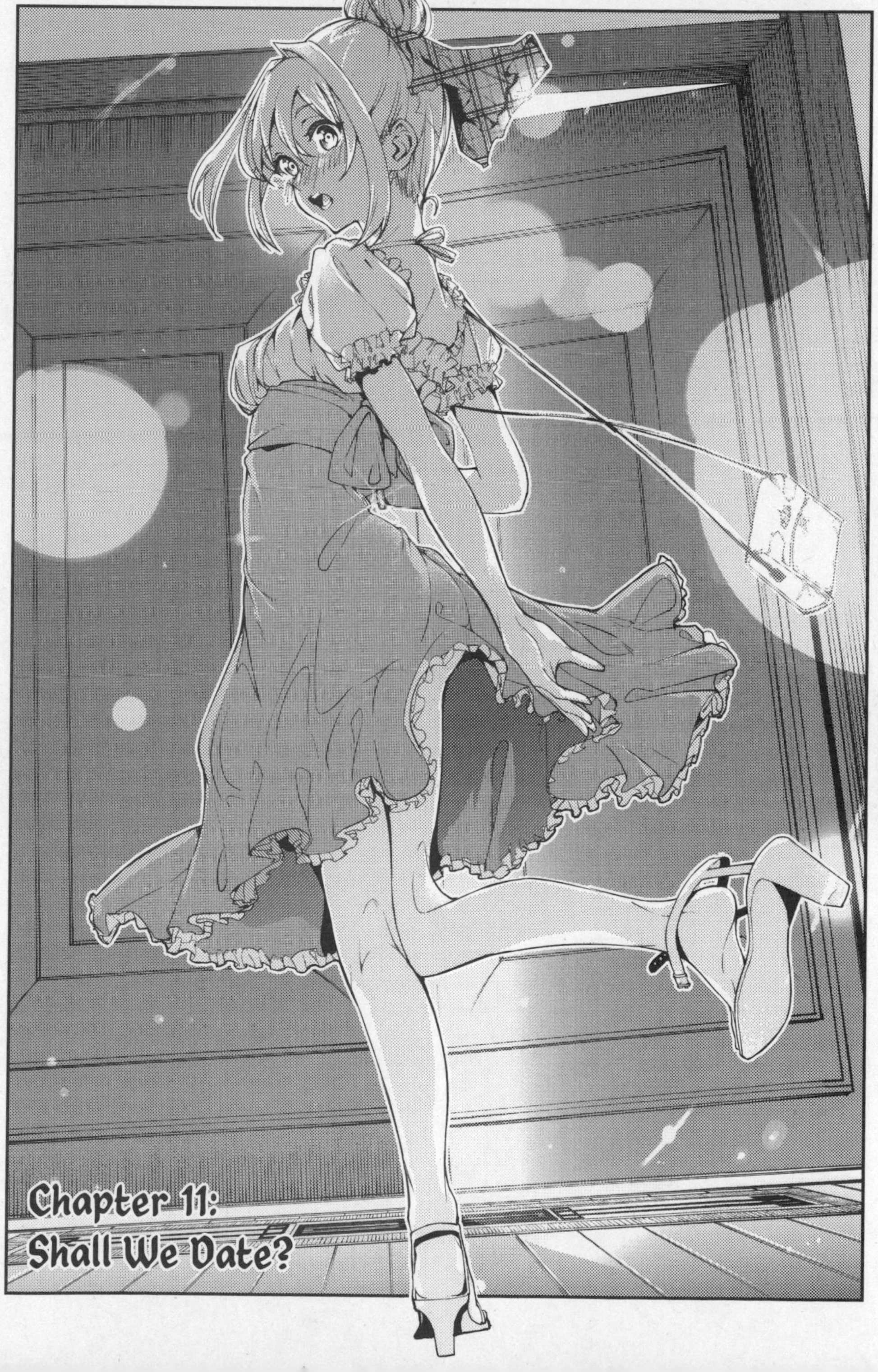
Chapter 11:
Shall We Date?

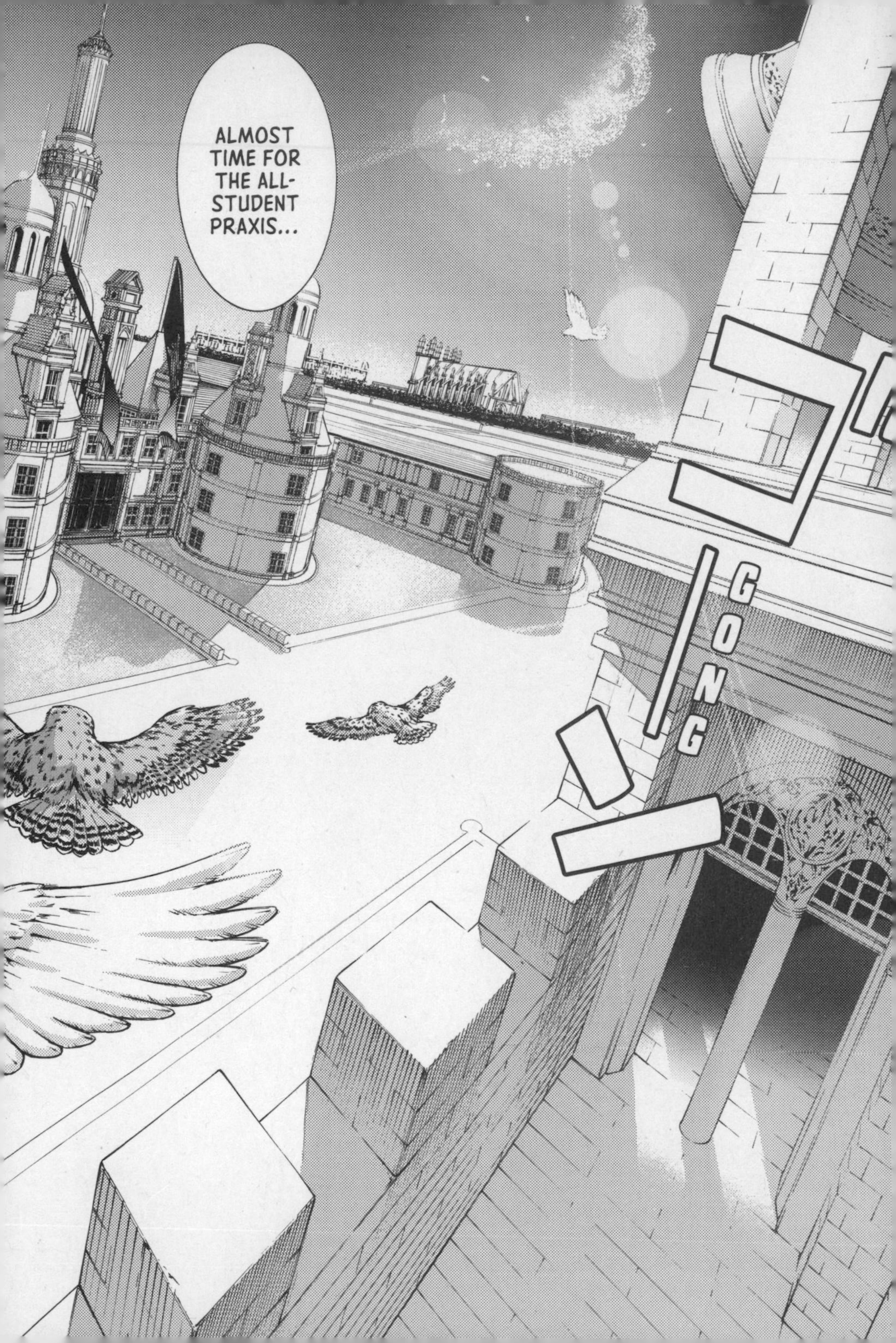
ALMOST TIME FOR THE ALL-STUDENT PRAXIS...
GONG

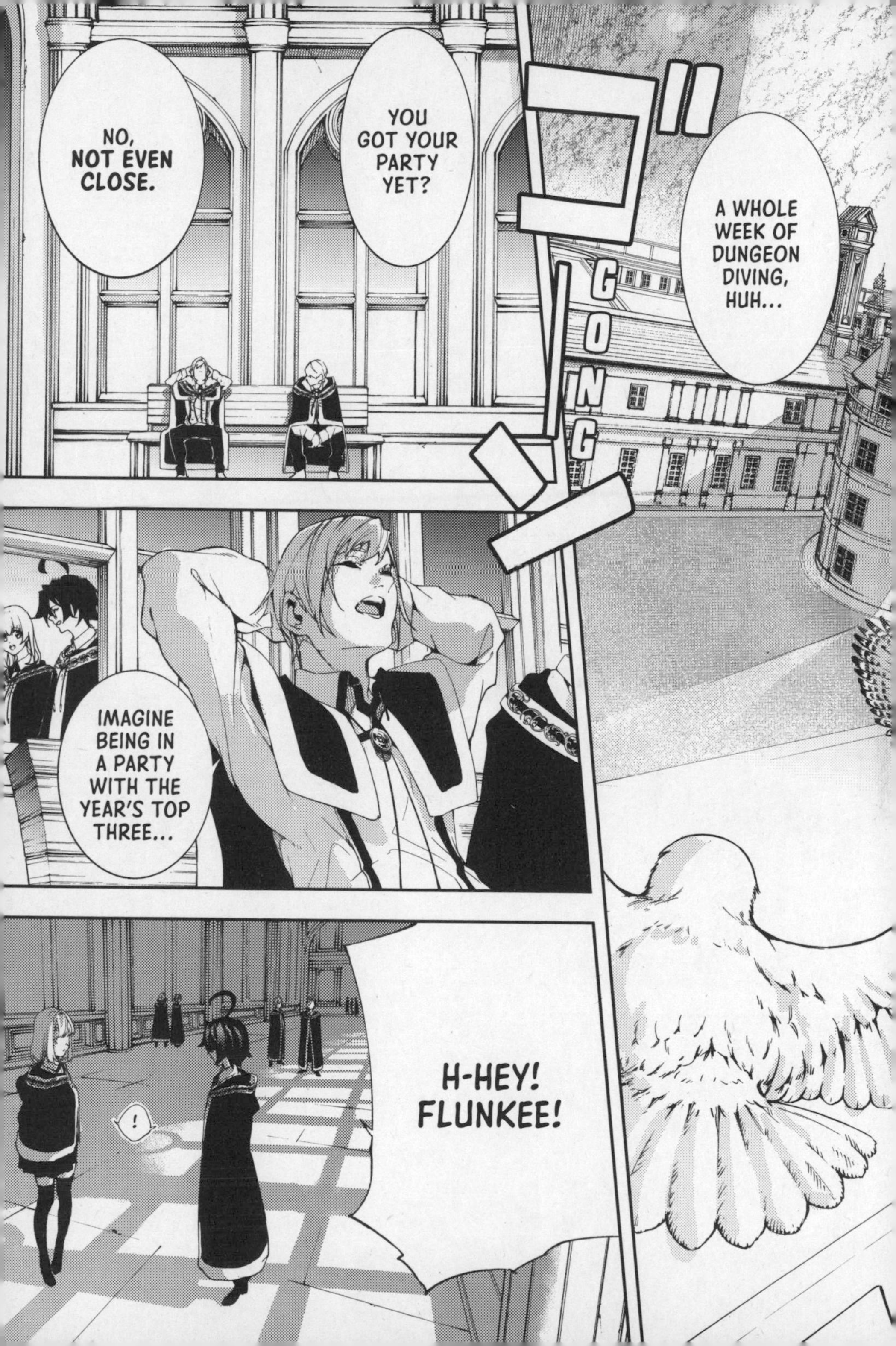
GONG
A WHOLE WEEK OF DUNGEON DIVING, HUH...
YOU GOT YOUR PARTY YET?
NO, NOT EVEN CLOSE.
IMAGINE BEING IN A PARTY WITH THE YEAR'S TOP THREE...
H-HEY! FLUNKEE!
!

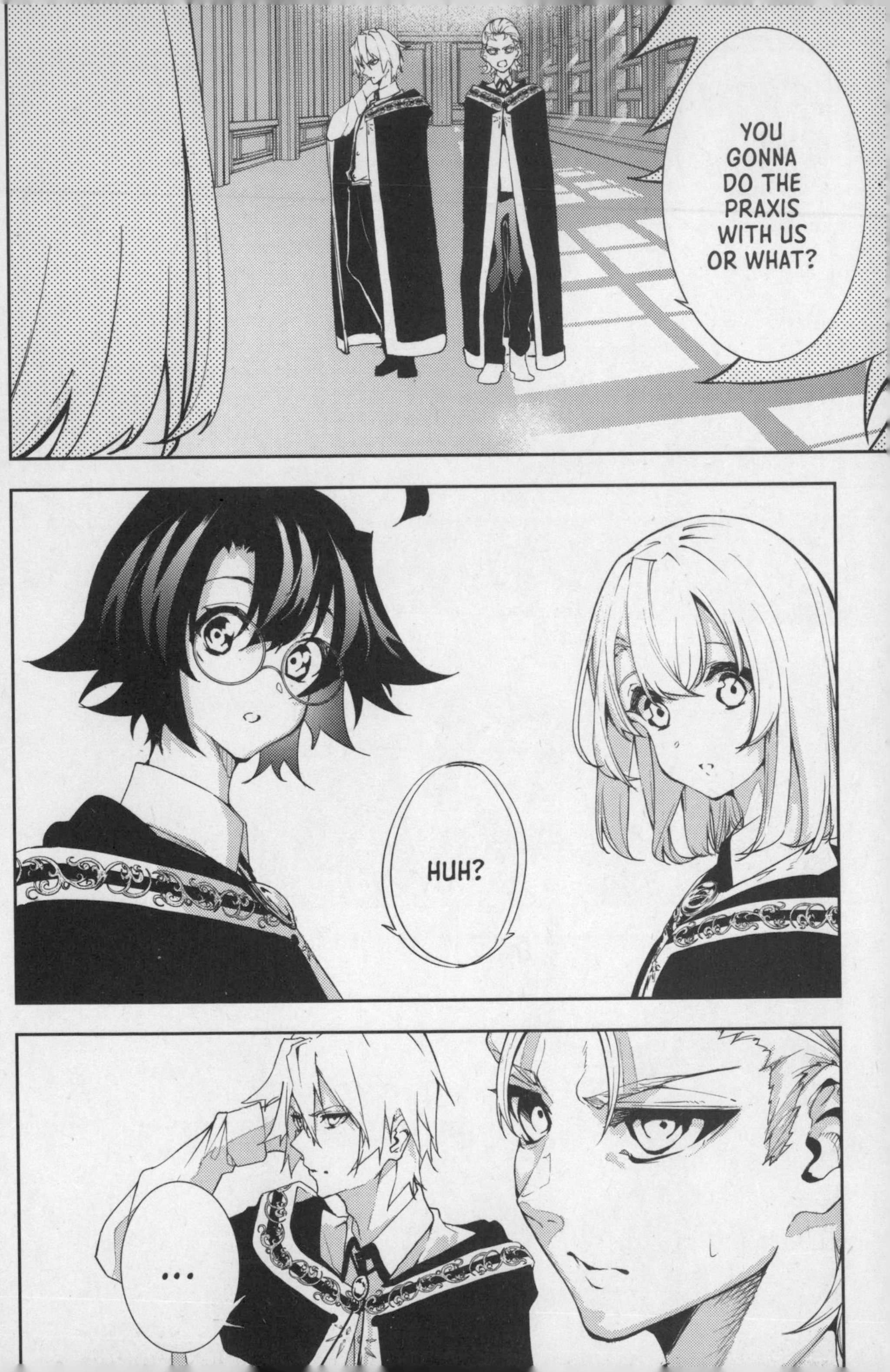
YOU GONNA DO THE PRAXIS WITH US OR WHAT?
HUH?
...

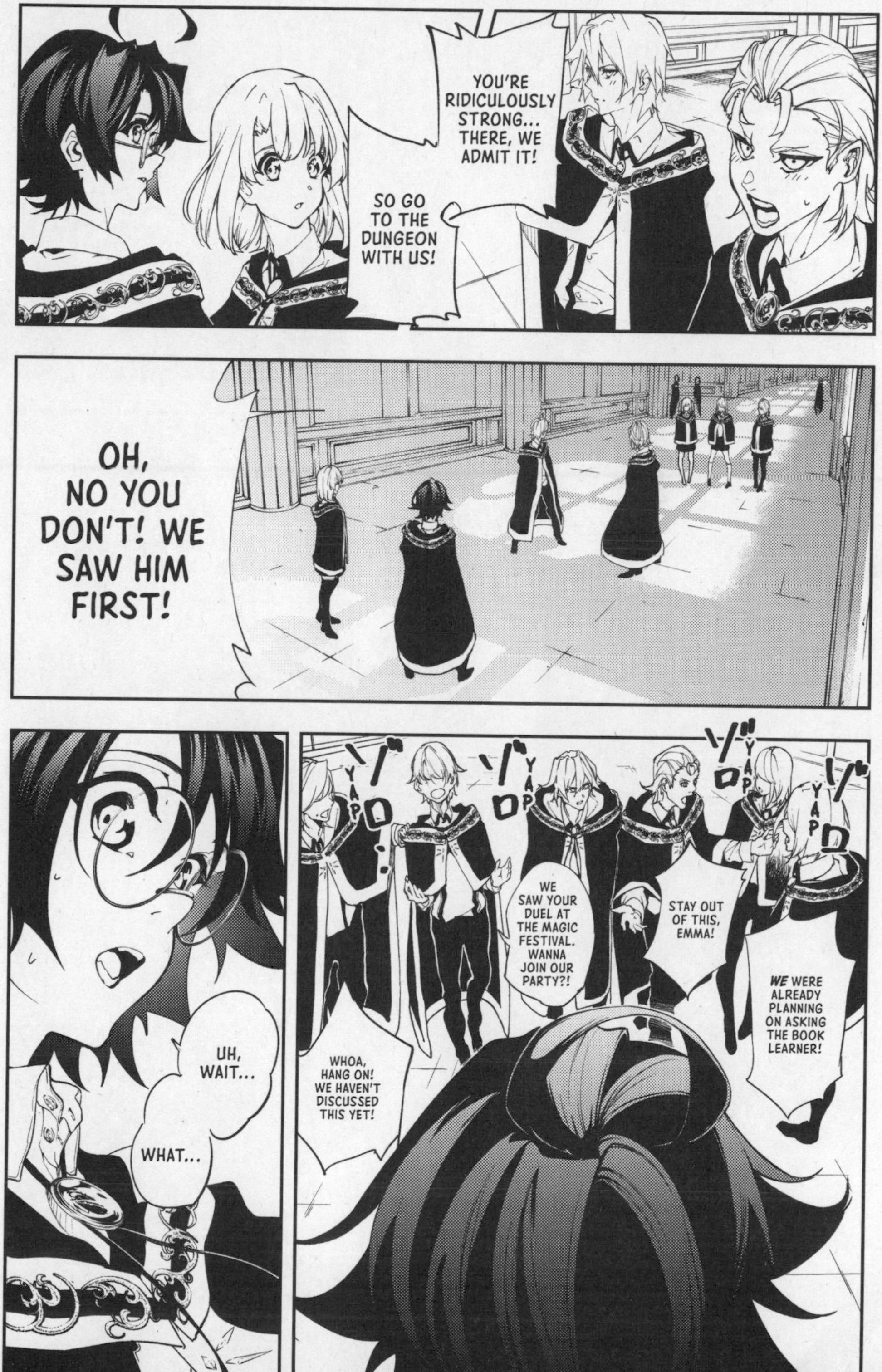
YOU'RE RIDICULOUSLY STRONG... THERE, WE ADMIT IT!
SO GO TO THE DUNGEON WITH US!
OH, NO YOU DON'T! WE SAW HIM FIRST!
YAP
YAP
YAP
YAP
WE WERE ALREADY PLANNING ON ASKING THE BOOK LEARNER!
STAY OUT OF THIS, EMMA!
WE SAW YOUR DUEL AT THE MAGIC FESTIVAL. WANNA JOIN OUR PARTY?!
WHOA, HANG ON! WE HAVEN'T DISCUSSED THIS YET!
UH, WAIT...
WHAT...

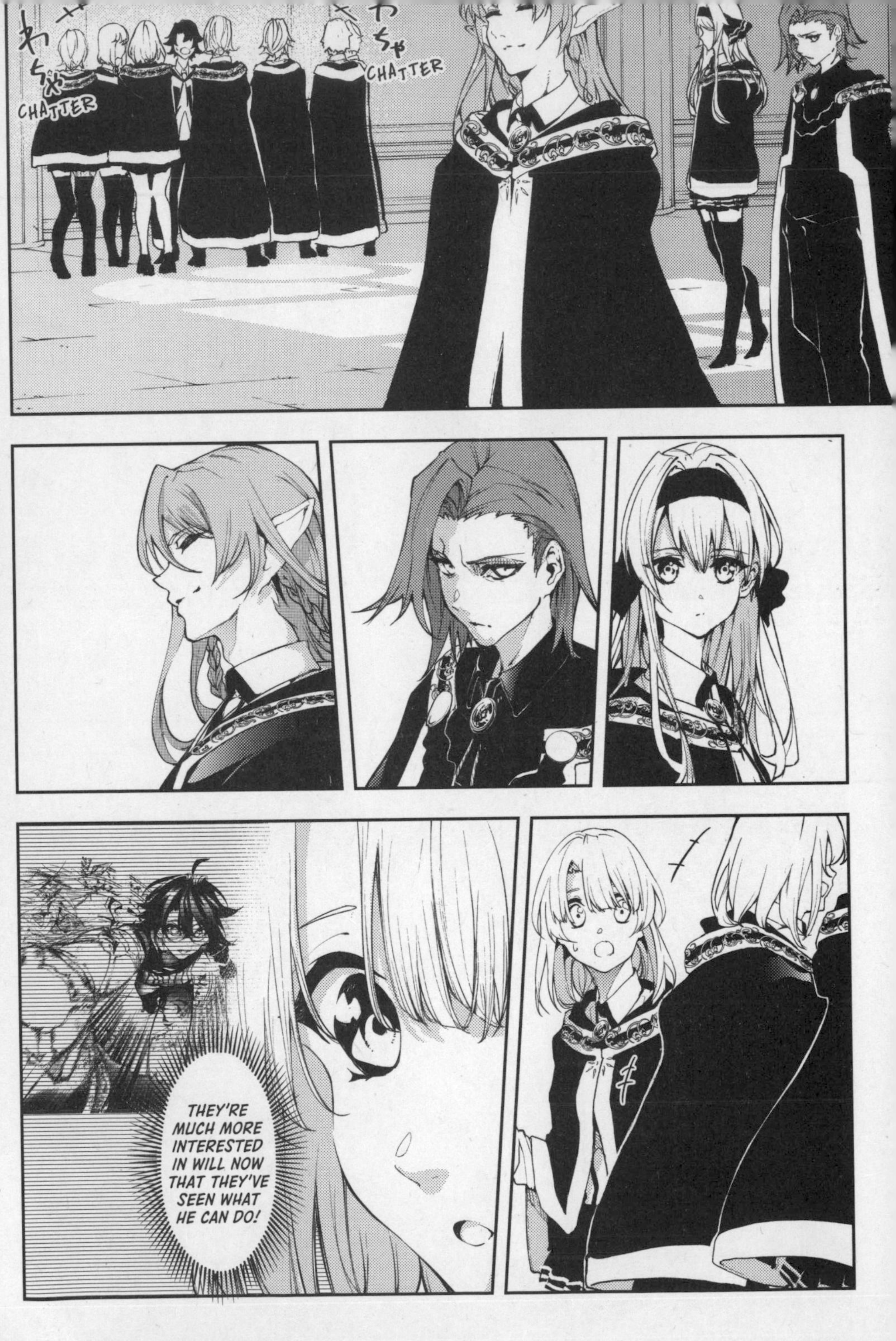
CHATTER
CHATTER
THEY'RE MUCH MORE INTERESTED IN WILL NOW THAT THEY'VE SEEN WHAT HE CAN DO!

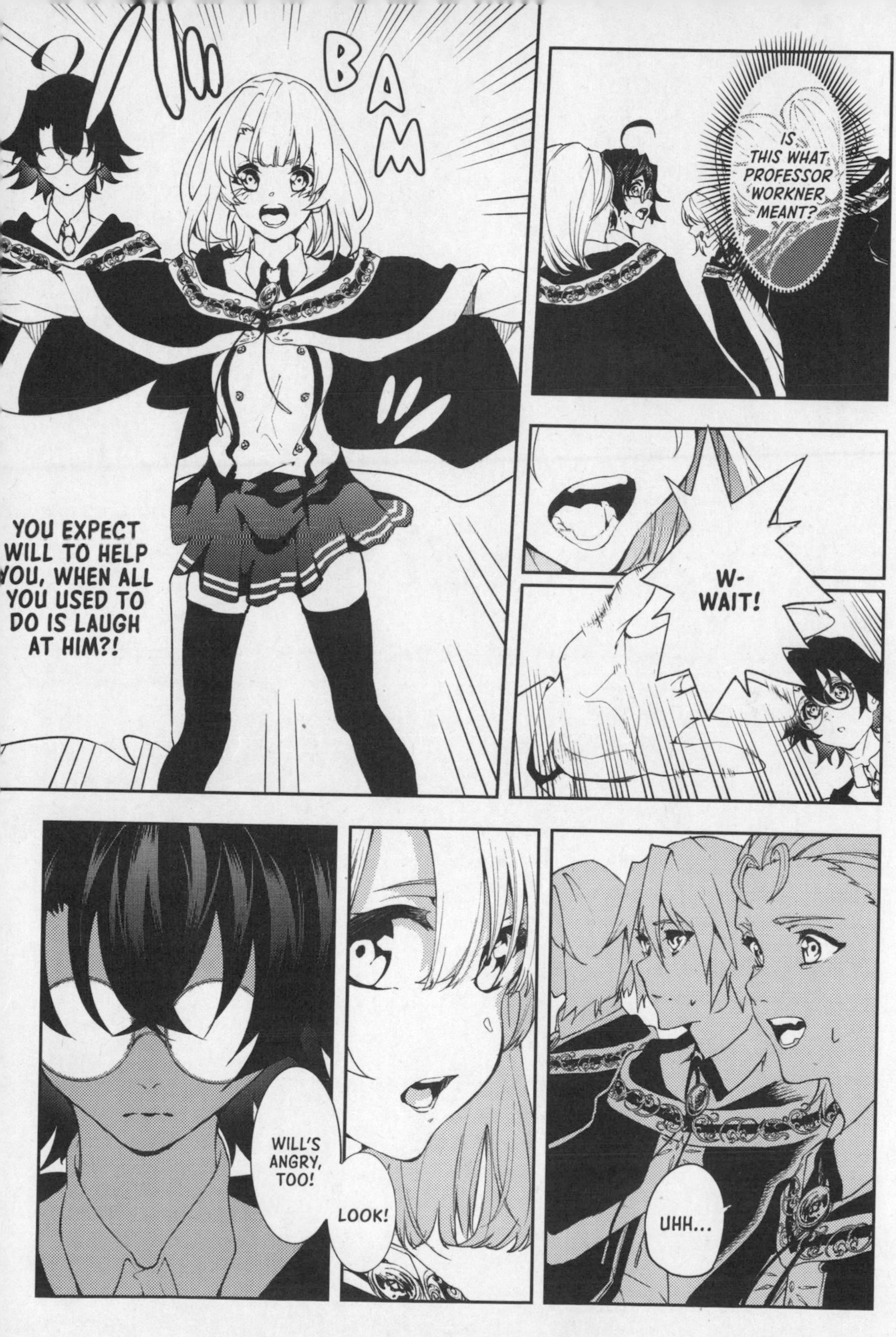
IS THIS WHAT PROFESSOR WORKNER MEANT?
W- WAIT!
BAM
YOU EXPECT WILL TO HELP YOU, WHEN ALL YOU USED TO DO IS LAUGH AT HIM?!
UHH...
LOOK!
WILL'S ANGRY, TOO!

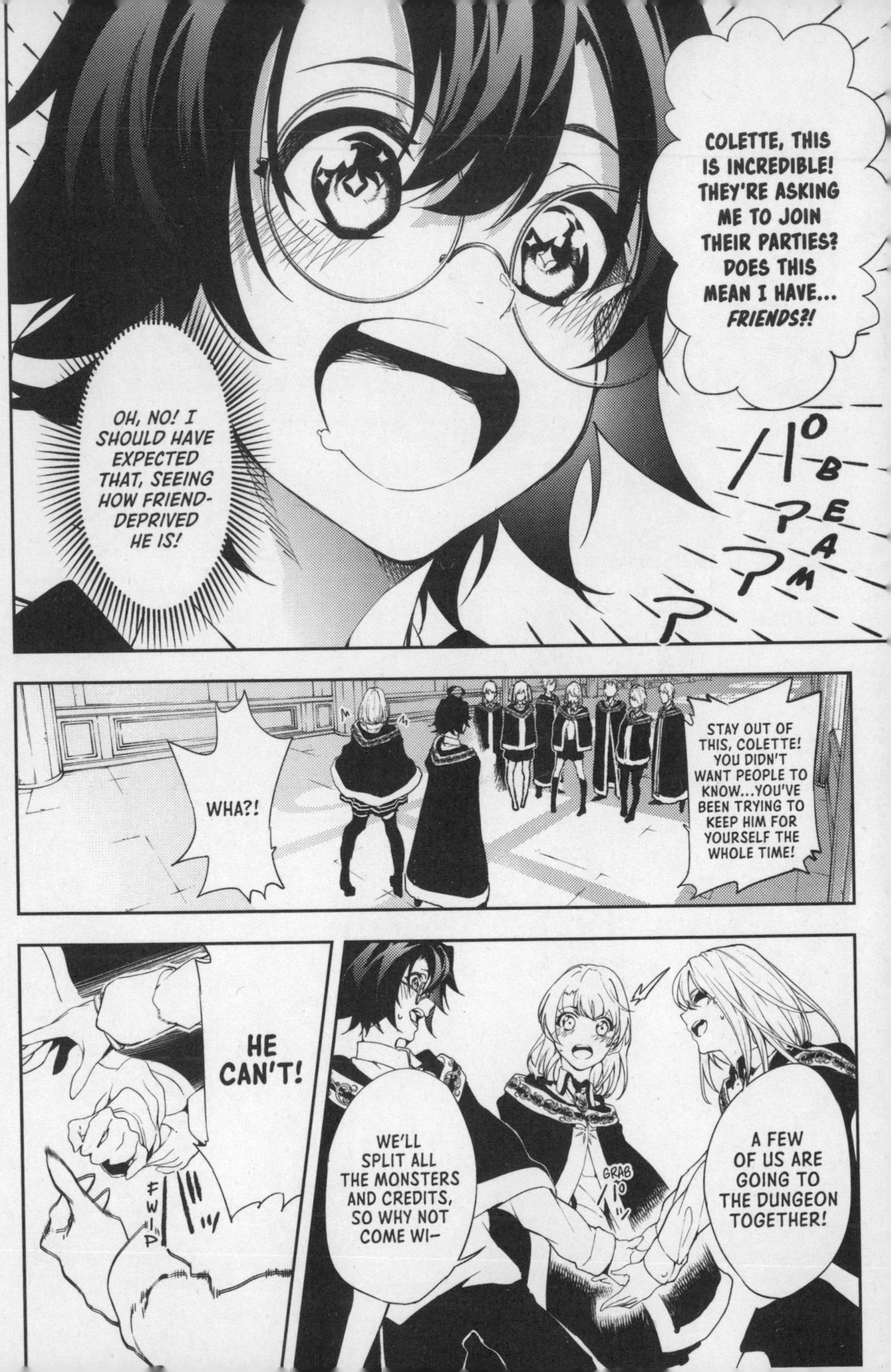
COLETTE, THIS IS INCREDIBLE! THEY'RE ASKING ME TO JOIN THEIR PARTIES? DOES THIS MEAN I HAVE... *FRIENDS?!*
BEAM
OH, NO! I SHOULD HAVE EXPECTED THAT, SEEING HOW FRIEND-DEPRIVED HE IS!
STAY OUT OF THIS, COLETTE! YOU DIDN'T WANT PEOPLE TO KNOW...YOU'VE BEEN TRYING TO KEEP HIM FOR YOURSELF THE WHOLE TIME!
WHA?!
A FEW OF US ARE GOING TO THE DUNGEON TOGETHER!
GRAB
WE'LL SPLIT ALL THE MONSTERS AND CREDITS, SO WHY NOT COME WI—
HE CAN'T!
FWIP

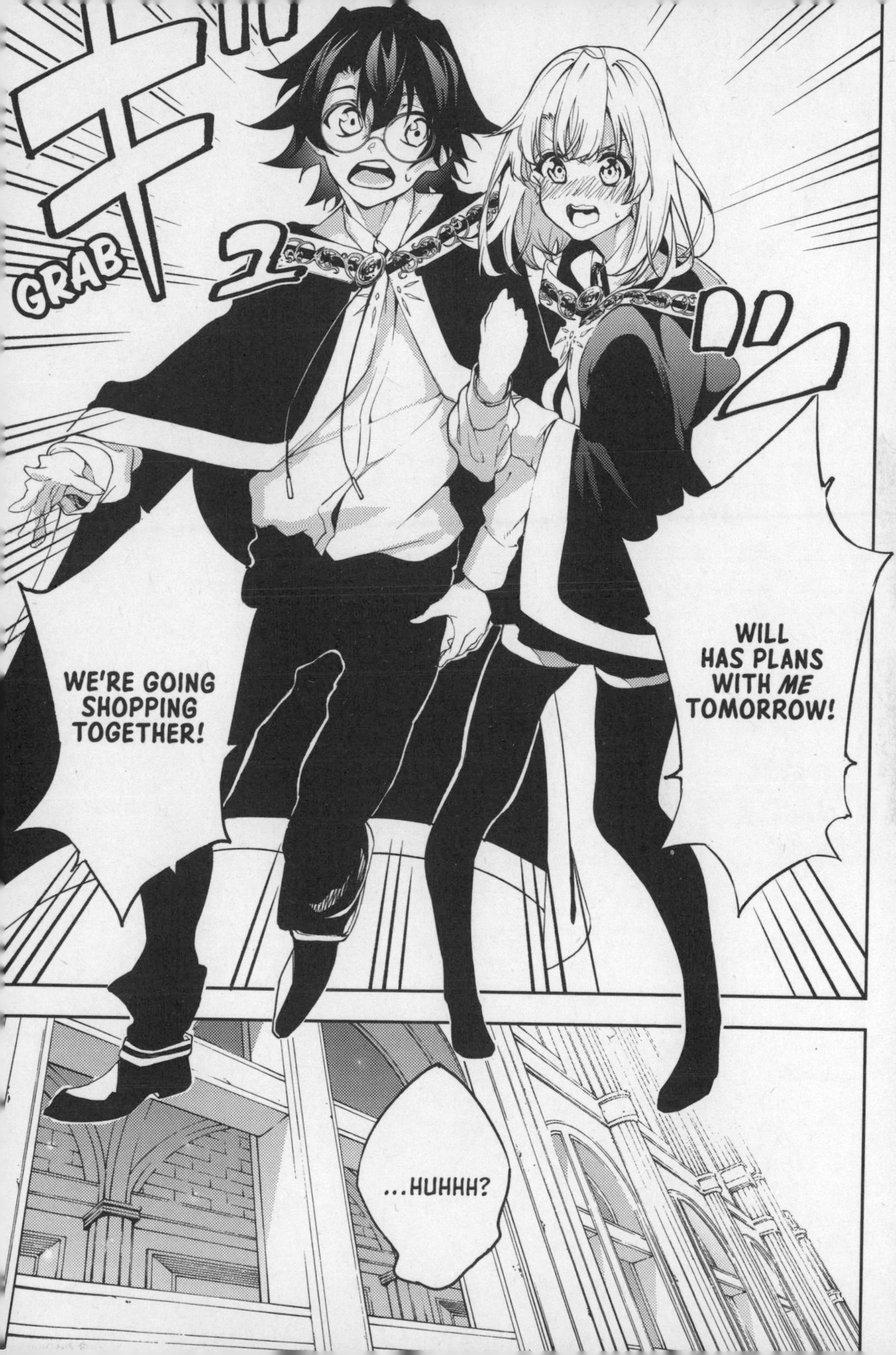
GRAB
WILL HAS PLANS WITH *ME* TOMORROW!
WE'RE GOING SHOPPING TOGETHER!
...HUHHH?

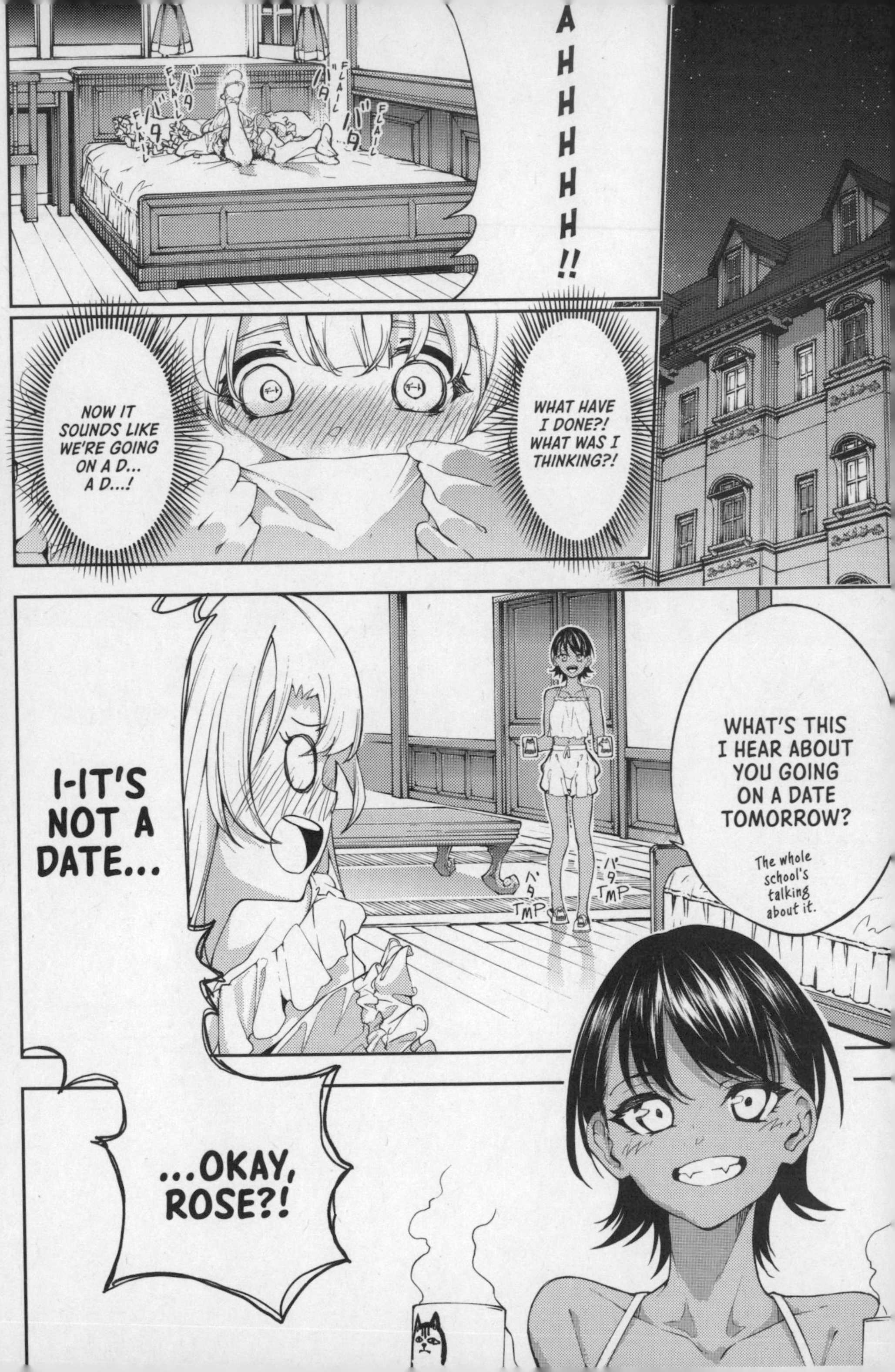
AHHHHHH!!
FLAIL
FLAIL
FLAIL
FLAIL
WHAT HAVE I DONE?! WHAT WAS I THINKING?!
NOW IT SOUNDS LIKE WE'RE GOING ON A D... A D...!
WHAT'S THIS I HEAR ABOUT YOU GOING ON A DATE TOMORROW?
The whole school's talking about it.
TMP
TMP
I-IT'S NOT A DATE...
...OKAY, ROSE?!

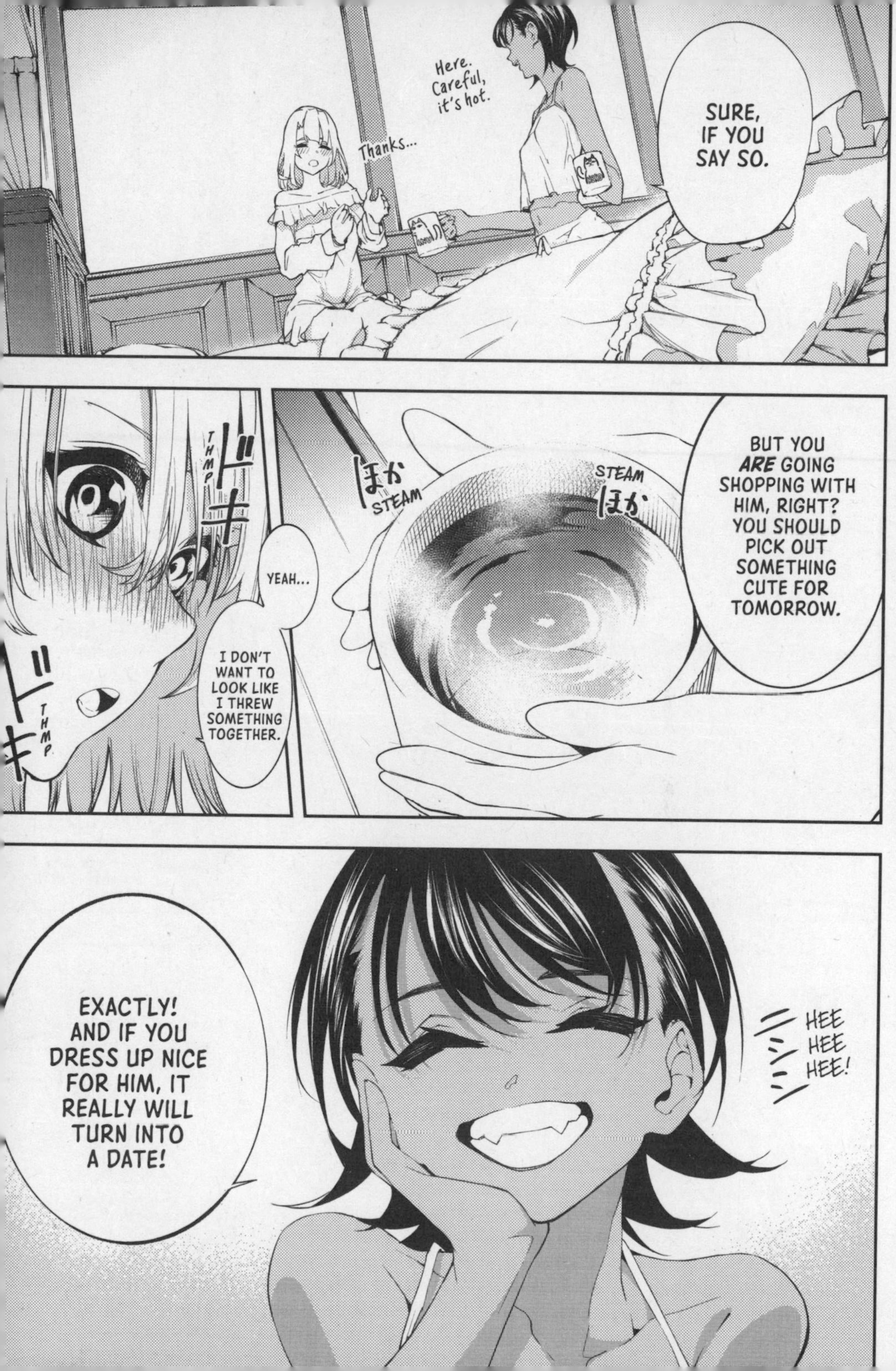
SURE, IF YOU SAY SO.
Here. Careful, it's hot.
Thanks...
BUT YOU ***ARE*** GOING SHOPPING WITH HIM, RIGHT? YOU SHOULD PICK OUT SOMETHING CUTE FOR TOMORROW.
ほか STEAM
ほか STEAM
ドキ THMP
YEAH...
I DON'T WANT TO LOOK LIKE I THREW SOMETHING TOGETHER.
ドキ THMP
HEE HEE HEE!
EXACTLY! AND IF YOU DRESS UP NICE FOR HIM, IT REALLY WILL TURN INTO A DATE!

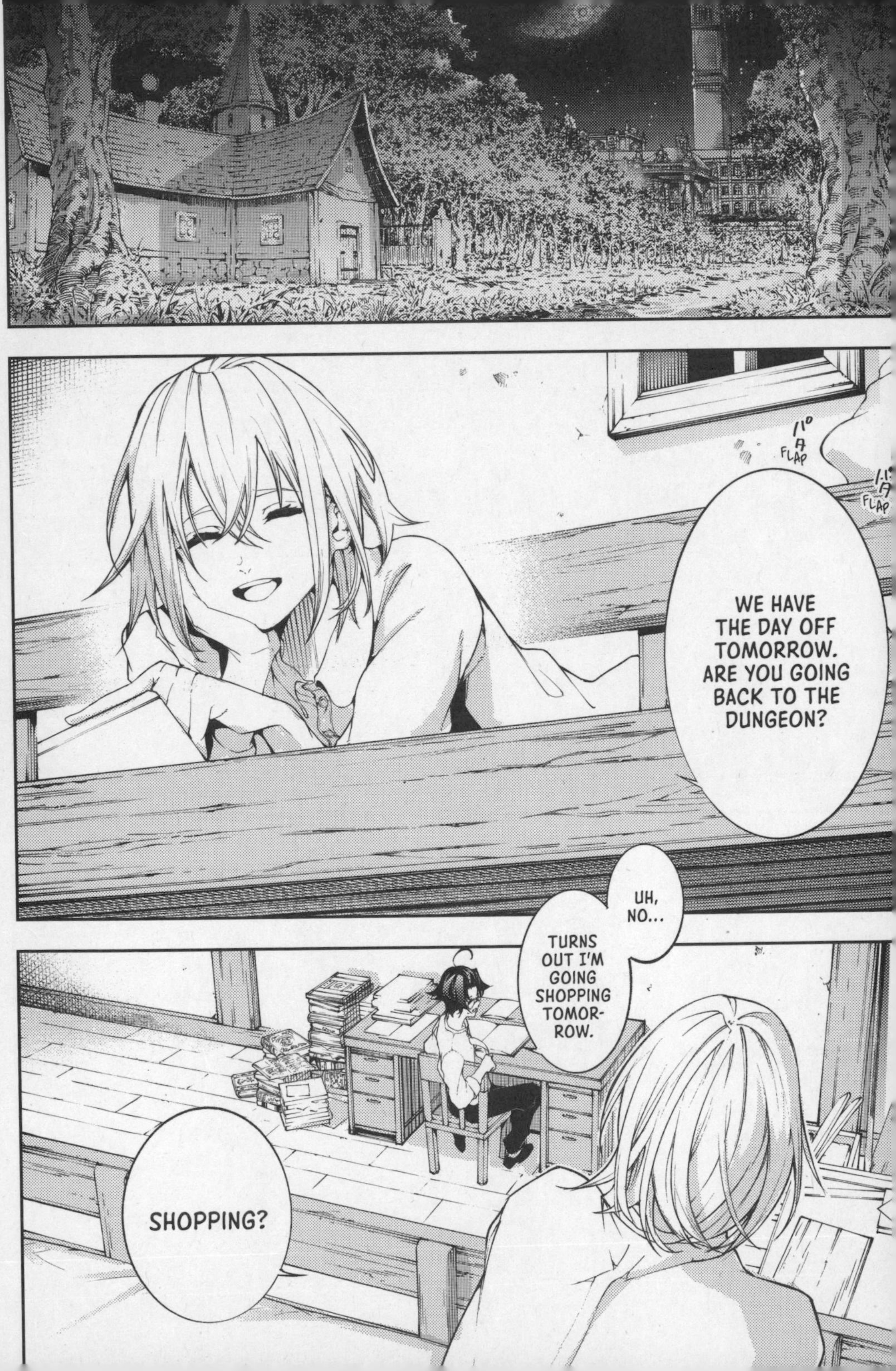
パタ FLAP
パタ FLAP
WE HAVE THE DAY OFF TOMORROW. ARE YOU GOING BACK TO THE DUNGEON?
UH, NO...
TURNS OUT I'M GOING SHOPPING TOMOR-ROW.
SHOPPING?

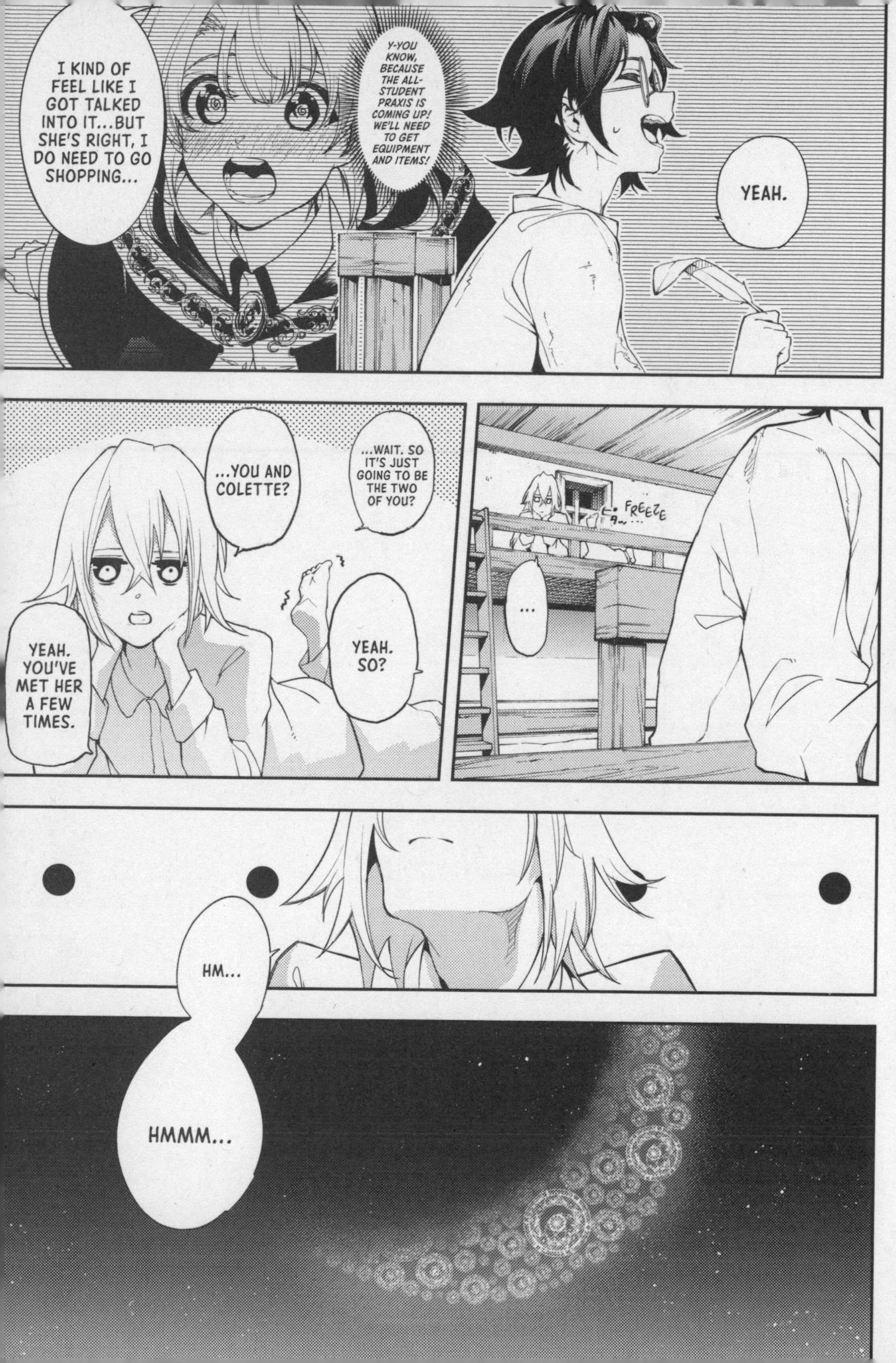
YEAH.
Y-YOU KNOW, BECAUSE THE ALL-STUDENT PRAXIS IS COMING UP! WE'LL NEED TO GET EQUIPMENT AND ITEMS!
I KIND OF FEEL LIKE I GOT TALKED INTO IT...BUT SHE'S RIGHT, I DO NEED TO GO SHOPPING...
FREEZE
...
...WAIT. SO IT'S JUST GOING TO BE THE TWO OF YOU?
...YOU AND COLETTE?
YEAH. SO?
YEAH. YOU'VE MET HER A FEW TIMES.
HM...
HMMM...

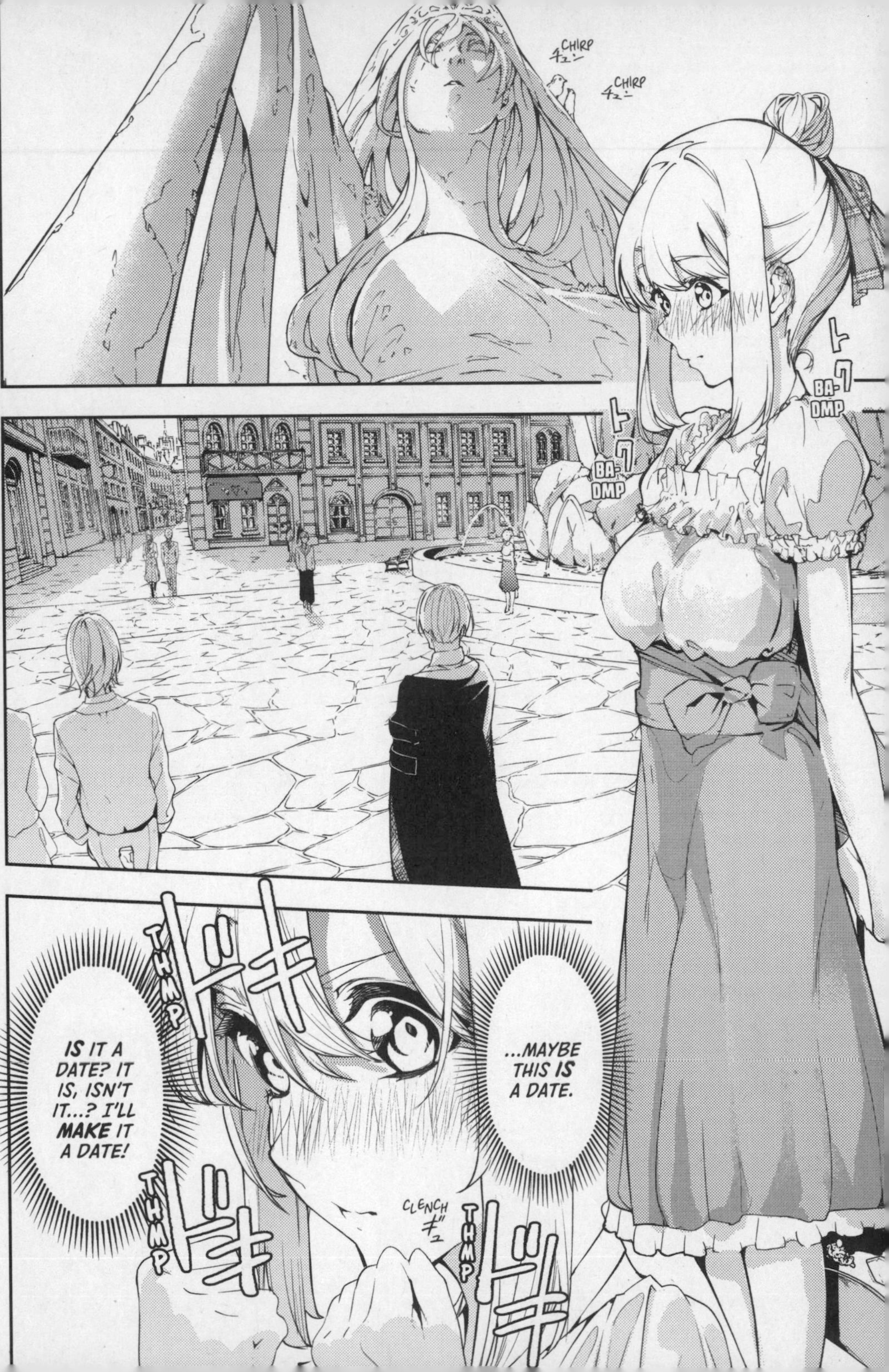
BA-DMP
トク
BA-DMP
トク
CHIRP
チュン
CHIRP
チュン
...MAYBE THIS **IS** A DATE.
THMP
ドキ
IS IT A DATE? IT IS, ISN'T IT...? I'LL **MAKE** IT A DATE!
THMP
ドキ
THMP
ドキ
CLENCH
ギュ

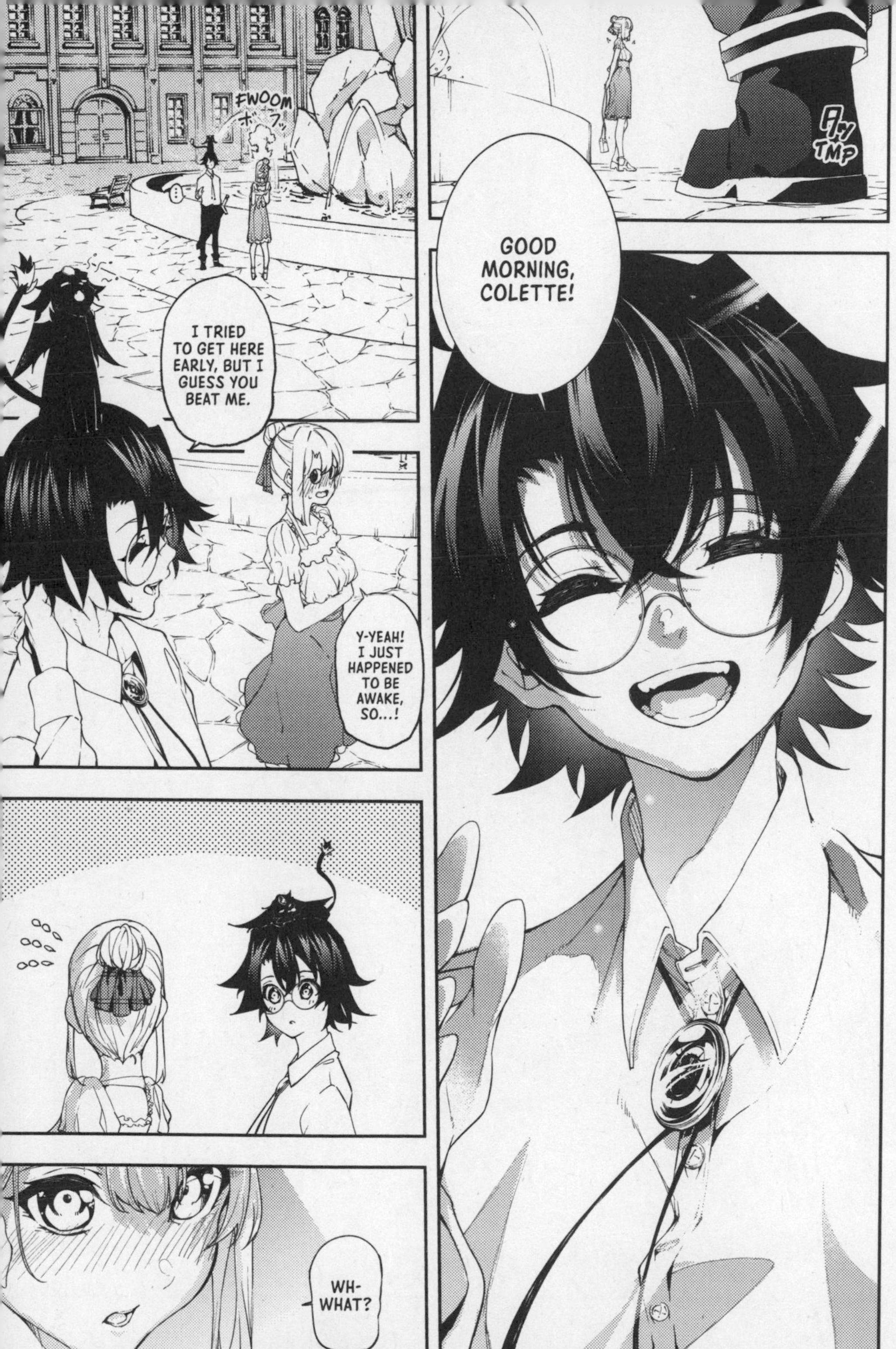
TMP
FWOOM
ボフッ
GOOD MORNING, COLETTE!
I TRIED TO GET HERE EARLY, BUT I GUESS YOU BEAT ME.
Y-YEAH! I JUST HAPPENED TO BE AWAKE, SO...!
WH-WHAT?

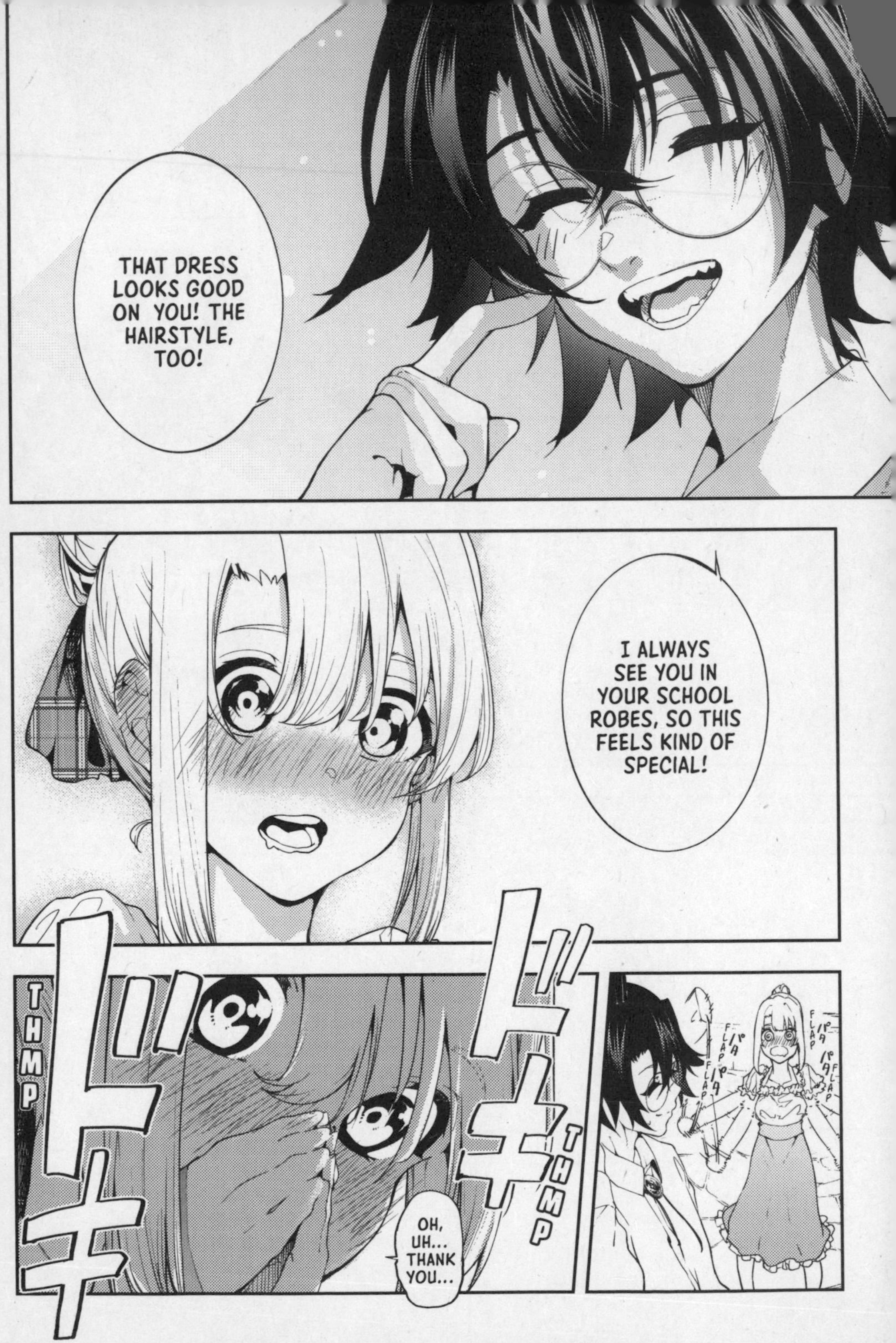
THAT DRESS LOOKS GOOD ON YOU! THE HAIRSTYLE, TOO!
I ALWAYS SEE YOU IN YOUR SCHOOL ROBES, SO THIS FEELS KIND OF SPECIAL!
FLAP
FLAP
FLAP
FLAP
THMP
THMP
OH, UH... THANK YOU...

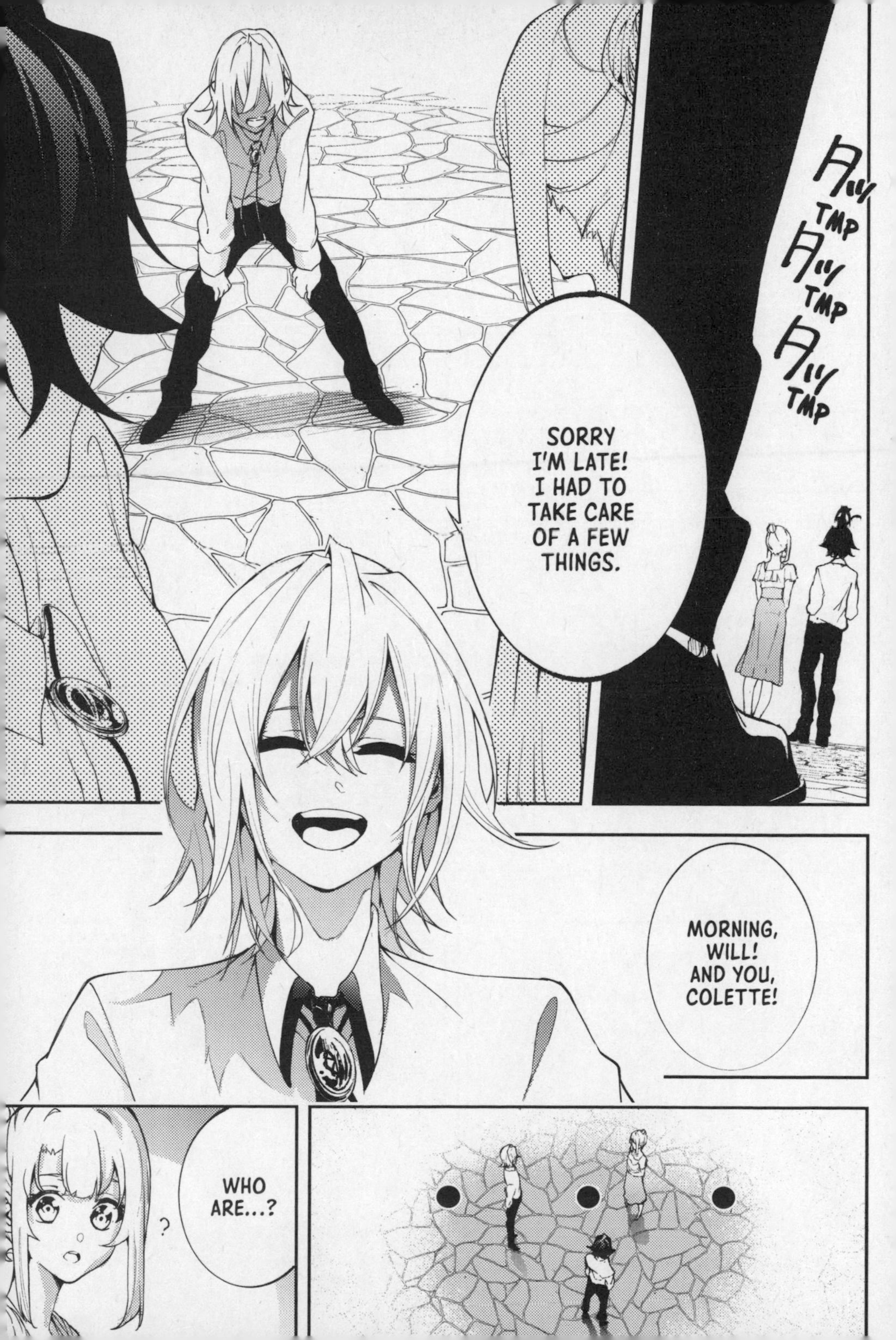
TMP
TMP
TMP
SORRY I'M LATE! I HAD TO TAKE CARE OF A FEW THINGS.
MORNING, WILL! AND YOU, COLETTE!
WHO ARE...?
?

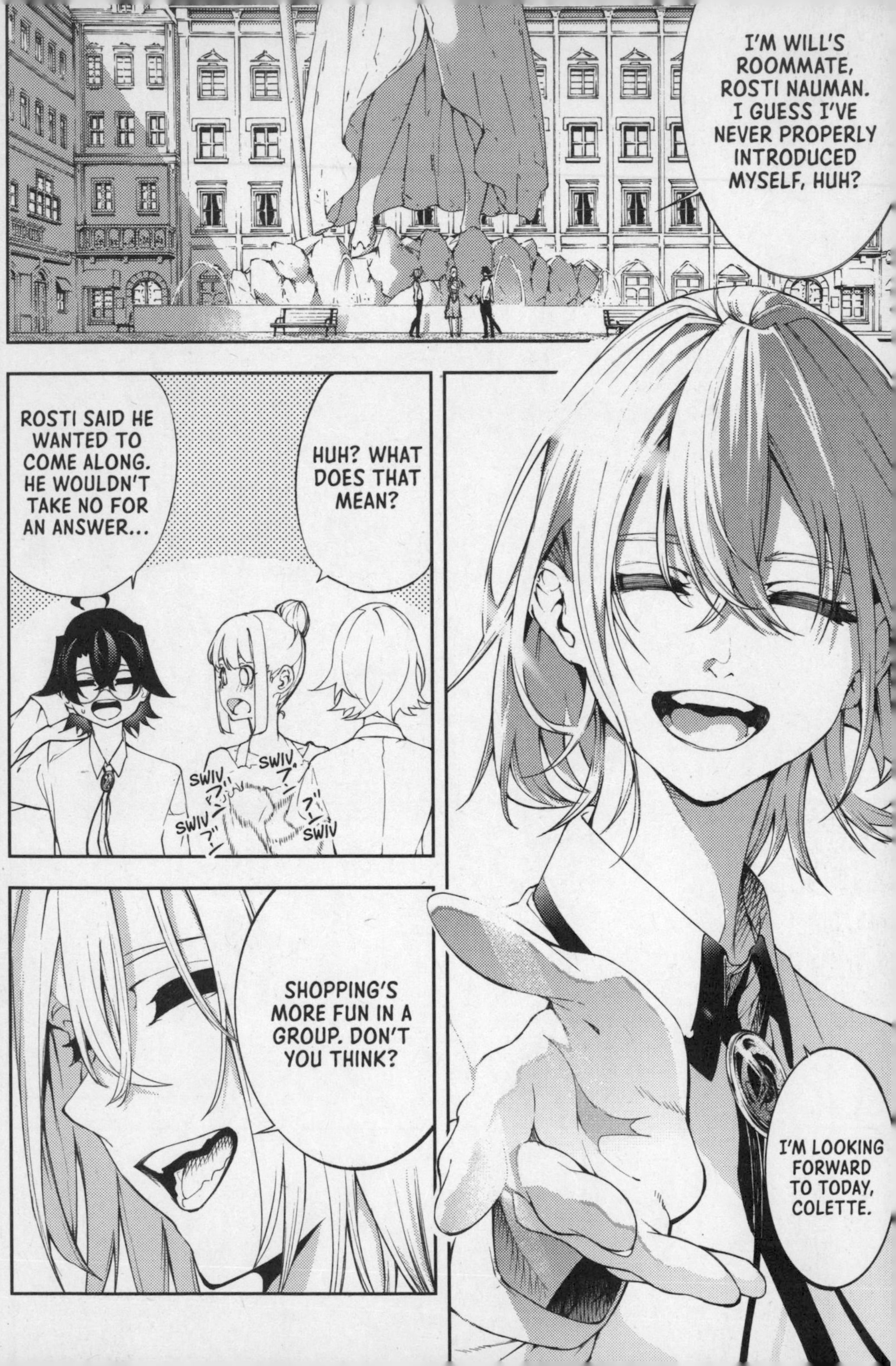
I'M WILL'S ROOMMATE, ROSTI NAUMAN. I GUESS I'VE NEVER PROPERLY INTRODUCED MYSELF, HUH?
I'M LOOKING FORWARD TO TODAY, COLETTE.
HUH? WHAT DOES THAT MEAN?
ROSTI SAID HE WANTED TO COME ALONG. HE WOULDN'T TAKE NO FOR AN ANSWER...
SWIV
SWIV
SWIV
SWIV
SHOPPING'S MORE FUN IN A GROUP. DON'T YOU THINK?

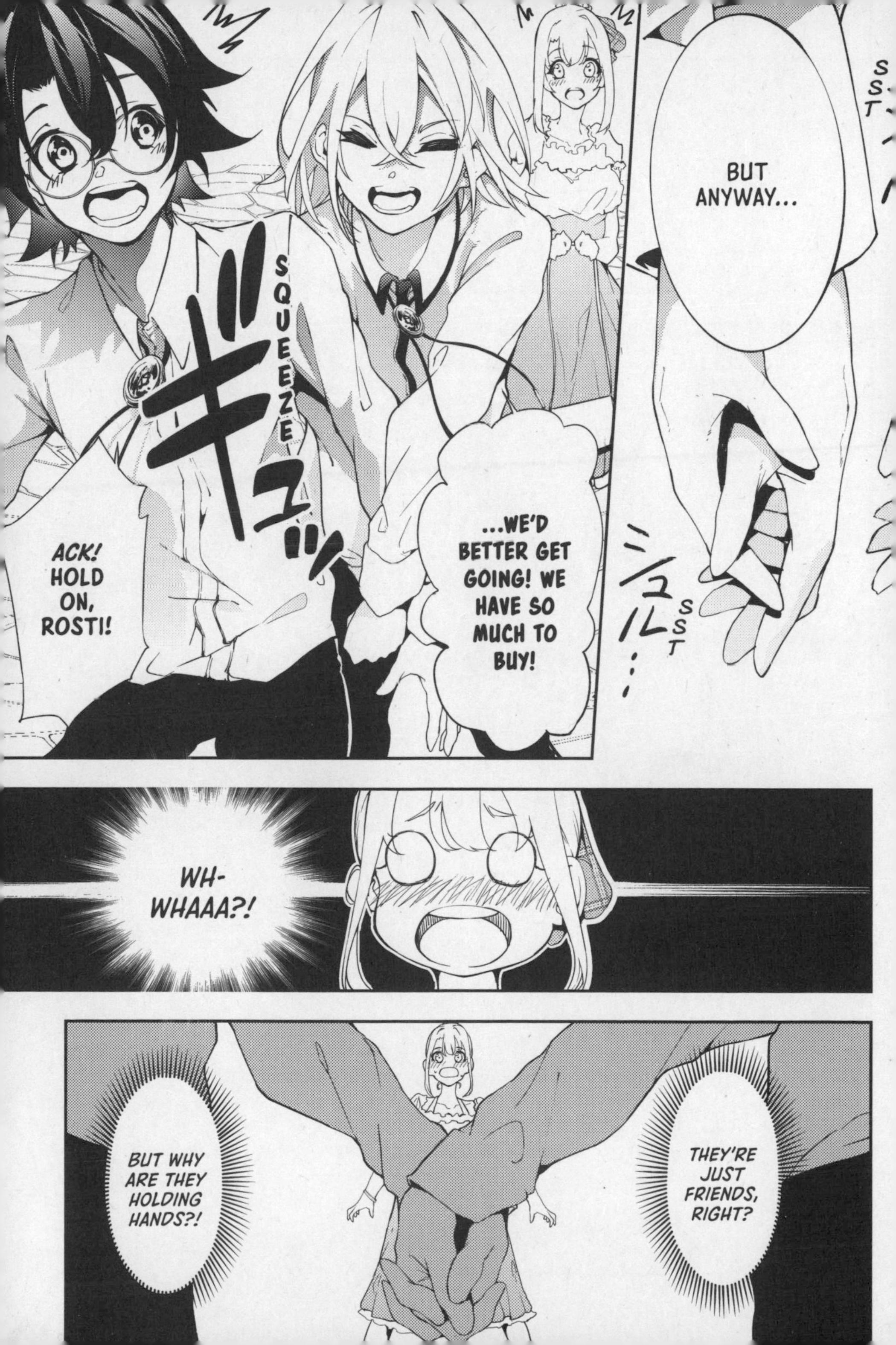
SST
BUT ANYWAY...
シュル
SST
...WE'D BETTER GET GOING! WE HAVE SO MUCH TO BUY!
SQUEEZE
ギュッ
ACK! HOLD ON, ROSTI!
WH- WHAAA?!
THEY'RE JUST FRIENDS, RIGHT?
BUT WHY ARE THEY HOLDING HANDS?!

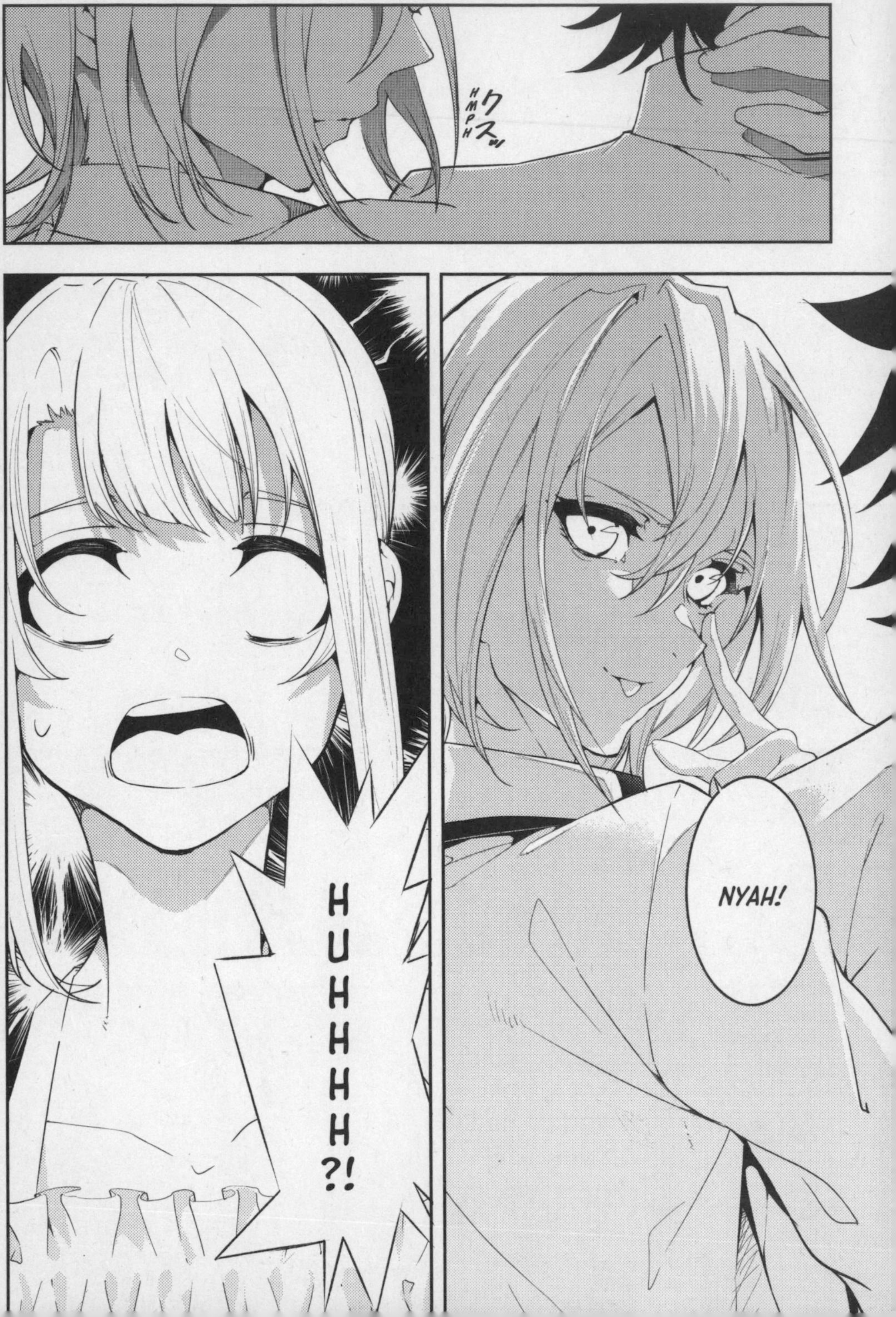
HMPH
クスッ
NYAH!
HUHHHHH?!

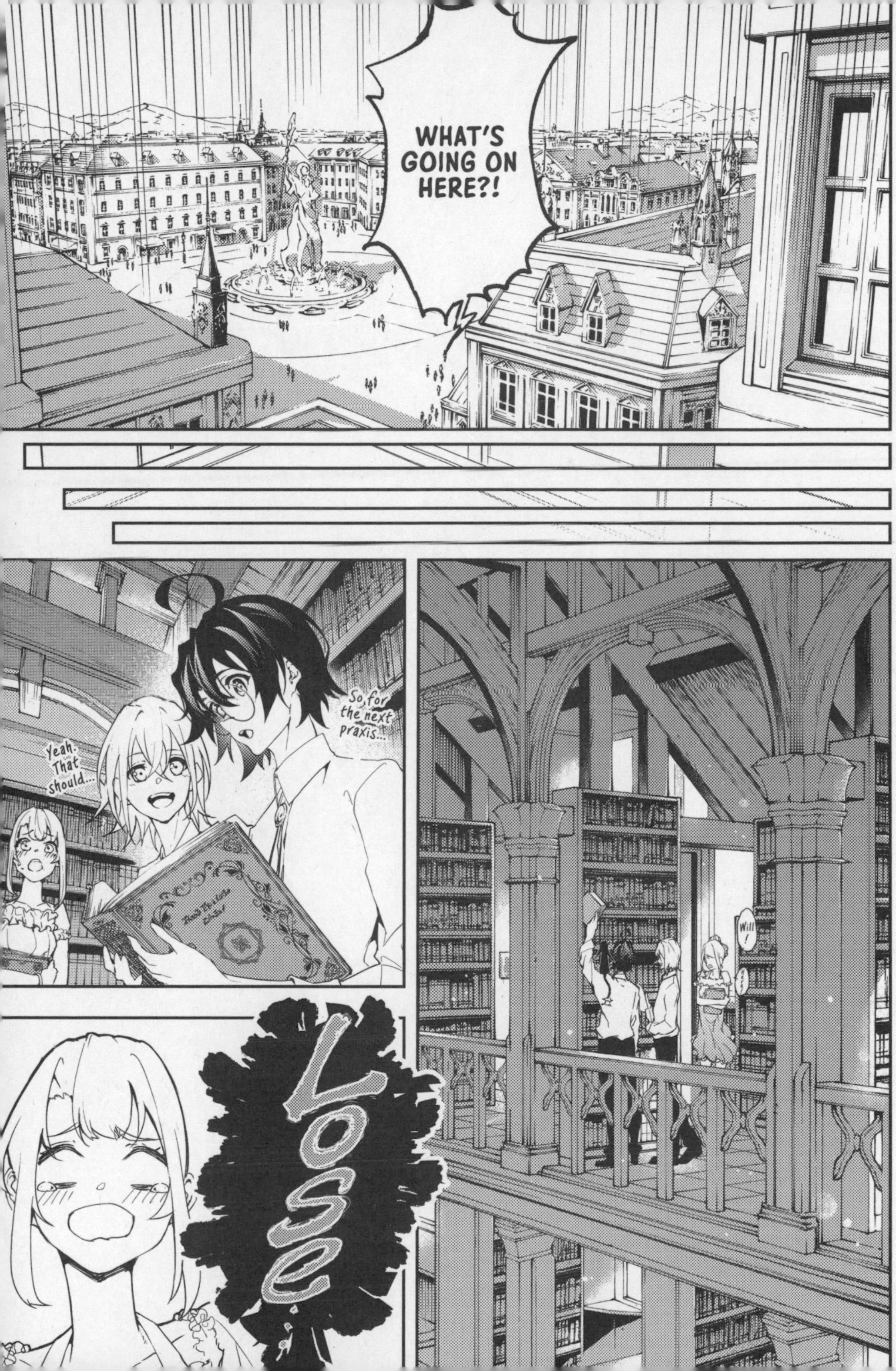
WHAT'S GOING ON HERE?!
Will!
Here!
So, for the next praxis...
Yeah. That should...
LOSE

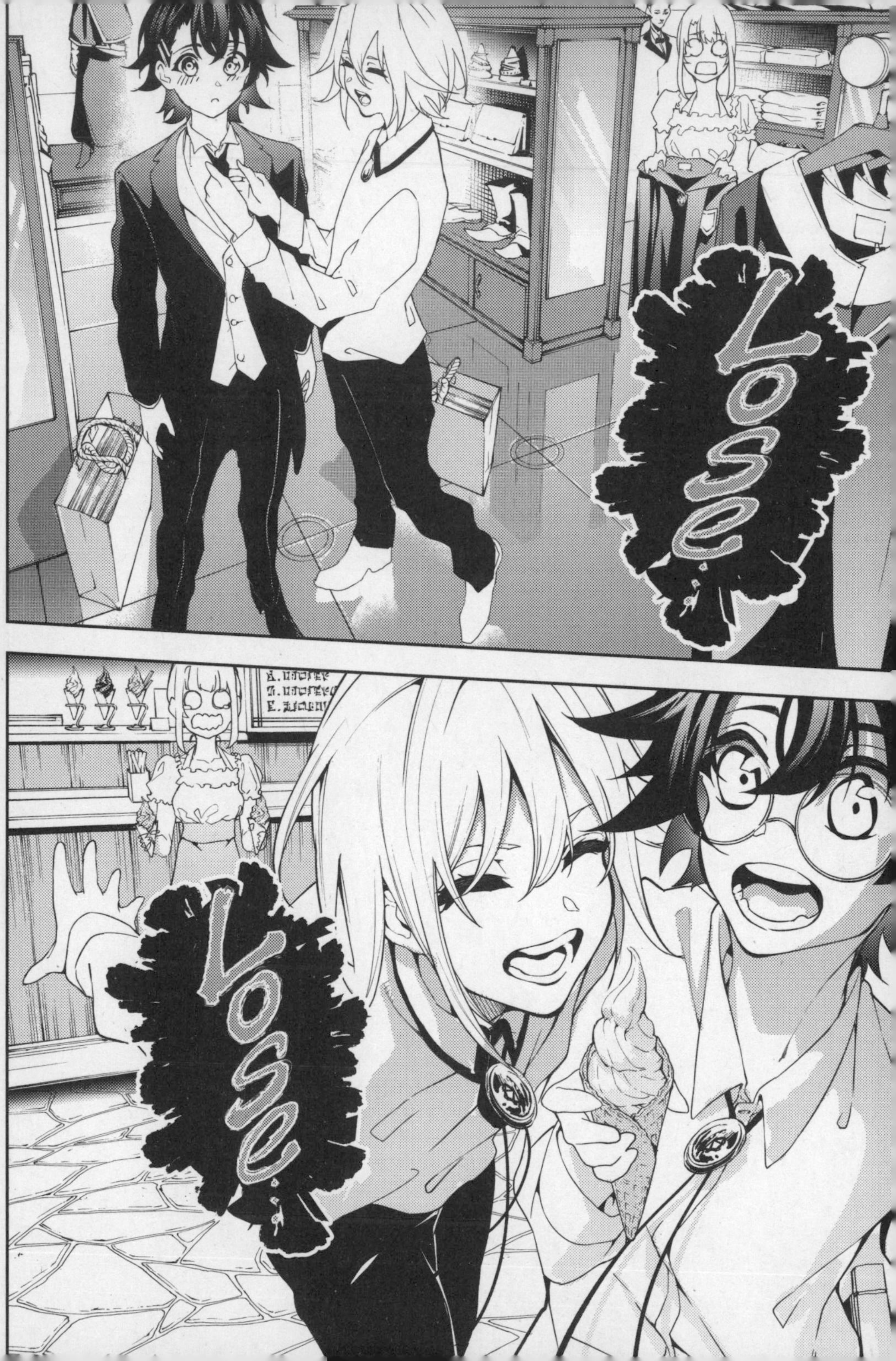
LOSE
LOSE

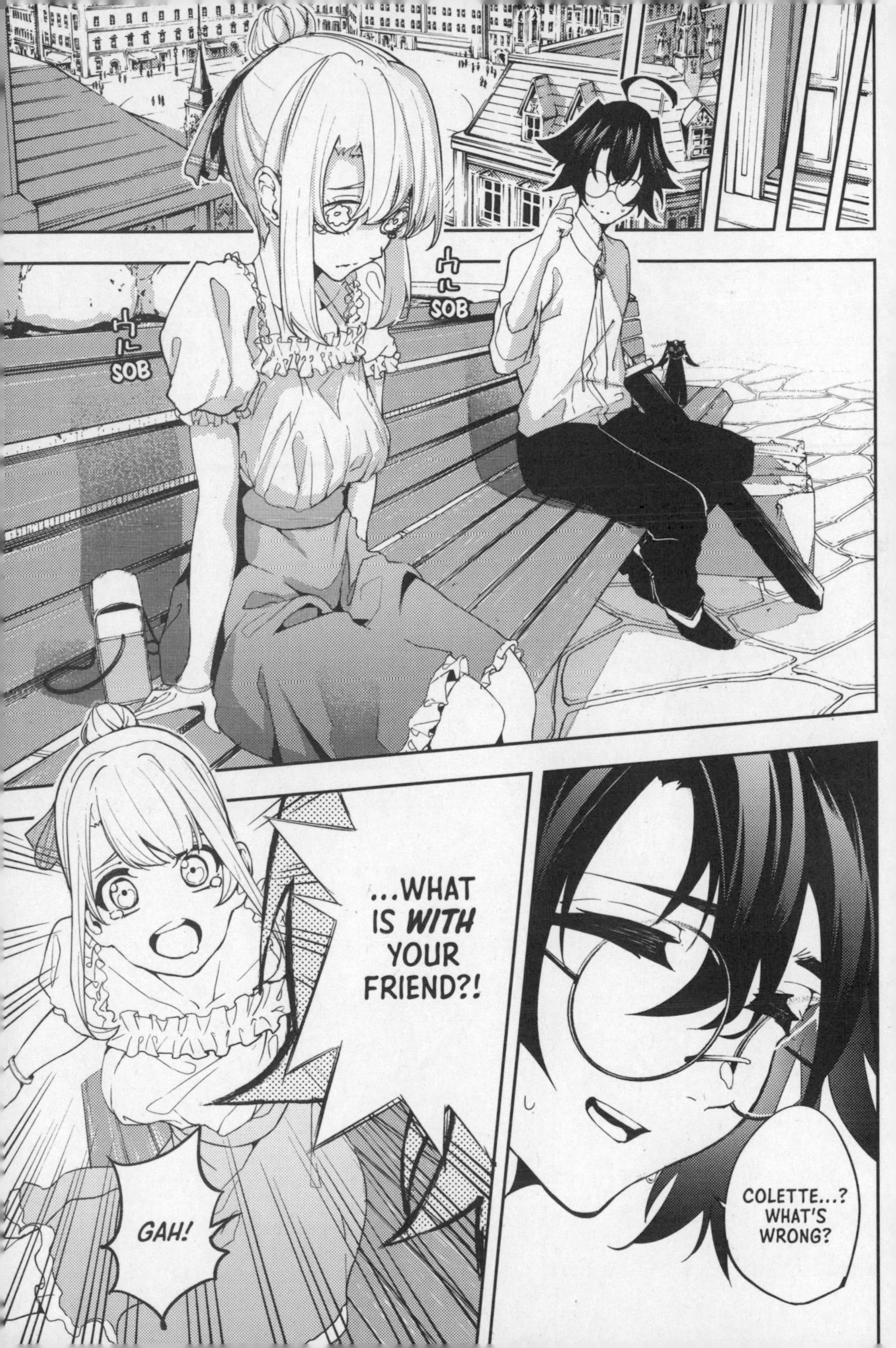
ウル
SOB
ウル
SOB
COLETTE...? WHAT'S WRONG?
GAH!
...WHAT IS WITH YOUR FRIEND?!

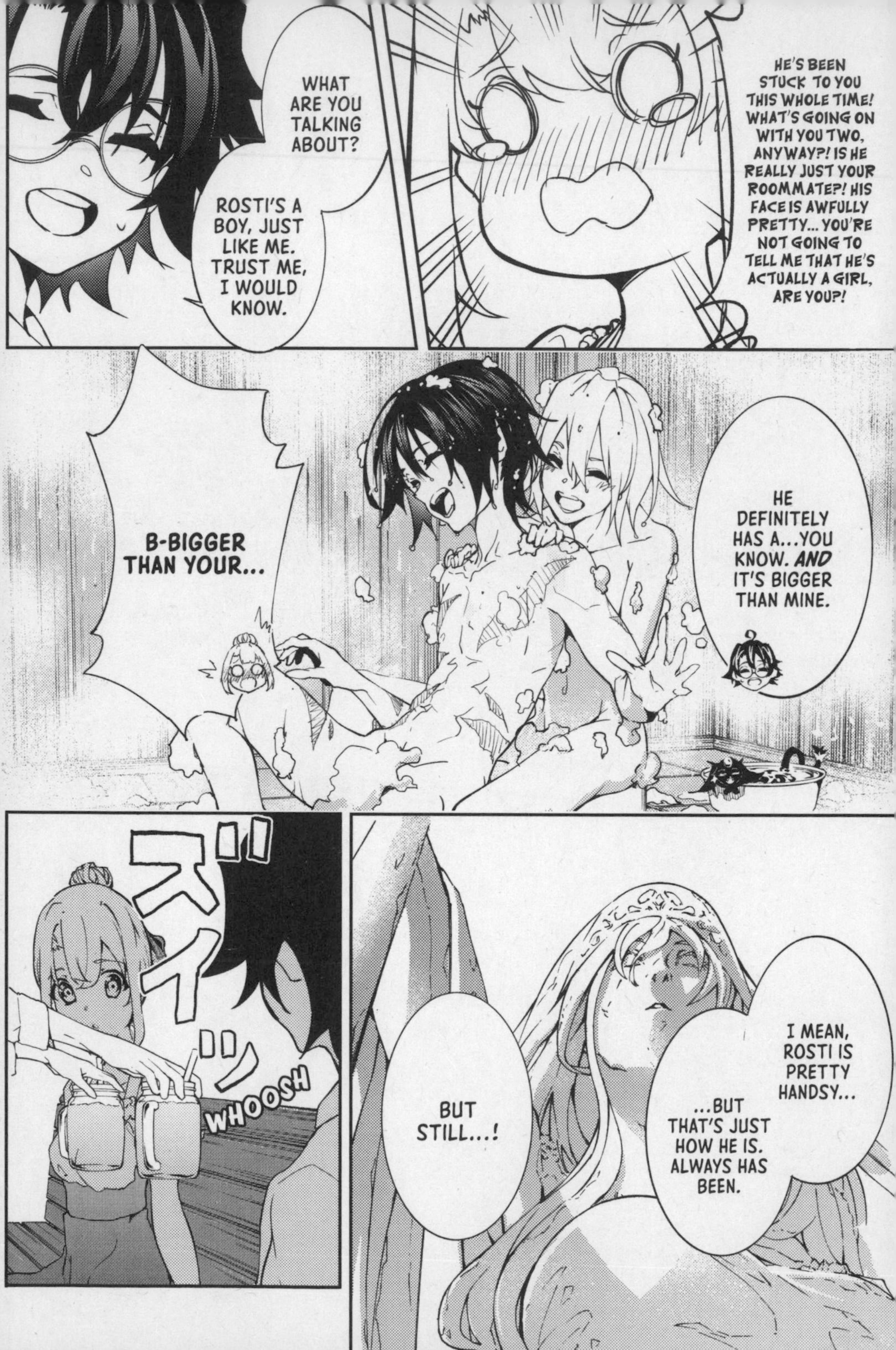
HE'S BEEN STUCK TO YOU THIS WHOLE TIME! WHAT'S GOING ON WITH YOU TWO, ANYWAY?! IS HE REALLY JUST YOUR ROOMMATE?! HIS FACE IS AWFULLY PRETTY... YOU'RE NOT GOING TO TELL ME THAT HE'S ACTUALLY A GIRL, ARE YOU?!
WHAT ARE YOU TALKING ABOUT?
ROSTI'S A BOY, JUST LIKE ME. TRUST ME, I WOULD KNOW.
HE DEFINITELY HAS A...YOU KNOW. *AND* IT'S BIGGER THAN MINE.
B-BIGGER THAN YOUR...
I MEAN, ROSTI IS PRETTY HANDSY...
...BUT THAT'S JUST HOW HE IS. ALWAYS HAS BEEN.
BUT STILL...!
ズイッ
WHOOSH

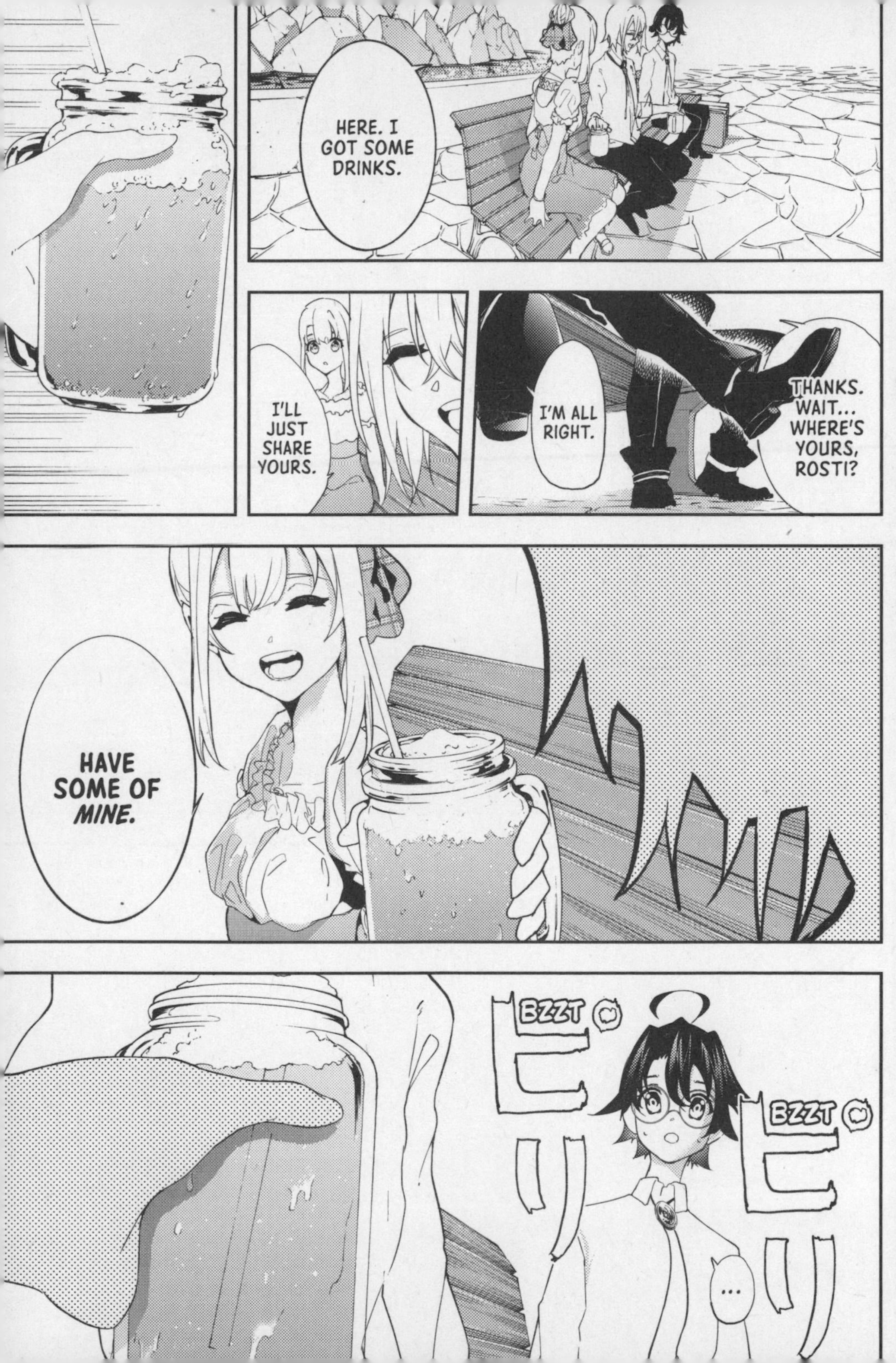
HERE. I GOT SOME DRINKS.
THANKS. WAIT... WHERE'S YOURS, ROSTI?
I'M ALL RIGHT.
I'LL JUST SHARE YOURS.
HAVE SOME OF *MINE.*
BZZT
ビリ
BZZT
ビリ
...

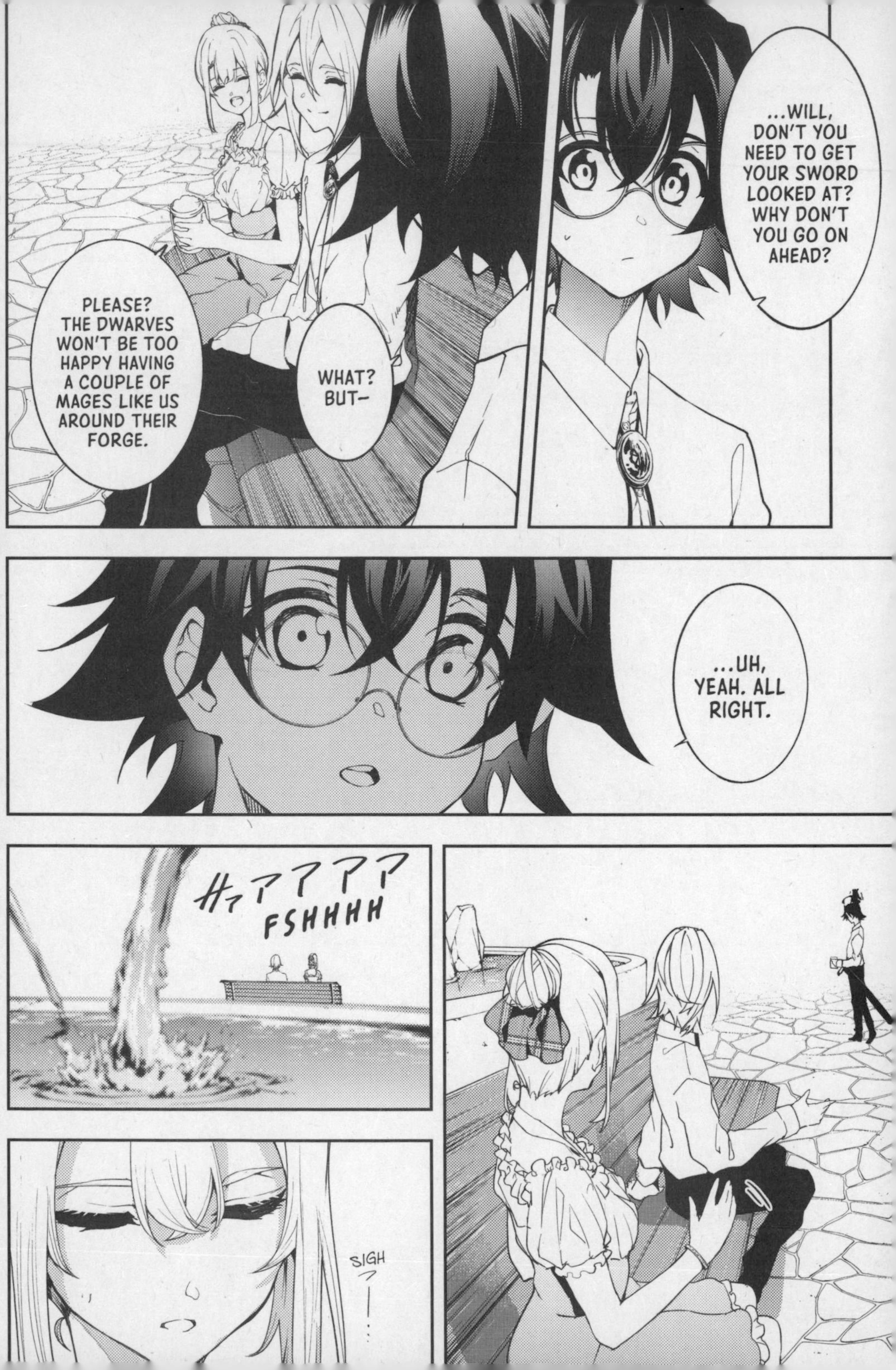
...WILL, DON'T YOU NEED TO GET YOUR SWORD LOOKED AT? WHY DON'T YOU GO ON AHEAD?
WHAT? BUT–
PLEASE? THE DWARVES WON'T BE TOO HAPPY HAVING A COUPLE OF MAGES LIKE US AROUND THEIR FORGE.
...UH, YEAH. ALL RIGHT.
FSHHHH
SIGH

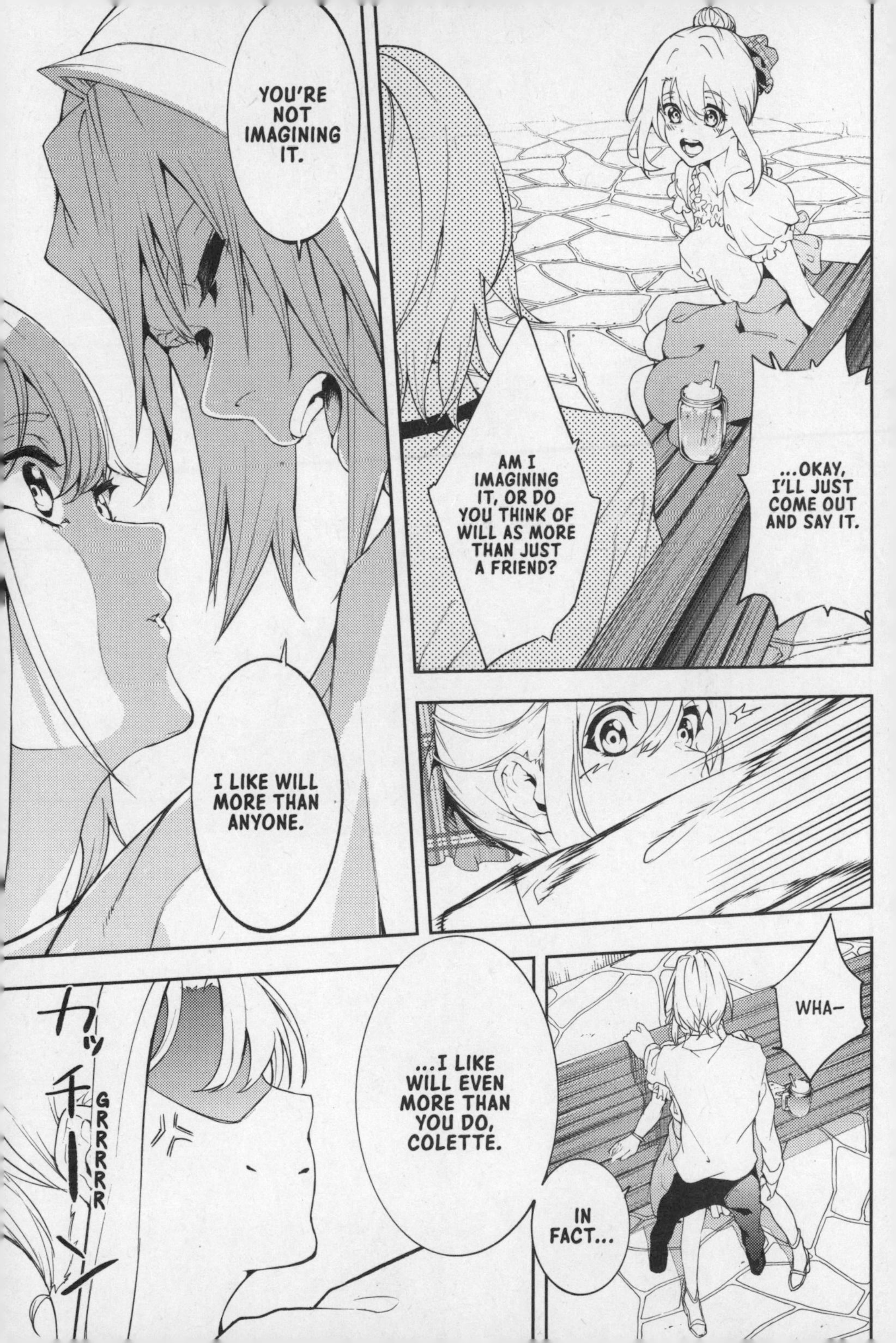
...OKAY, I'LL JUST COME OUT AND SAY IT.
AM I IMAGINING IT, OR DO YOU THINK OF WILL AS MORE THAN JUST A FRIEND?
YOU'RE NOT IMAGINING IT.
I LIKE WILL MORE THAN ANYONE.
WHA-
IN FACT...
...I LIKE WILL EVEN MORE THAN YOU DO, COLETTE.
カッチーン
GRRRRR

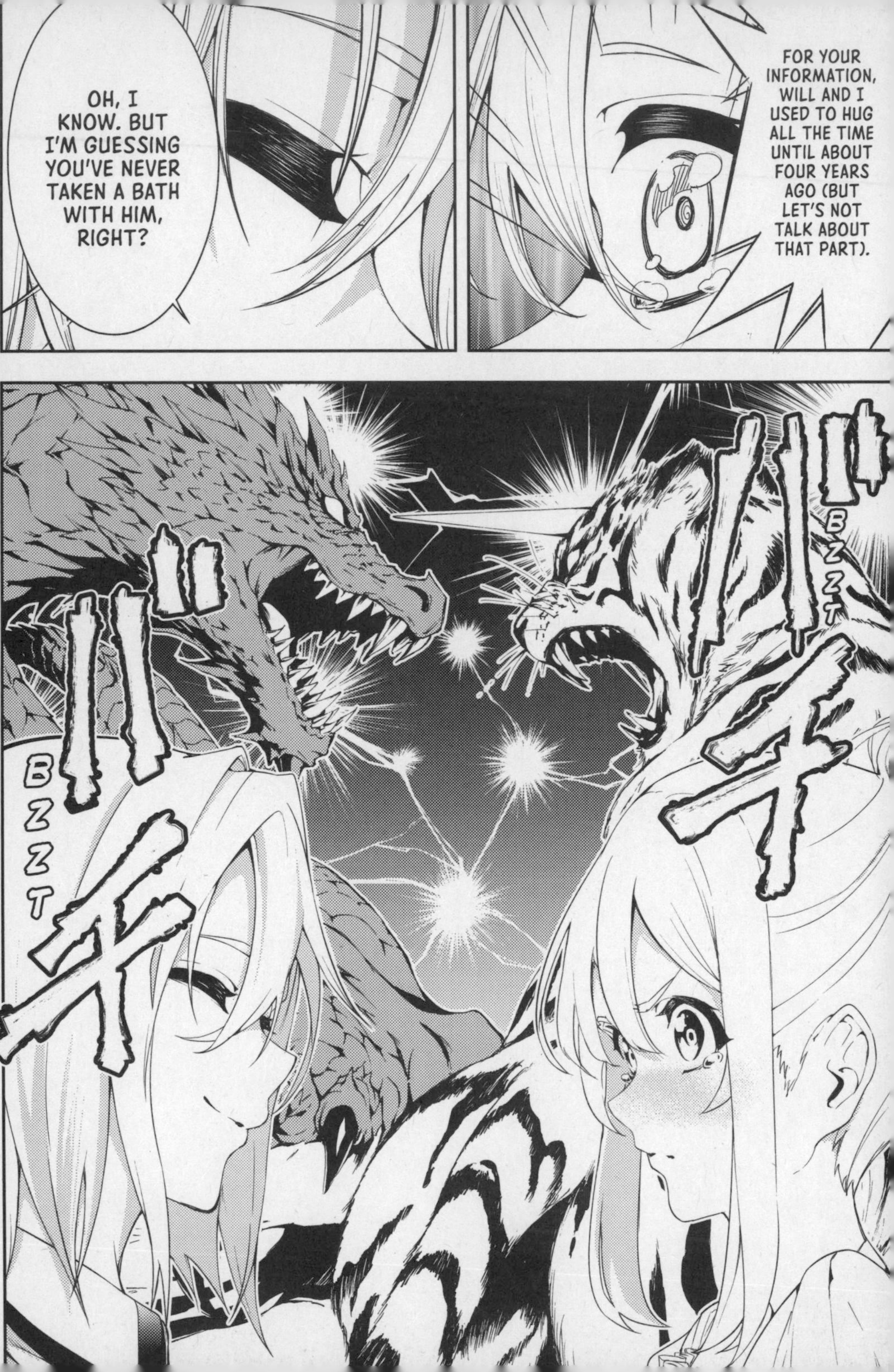
FOR YOUR INFORMATION, WILL AND I USED TO HUG ALL THE TIME UNTIL ABOUT FOUR YEARS AGO (BUT LET'S NOT TALK ABOUT THAT PART).
OH, I KNOW. BUT I'M GUESSING YOU'VE NEVER TAKEN A BATH WITH HIM, RIGHT?
BZZT
BZZT

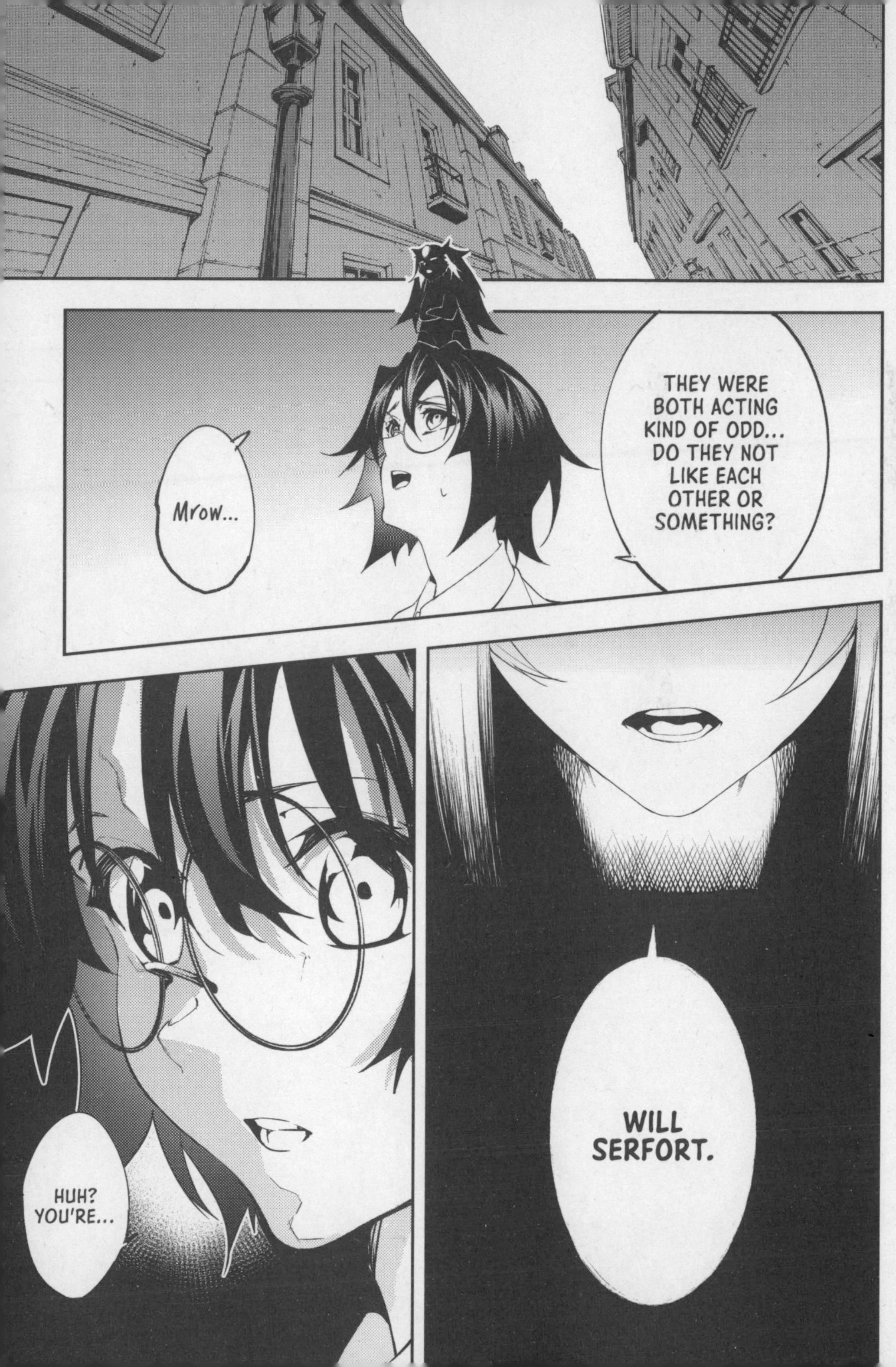
THEY WERE BOTH ACTING KIND OF ODD... DO THEY NOT LIKE EACH OTHER OR SOMETHING?
Mrow...
WILL SERFORT.
HUH? YOU'RE...

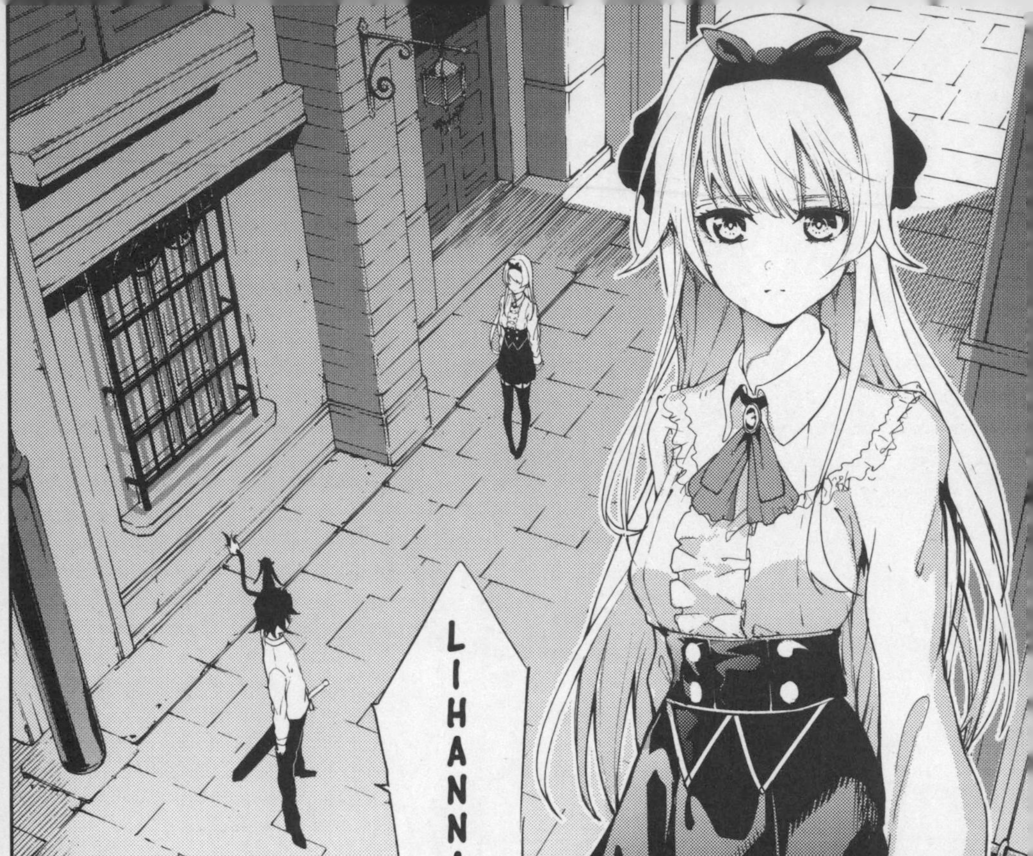
LIHANNA?!
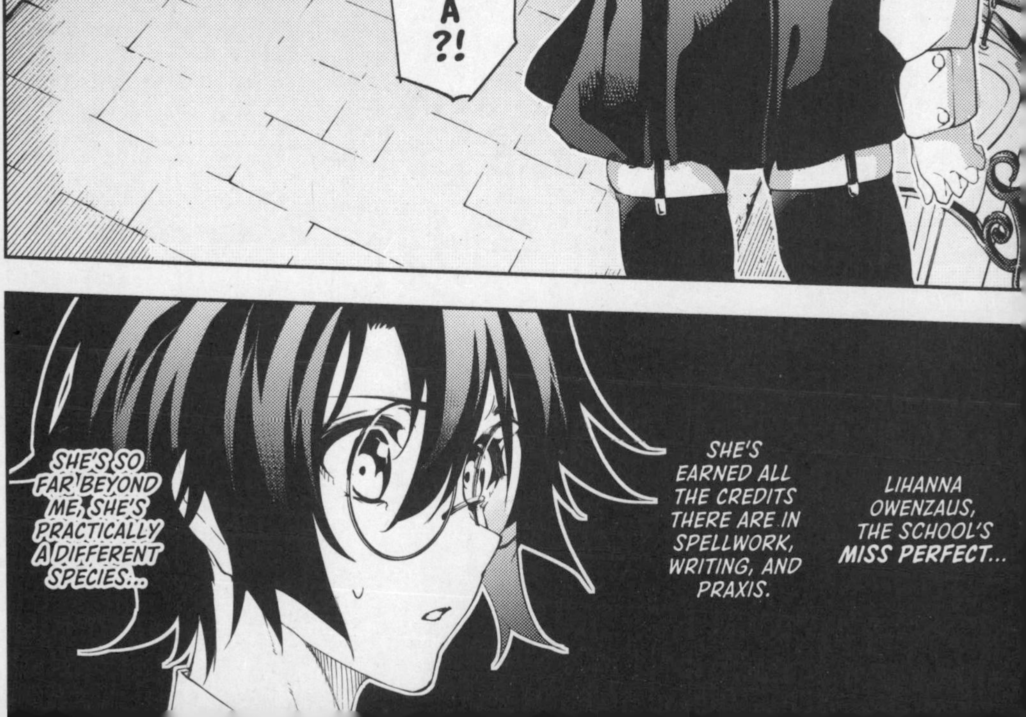
LIHANNA OWENZAUS, THE SCHOOL'S MISS PERFECT...
SHE'S EARNED ALL THE CREDITS THERE ARE IN SPELLWORK, WRITING, AND PRAXIS.
SHE'S SO FAR BEYOND ME, SHE'S PRACTICALLY A DIFFERENT SPECIES...

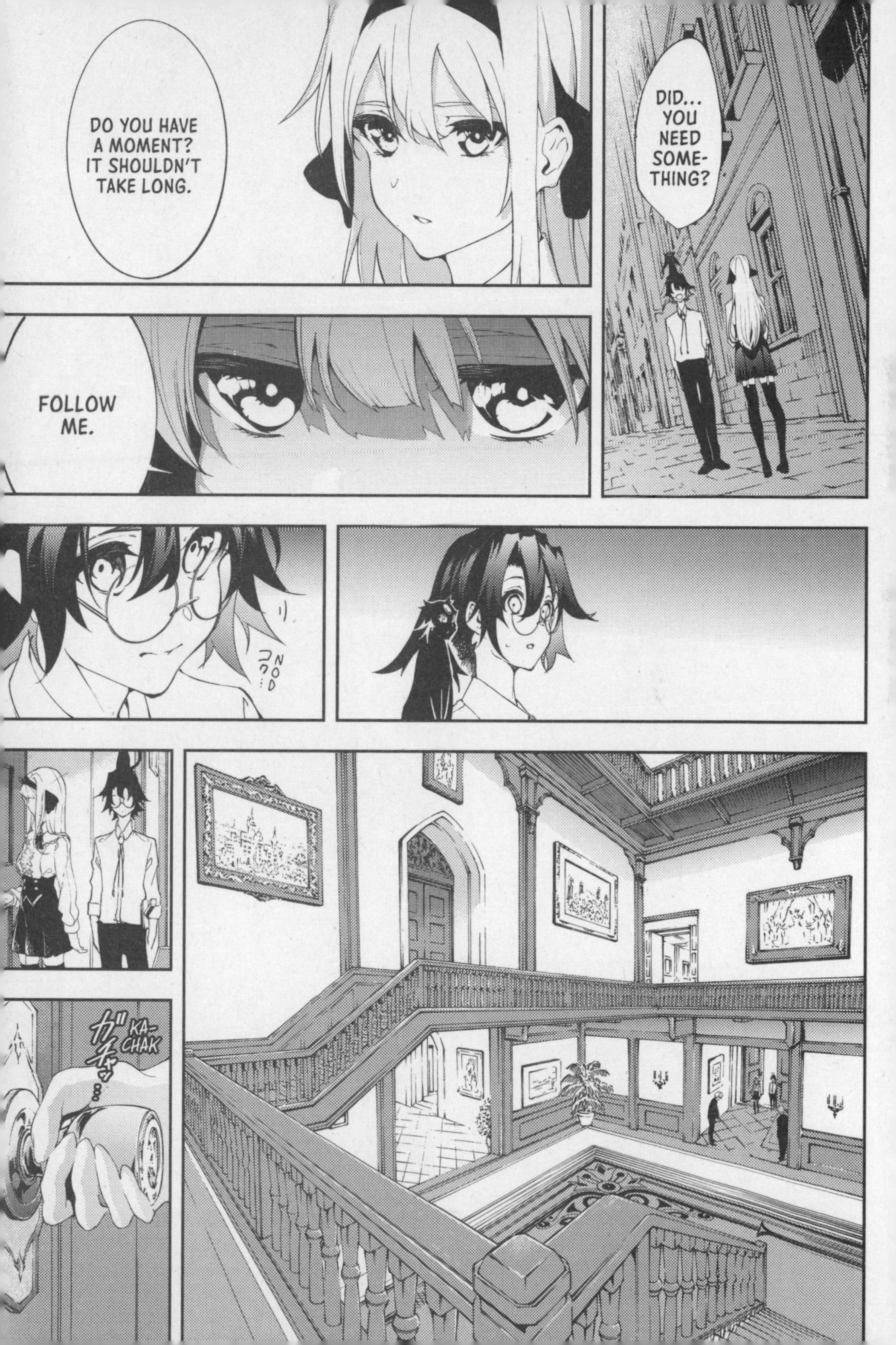
DID... YOU NEED SOMETHING?
DO YOU HAVE A MOMENT? IT SHOULDN'T TAKE LONG.
FOLLOW ME.
NOD NOD...
KA-CHAK

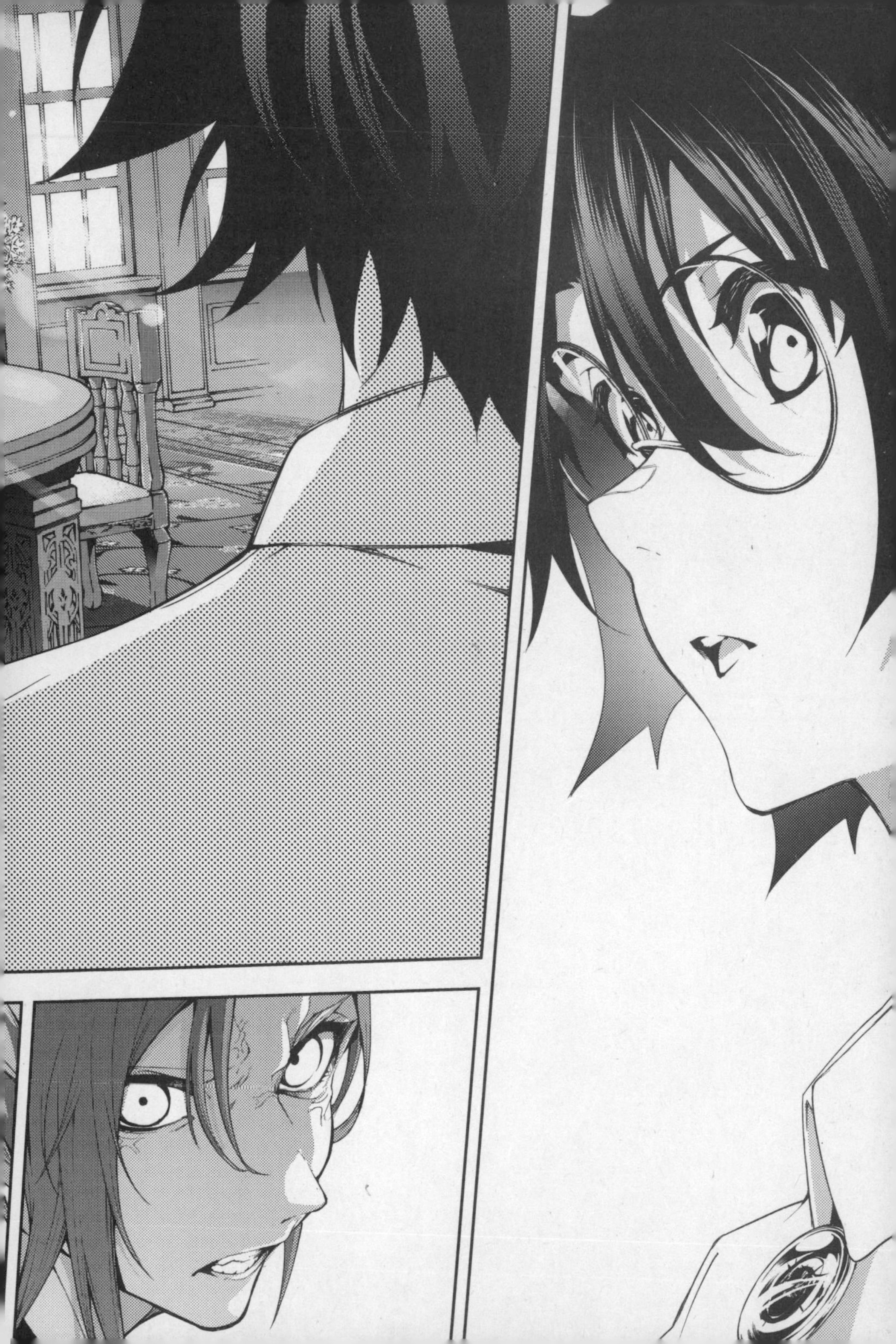

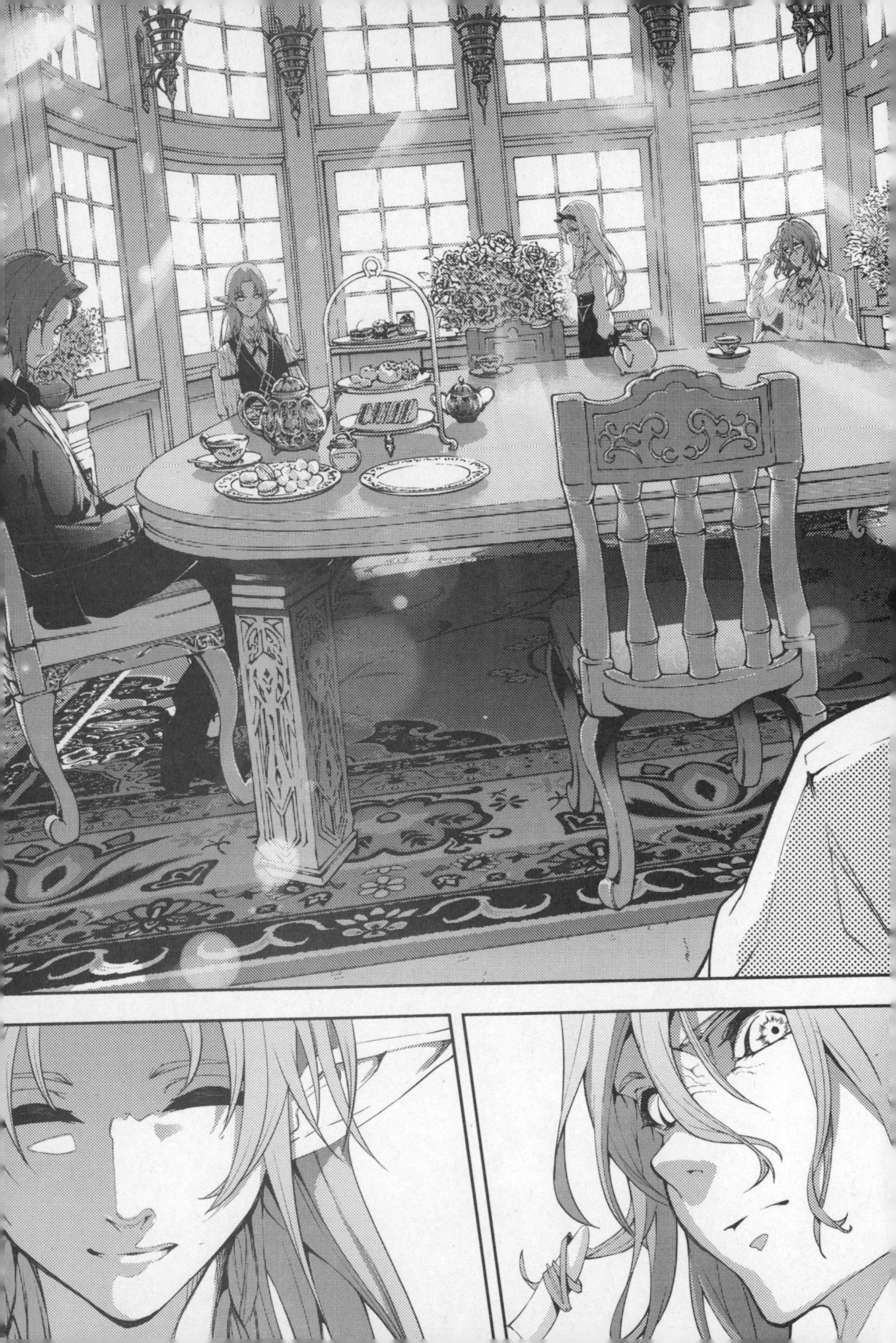

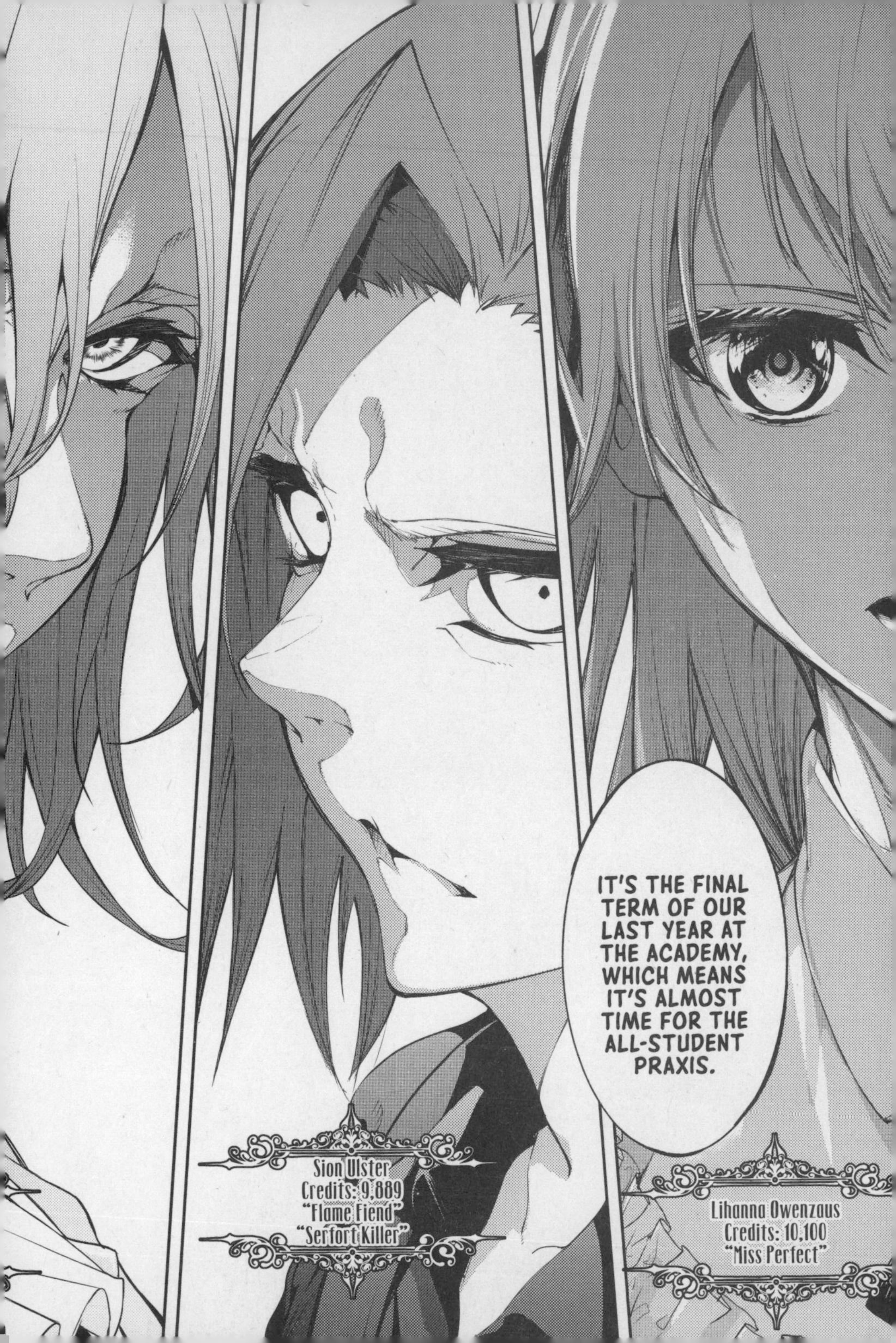
IT'S THE FINAL TERM OF OUR LAST YEAR AT THE ACADEMY, WHICH MEANS IT'S ALMOST TIME FOR THE ALL-STUDENT PRAXIS.
Lihanna Owenzaus Credits: 10,100 "Miss Perfect"
Sion Ulster Credits: 9,889 "Flame Fiend" "Serfort Killer"

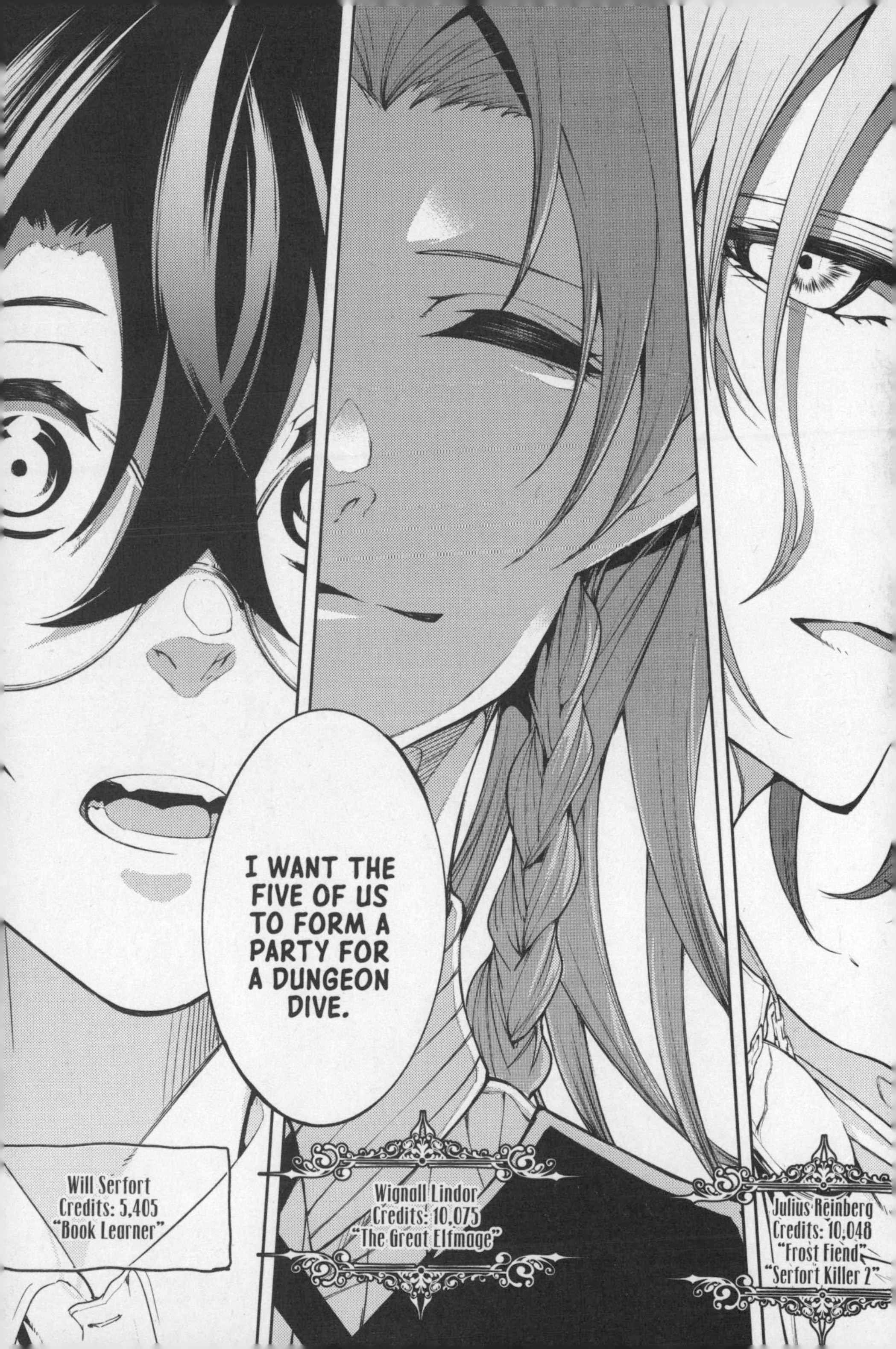
Julius Reinberg
Credits: 10,048
"Frost Fiend"
"Serfort Killer 2"
Wignall Lindor
Credits: 10,075
"The Great Elfmage"
I WANT THE FIVE OF US TO FORM A PARTY FOR A DUNGEON DIVE.
Will Serfort
Credits: 5,405
"Book Learner"

Wistoria
Wand and Sword

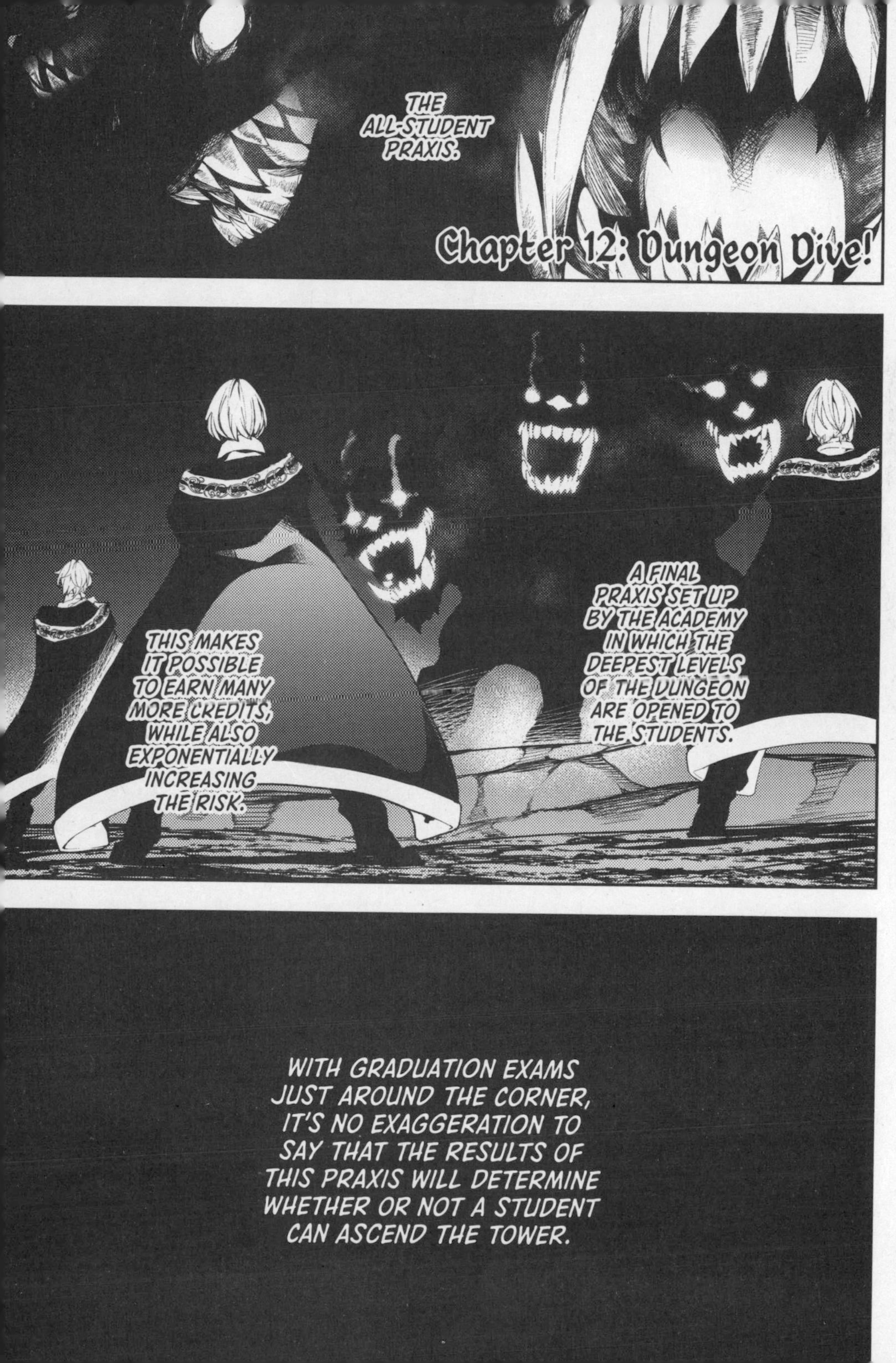
THE ALL-STUDENT PRAXIS.
Chapter 12: Dungeon Dive!
A FINAL PRAXIS SET UP BY THE ACADEMY IN WHICH THE DEEPEST LEVELS OF THE DUNGEON ARE OPENED TO THE STUDENTS.
THIS MAKES IT POSSIBLE TO EARN MANY MORE CREDITS, WHILE ALSO EXPONENTIALLY INCREASING THE RISK.
WITH GRADUATION EXAMS JUST AROUND THE CORNER, IT'S NO EXAGGERATION TO SAY THAT THE RESULTS OF THIS PRAXIS WILL DETERMINE WHETHER OR NOT A STUDENT CAN ASCEND THE TOWER.

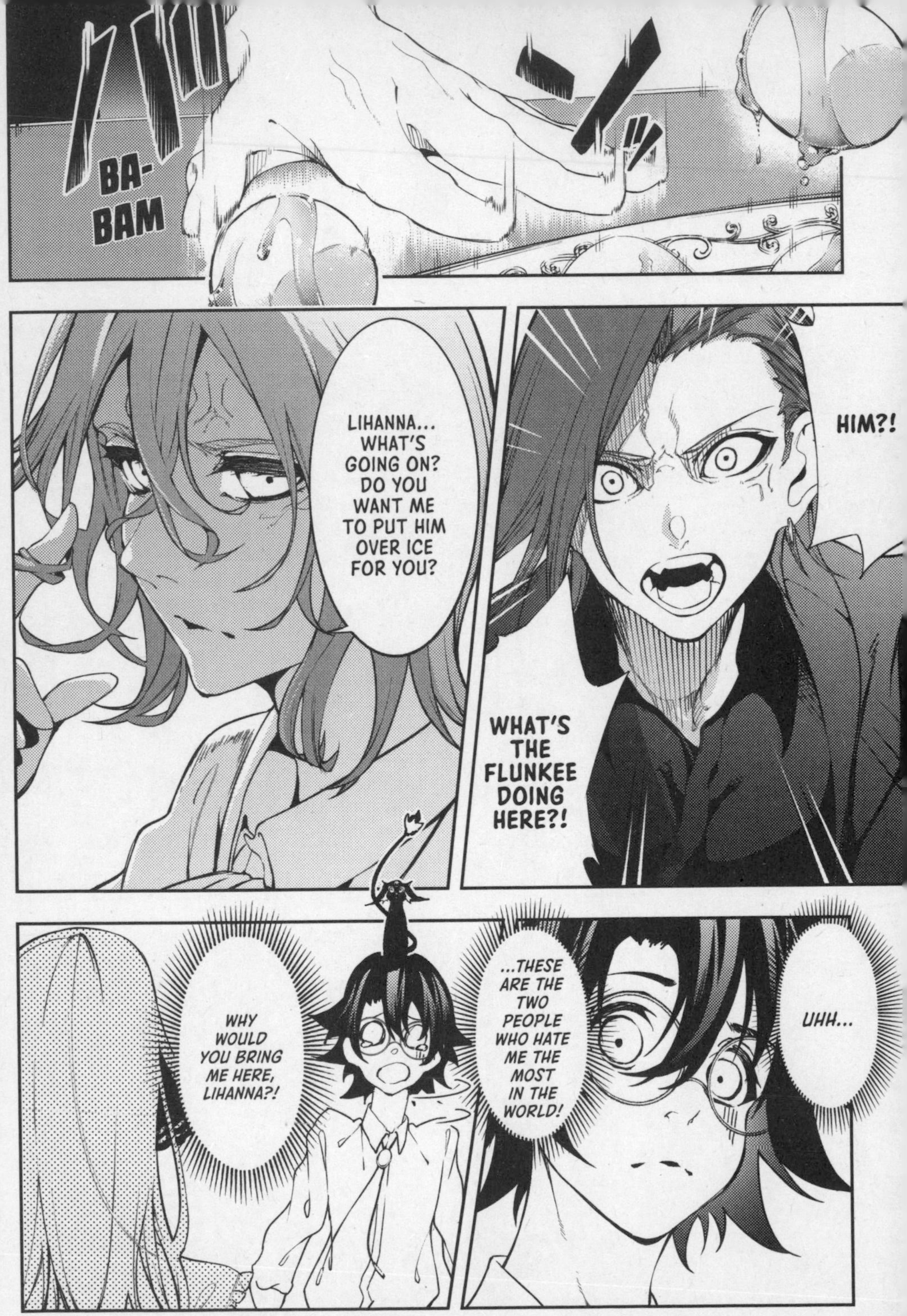
BA-BAM
HIM?!
WHAT'S THE FLUNKEE DOING HERE?!
LIHANNA... WHAT'S GOING ON? DO YOU WANT ME TO PUT HIM OVER ICE FOR YOU?
UHH...
...THESE ARE THE TWO PEOPLE WHO HATE ME THE MOST IN THE WORLD!
WHY WOULD YOU BRING ME HERE, LIHANNA?!

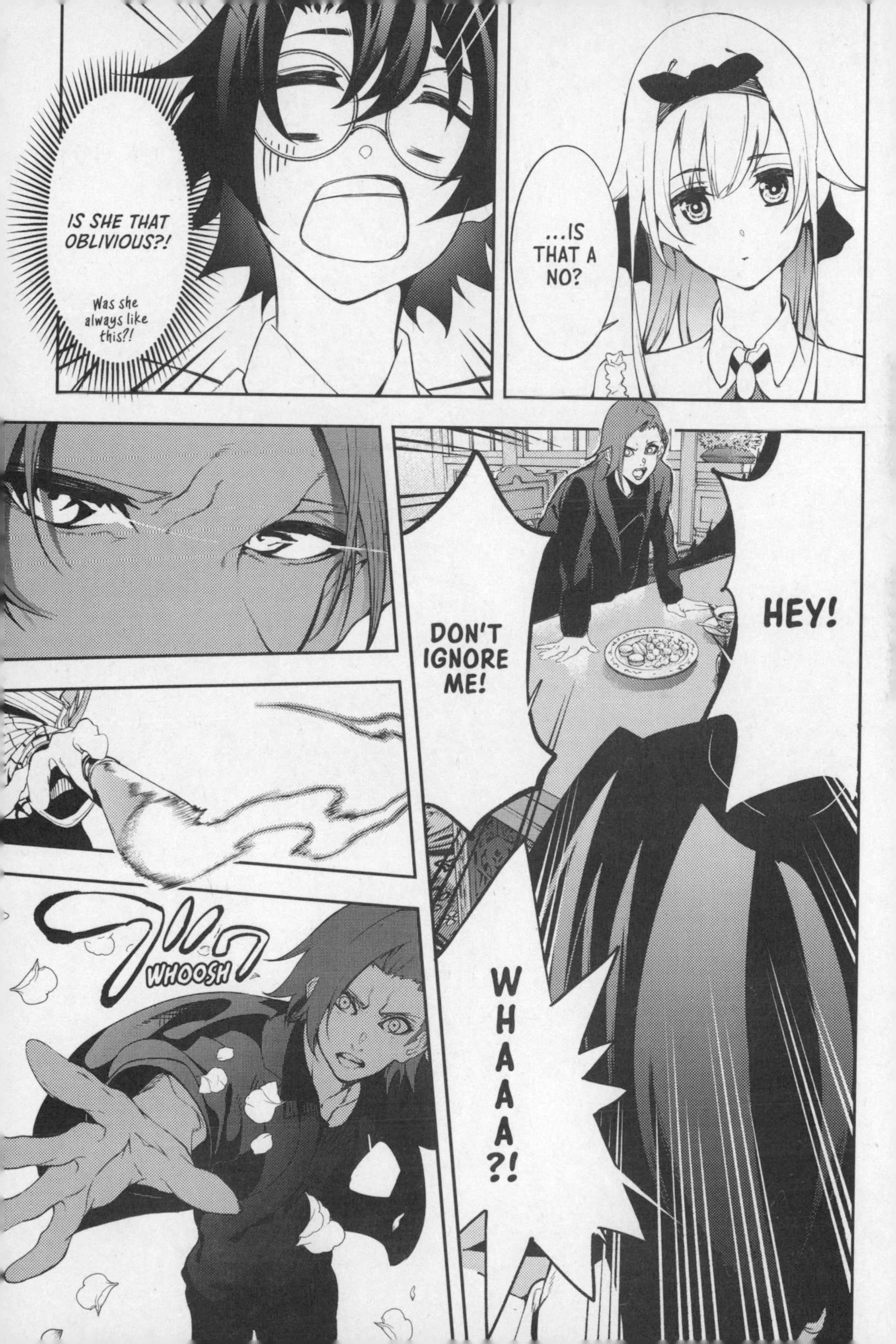
...IS THAT A NO?
IS SHE THAT OBLIVIOUS?!
Was she always like this?!
HEY!
DON'T IGNORE ME!
WHAAAA?!
WHOOSH

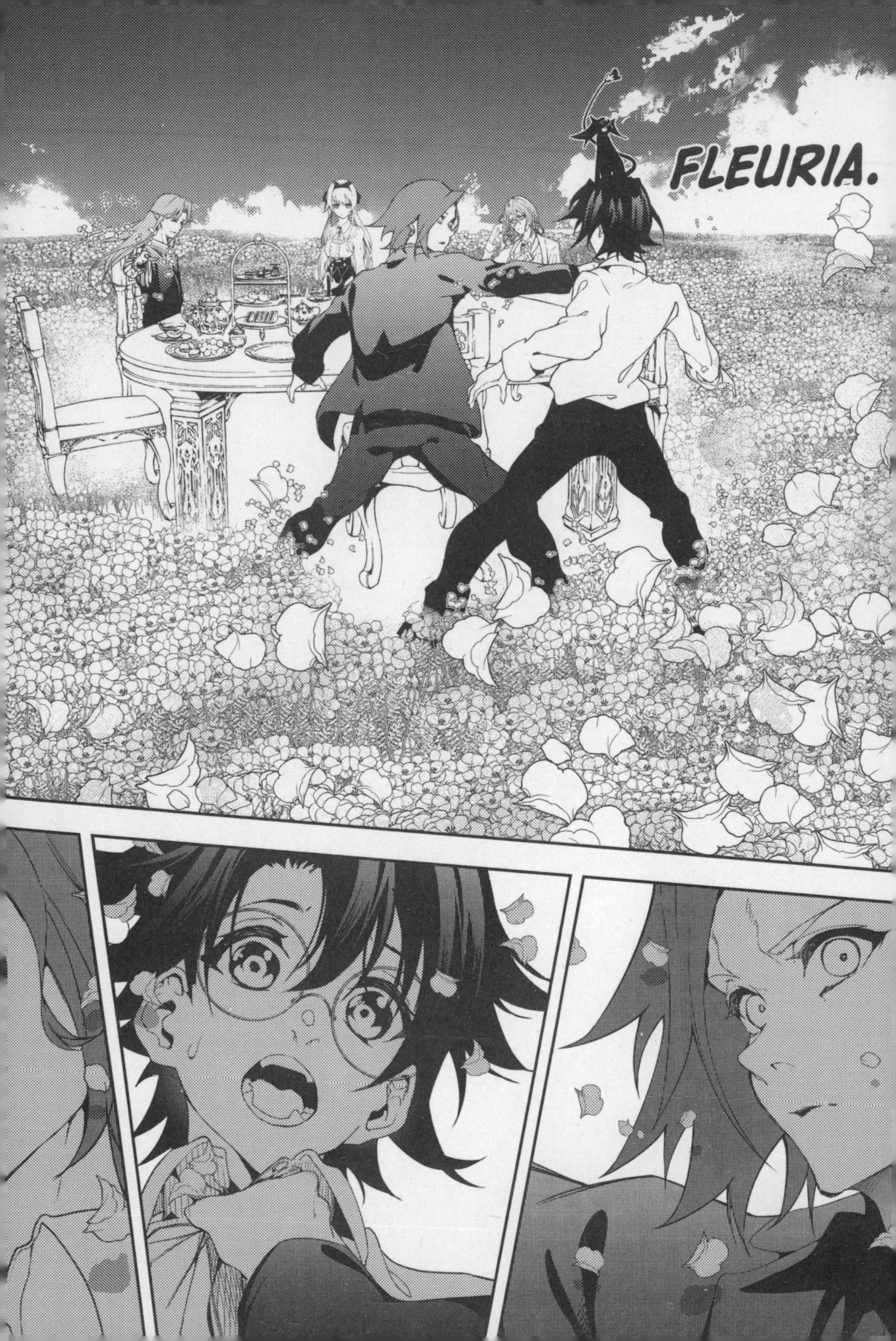
FLEURIA.

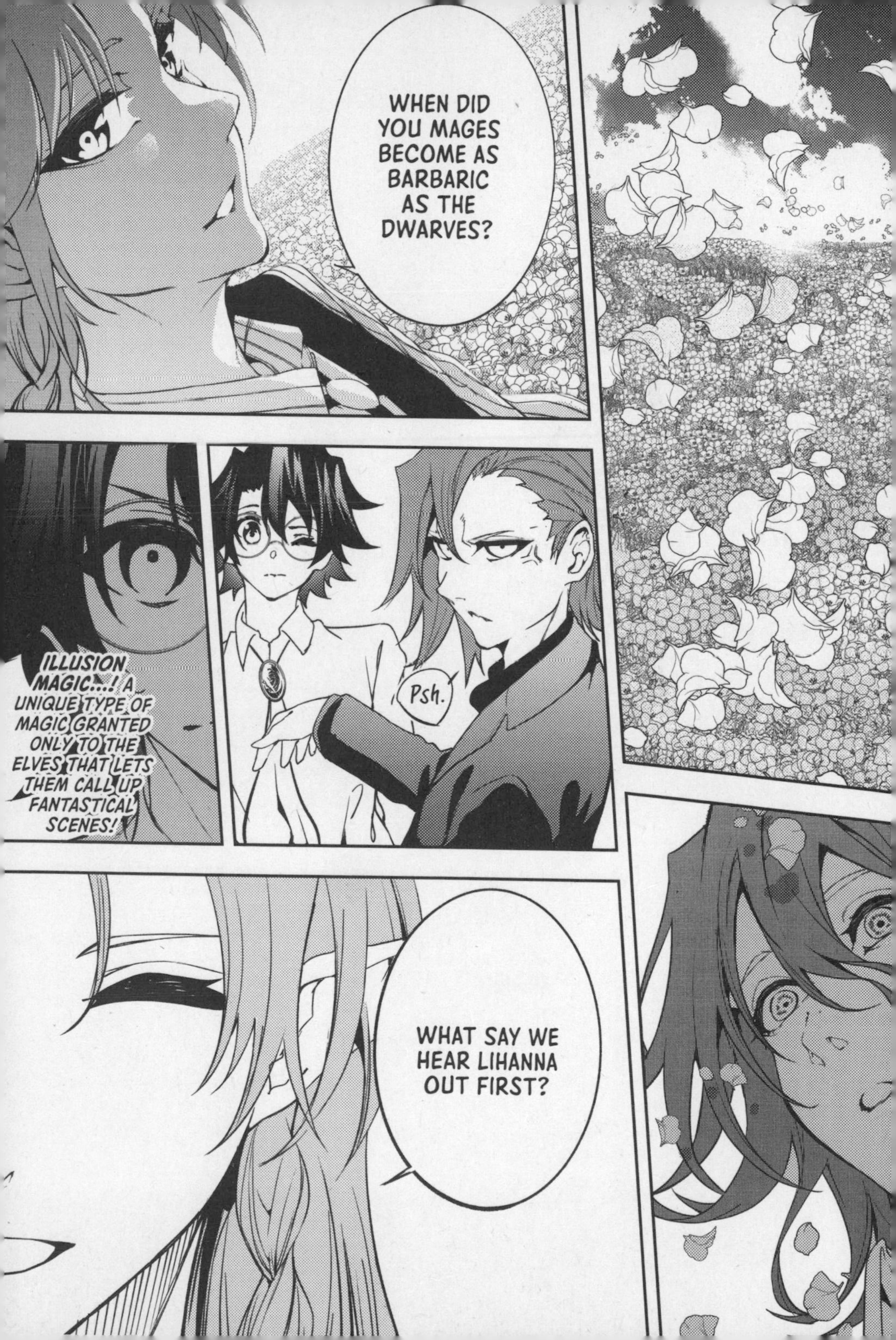
WHEN DID YOU MAGES BECOME AS BARBARIC AS THE DWARVES?
Psh.
ILLUSION MAGIC...! A UNIQUE TYPE OF MAGIC GRANTED ONLY TO THE ELVES THAT LETS THEM CALL UP FANTASTICAL SCENES!
WHAT SAY WE HEAR LIHANNA OUT FIRST?

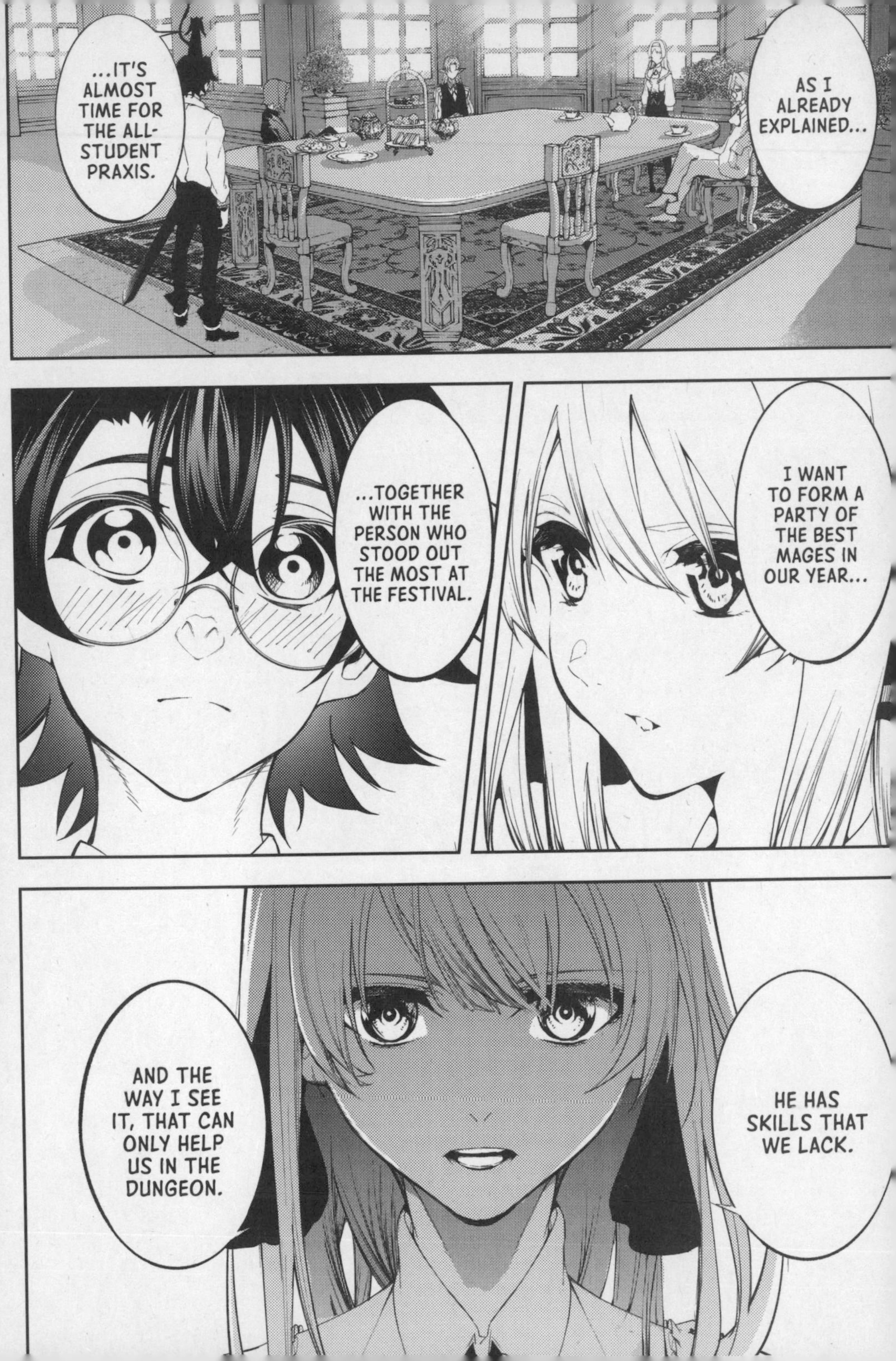
AS I ALREADY EXPLAINED...
...IT'S ALMOST TIME FOR THE ALL-STUDENT PRAXIS.
I WANT TO FORM A PARTY OF THE BEST MAGES IN OUR YEAR...
...TOGETHER WITH THE PERSON WHO STOOD OUT THE MOST AT THE FESTIVAL.
HE HAS SKILLS THAT WE LACK.
AND THE WAY I SEE IT, THAT CAN ONLY HELP US IN THE DUNGEON.

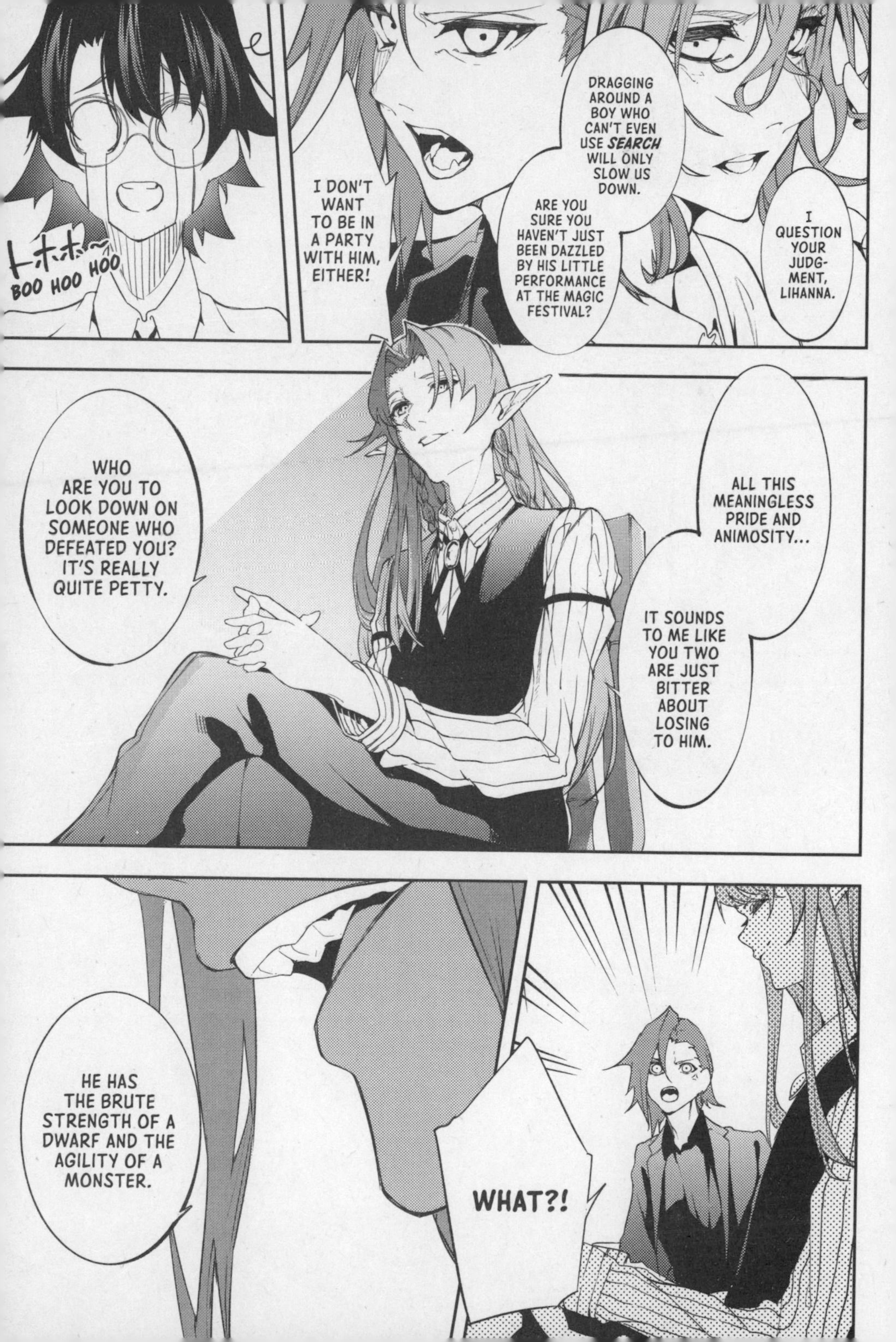
I QUESTION YOUR JUDGMENT, LIHANNA.
DRAGGING AROUND A BOY WHO CAN'T EVEN USE ***SEARCH*** WILL ONLY SLOW US DOWN.
ARE YOU SURE YOU HAVEN'T JUST BEEN DAZZLED BY HIS LITTLE PERFORMANCE AT THE MAGIC FESTIVAL?
I DON'T WANT TO BE IN A PARTY WITH HIM, EITHER!
トホホ～
BOO HOO HOO
ALL THIS MEANINGLESS PRIDE AND ANIMOSITY...
IT SOUNDS TO ME LIKE YOU TWO ARE JUST BITTER ABOUT LOSING TO HIM.
WHO ARE YOU TO LOOK DOWN ON SOMEONE WHO DEFEATED YOU? IT'S REALLY QUITE PETTY.
WHAT?!
HE HAS THE BRUTE STRENGTH OF A DWARF AND THE AGILITY OF A MONSTER.

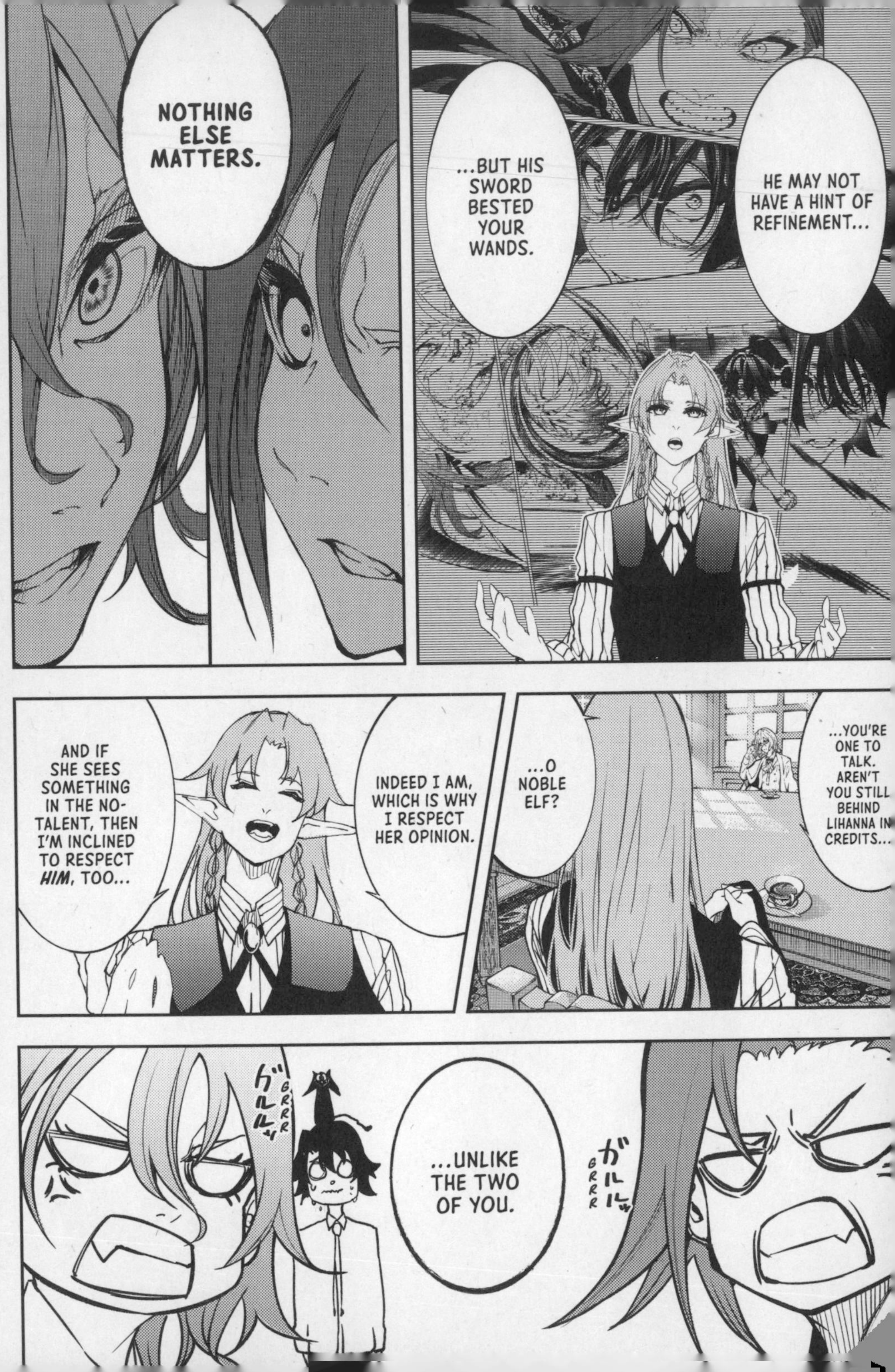
HE MAY NOT HAVE A HINT OF REFINEMENT...
...BUT HIS SWORD BESTED YOUR WANDS.
NOTHING ELSE MATTERS.
...YOU'RE ONE TO TALK. AREN'T YOU STILL BEHIND LIHANNA IN CREDITS...
...O NOBLE ELF?
INDEED I AM, WHICH IS WHY I RESPECT HER OPINION.
AND IF SHE SEES SOMETHING IN THE NO-TALENT, THEN I'M INCLINED TO RESPECT *HIM*, TOO...
ガルルッ GRRR
...UNLIKE THE TWO OF YOU.
グルルッ GRRR

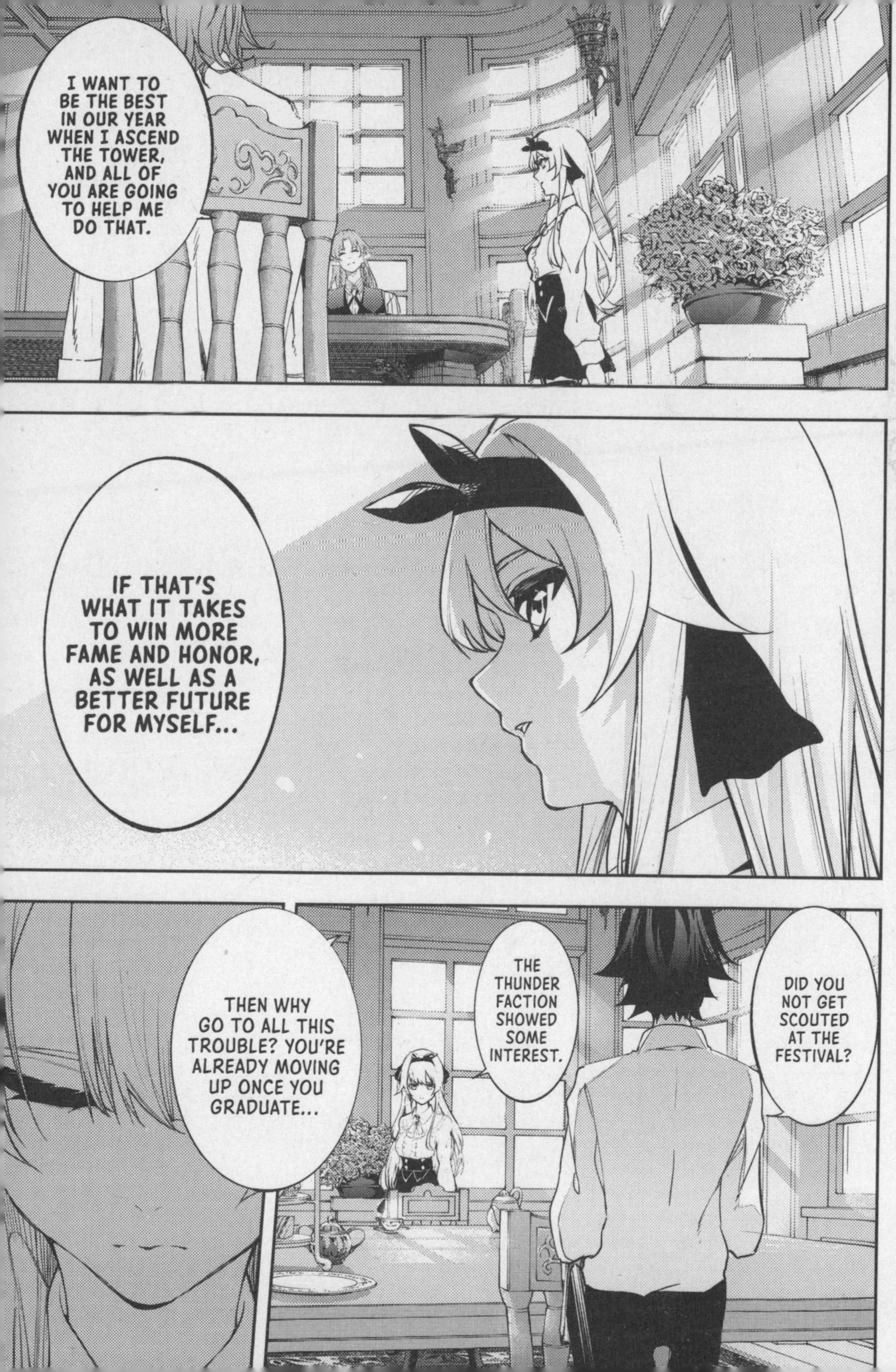
I WANT TO BE THE BEST IN OUR YEAR WHEN I ASCEND THE TOWER, AND ALL OF YOU ARE GOING TO HELP ME DO THAT.
IF THAT'S WHAT IT TAKES TO WIN MORE FAME AND HONOR, AS WELL AS A BETTER FUTURE FOR MYSELF...
DID YOU NOT GET SCOUTED AT THE FESTIVAL?
THE THUNDER FACTION SHOWED SOME INTEREST.
THEN WHY GO TO ALL THIS TROUBLE? YOU'RE ALREADY MOVING UP ONCE YOU GRADUATE...

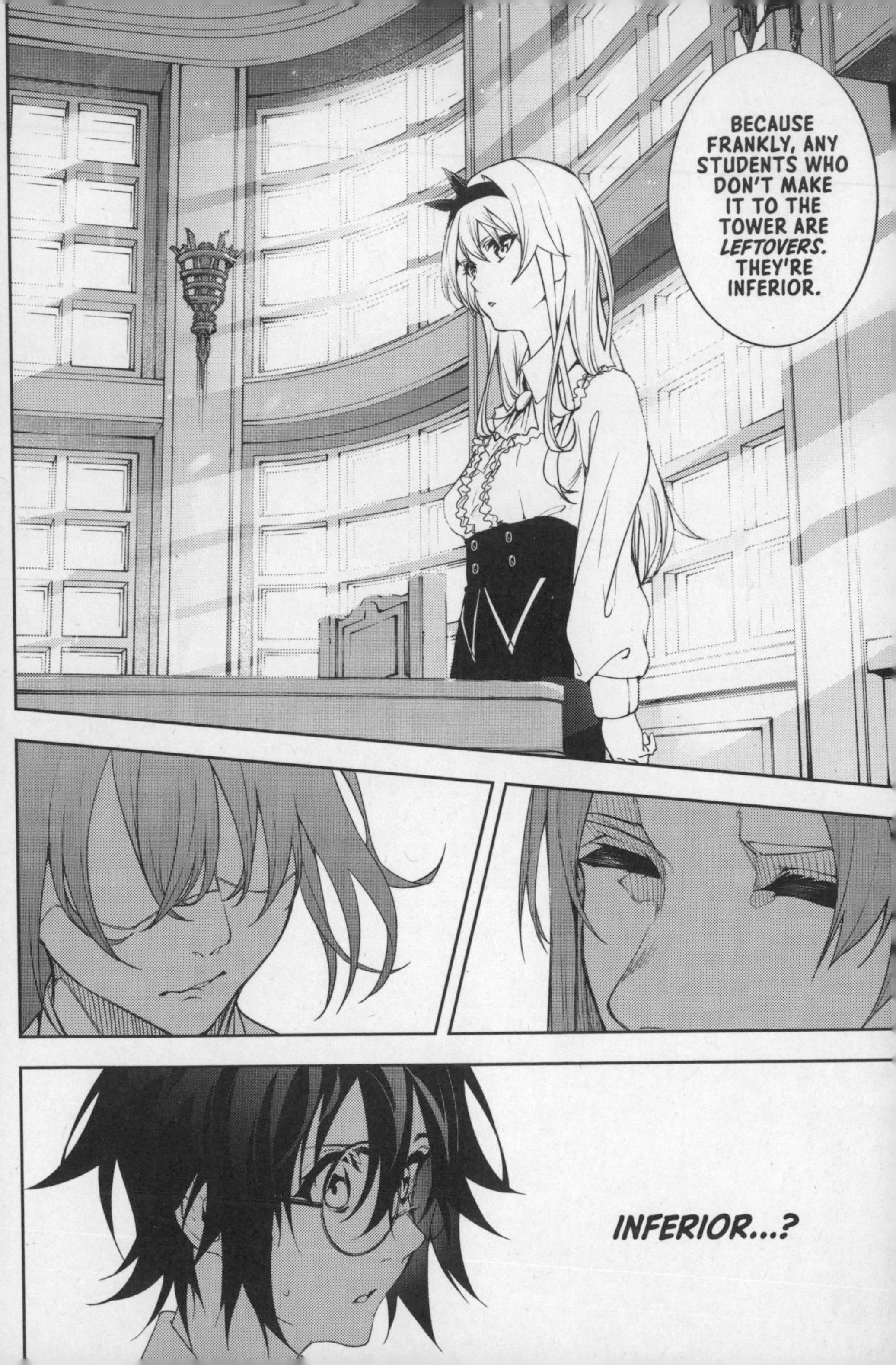
BECAUSE FRANKLY, ANY STUDENTS WHO DON'T MAKE IT TO THE TOWER ARE *LEFTOVERS*. THEY'RE INFERIOR.
INFERIOR...?

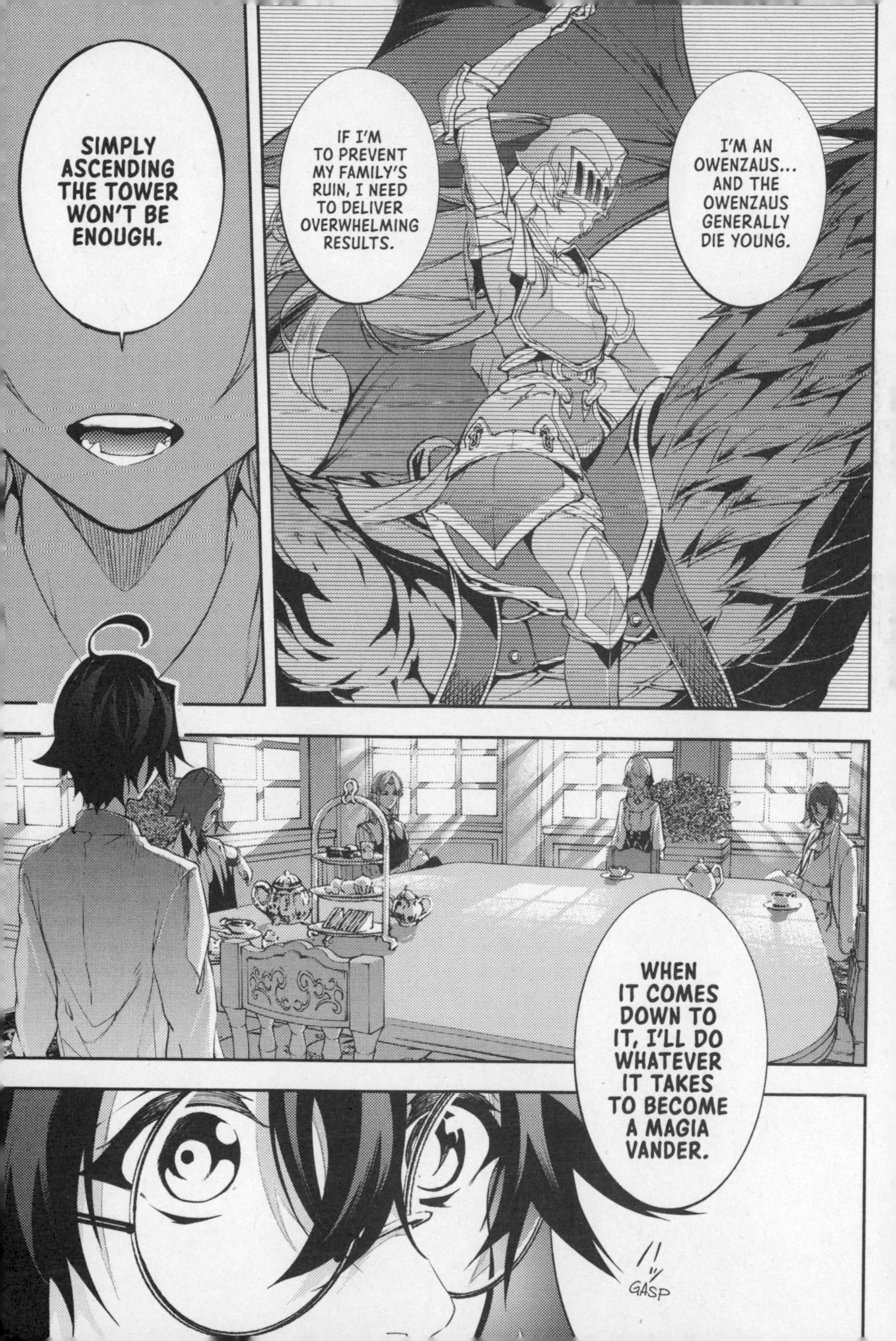
I'M AN OWENZAUS... AND THE OWENZAUS GENERALLY DIE YOUNG.
IF I'M TO PREVENT MY FAMILY'S RUIN, I NEED TO DELIVER OVERWHELMING RESULTS.
SIMPLY ASCENDING THE TOWER WON'T BE ENOUGH.
WHEN IT COMES DOWN TO IT, I'LL DO WHATEVER IT TAKES TO BECOME A MAGIA VANDER.
GASP

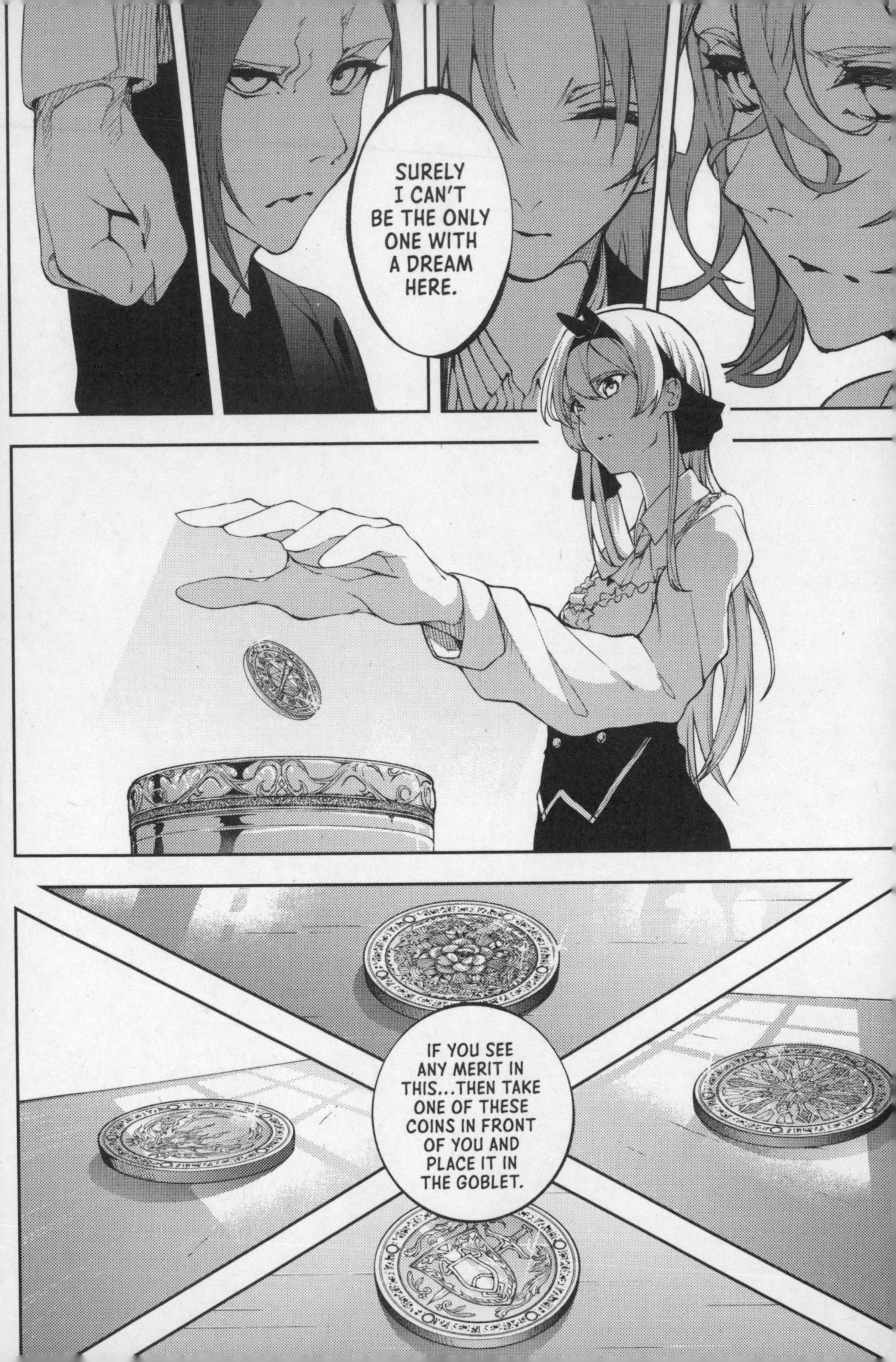
SURELY I CAN'T BE THE ONLY ONE WITH A DREAM HERE.
IF YOU SEE ANY MERIT IN THIS...THEN TAKE ONE OF THESE COINS IN FRONT OF YOU AND PLACE IT IN THE GOBLET.

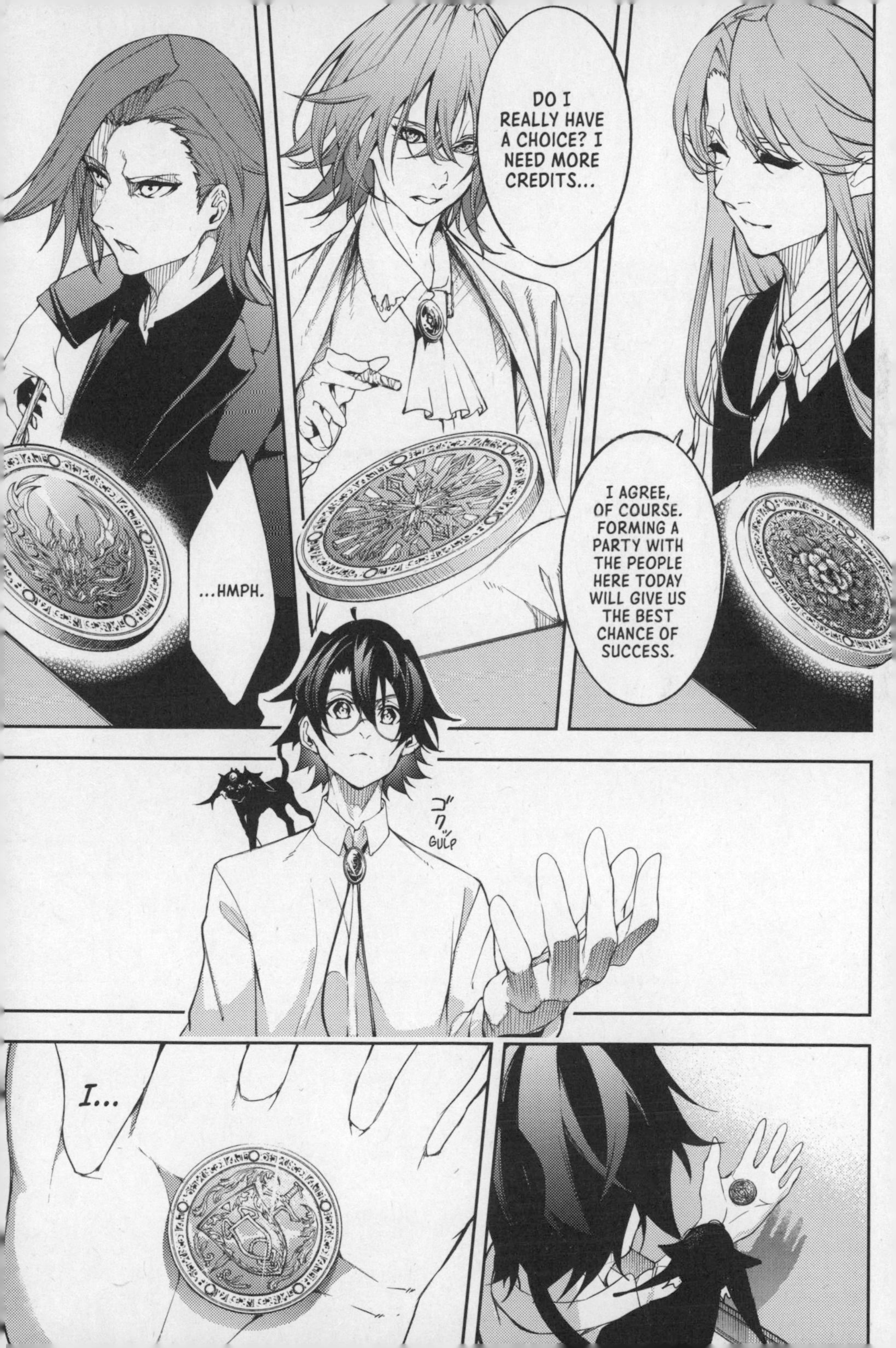
I AGREE, OF COURSE. FORMING A PARTY WITH THE PEOPLE HERE TODAY WILL GIVE US THE BEST CHANCE OF SUCCESS.
DO I REALLY HAVE A CHOICE? I NEED MORE CREDITS...
...HMPH.
ゴクッ
GULP
I...

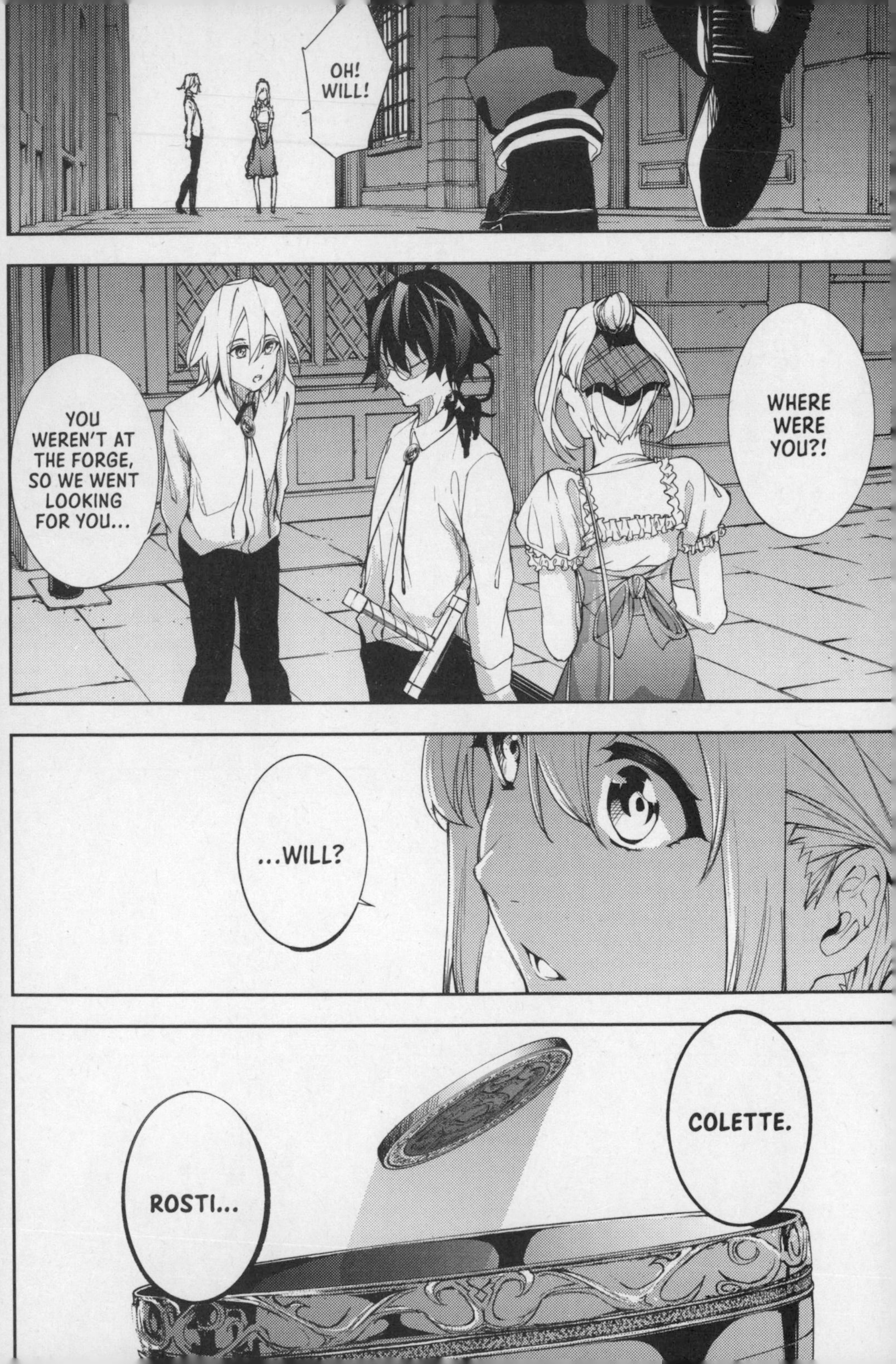
OH! WILL!
WHERE WERE YOU?!
YOU WEREN'T AT THE FORGE, SO WE WENT LOOKING FOR YOU...
...WILL?
COLETTE.
ROSTI...

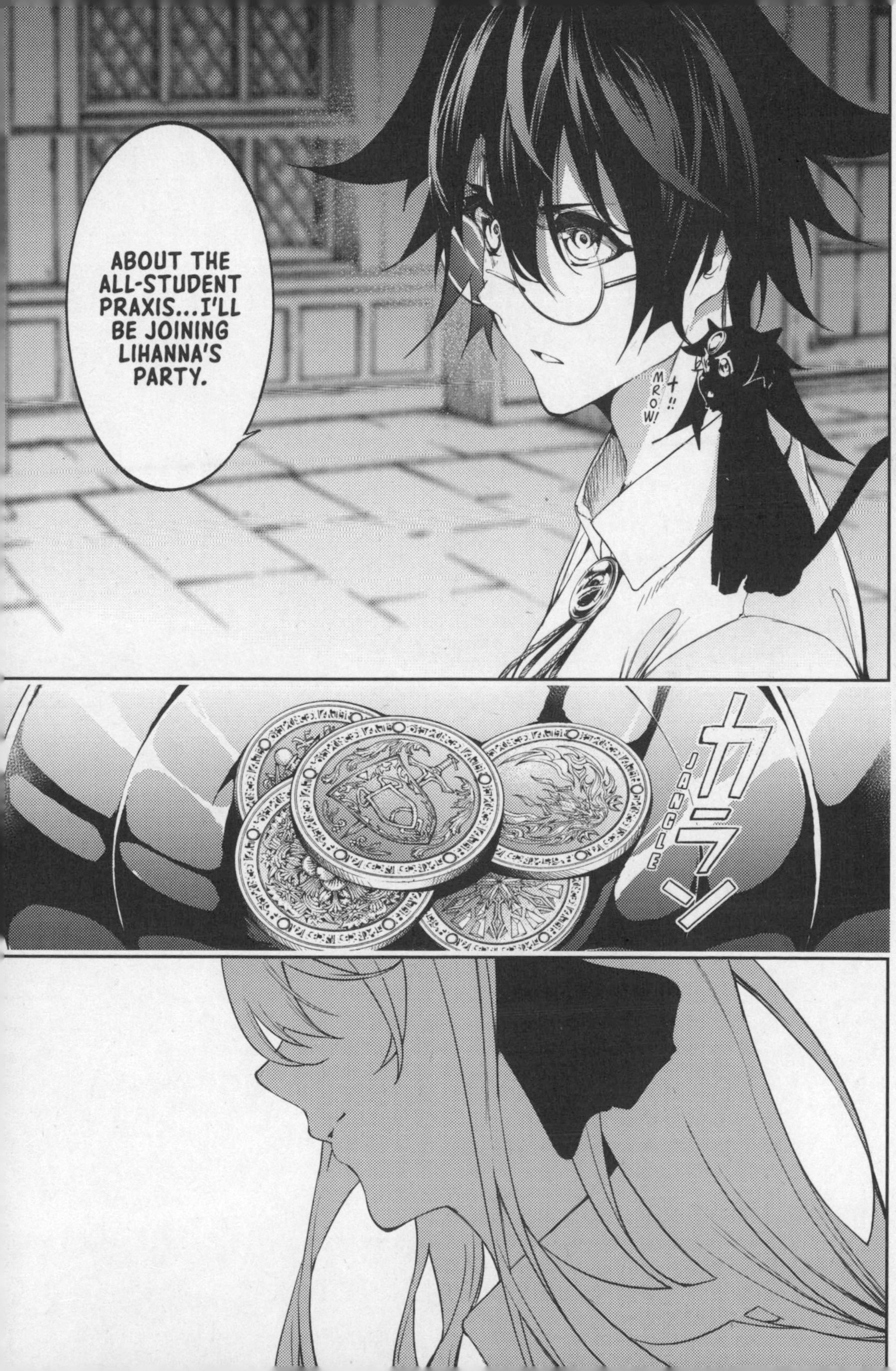
ABOUT THE ALL-STUDENT PRAXIS...I'LL BE JOINING LIHANNA'S PARTY.
MROW!
JANGLE

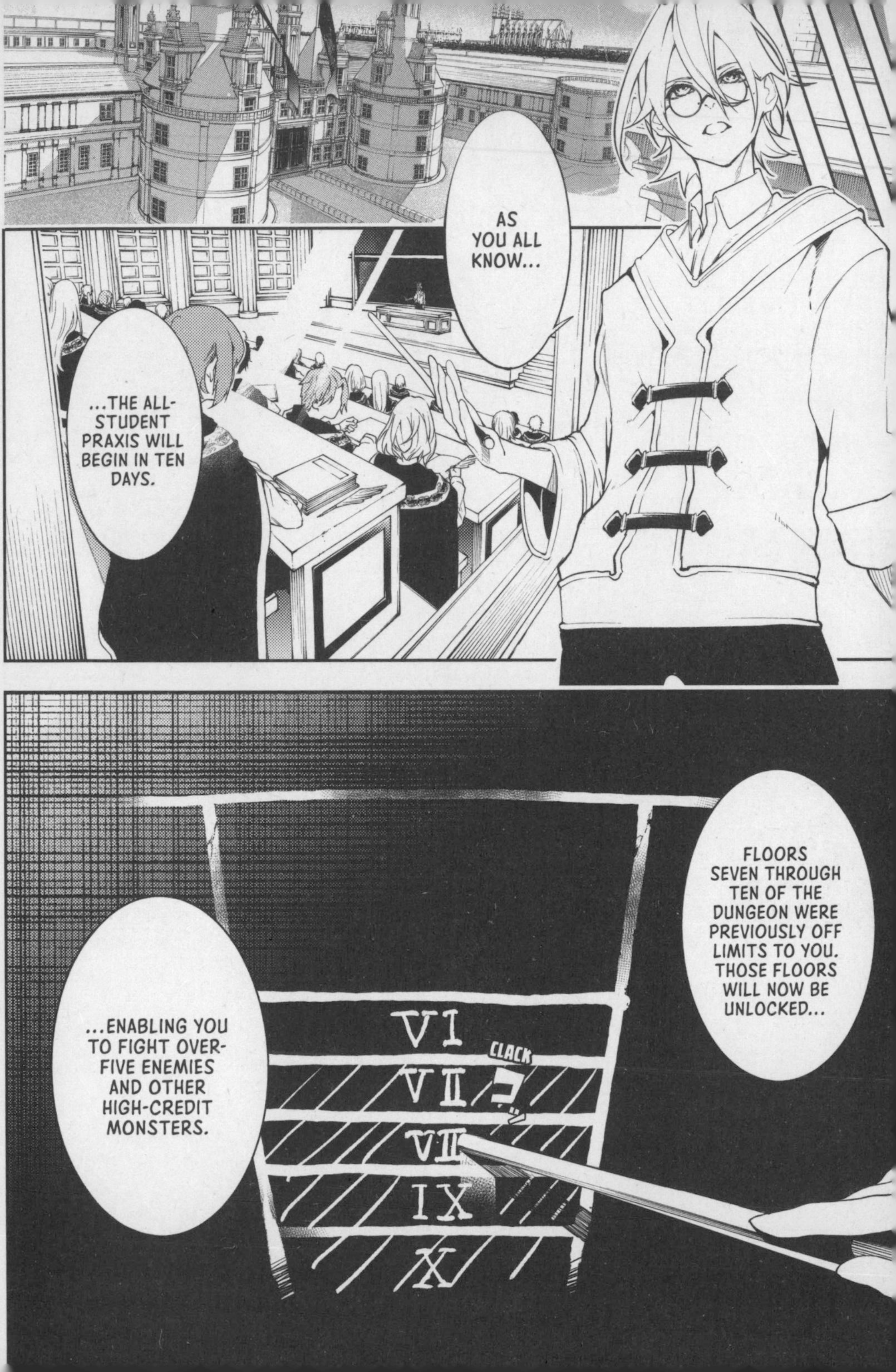
AS YOU ALL KNOW...
...THE ALL-STUDENT PRAXIS WILL BEGIN IN TEN DAYS.
FLOORS SEVEN THROUGH TEN OF THE DUNGEON WERE PREVIOUSLY OFF LIMITS TO YOU. THOSE FLOORS WILL NOW BE UNLOCKED...
CLACK
VI
VII
VIII
IX
X
...ENABLING YOU TO FIGHT OVER-FIVE ENEMIES AND OTHER HIGH-CREDIT MONSTERS.

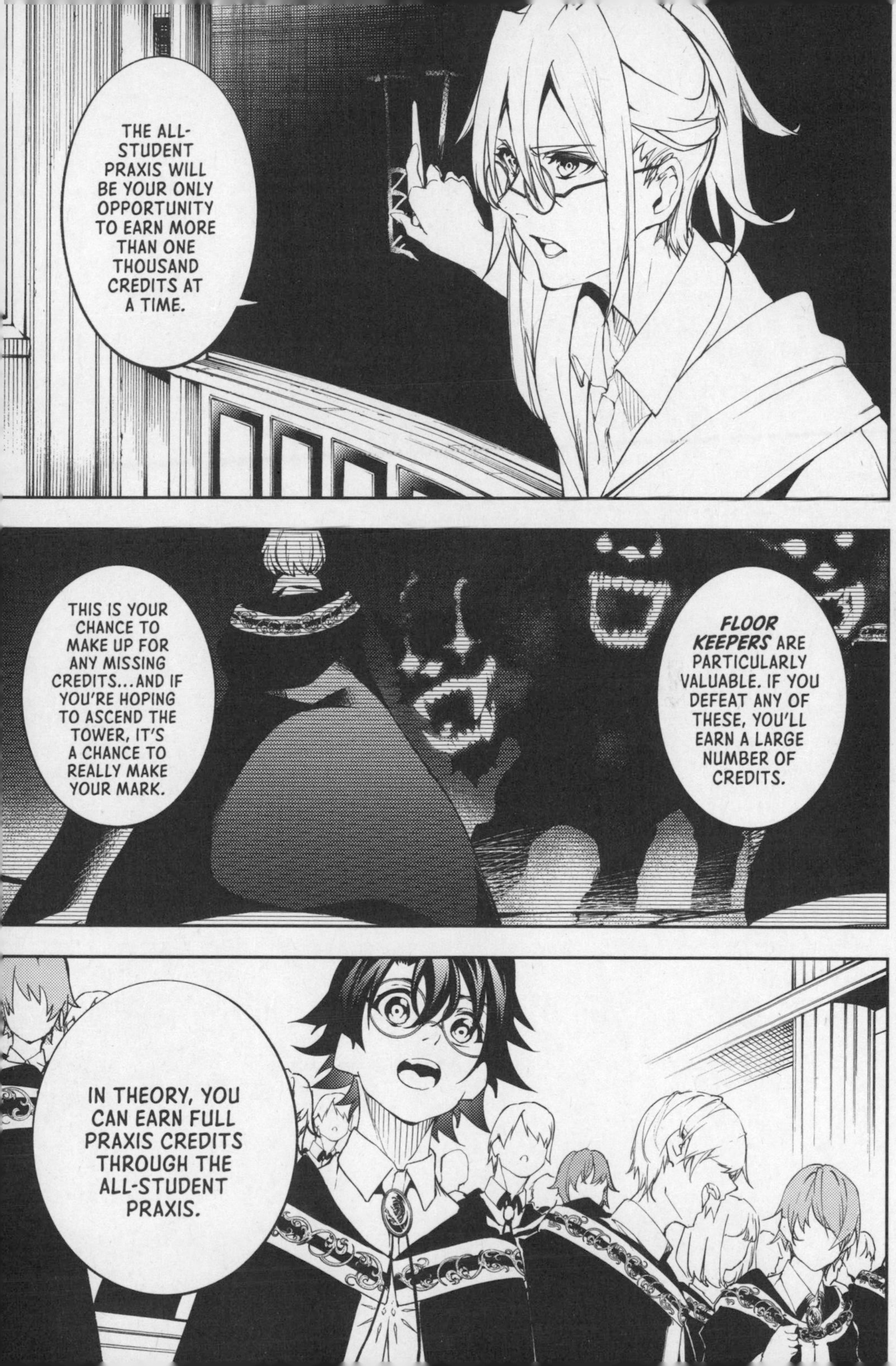
THE ALL-STUDENT PRAXIS WILL BE YOUR ONLY OPPORTUNITY TO EARN MORE THAN ONE THOUSAND CREDITS AT A TIME.
FLOOR KEEPERS ARE PARTICULARLY VALUABLE. IF YOU DEFEAT ANY OF THESE, YOU'LL EARN A LARGE NUMBER OF CREDITS.
THIS IS YOUR CHANCE TO MAKE UP FOR ANY MISSING CREDITS...AND IF YOU'RE HOPING TO ASCEND THE TOWER, IT'S A CHANCE TO REALLY MAKE YOUR MARK.
IN THEORY, YOU CAN EARN FULL PRAXIS CREDITS THROUGH THE ALL-STUDENT PRAXIS.

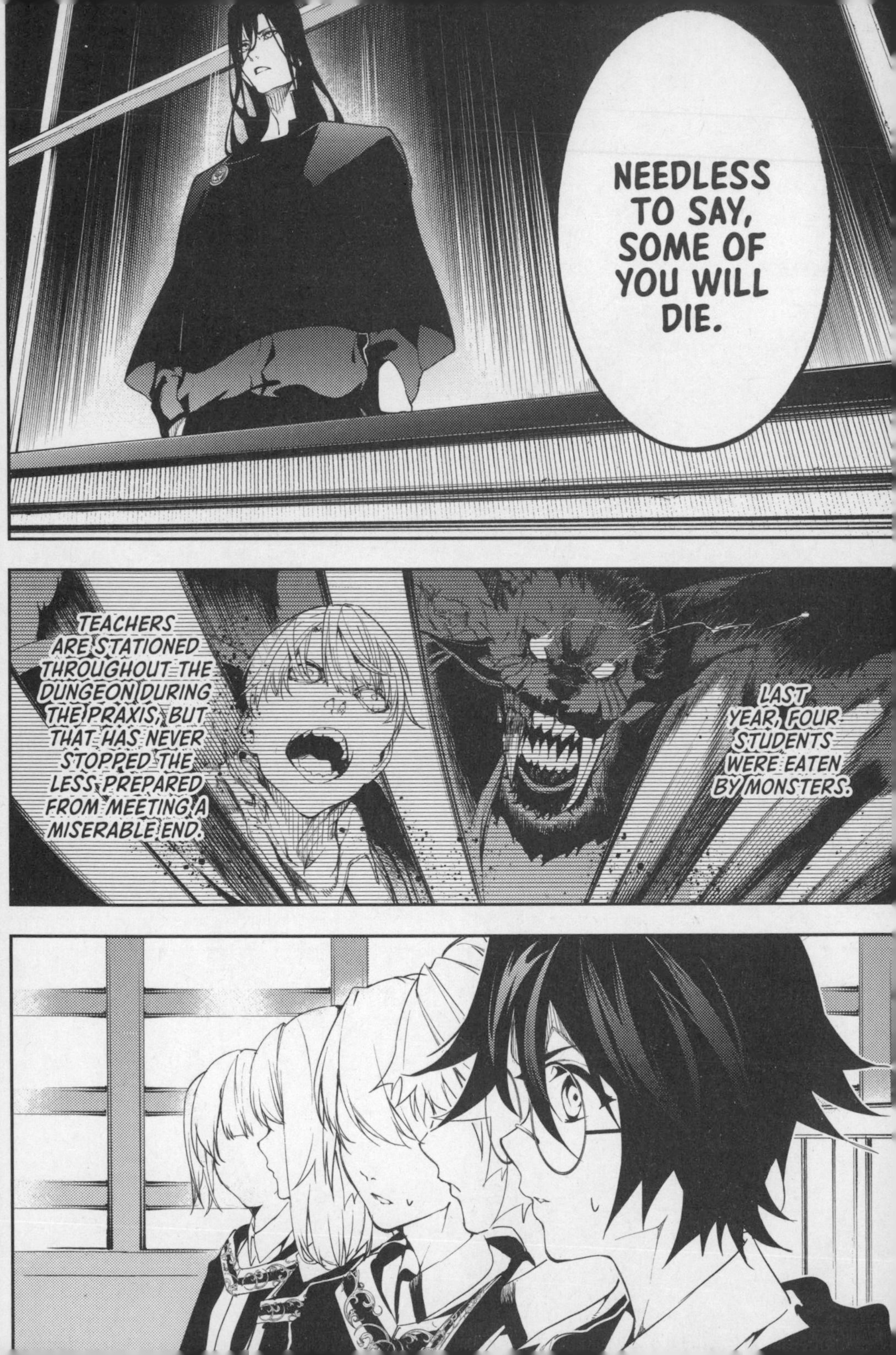
NEEDLESS TO SAY, SOME OF YOU WILL DIE.
LAST YEAR, FOUR STUDENTS WERE EATEN BY MONSTERS.
TEACHERS ARE STATIONED THROUGHOUT THE DUNGEON DURING THE PRAXIS, BUT THAT HAS NEVER STOPPED THE LESS PREPARED FROM MEETING A MISERABLE END.

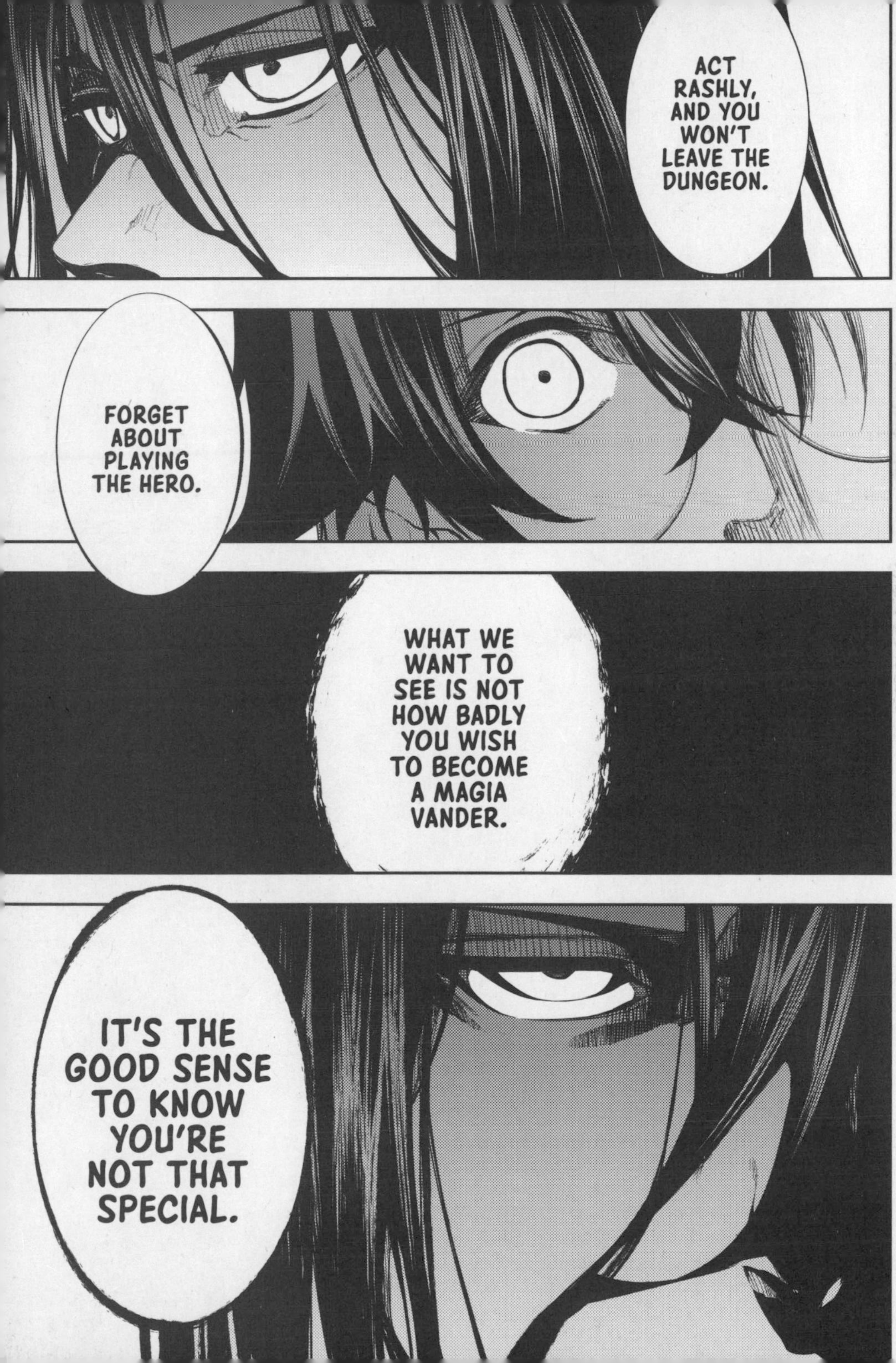
ACT RASHLY, AND YOU WON'T LEAVE THE DUNGEON.
FORGET ABOUT PLAYING THE HERO.
WHAT WE WANT TO SEE IS NOT HOW BADLY YOU WISH TO BECOME A MAGIA VANDER.
IT'S THE GOOD SENSE TO KNOW YOU'RE NOT THAT SPECIAL.

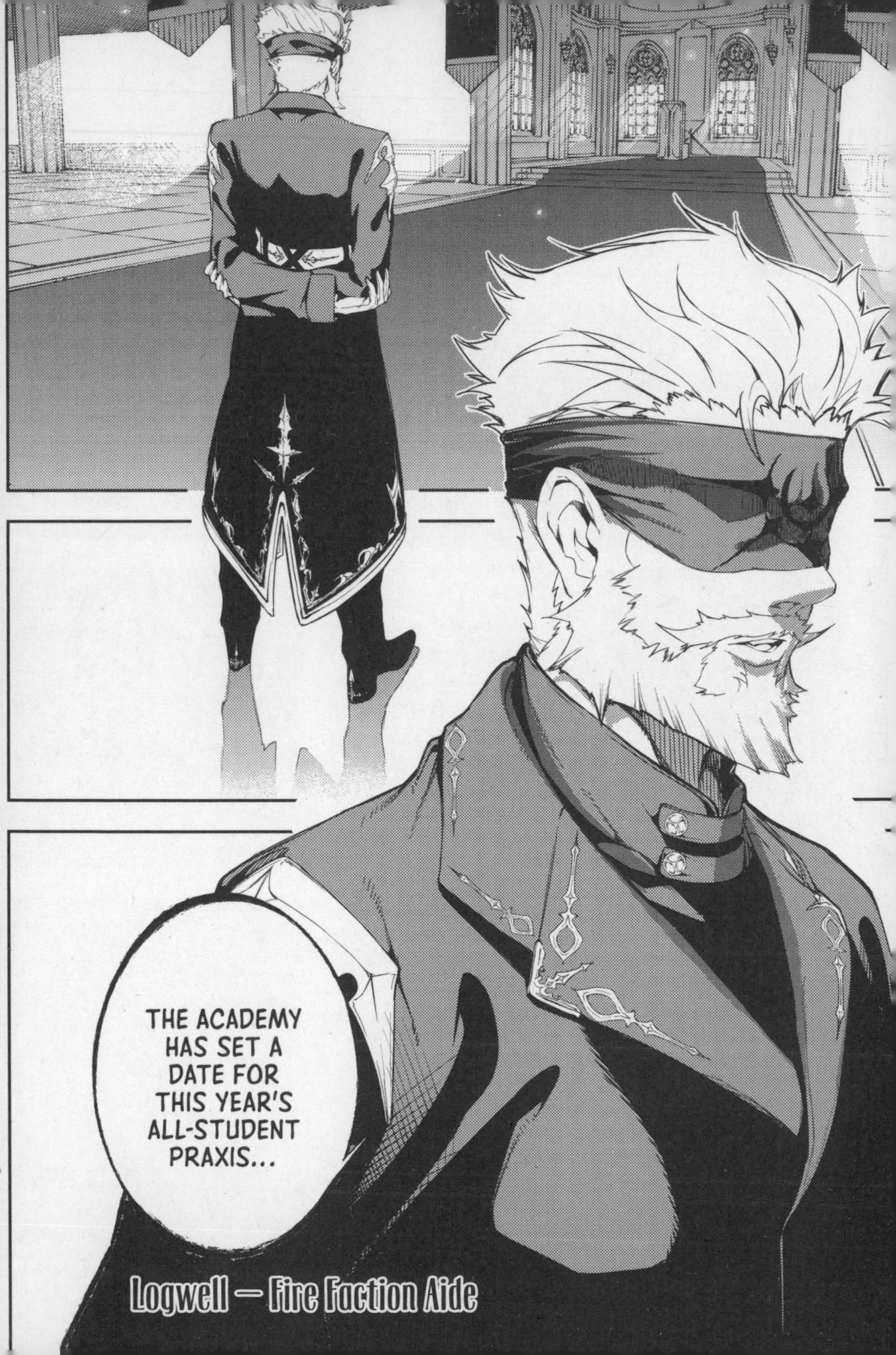
THE ACADEMY HAS SET A DATE FOR THIS YEAR'S ALL-STUDENT PRAXIS...
Logwell — Fire Faction Aide

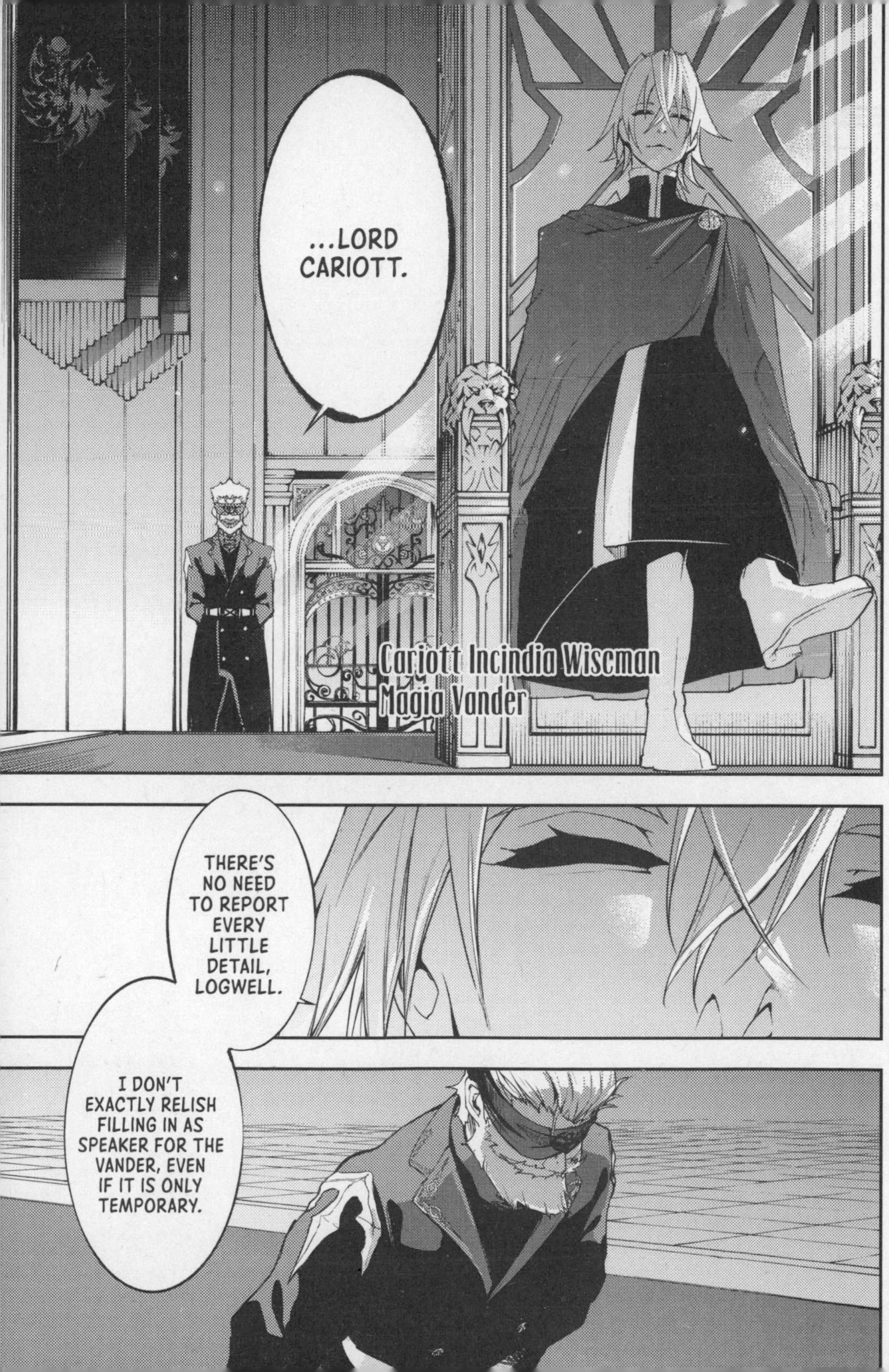
...LORD CARIOTT.
Cariott Incindia Wiscman
Magia Vander
THERE'S NO NEED TO REPORT EVERY LITTLE DETAIL, LOGWELL.
I DON'T EXACTLY RELISH FILLING IN AS SPEAKER FOR THE VANDER, EVEN IF IT IS ONLY TEMPORARY.

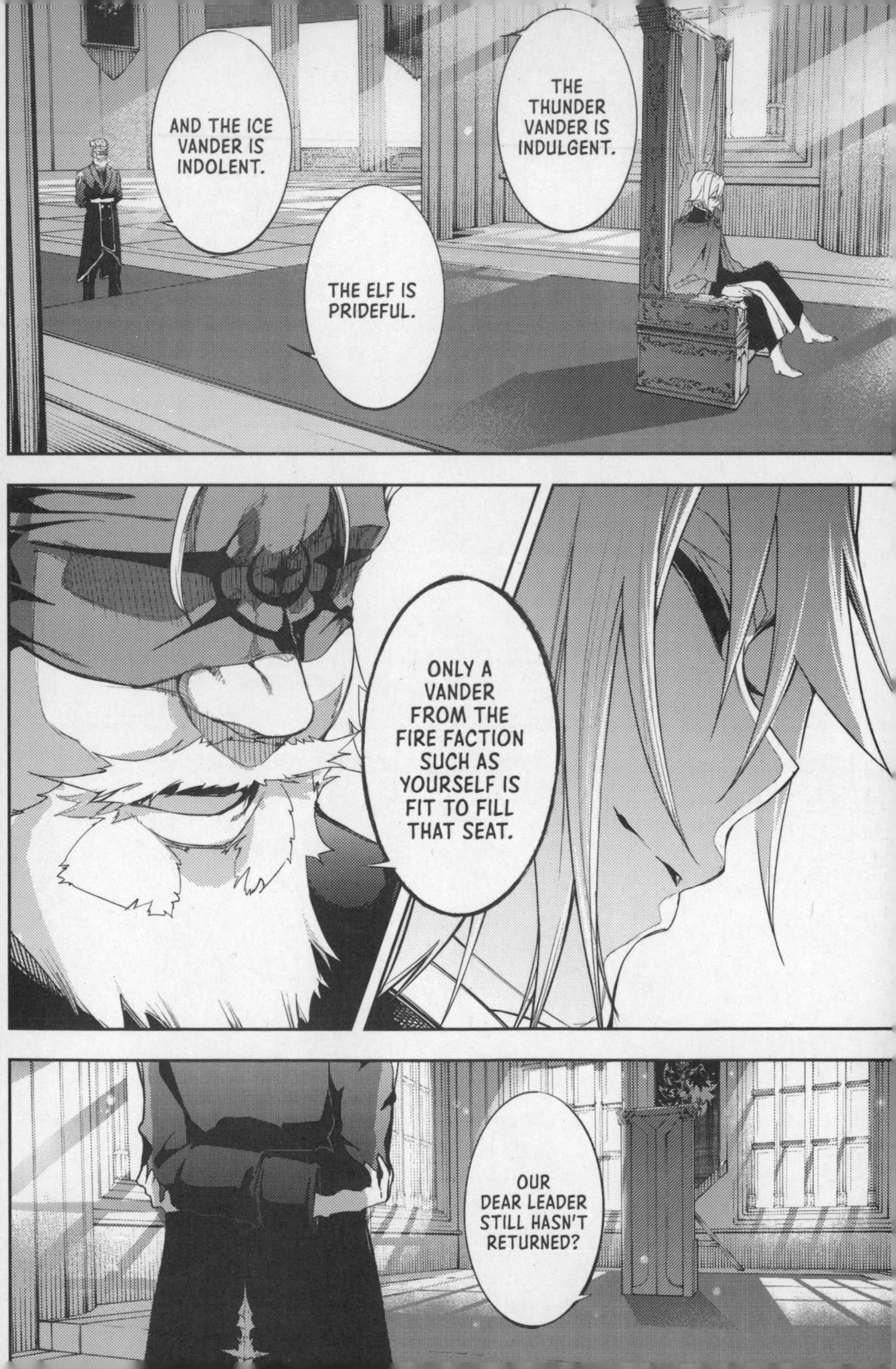
THE THUNDER VANDER IS INDULGENT.
THE ELF IS PRIDEFUL.
AND THE ICE VANDER IS INDOLENT.
ONLY A VANDER FROM THE FIRE FACTION SUCH AS YOURSELF IS FIT TO FILL THAT SEAT.
OUR DEAR LEADER STILL HASN'T RETURNED?

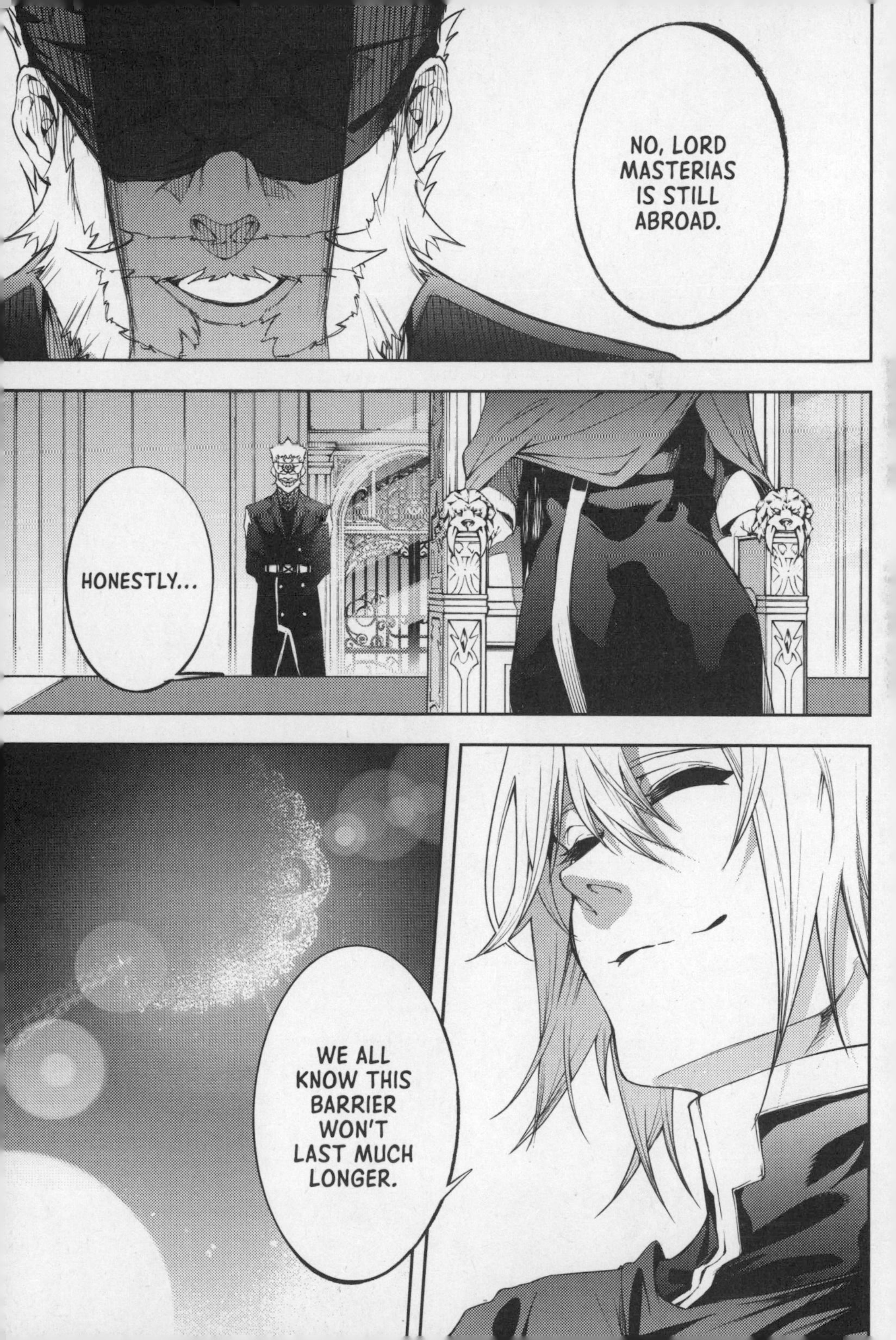
NO, LORD MASTERIAS IS STILL ABROAD.
HONESTLY...
WE ALL KNOW THIS BARRIER WON'T LAST MUCH LONGER.

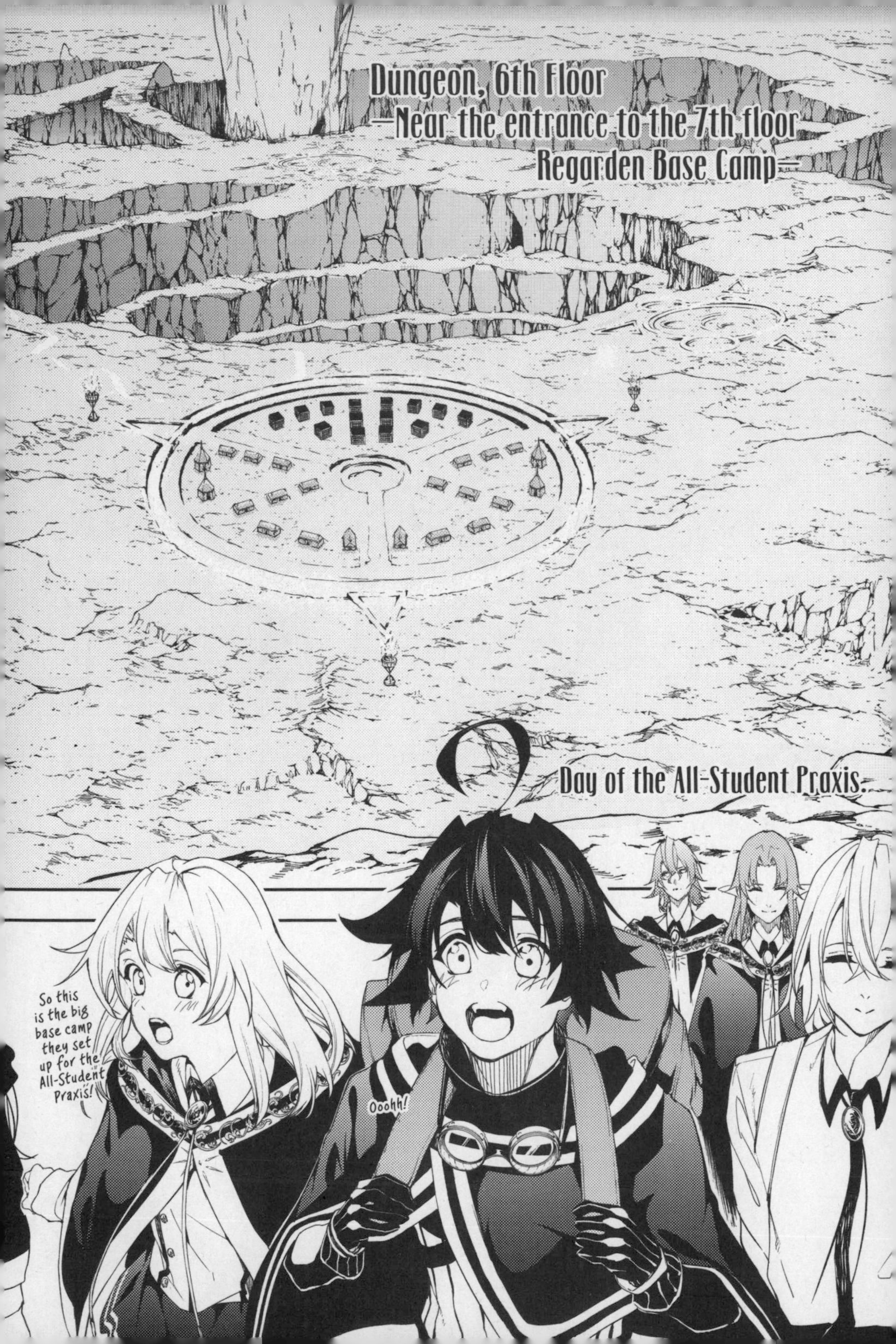
Dungeon, 6th Floor
—Near the entrance to the 7th floor
Regarden Base Camp—
Day of the All-Student Praxis...
Ooohh!
So this is the big base camp they set up for the All-Student Praxis!

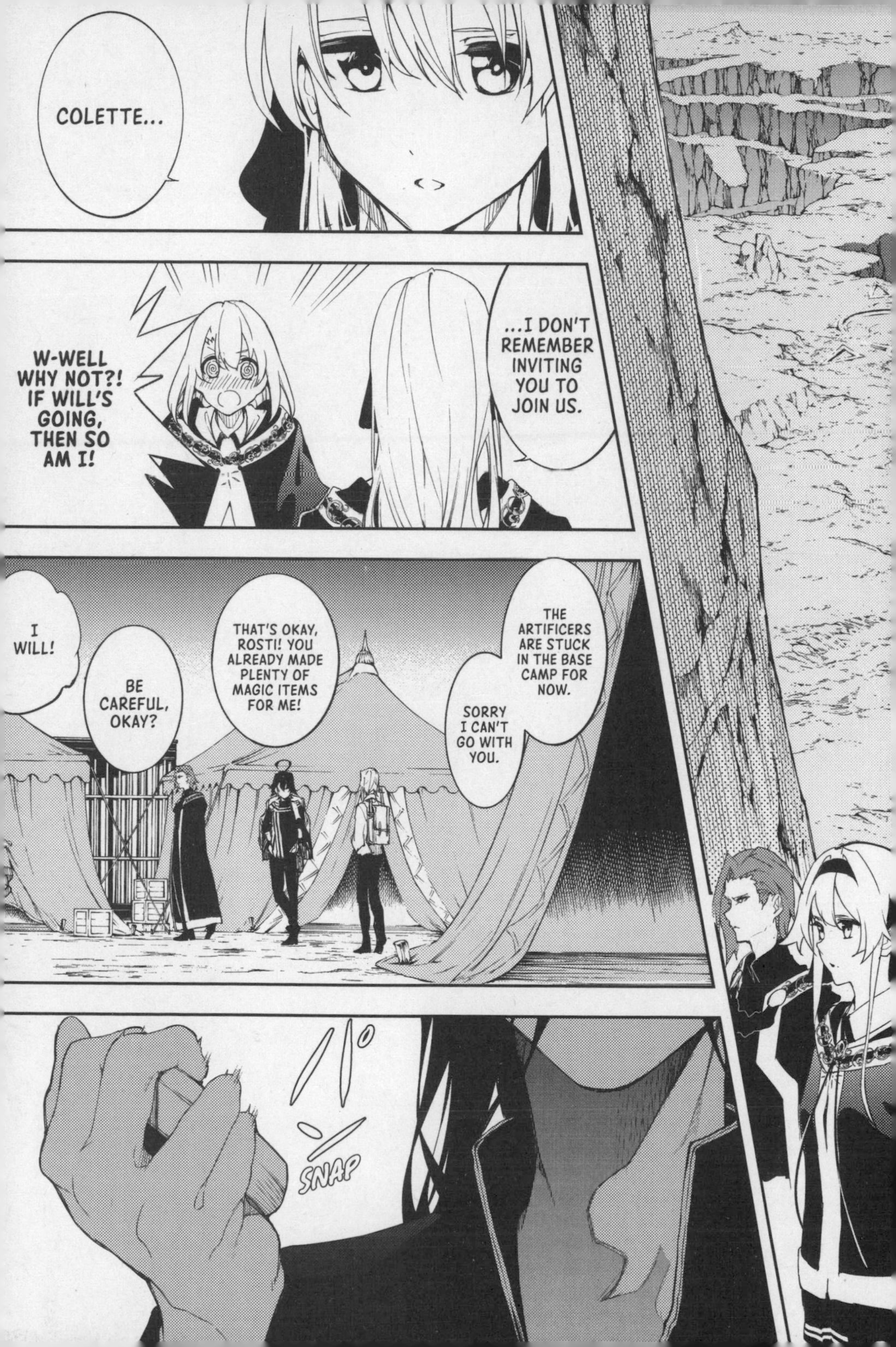
COLETTE...
...I DON'T REMEMBER INVITING YOU TO JOIN US.
W-WELL WHY NOT?! IF WILL'S GOING, THEN SO AM I!
THE ARTIFICERS ARE STUCK IN THE BASE CAMP FOR NOW.
SORRY I CAN'T GO WITH YOU.
THAT'S OKAY, ROSTI! YOU ALREADY MADE PLENTY OF MAGIC ITEMS FOR ME!
BE CAREFUL, OKAY?
I WILL!
SNAP

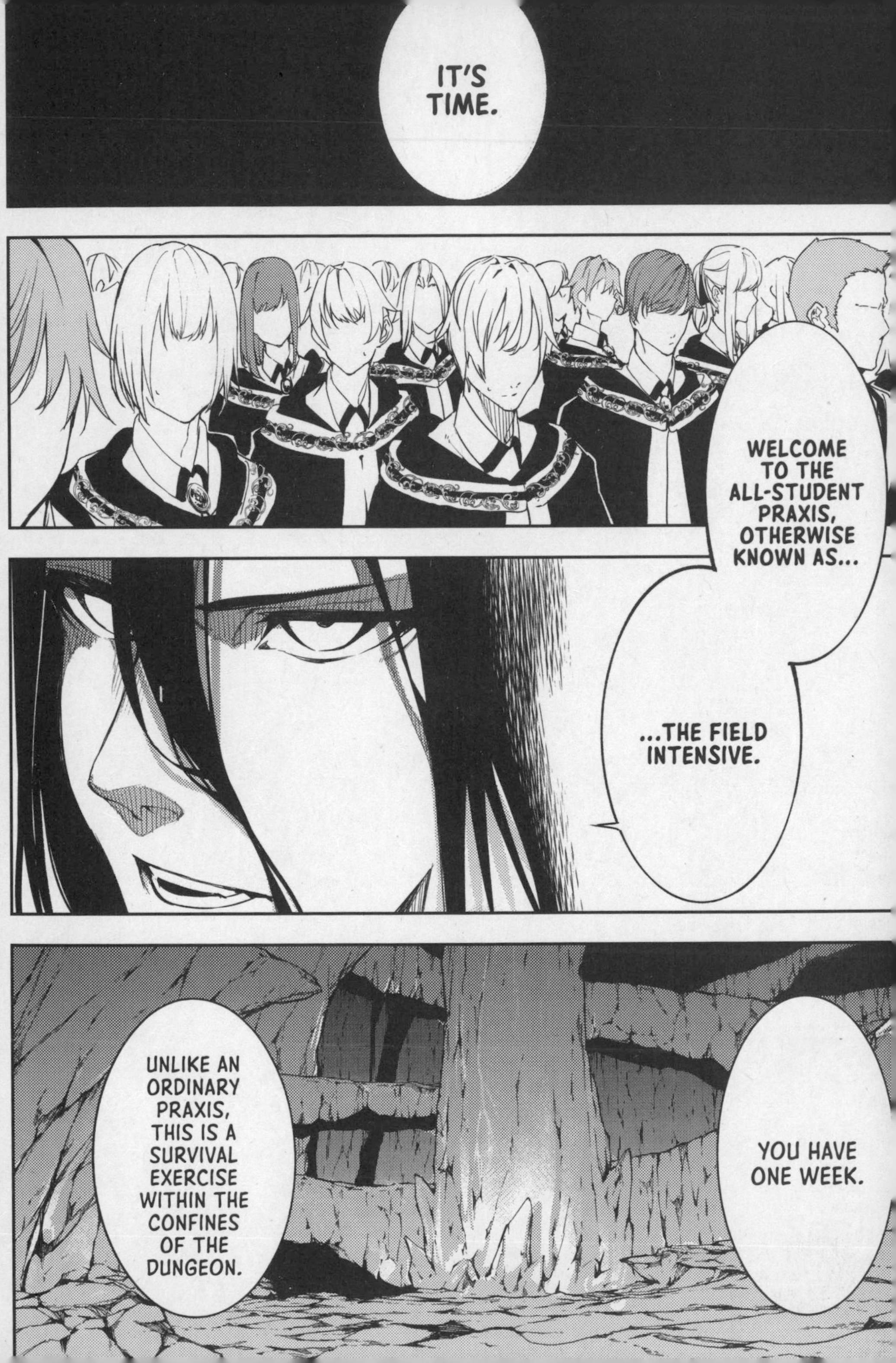
IT'S TIME.
WELCOME TO THE ALL-STUDENT PRAXIS, OTHERWISE KNOWN AS...
...THE FIELD INTENSIVE.
YOU HAVE ONE WEEK.
UNLIKE AN ORDINARY PRAXIS, THIS IS A SURVIVAL EXERCISE WITHIN THE CONFINES OF THE DUNGEON.

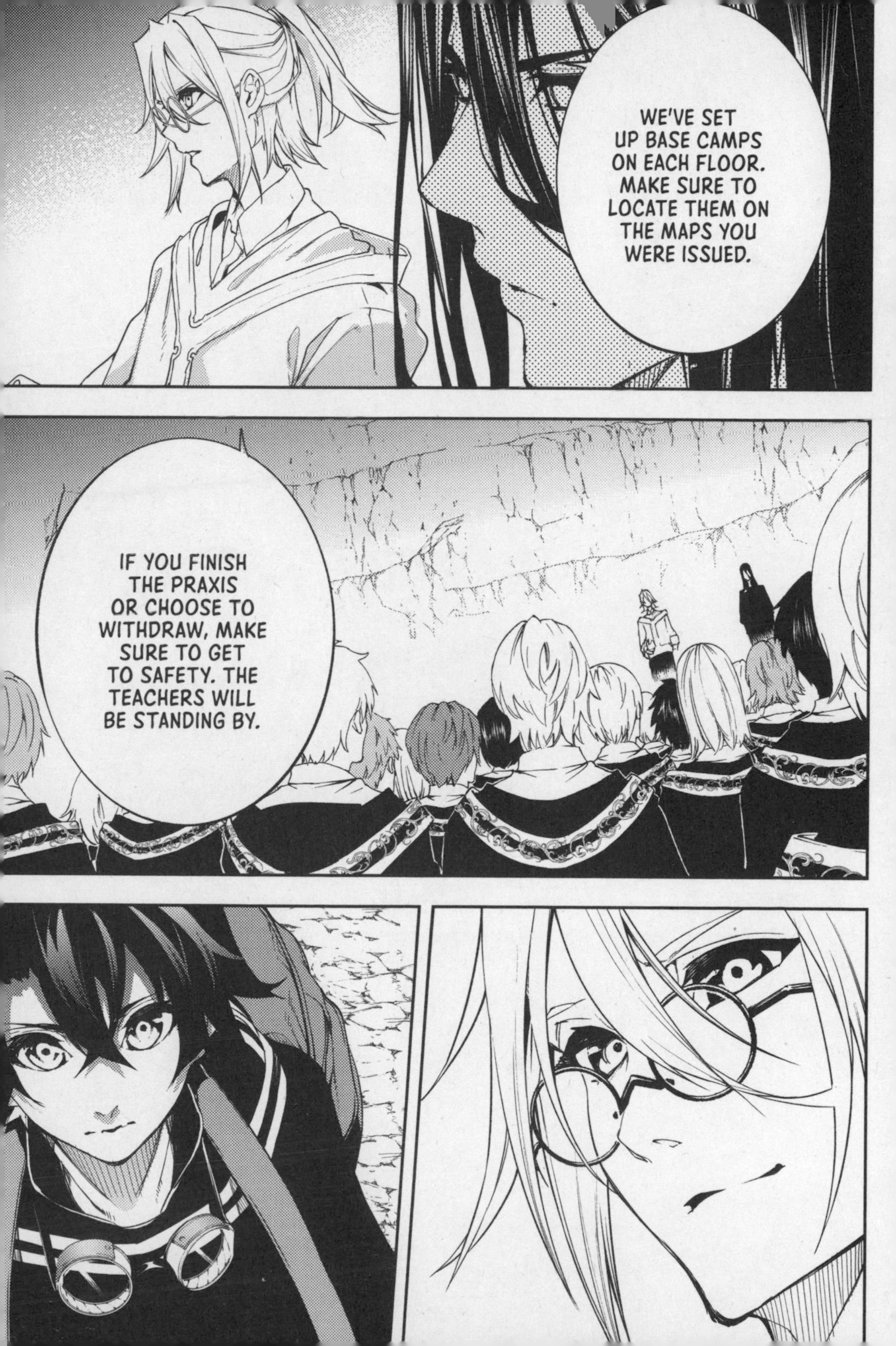
WE'VE SET UP BASE CAMPS ON EACH FLOOR. MAKE SURE TO LOCATE THEM ON THE MAPS YOU WERE ISSUED.
IF YOU FINISH THE PRAXIS OR CHOOSE TO WITHDRAW, MAKE SURE TO GET TO SAFETY. THE TEACHERS WILL BE STANDING BY.

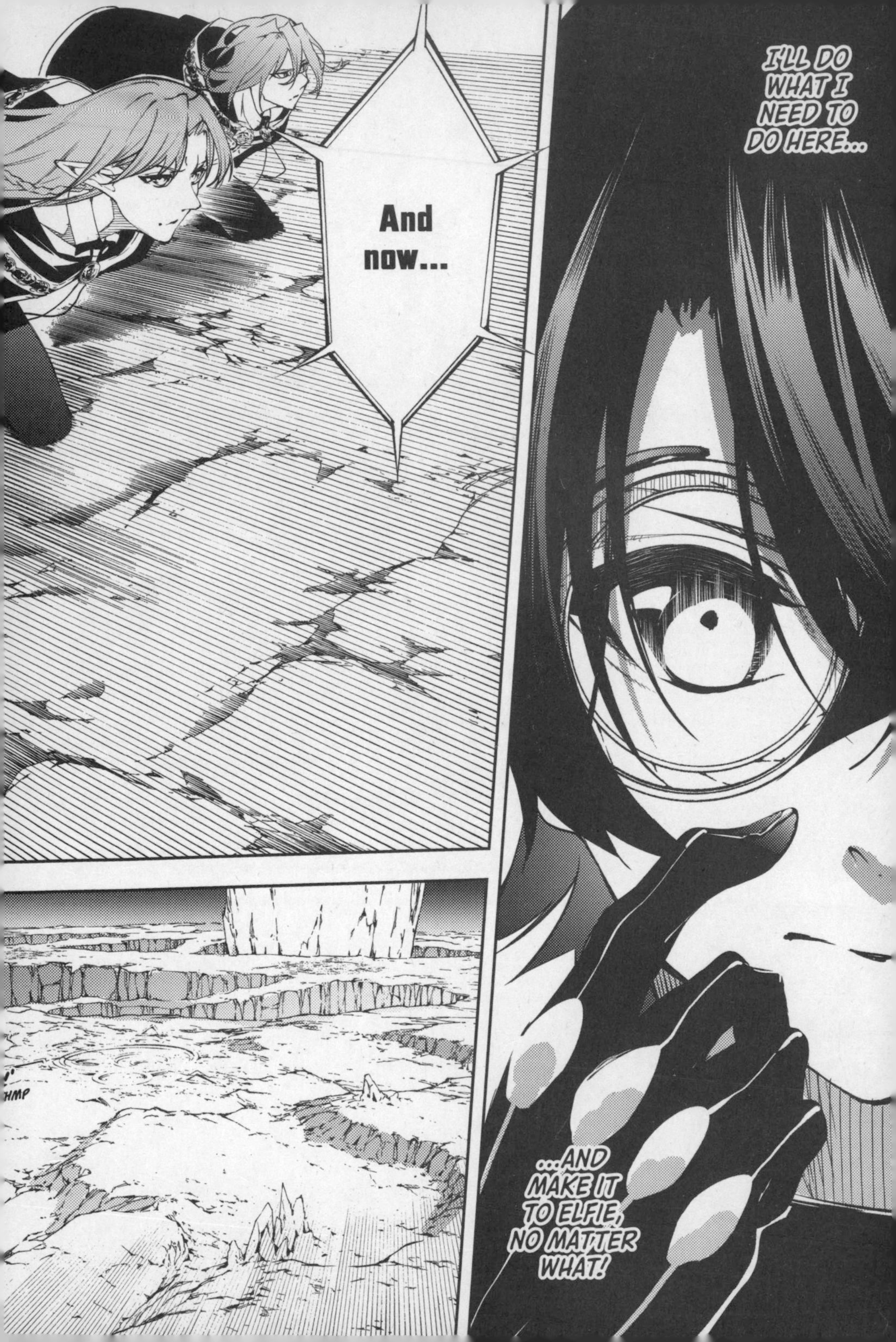
I'LL DO WHAT I NEED TO DO HERE...
...AND MAKE IT TO ELFIE, NO MATTER WHAT!
And now...
THMP

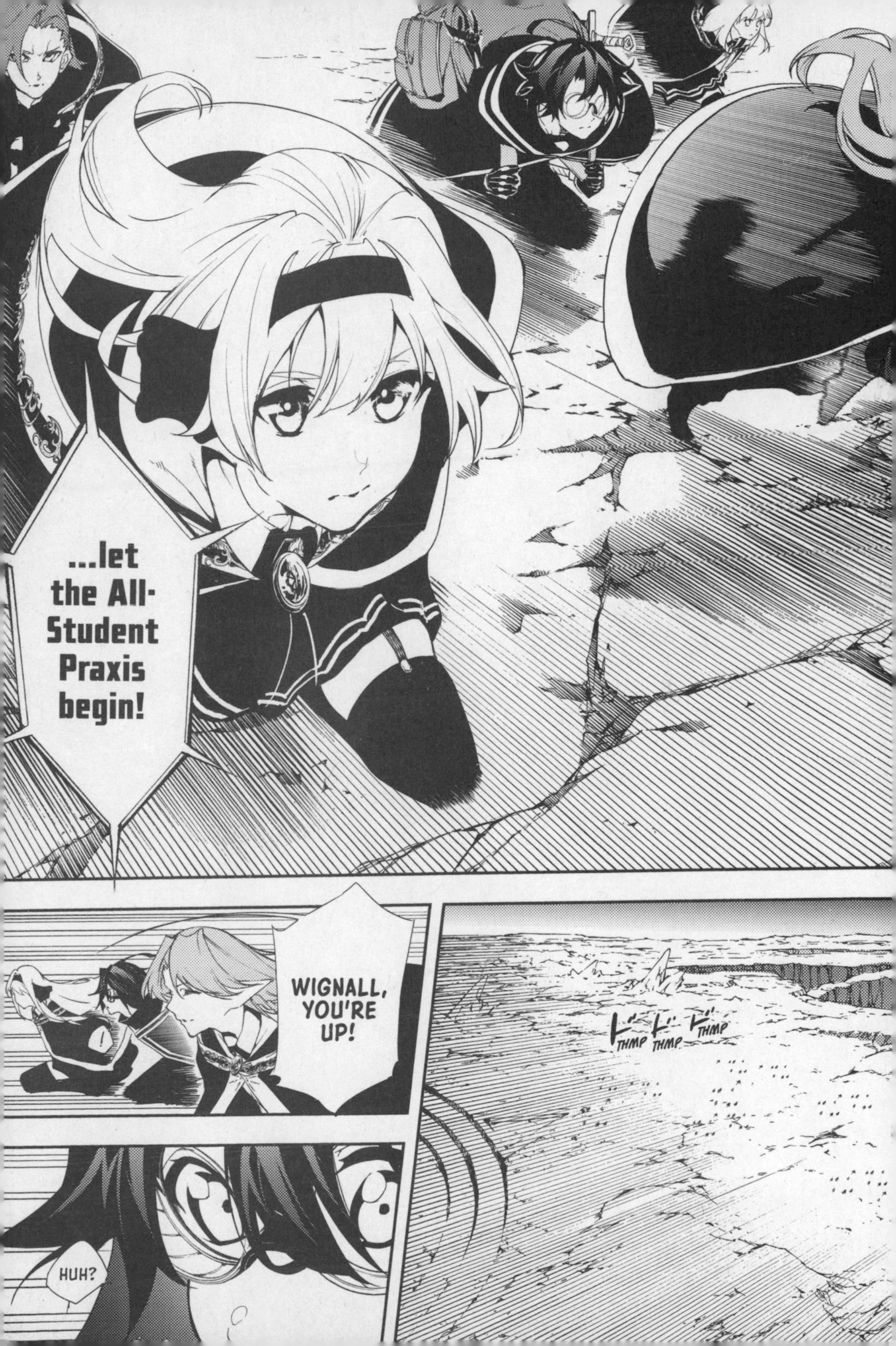
...let the All-Student Praxis begin!
ド THMP
ド THMP
ド THMP
WIGNALL, YOU'RE UP!
!
HUH?

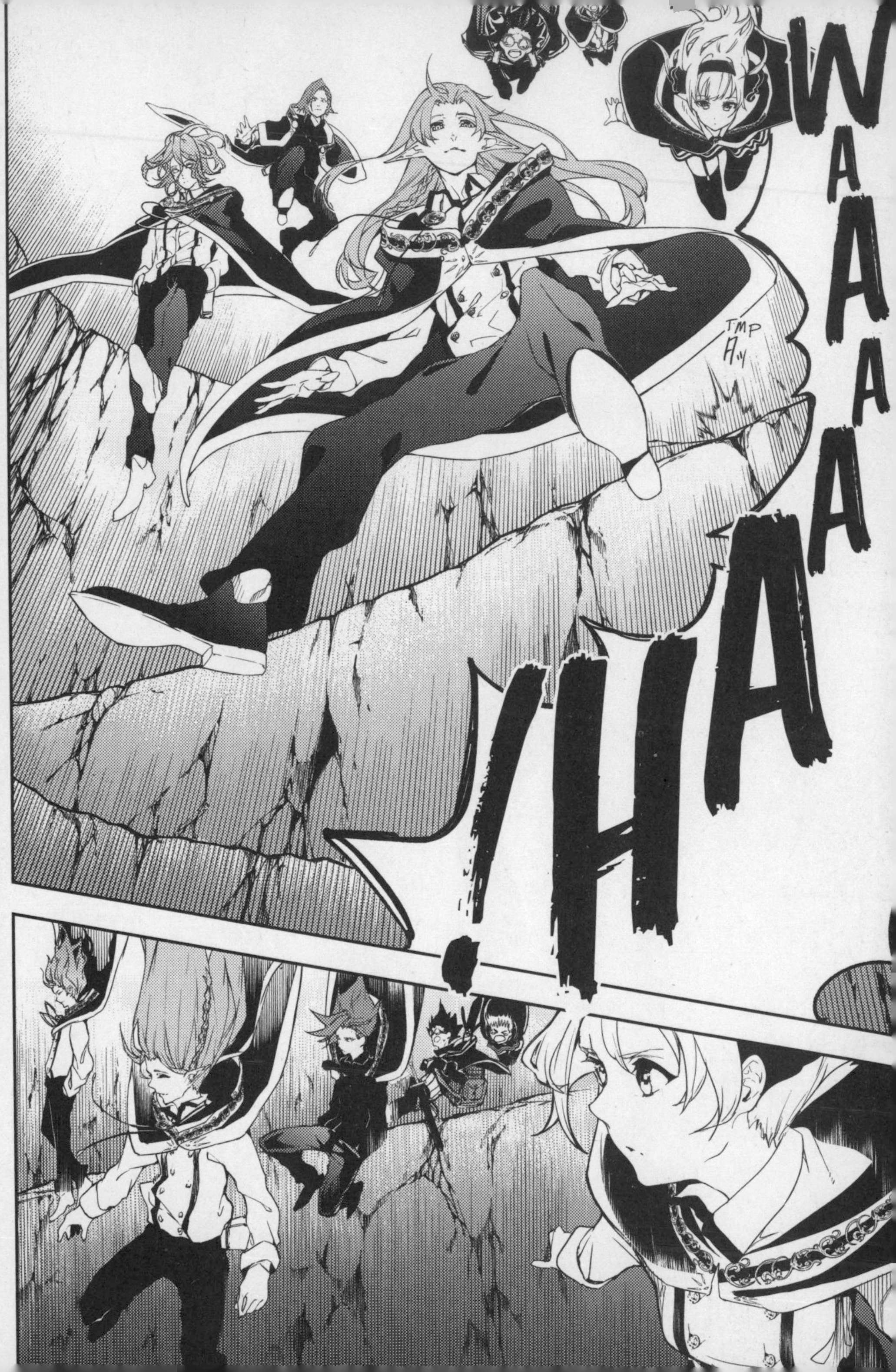
WAAAAAH!!
TMP

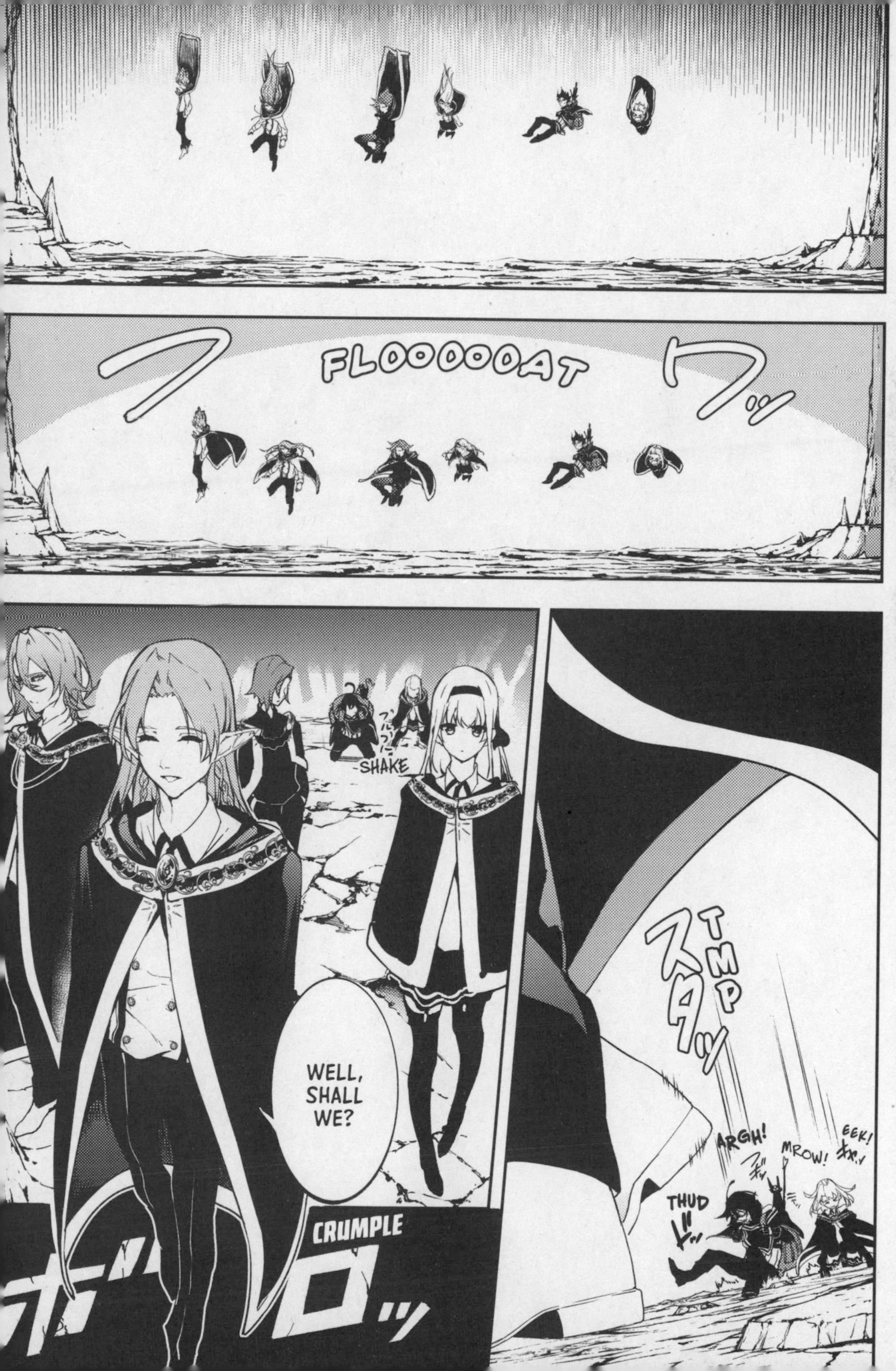

FLOOOOOAT
TMP
EEK!
MROW!
ARGH!
THUD
SHAKE
WELL, SHALL WE?
CRUMPLE

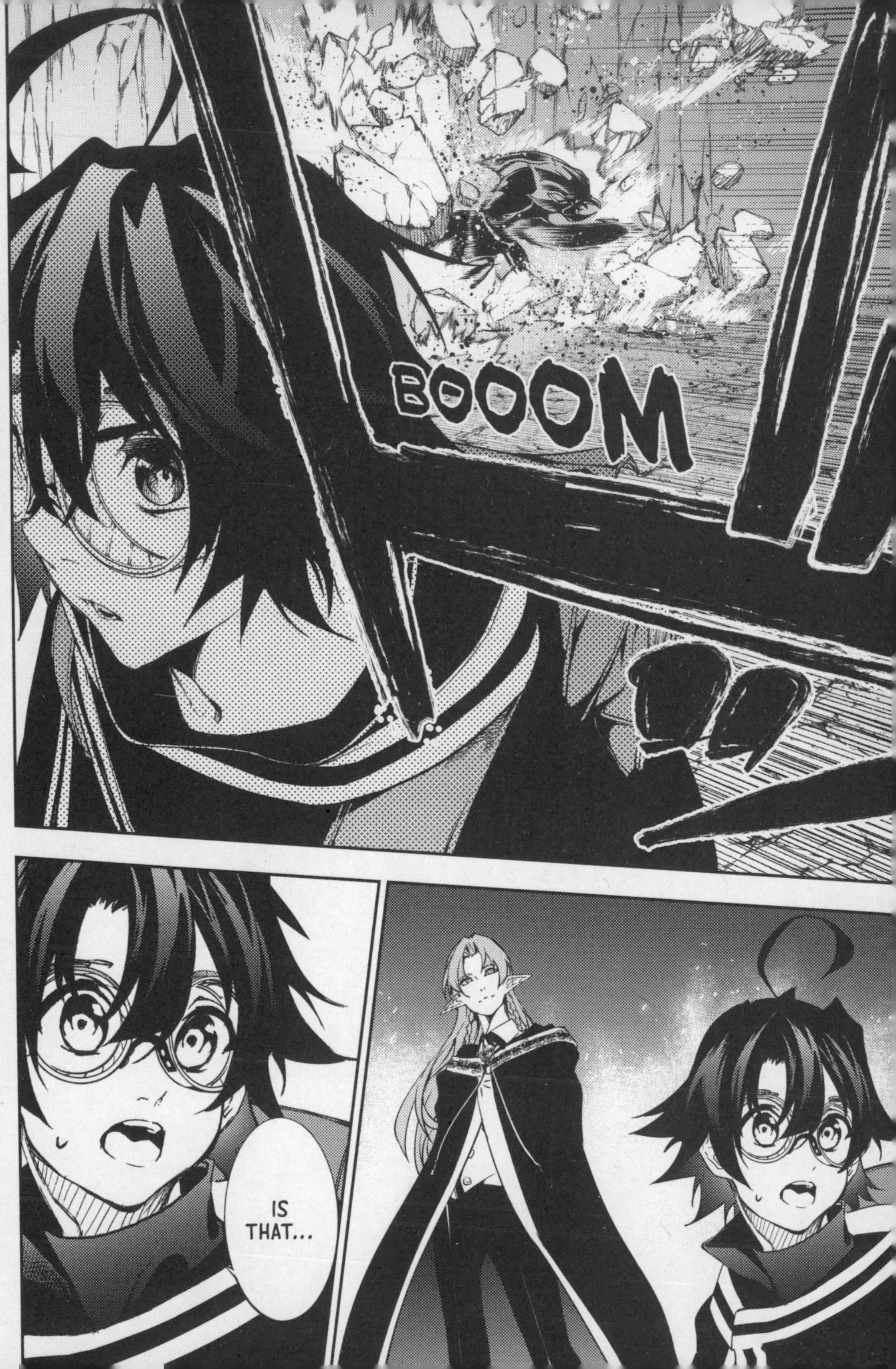
BOOOM
IS THAT...

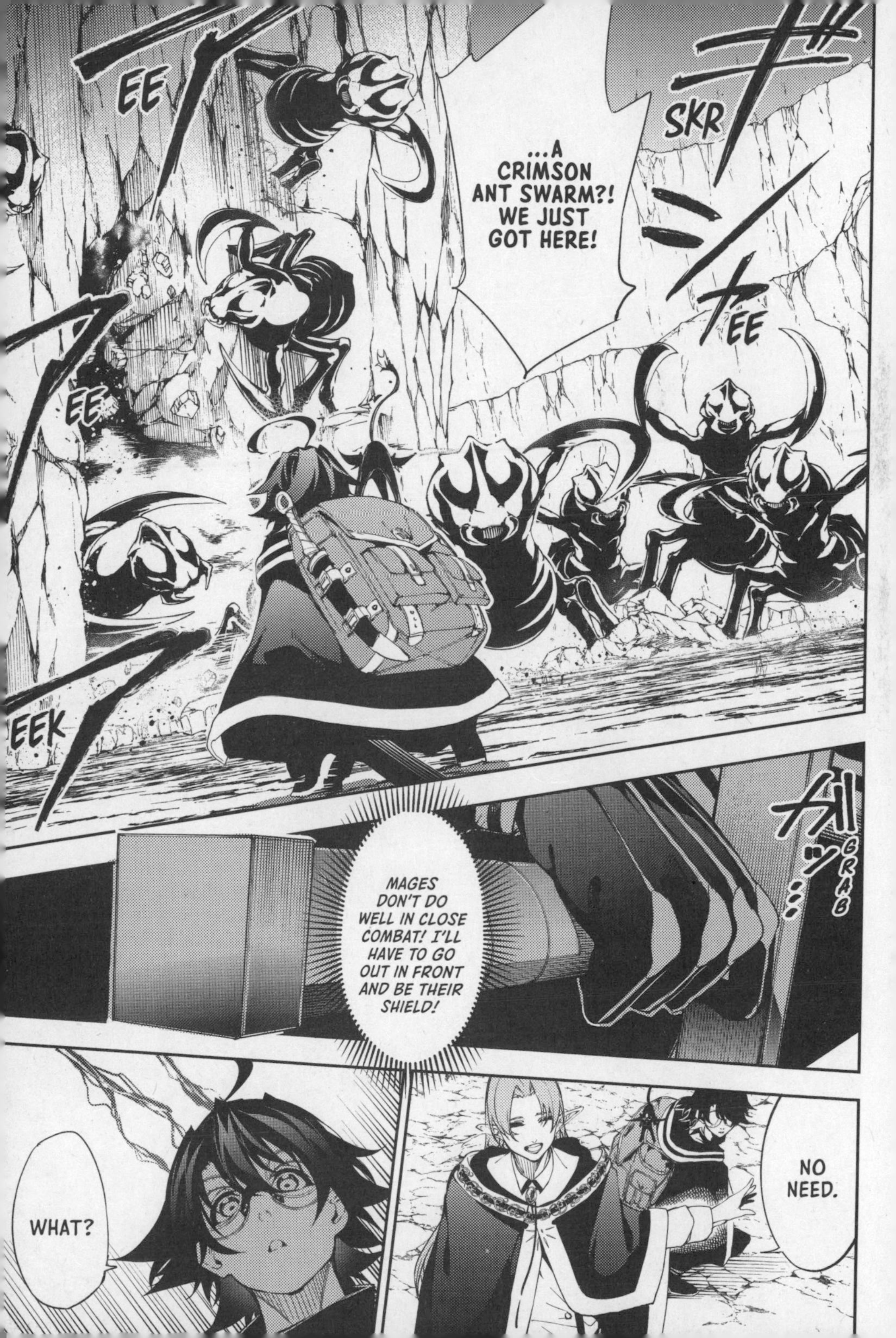
SKR
...A CRIMSON ANT SWARM?! WE JUST GOT HERE!
EE
EE
EE
EEK
GRAB
MAGES DON'T DO WELL IN CLOSE COMBAT! I'LL HAVE TO GO OUT IN FRONT AND BE THEIR SHIELD!
NO NEED.
WHAT?

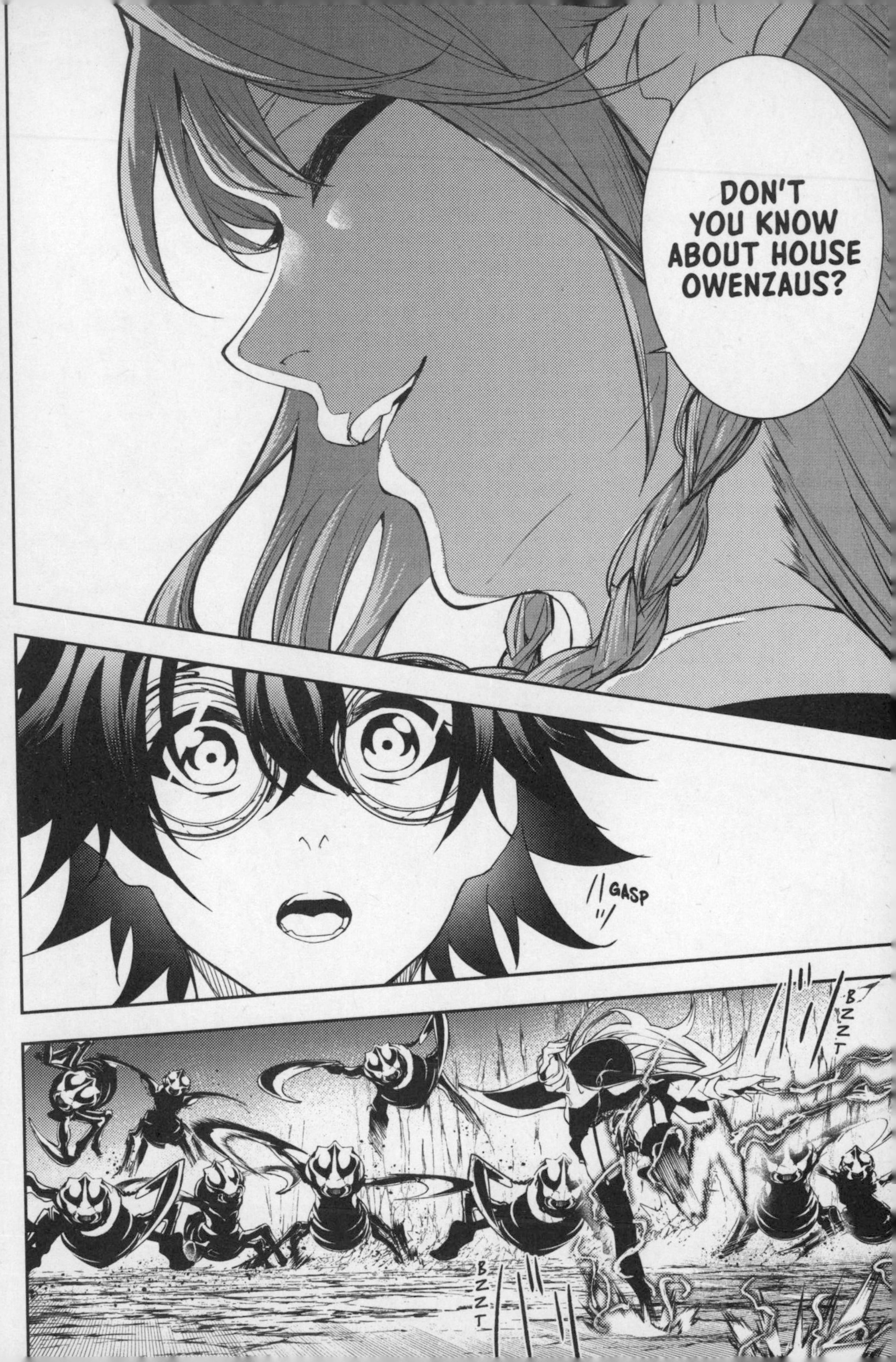
DON'T YOU KNOW ABOUT HOUSE OWENZAUS?
GASP
BZZT
BZZT

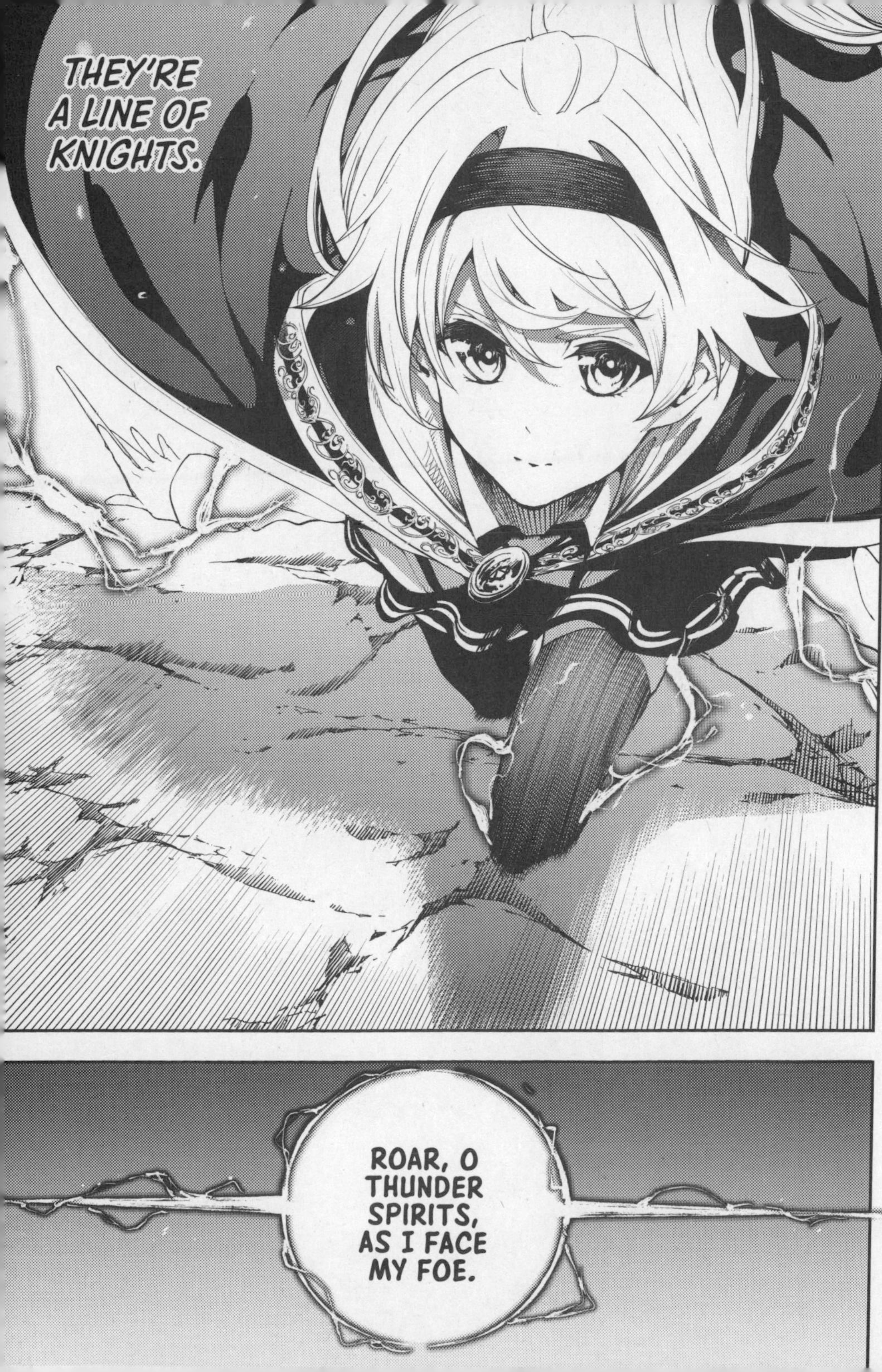
THEY'RE A LINE OF KNIGHTS.
ROAR, O THUNDER SPIRITS, AS I FACE MY FOE.

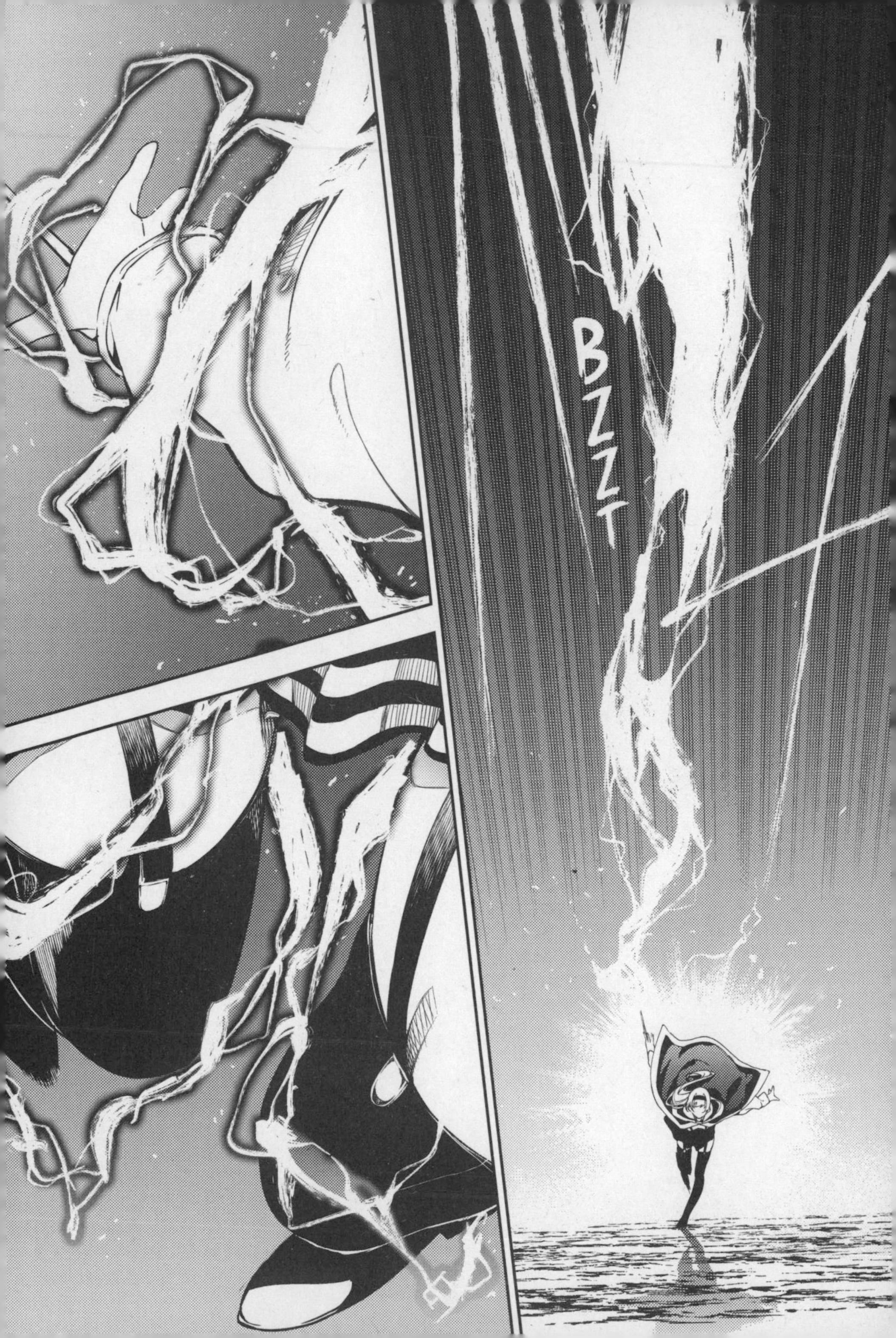
BZZT

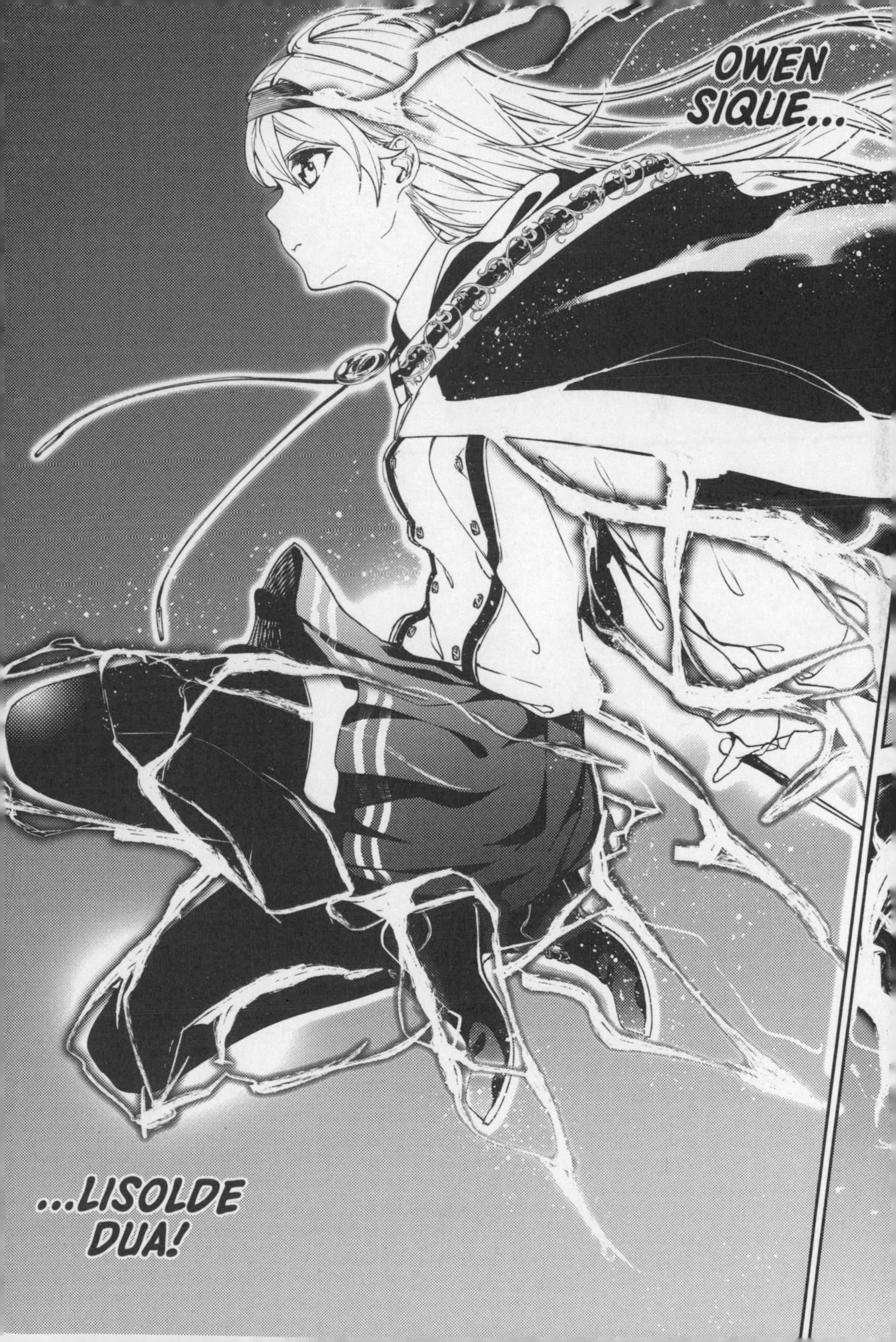
OWEN SIQUE...
...LISOLDE DUA!

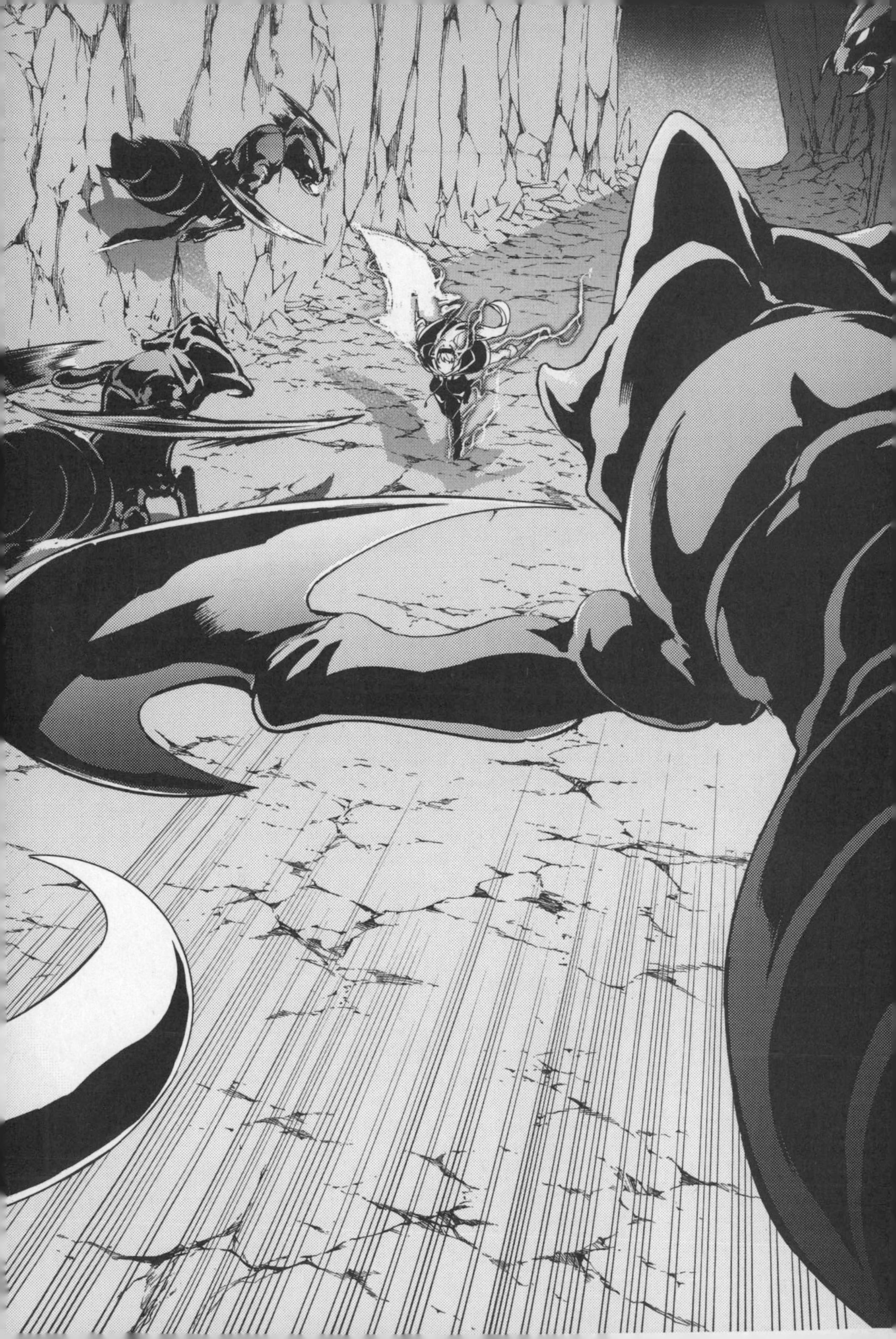

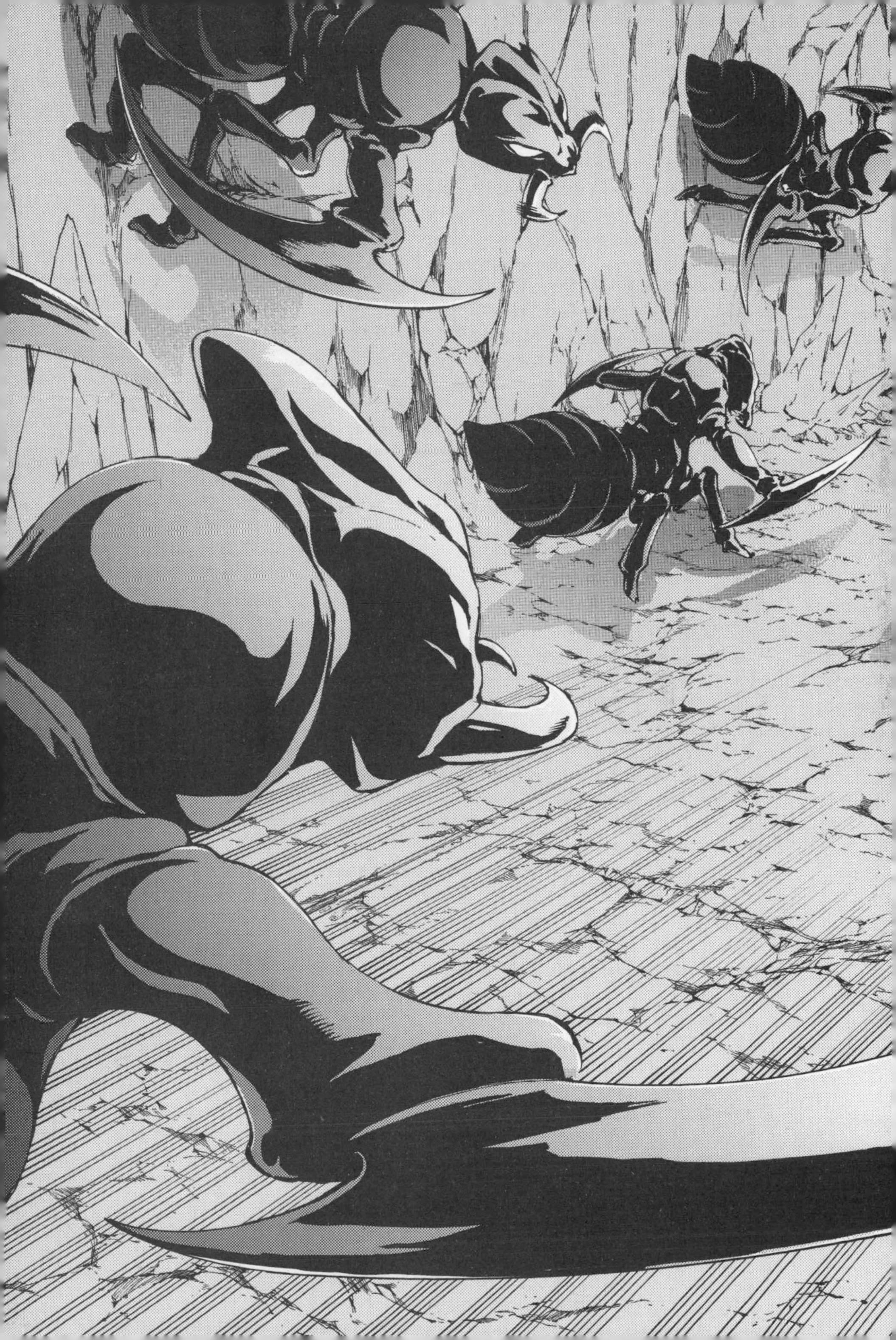

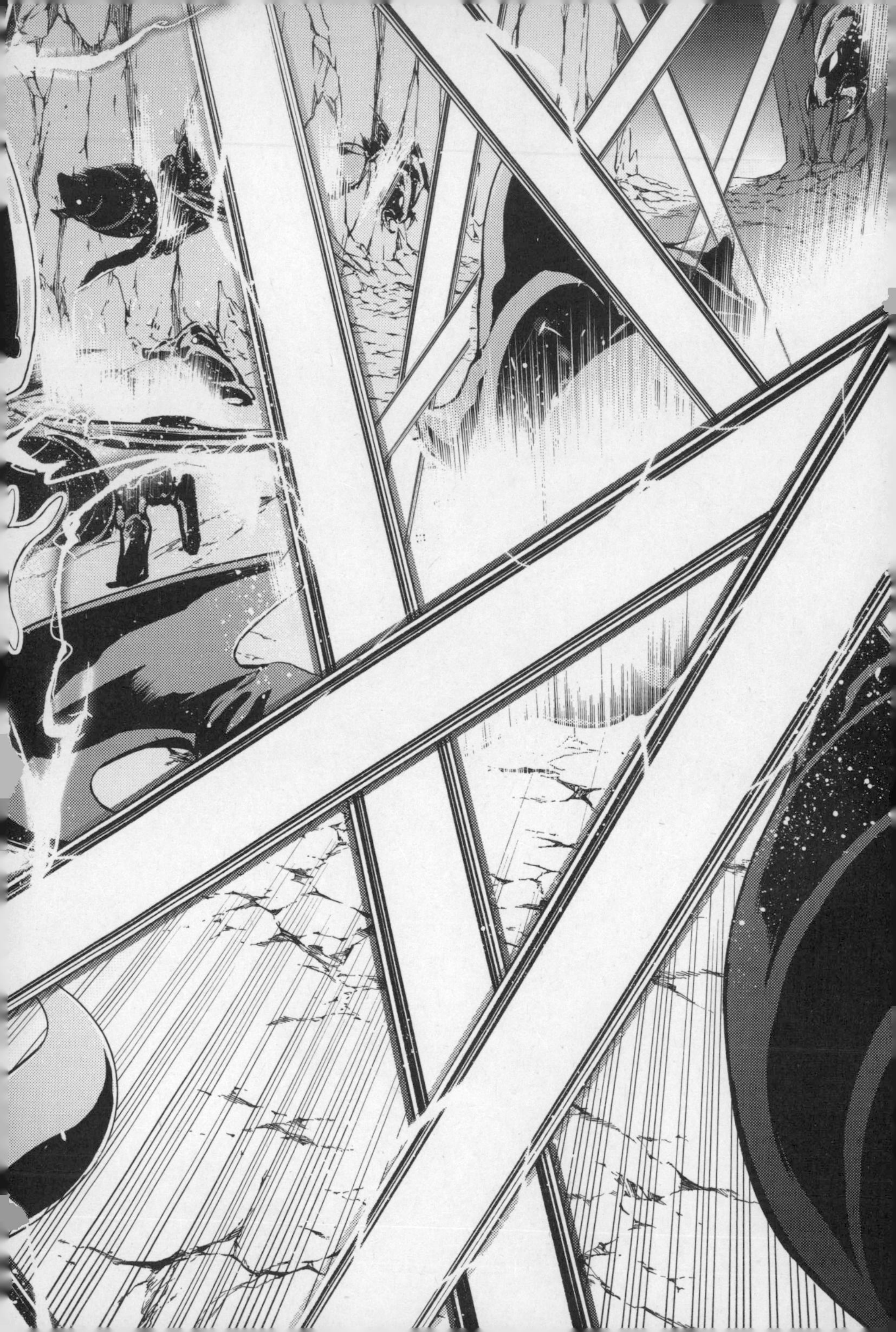

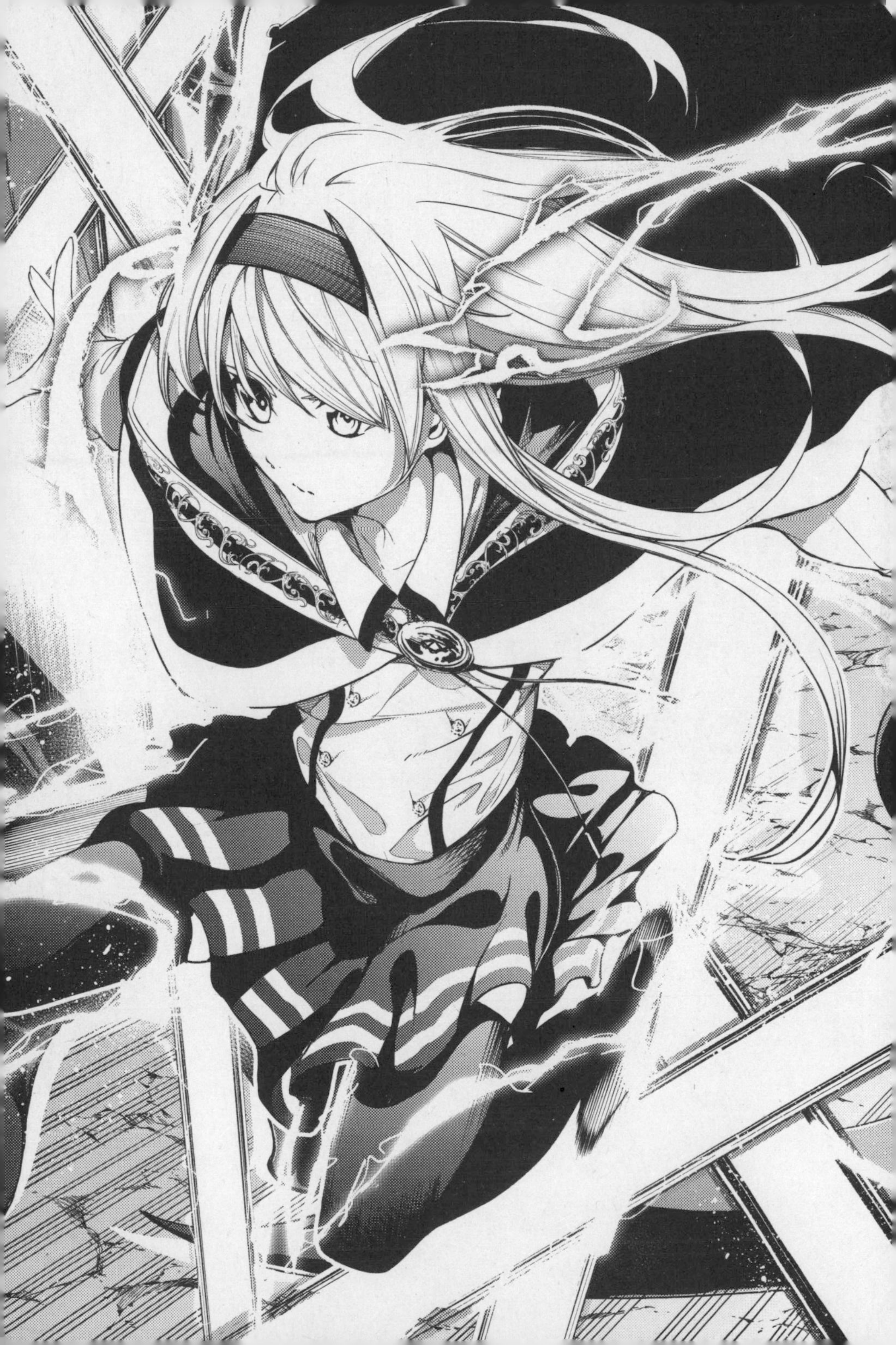

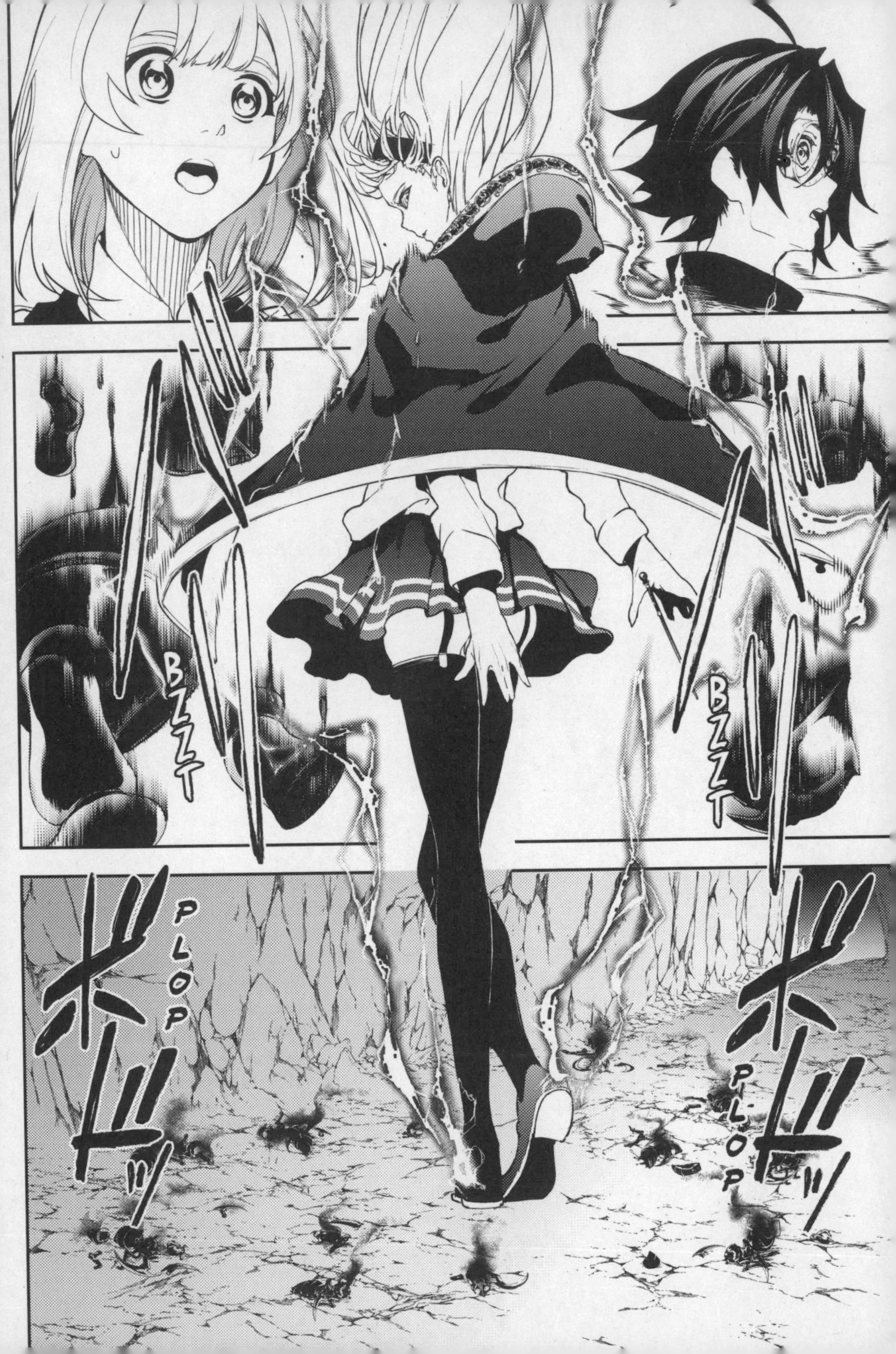
BZZT
BZZT
PLOP
PLOP

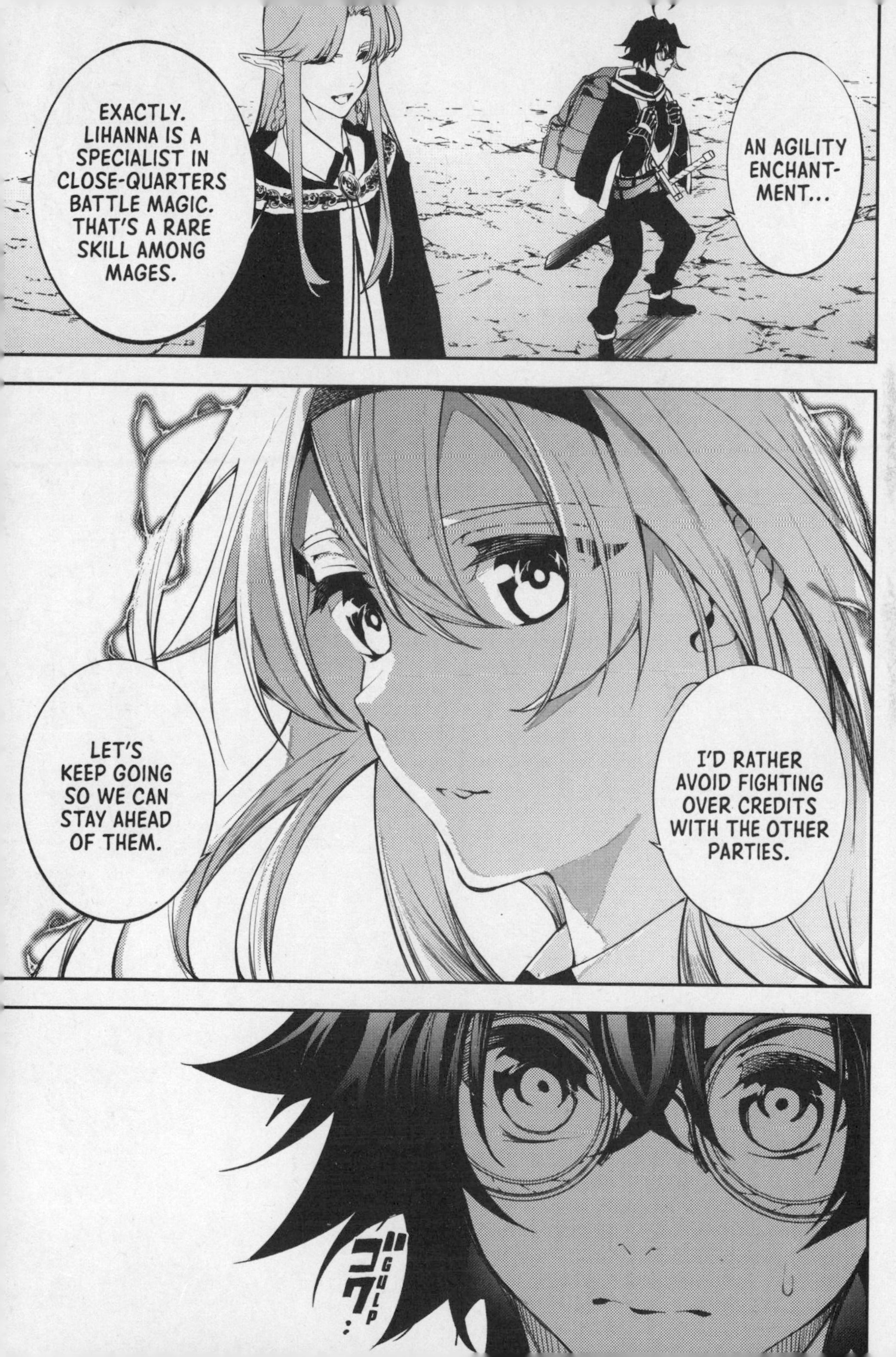
AN AGILITY ENCHANT-MENT...
EXACTLY. LIHANNA IS A SPECIALIST IN CLOSE-QUARTERS BATTLE MAGIC. THAT'S A RARE SKILL AMONG MAGES.
I'D RATHER AVOID FIGHTING OVER CREDITS WITH THE OTHER PARTIES.
LET'S KEEP GOING SO WE CAN STAY AHEAD OF THEM.
GULP

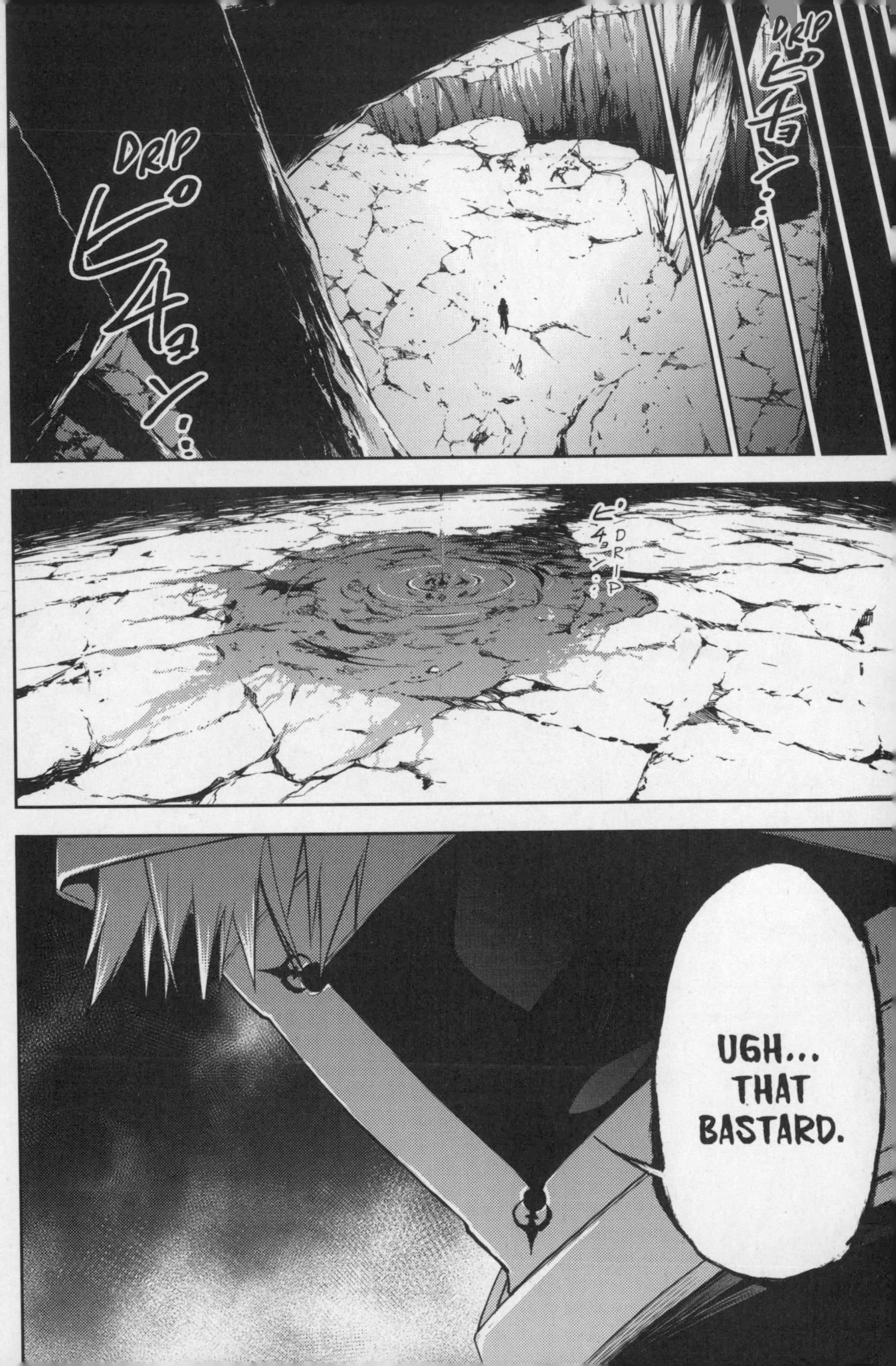
DRIP
ピチョン…
DRIP
ピチョン…
DRIP
ピチョン…
UGH... THAT BASTARD.

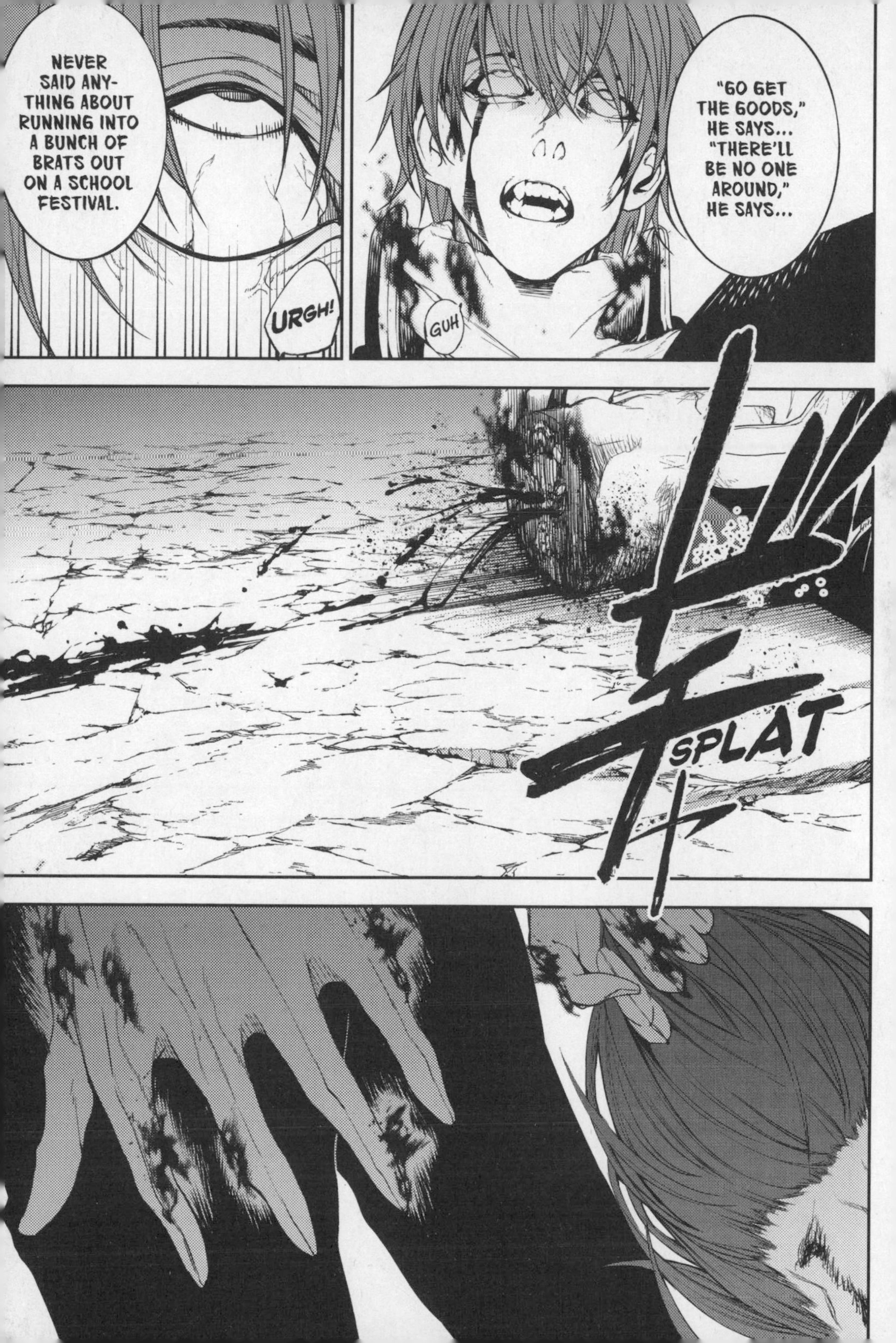
"GO GET THE GOODS," HE SAYS... "THERE'LL BE NO ONE AROUND," HE SAYS...
GUH
NEVER SAID ANY-THING ABOUT RUNNING INTO A BUNCH OF BRATS OUT ON A SCHOOL FESTIVAL.
URGH!
SPLAT

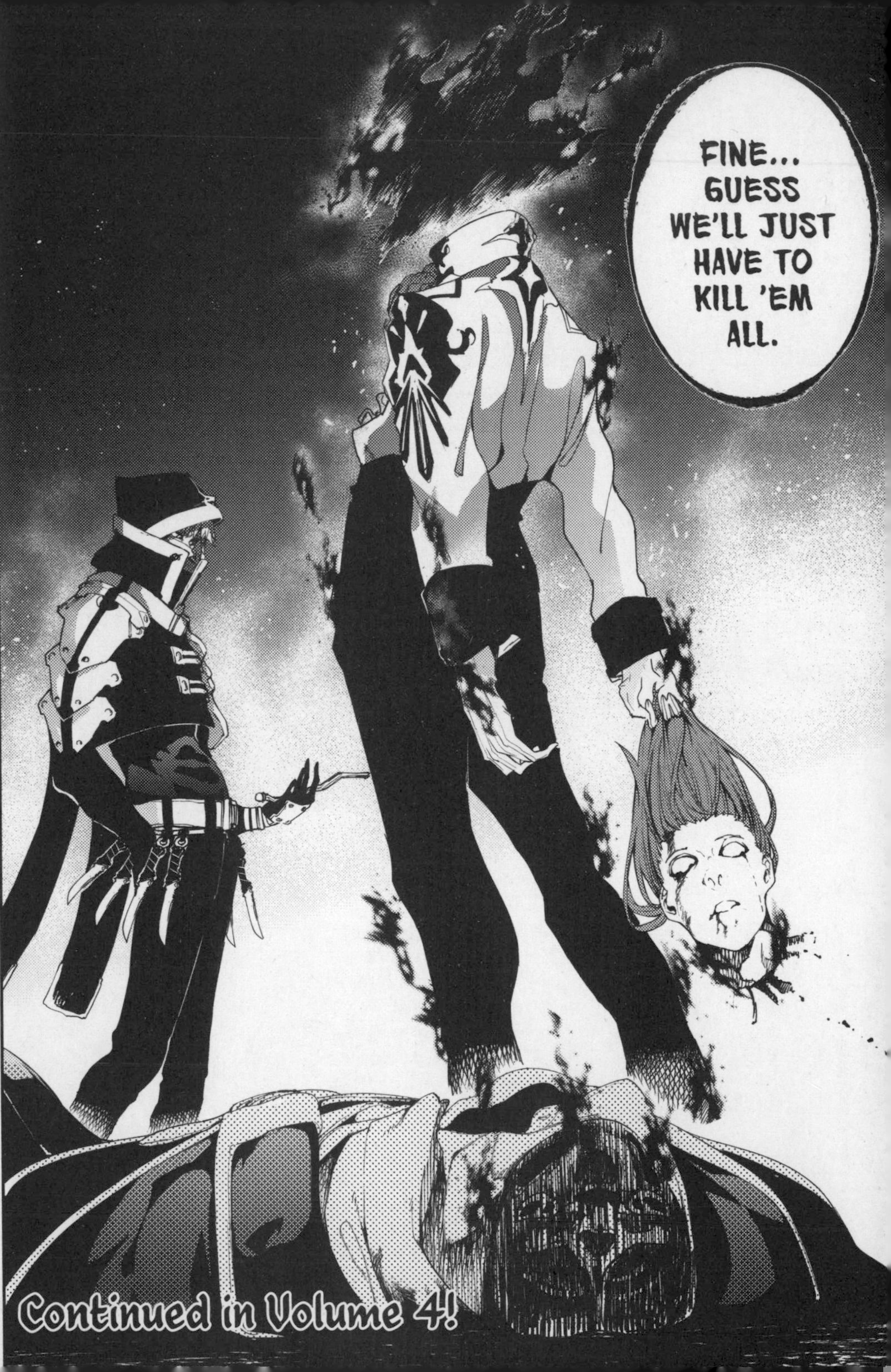
FINE... GUESS WE'LL JUST HAVE TO KILL 'EM ALL.
Continued in Volume 4!

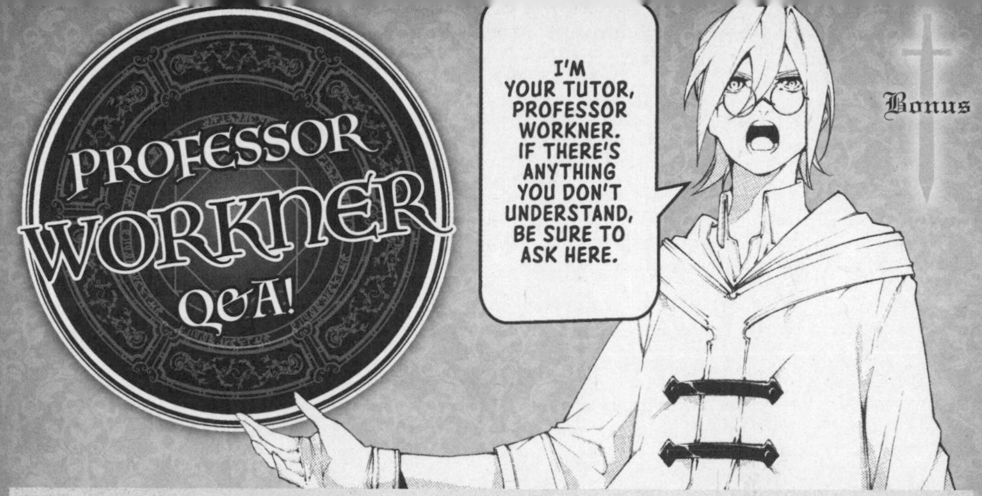
PROFESSOR WORKNER Q&A!
I'M YOUR TUTOR, PROFESSOR WORKNER. IF THERE'S ANYTHING YOU DON'T UNDERSTAND, BE SURE TO ASK HERE.

Q. COULD YOU TALK A LITTLE BIT ABOUT THE TOWER AND THE ADVANCEMENT PROCESS?

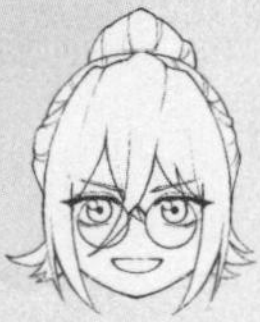

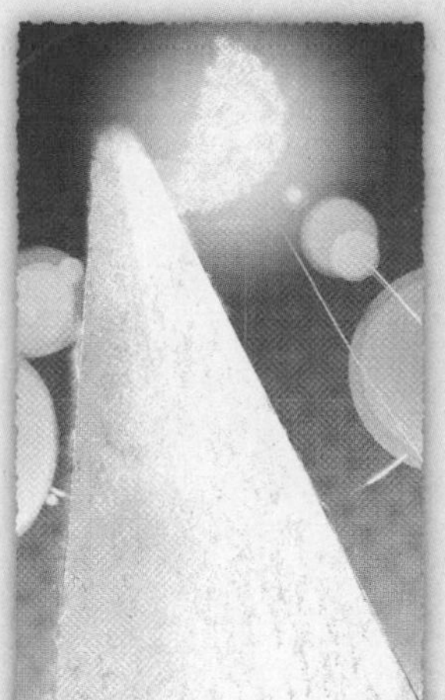

Mercedes Caulis, also known as the Tower, serves a dual purpose. As the home of the Upper Institute, our highest seat of learning, the Tower stands at the forefront of magical research. It also serves as a fortress in defense of our world. The mighty Magia Vander reside in the upper levels of the Tower.

To advance to the Upper Institute, students at Regarden Magical Academy must either invent a new spell or earn at least 7,200 credits. Those who succeed in advancing are recognized as High Mages, while Ascendants, or those who reach the highest floor of the Tower, earn the right to become a Magia Vander.

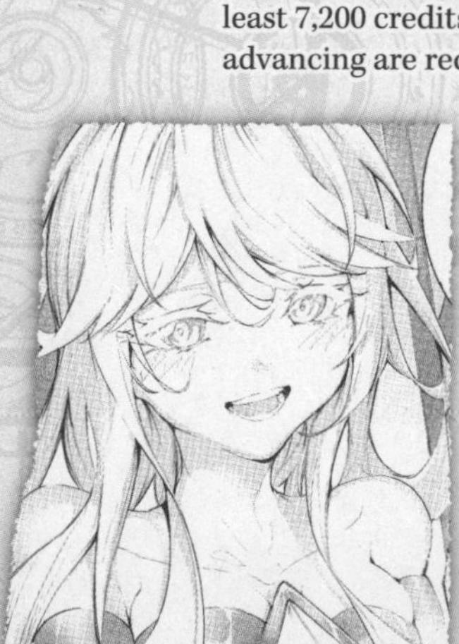

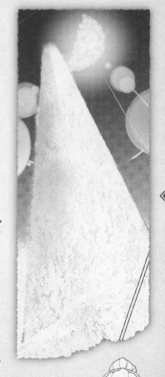

As in the case of a rare prodigy like Elfaria, students may be singled out for ascension while still enrolled at the academy. However, such cases are few and far between.

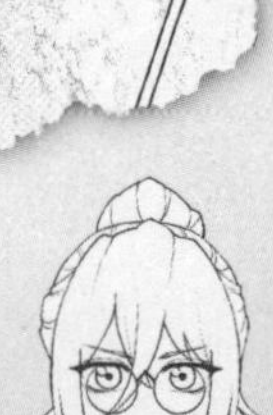

Q. HOW MANY CREDITS DOES THE ACADEMY OFFER, AND HOW ARE THEY DIVIDED UP?

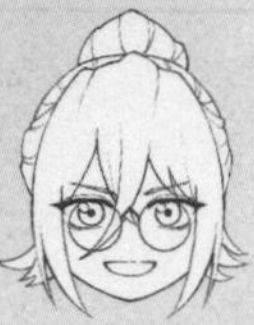

Students can earn a maximum of 12,000 credits, which are broken down as follows:
- Writing (written exams): 3,600
- Spellwork (magical exercises, demonstrations): 4,800
- Praxis (defeating dungeon monsters): 3,600

You would be correct in assuming that the reason more points are awarded for spellwork is to help the Upper Institute identify promising students. The Upper Institute is always on the lookout for mages with the most polished magical abilities to assist in their research.

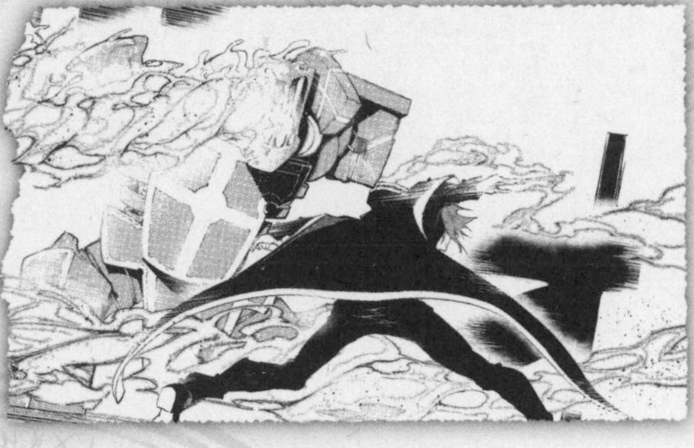

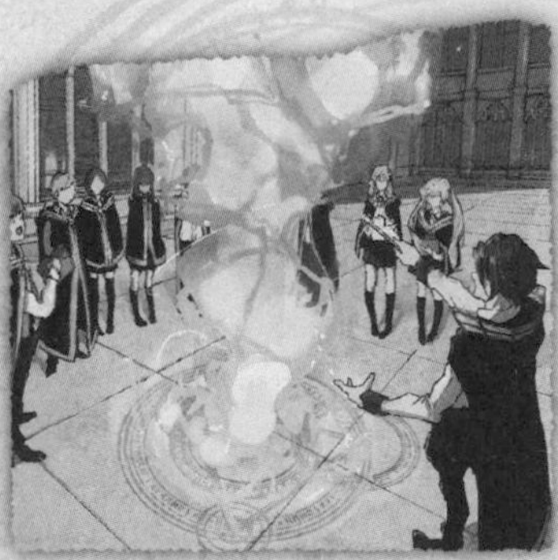

It's worth noting that students must earn 1,000 credits annually in order to advance to the next year at the academy. In other words, you need 2,000 credits to become a third year, 3,000 to become a fourth year, etc. If your only goal is to graduate from the academy, you only need to earn 6,000 credits. This should be enough to give you a wide range of job opportunities, even if you don't intend to continue on to the Upper Institute.

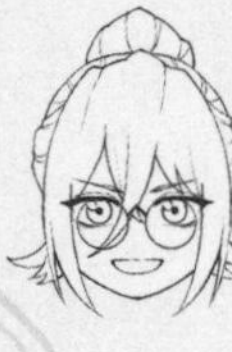

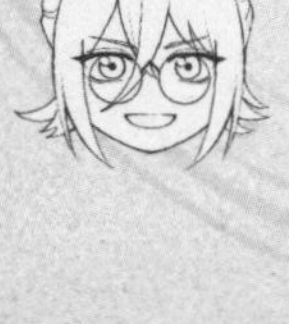

...There is a certain "problem child" who hopes to ascend the Tower on writing and praxis credits alone. As he is unable to earn any spellwork credits, he must earn every other credit he can. **I'm so worried, I can't help spying on him**... I mean, never mind. Forget I said anything.

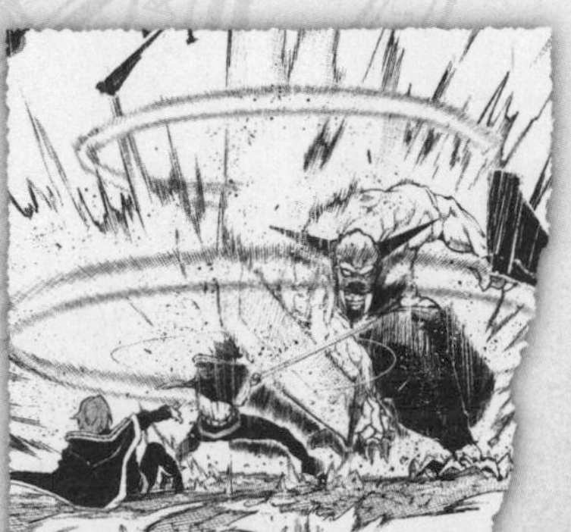

STORY   **FUJINO OMORI**   @fujinoomori

STUDIO AOI

STAFF

KATSUROU

SNS @ _katsurou_

HARON-SAN EIGHT

AYUMU TAKEFUJI

AYAHIRO

@pho1210

RYOUTARO MASUYA

@masuya0403

AKISUKE

@Gera4nium

RYOUTA SHIMOUCHI

-XEVEC
Weekly Shonen Magazine
3 volumes on sale now
-Tsugunai Mahou Shoujo Carenza
Ongoing series in *Manga One*
@BllSUKE18

SPECIAL THANKS

KOUTA SANNOMIYA

-Tesla Note
Ongoing series in *Magazine Pocket*
Volumes 1+ on sale now

@sanchecheco

COMIC   **TOSHI AOI**   @Aoi_00008

WISTORIA
WAND AND SWORD

AND YOU

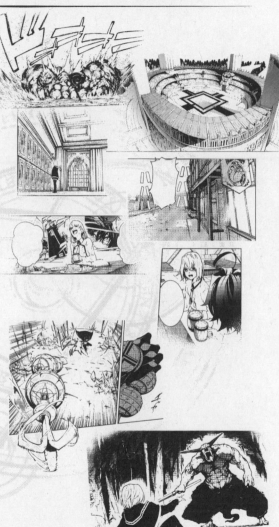

ROSTI NAUMAN

Race: Lyzance
Age: 16
Height: 5'7"

Birthday: 10th of Hallasmoon
(July 10th, in our world)

Likes: Everything about Will Serfort

Dislikes: · Fire
· Flame spells

First love: Will Serfort

Lowest dungeon floor reached: 7th

Equipment: Gear wand

Specialty: Crafting magic items

A skilled magical artificer and Will's roommate. His boundless affection for Will is enough to make Colette nervous. While lacking any natural gift for artificing, he has become a great talent and often devises various magical items under the pretense of making them for Will.

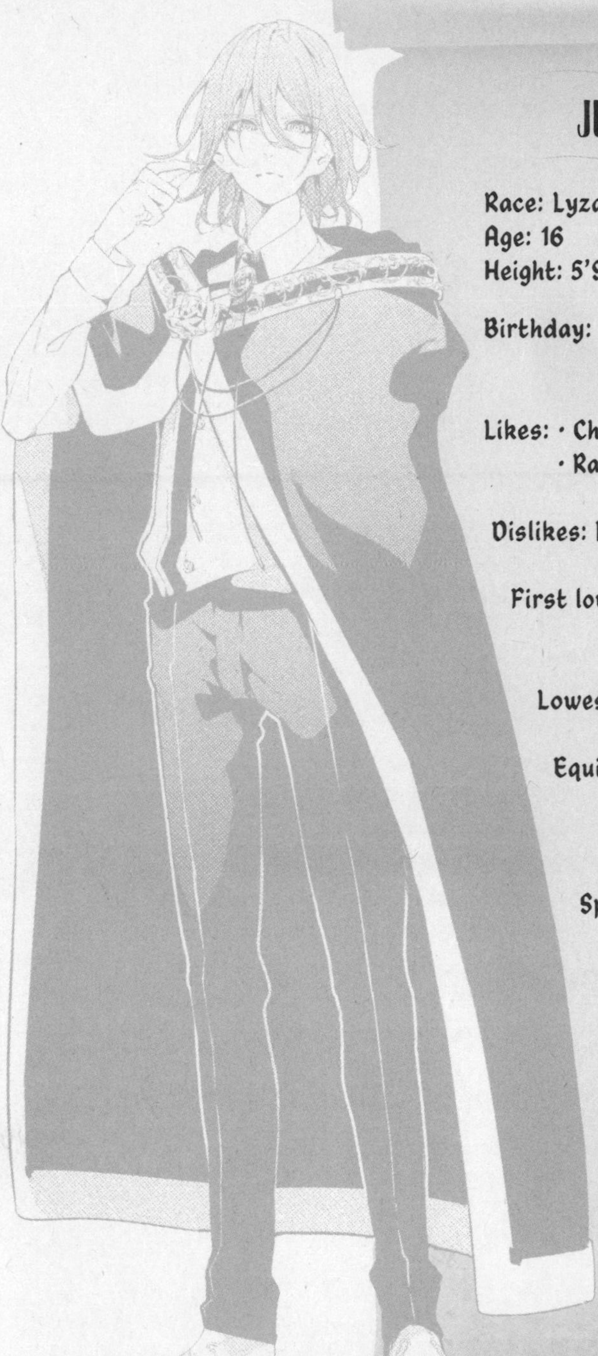

JULIUS REINBERG

Race: Lyzance

Age: 16

Height: 5'9"

Birthday: 23rd of Radelmoon
(February 23rd, in our world)

Likes: · Chilled cream of potato soup
· Raspberry sherbet

Dislikes: Peppers

First love: The family maid
(ended in heartbreak)

Lowest dungeon floor reached: 6th

Equipment: · Bluemirror wand
· Talisman given to him
by a certain maid

Specialty: · Low- to mid-level
ice magic
· El One: Ars Weiss*

An ice mage and one of the
top three students in Will's
year. He is a typical noble,
with pride and self-assurance
to spare. Since the incident
at the Magic Festival, he
has been forced to work
at Gina's bar.

*Albeit in an imperfect form
inferior to the original.

A Kodansha Trade Paperback Original

Wistoria: Wand and Sword 3 copyright © 2021 Fujino Omori/Toshi Aoi
English translation copyright © 2023 Fujino Omori/Toshi Aoi

Published in the United States by
Kodansha USA Publishing, LLC, New York.

Publication rights for this English edition arranged through
Kodansha Ltd., Tokyo.

First published in Japan in 2021 by Kodansha Ltd., Tokyo
as *Tsue to tsurugi no wistoria*, volume 3.

ISBN 978-1-64651-742-8

Printed in the United States of America.

9 8 7 6 5 4 3 2 1

Translation: Alethea and Athena Nibley
Lettering: AndWorld Design
Editing: Andres Oliver
Kodansha USA Publishing edition cover design by Pekka Luhtala

Publisher: Kiichiro Sugawara

Director of Publishing Services: Ben Applegate
Director of Publishing Operations: Dave Barrett
Associate Director of Publishing Operations: Stephen Pakula
Publishing Services Managing Editors: Alanna Ruse, Madison Salters,
with Grace Chen
Production Manager: Emi Lotto

KODANSHA.US

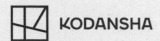

KODANSHA